LEGITIMACY IN PUBLIC ADMINISTRATION

 Advances
in Public
Administration

Sponsored by
the **Public Administration Theory Network**
and **College of Urban and Public Affairs**
Portland State University

Advances in Public Administration is a series of books designed both to encourage and to contribute to the vital processes of rethinking public administration and reconceptualizing various aspects of the field in an insightful manner that goes well beyond traditional approaches.

O. C. McSwite

LEGITIMACY IN PUBLIC ADMINISTRATION

A Discourse Analysis

 Advances in Public Administration

Sponsored by the **Public Administration Theory Network** and supported by **Portland State University**

SAGE Publications
International Educational and Professional Publisher
Thousand Oaks   London   New Delhi

For information:

SAGE Publications, Inc.
2455 Teller Road
Thousand Oaks, California 91320
E-mail: order@sagepub.com

SAGE Publications Ltd.
6 Bonhill Street
London EC2A 4PU
United Kingdom

SAGE Publications India Pvt. Ltd.
M-32 Market
Greater Kailash I
New Delhi 110 048 India

Printed in the United States of America

Library of Congress Cataloging-in-Publication Data

McSwite, O. C.
    Legitimacy in public administration: A discourse analysis /
O. C. McSwite
      p. cm,—(Advances in public administration)
    Includes bibliographical references (p.   ) and index.
    ISBN 0-7619-0273-2 (cloth: acid-free paper).—ISBN
0-7619-0274-0 (pbk.: acid-free paper)
    1. Public administration. 2. Public administration—
United States—History. 3. Discourse analysis. I. Title
II. Series.
JF1351.M26 1997   96-51270
351—dc21

97 98 99 00 01 02 03 10 9 8 7 6 5 4 3 2 1

Acquiring Editor:	Catherine Rossbach
Editorial Assistant:	Kathleen Derby
Production Editor:	Diana E. Axelsen
Production Assistant:	Denise Santoyo
Typesetter/Designer:	Marion Warren
Indexer:	Edwin Durbin
Print Buyer:	Anna Chin

Contents

This book is dedicated

To Warren and June McSwain,
For all they have taught me

and

To Phyllis and Orion,
For all they have taught me.

Preface

■ IT IS MORE IMPORTANT THAN USUAL that the reader approach this book from a special perspective appropriate to it. The first thing the reader should bear in mind is the subject matter: The book is about dialogue—specifically, the theory dialogue that takes place in the field of public administration. Its purpose is to work toward changing the nature of the present dialogue, to change *what* public administration theorists are talking about and *how* they are talking about it to each other.

Given this purpose, I face the problem that writing a book is a contradictory thing to do, an action that works against my purpose. This is so because it is primarily books that set the kind of theory dialogue we now carry on in the field. Whether books make extended arguments or provide research descriptions, they usually are attempts to convince someone of something. They are met with varying degrees of acceptance or rejection, but the discussion is always in terms of the effectiveness of the effort to convince. The implicit effect is to shift the focus off the point of the book and onto the question of the competence of the author, which is generally a matter of no lasting importance. Thus, this sub rosa diversion is pointless and destructive, and in the case of the present book especially so.

The other thing books do is make it seem as if changes in the content of what we consider true are easily possible. The illusion created is that all one has to do to change things is get together a convincing argument and write it into a book. Books rarely convince people of anything, though. They generally are agreed to by people who are already disposed to agree with them and rejected by those who do not want to agree. In the process, what we consider the truth stays pretty much the same, and, most important, we keep believing that *there is truth*—if someone would just say convincingly what it is! So the more things change (the more books that are written), the more things stay the same.

The content of this book is problematic in this regard. A great deal of the content is historical. My original intention, following the traditional approach to book writing, was to marshal so much historical evidence that no one could disagree with my argument. Then three things happened: (a) I found there was far more historical evidence than I could ever assimilate or digest; (b) I found that there was not enough space to present even the evidence I could get together; and (c) I realized that in seeking to make an undeniably convincing argument, I was working against my primary purpose.

So what about the content? How should it be regarded? This book appears in a series that seeks to present "new concepts" in the field of public administration. The series is supposed to consist of evocative "idea" books. Therefore, space limitations are imposed. Although this limitation was dismaying at first, I saw ultimately that it works to my purpose. It allows me to tell readers that I cannot and do not hope to compel them to agree with the argument. Rather, what I set out here is the *template* of an argument, one that is deliberately incomplete. Though I have done the best I can in making it, and will certainly elaborate it as strenuously as I can if you ever want to talk with me about it, it is incomplete and ultimately unconvincing. Also, I know that it is wrong. How do I know this? Because in my experience, all books are wrong. I have never read one that was really, truly "right." Why should this one be any different?

What am I up to then, writing a book that I know is wrong? One way of answering this question is by referring to an excellent recent book by David Farmer (1995), a public administration theorist at Virginia Commonwealth University. He writes from a postmodern perspective that denies that any line of discourse should be regarded as holding a metatheoretical position from which it can state the truth. He reads things sensitively and delightfully and points out (a) that they are wrong and (b) that there is much that is useful in them. This is the kind of arrangement that I want this book to have with the reader: Read me to find out how I am wrong, and then to see how what I say is useful, so that we have something to continue to talk about with each other. I, like David Farmer, am a postmodernist in just this sense.

This last point leads to a final one. This book, as the title says, is a "discourse analysis," an unmasking of an ideology as a tissue of distortions and fabrications. As a postmodernist who believes there is no position from which to do such an unmasking, how could I pretend to do this? This is a good question, but it presumes that discourse analysis can only be showing how a theory that represents itself as the truth is really not the truth—that it does not correspond to "reality" in some way and is therefore misleading us all. I am not working from such a presumption. My idea of ideology follows the school of thought that says ideology is not simply a composition of misrepresentations, but a set of assumptions that renders sensible the practices that enable a given social reality to continue to reproduce itself, and that gains the power to do this by virtue of the fact that these assumptions are held *unconsciously*. To unmask an ideology in this sense is simply to bring any such assumptions to the surface and, by making them conscious, to disempower them, thereby making it difficult or impossible to reproduce the status quo.

This brings us back to the point of the book: to change theory dialogue in the field of public administration. One thing structuring this dialogue at present is an unconsciously held assumption that makes it seem sensible to listen only to some (the wise and worthy) and not to others. Engagement in this dialogue is a process of jockeying for the position of "he who should be listened to and believed" and avoiding being forced into the position of "she who must listen because she has nothing to say," or "he who should be ignored because what he says is wrong." I want a dialogue in which we all talk, and we all listen, and we all get to be in on coming up with what we do next.

Acknowledgments

IT IS PLEASURABLE AND EVEN JOYFUL to contemplate the rich set of human relationships that produced this book. Most of the initial draft of the manuscript was written while we were on sabbatical research leave at the University of Leiden in the Netherlands. Taking this leave would scarcely have been possible without the personal support that John McSwain provided in helping us manage our lives during a protracted absence from home. We sincerely appreciate his help. We want to thank The George Washington University and Virginia Tech University for providing our sabbatical time, making it possible for us to teach at Leiden and to live at the other places in Europe where we stayed during that year. Our colleagues at Leiden were warm and welcoming and created a context that opened and inspired us. The time there was great fun and highly developmental.

The argument of this book is nothing if not heterodox, and it could not have been conceived in some academic contexts. Our colleagues in the Department of Public Administration and the Center for Public Administration and Policy have the intellectual and emotional range of heart and mind not only to accept and support us and our work but to encourage us and help us sharpen the ideas that went into the book

x

through a continuing dialogue. Our relationships with them are to us living evidence that effective discourse is possible even in highly diverse contexts.

In a similar vein, we want to thank Bud Kass, the general editor of this Sage series, for the vision and scope of intellect that he showed in seeing potential in the proposal for a book that we submitted to him. His reflective feedback and consistent encouragement have done much to sustain us through the long haul of completing the work. He is definitely an appropriate scholar to edit a series of books presenting "new concepts" in the field.

We also want to extend our deep appreciation to the members of the Public Administration Theory Network, our intellectual "family." They have supported, cared for, and variously agreed and argued with us in the best family tradition. This book is an effort on our part to honor the members of the network and to contribute to our ongoing dialogue.

We have been given much intellectual support, stimulation, and inspiration by our participation in the ongoing Lacan-Zizek Reading Seminar in the Department of English at The George Washington University and in the continuing Human Subjectivity Seminar at the Center for Public Administration and Policy at Virginia Tech University. Discussions in these two venues (especially with Janet Cummings and Allan Jones) have gone to the heart of the matter that is the focus of the important last chapter of the work.

We have benefited from excellent, skilled assistance in the gritty details of the research process. Tamela Griffin, Tammy Hall, Monika Suarez, and Suzanne Payne all provided much help to us as research assistants.

Specific parts of the manuscript were read by Larry Kirkhart, Fran Emory, Ed Banas, and Gary Marshall. Their informative comments and insightful feedback were of direct help in refining our final argument. Readers who know Larry's work and who are aware of our long-term relationship with him will see more than a little of his influence in the ideas in this book. Fran and Ed also provided one of the laptop computers we used while working in Europe.

The entire manuscript was read by Bayard Catron and Michael Harmon, and we spent many hours discussing it with them both in general and in specific. These discussions, however, were simply an extension of our ongoing personal intellectual connection with these two colleagues. The differences between the interests, intellectual style, and perspectives of each of us are clear, but at the same time it is often difficult to see where one of us ends and the other begins. Our relationship with them is so synergistic that thanking them for the enhancement they have made to this book seems superfluous.

On the topic of enhancement, simply not enough can be said about the contribution made to the manuscript by our immediate supervising editor, Camilla Stivers. We have the highest respect for Cam's level of scholarship, and it was not only reassuring but gratifying to have her give it the two careful readings and edits that she did. Her stylistic and editorial help was invaluable, and the substantive discussions we had with her about the content of the work enabled us not only to make the argument remarkably more vivid but to elaborate it in directions that strengthened it.

At the even more intimate level of the day-to-day grind of giving the essay its final shape and producing the manuscript, we cannot thank Tracy Smith Hall, of the Center for Public Administration and Policy, enough. As a member of the Human Subjectivity Seminar, not only did she give us intellectual inspiration and support, but in addition she read and provided valuable feedback about specific parts of the manuscript. Also, at another level, she employed her amazing computer skills to the daunting work of accomplishing the hundreds of detailed tasks that putting the final manuscript together involved.

Last, though, we must acknowledge and give our deepest thanks to O. C. McSwite—who, after all, is the one who did it.

Do you think I am trying to weave a spell? Perhaps I am; but remember your fairy tales. Spells are used for breaking enchantments as well as to induce them.

C. S. Lewis

The Legitimacy Issue and Academic Discourse

I do not know which of us has written this page.
Jorge Luis Borges

Most of us, it seems—up to 98 percent, according to
some recovery gurus—grew up in dysfunctional families.
Beryl Lieff Benderly

THE GENESIS OF THIS BOOK is quite specific. At the 1991
conference of the Public Administration Theory Network, I
delivered a paper entitled "The Semiotic Way of Knowing and Public
Administration" (White, 1991). The paper was written on the specific
theme set for this meeting as a result of the dialogue at the preceding
year's conference. During those discussions, members had acknowl-

AUTHOR'S NOTE: This chapter's epigraph by Beryl Lieff Benderly is taken from her
article "Everybody's Got Troubles," in *Washington Post Book World*, July 5, 1992, p. 6.
Copyright 1992, Washington Post Book World Service/Washington Post Writers Group;
reprinted with permission. The excerpt from "Little Gidding" in *Four Quartets*, copyright 1943 by T. S. Eliot and renewed 1971 by Esme Valerie Eliot, is reprinted by
permission of Harcourt Brace & Company.

edged that our discourse had been distorted and entangled by the philosophical commitments (in most instances, the epistemological commitments) that underlay our various intellectual positions. These commitments, despite their centrality to the discussion, remained implicit, undisclosed, and undiscussed.

In the interest of improving the quality of theory dialogue in the field, the group resolved to focus on such commitments specifically at the next conference. Rather than invoke the generally deplored prospect of creating a debate on epistemology, the organizers of the 1991 conference chose the more general theme of "Ways of Knowing in Public Administration." The idea was to create a forum where those who wished to do so could set out in detail, while the rest of the theory community listened, the foundational assumptions that underpinned their ways of understanding the theoretical issues with which we in the field struggle. This was intended to foster a common understanding on which the further dialogue of the community could be based. I remember leaving the planning session with a rare and palpably positive feeling that the theory community was going to accomplish a major scholarly development. I thought that perhaps the next conference could create a coherent quality of dialogue that would be marked by understanding and acknowledging the positions of others. I looked forward to this, as I felt I had never yet experienced such grounded dialogue in my academic career.

What happened at the subsequent conference did not fulfill this lofty promise. Many of the papers presented simply ignored the theme. Although this is a common occurrence at academic conferences that attempt thematic integration, in this case I found it a rather stinging disappointment. The biggest failure of the meeting, however, came in the texture of the dialogue about those papers that did seek to meet the intent of the conference. Rather than listening to the various perspectives on knowing with an eye to learning how to "indwell" in them (Buscemi, 1978)—that is, learning to see how the world looks from within them—the audience sought to shape the perspectives into categories that were familiar so that they could then find a basis for *agreeing* or *disagreeing* with them. There was very little exploration of the approaches, very little neutral mulling over of foundational assumptions. Since it is so rare that academics lay out the root assumptions that underpin their work, and since in my view it is so important to acknowledge these, I felt that a precious opportunity was going unrealized. The discussion was being pressed into the same old, tired channels I had watched it flow through during the entire thirty-four years of my attending academic conferences in political science and public administration.

The luncheon arrangement at this conference was for informal groups of conferees to eat together while holding more casual conversations about the conference proceedings. As I sat down at the table with a group of some people I knew and some I did not, the frustration and disappointment I was feeling popped out. I said something like

> Isn't it incredible how these discussions are going? The same old topics are coming up again! I've heard these same conversations about these same issues at panels at public administration and political science meetings for the past thirty-four years—over and over. If we were a family, people would certainly say we were dysfunctional and ought to go see a therapist!

There was a prolonged silence, and then one of my luncheon partners said, "But it's these very issues that hold us together." I thought to myself that indeed, yes, we were just like a dysfunctional family, held together by our problems. It was this interchange that set off a chain of mental events and conversations that resulted, ultimately, in the writing of this book.

The experience of the conference led to a protracted introspection. It was only a short while after the meeting that I came to the realization that the dialogue around the papers was quite normal, really, and my evaluation of it an overreaction. Indeed, in light of my general experience at professional conferences, this one had to be judged a rather remarkable success. Why did I expect and want the discussion to be different? In particular, why did I feel such an intense distress when it did not come closer to my expectations? I found myself returning to feelings I had often noticed during my academic career, feelings of dissatisfaction with the quality of intellectual relationship that I found characteristic of most faculty collegiality throughout the university, not just within my departments of public administration and political science.

My intention as a young person had not been to become an academic, and, like most people, I had virtually no idea of what academic life was or was supposed to be. Jumping around among various jobs after college eventually landed me in graduate school in a political science program, and I began to take on the role behaviors of a graduate student. The distillation of my naïveté and youthful confusion into a sense of purpose, or at least the beginnings of one, came late in my graduate career when my dissertation supervisor made a casual remark to the effect that what university faculties were paid to do was provide a "special kind of conversation that was not available anywhere else in society." When I asked what was special about this conversation, he replied, "It is a conversation that is aware of itself." I pretended to know what this meant and have pondered the statement ever since. As I reflected on my reaction to the dialogue at the theory conference, it occurred to me that the texture of academic discourse was the primary disappointment I had experienced as a university professor.

I could think of very few times that I had engaged in a conversation in an academic setting that showed more than a minimal awareness of itself. It was more typical to hear major undisclosed assumptions reflected in rhetorical manipulation and even outright prejudice. This is not to say that colleagues have not been of sufficient intelligence or background to carry on a self-aware dialogue. Indeed, the reverse is true. In most cases, the people I have worked with in universities are of superior intelligence and superb educational background. Why, then, was my experience in academic dialogue so disappointing? I have no definitive answer to this question, but I have begun to see that the answer involves more than the personal characteristics of academics themselves.

A venerable axiom in the analysis of social process is that if a pattern exists in a social system, even a problematic pattern, it is serving some manifest, latent, or vestigial function (Merton, 1949; Parsons, 1949). If poverty, for example, continues to exist, it is because it produces benefits in increased viability for the system that outweigh its detriments (Gans, 1971). Although this mode of explanation is in popular eclipse (Black, 1961), as I reflected on the issue of academic dialogue I returned to it over and over as a plausible account of the type of discourse I have encountered. I wondered what interpretation an insightful outsider would give of the sort of academic dialogue I have experienced. Certainly, a therapeutically minded observer would see the dialogue as a way of maintaining the equilibrium of the social system in which it occurred (Friedman, 1985). Just as in dysfunctional families, painful patterns of interaction are reassuring because they are familiar and predictable. They allow the family members to avoid the pain and uncertainty entailed by even positive change (Berne, 1961).

This is probably what my colleague meant when he responded that it was the set of issues—the same old set of unresolved issues—that was holding us together. Such a view does not answer the question, though, of why such a dialogue, especially the dysfunctional, nonproductive dialogue of academia, is supported by the larger society. In other words, what function does typical academic discourse—closed, narrow, and static—serve in maintaining the social system? Academic institutions have enjoyed a certain security of support, at a high enough level, to occasion the question: Why?

The usual answer to this question is rendered insufficient when we consider that the question entails a more profound issue—that is, the *content* of the dialogue. Indeed, the content of what is taught at least in the liberal arts is regularly attacked in popular culture (Bloom, 1987). If academics were judged on content alone, I fear we would have long ago been given the hook and be off the stage. Hence, I was led to the thought that the nature of the dialogue itself—what I was calling, contrary to my old professor's thought, the *unreflexive, unaware* nature of this dialogue—must be serving some broader social purpose than the official one of knowledge construction and transmission. It is clear to me that academic discourse usually entails redundant, repetitious discussions about standard, well-recognized issues conducted by the same old familiar faces of the sort that evoked my reflections at the conference in 1991 and to which everyone who regularly attends professional conferences is all too accustomed.

The temptation in following such a line of thought, though, is to assert that all social processes representing the status quo simply maintain those who are in advantaged positions of privilege and control. This way of thinking is appealing as a device of political rhetoric; it has a certain compelling face validity to it, and it evokes maximum heat in the discourse, the kind of heat that leads directly to political activism. Ultimately, however, I find this argument unsatisfying. I am not convinced that self-interest or pure greed alone, even greed on a scale that would produce a monopoly of material goods, physical satisfactions, and human deference, could provide enough ideological power and acuity to produce the pervasively integrated pattern of repression that one sees in the world. Greed can only produce, in my opinion, a sort of medieval pattern of social organization, one of decentralized monopolies. This is all that would be required if the personal motives of specific people were the only drives seeking gratification. There must be a broader and darker purpose than even greed at work to produce the pervasive pattern that I saw in my tiny corner of human experience, a purpose that structured the dialogue of a few relatively esoteric and isolated academics as they talked to each other. What is this dark purpose, this deep stake underlying our very pattern of academic social organization and process?

I came to the conclusion that what is at stake is a style of mind, a pattern of consciousness, a way of building a representation of human experience. My reflection led me to see this consciousness as the ultimate political stake, the interest from which all others derive. It is not avarice per se, but a given *pattern* of greed, one that takes the form of a mind-set. Since greed is energized by the physical drives that define it, it can only produce a kind of social organization that reflects the necessity of satiating the drives of a given person or elite group. Consciousness, however, *defines* these drives, so consciousness as a political interest is capable of creating a social system that completely transcends the drive-based greed of any group, even a sizable one. The "need" of consciousness is for *totality*, for a transcendent integrity that denies all exception or even the possibility of exception. Greed-based social systems can achieve only authoritarianism; systems oriented to the stake of a pattern of consciousness demand totalitarianism. Any deviation from the pattern that defines the system is a threat to its hegemony. The gratification of specific drives in this light becomes incidental, a subordinate concern.

What had bothered me about the dialogue at the theory conference was that the same old issues were being discussed in the same old ways they had been for years, with the same old positions being taken and miscommunicated, and everyone either seemed to be unaware that this was happening or simply accepted it as the only possibility for our discourse—just as in any dysfunctional group, work team, or family. It was the "feeling texture" of the meeting, the emotional ambience of the dialogue we were creating, however, that was the source of my personal distress. If the discourse at the meeting was serving the dark purpose of maintaining a specific pattern, even a dysfunctional one, of social organization and process, as I have just been suggesting, then its achievement apparently required participants in the dialogue to assume a certain existential posture toward themselves and each other. To me, this stance and the emotional texture that accompanied it were essentially characterized by *a commitment to a permanent sense of irresolvable problem and a willingness to live with the inevitable interpersonal distress that this sense of intractable problem generates.*

This realization drew my attention directly back to my experience with public administration. I remembered that when I began graduate school at the University of Texas, studying mainly with Emmette

Redford in the Department of Government, there was tension over the advent of the behavioral approach in political science. My sense of this tension sharpened as I continued graduate school in political science at Indiana University, studying there with Charles Hyneman, a contemporary of Redford's but one who stood on the other side of the political fence and supported the new "empirical" behavioral approach. In further graduate work, at the University of North Carolina at Chapel Hill, I found the same tension existing between the public administration program and the political science department within which it resided. The distress that I felt at the theory conference reminded me of the tensions that afflicted dialogue in these graduate programs.

It also became clear to me how deeply public administration as a field of inquiry and practice embodies the broader problem of social consciousness and the forms of social organization and process that a collective pattern of consciousness creates. Emmette Redford represented the idea that effective governance, performed by responsible officials and of which administration was an indispensable and legitimate part, was a vital part of social life and societal well-being. Charles Hyneman, as an American political conservative, resisted this view. He held to a deep and general doubt that authoritative action through government could ever be efficacious and truly responsible. He had great disdain for Redford's faith in the possibility for government to set baseline standards by which the general well-being could be determined and protected. (Hyneman always pronounced the word *standards* with great derision when he quoted Redford or discussed this idea.) His preference for the new empirical approaches to the study of politics was grounded in his conservative political theory. He felt that liberal faith in the efficacy of government was maintained and protected by an interlocking set of myths that misdescribed how social, economic, and political institutions functioned, and that these myths could be debunked through empirical study of "how things really work."

The rebuttal by Redford and the more traditional school he represented was that the "empirical" approach actually was not sufficiently empirical at all. Redford's direct experience in government had convinced him that the world of government was too complex to be apprehended through what he saw as the limited techniques of the abstracted empiricism emerging in the behavioral sciences (Mills, 1959). The only appropriate response to this real-world complexity was a deference to it that required accepting a substantial degree of approximateness in understanding (Stein, 1952b). This posture of humility and tentativeness before the complexity of government was captured best, Redford felt, in the very myths—which, after all, attain mythic status because they represent certain fundamental truths— that Hyneman wanted to debunk (White & McSwain, 1990).

The purpose of recounting this is to convey something of the source of the "dialogic distress" I am discussing. As I progressed in my graduate school experience, it became clear to me that the main source of meaning in the studies that my fellow graduate students and I found available to us was the disagreements between our professors and other figures in the field. The fact that people disagreed, then took positions that they defended and from which they attacked, seemed to reassure us as students. It gave us a sense that there was something about the all-too-often dry, bloodless material we were studying that was worth caring about, that had human meaning to it. In a sense, we graduate students were socialized to the idea that conflict and meaning were equivalent. To the extent that one wished to have an "intellectual identity," it seemed one would have to join one side or the other of an intellectual dispute and become part of an approach or school.

I wanted to have an identity, but I found myself experiencing a good deal of tension around the notion of having to commit to a position that necessarily included some people and excluded others. Though I did not see it at the time, the tension I was experiencing derived from the fact that my basic stance, the identity that I brought to graduate school, was that of the humanist. The fundamental issue for human- ism has always been to find an approach that does not make the kind of invidious distinctions that lead to inclusion and exclusion.

As I grappled with the problem of committing myself to an intel- lectual orientation, the basic nature of the dispute that I had observed between my mentors and among my graduate student peers became much clearer to me. Though it was extremely complex in the sense that it was expressed over many different and interlocked levels, at its foundation the dispute centered on the question of whether coopera- tion was desirable or possible in social life and, relatedly, whether an inevitable competitiveness in human relationships required establish- ing overhead control by an elite leadership. I realized that this same question was the basis of my ambivalence about declaring an intellec- tual stance.

As I continued graduate school at the University of North Carolina, the distress I felt was amplified. The issue there became embodied in relations among sectors of the faculty, specifically the American politics specialists and the public administration specialists. The

Americanists, as exemplars of the field of American political science generally, seemed to me to work from a worldview that saw competition as the center of human nature and social process. The game of politics—the winning and losing and the tensions and melodrama that surround the outcomes—seemed to grip their attention, to constitute meaning for them. The public administrationists appeared, on the other hand, to find meaning in the mundane, the day-to-day business of governance, and rather than focusing on winning and losing, they put their attention on questions that had to do with the results of government—what it did or did not contribute to social well-being.

The strangest part of the relations between these two groups was that the Americanists did not see public administration as a truly legitimate part of the enterprise of the department. For a time, I occupied a position between the two and had the confidence of both sides. The Americanists openly expressed disdain for public administration, including sometimes the wish that it would disappear. This attitude seemed to be based in a feeling that the political science view of the world was the predominant one. It was "hard-headed and realistic," and any "sensible intellectual" obviously saw competition as the essence of social process. The cooperation-based worldview of public administration was soft-headed, odd, and lacking in scholarly rigor and credibility.

As I reflected on this period of my life, I noticed something interesting. I realized that when I attended the various political science reading/discussion groups organized around special academic interests, the distress in this dialogue was very similar to that I experienced later at the public administration theory conference. The difference was that whereas the theory conference dialogue centered on the problem of understanding various ways of knowing, the Americanists' discourse was rather firmly grounded in a common way of knowing, which might be appropriately called a kind of "positivist behavioralism." Despite this, the Americanist discussions never resolved much; they were characterized primarily by posturing and defensiveness. The point seemed to be to create disagreement, to put whatever intellectual claim was being made into suspension, thus rendering it tentative. The most curious aspect of all this was that the way of knowing shared within a particular group had as its central ideal the possibility of arriving at a truth that is *not* tentative. The feeling that one gained from membership in such groups was a kind of camaraderie derived from sharing this ideal, paradoxically qualified by a strong underlying dissonance that came from the equally legitimate belief that any step toward realization of a truth must be resisted.

The disagreement I had witnessed at the theory conference, though, was not exactly of this sort. The issue in the theory group was rather more personal, a degree or two deeper, and quite specific to the field of public administration. It was a kind of angst, what Sartre might have called an existential anxiety or what R. D. Laing (1960, 1967) has called ontological insecurity. The questions that seemed to underlie all those discussions were "What is our place?" and "How are we to fit into the scheme of American democratic governance?" In their disjointed discourse, public administration theorists seemed to me to embody fundamental concerns of identity and role for the overall field. In their shared but beleaguered devotion to the realms of action and choice, their own deep distress revealed the central question of whether a focus on collaborative social process is possible as the foundation for an intellectual enterprise.

It was through this sort of reflection that I came to see academic public administration more broadly, not so much as a dysfunctional system in itself but as the "identified patient" of a larger dysfunctional system, entailing not only its parent discipline of political science but social science in general, and indeed governance itself. In systems theory, the person who becomes the problem in the sense of exhibiting destructive behaviors is simply showing or presenting the symptoms of the whole system. Though treatment starts with this identified patient, the cure aims at the entire system, because that is where the source of the problem lies (Bowen, 1978; Friedman, 1985; Gilmore, 1982; Guerin, 1976; Hirschorn & Gilmore, 1980; Kahn, 1979; Schaef, 1988).

In what sense could the situation be seen this way? How was public administration exhibiting symptoms, acting out, being destructive or self-destructive? As a person in the field who does academic theory but who has coupled this with a great deal of consulting work with public agencies, I have a rather definite answer in mind. To me, one of the more curious aspects of public administration as an academic field is the degree to which, historically, the official leadership of the field has been so compliant. There has been relatively little writing in major venues such as *Public Administration Review* that makes a positive case for administration or even defends it against the persistent, relentless, low- and high-grade criticism to which it is subjected. Public administration has simply accepted whatever changes were in vogue and attempted to adapt. Is cutback the new regime? Then let's invent new managerial tactics for cutback management. Is the problem that public bureaucrats' job benefits and pay are unnecessarily high?

Okay, let's reduce them. Are tighter, more pressurized controls and evaluation of budgets and personnel needed? We will invent or certainly implement them for you.

Defense, much less counterattack, has been virtually nonexistent. Public concern about the *net* effects of changes, the positive benefits and accomplishments of public bureaucracies, the constraints under which public organizations work, or the broader sociocultural patterns that might dispose us to place so much unproductive blame on public bureaucracies—these factors remain largely unaddressed. It seems ironic to me that academic public administrationists, who might be obvious sources for a vigorous theoretical counterattack, have often been the most conservative and restrained in responding to attacks on the field.

Notable exceptions to this passivity have been Larry Lane and James Wolf's book *The Human Resource Crisis in the Public Sector* (1990), Charles Goodsell's *The Case for Bureaucracy* (1994), and the other work of the so-called "Blacksburg Manifesto" group (Wamsley et al., 1990). Overall, though, the response of public administration to attacks on it from within the political arena has been quiescent and weak. The same is true for the field's relationship to the discipline of political science. Most public administrationists seem to try to ignore their second-class academic status and thereby to rise above the whole issue. Few, if any, have followed Dwight Waldo's (1971) lead and directly confronted it (Henry, 1987).

This passivity is a reflection of the fact that the field has never effectively come to terms with the fundamental question of how administration fits within the scheme of American democratic government. Neither, of course, has political science dealt with this question in the form that is appropriate to it—namely, to spell out a positive theory of governance for the American political system. Political science's default position has been to adopt the so-called empirical mode of analysis for political affairs and present itself thereby as simply describing how the system works. Just as when a family lacks a firm sense of itself as a set of stable relationships, and this ambivalence is embodied in a problem child who finds a role within the family system that expresses the distinctive kind of ambivalence that besets it, public administration embodies and expresses the ambivalence of political science about its identity. Since the political science problem seems to be an uncertainty about how far to go in being hard-nosed, rigorous, and "non-normative," public administration assumes a compensatory opposite posture and is "soft" in its methodology and passive both in defining its role and in fulfilling it in the actual process of governance.

Just as public administration is the presenting patient for the disciplinary system of political science, however, so is political science the presenting patient for the American political system and, more broadly, American society. Because Americans themselves are split or ambivalent about their idea of what positive role government is to play in public affairs, they have produced, through the pattern of support they have provided, a political science that expresses this problem. Since the issue for American society seems to be how far to stress commercial process and the competitive individualism on which it is grounded over the principle of human relationship and community, we have produced a political science that is fascinated with nothing more than the competition of the electoral process. Even the study of institutions seems to be carried out from the point of view of how institutional performances bear on electoral success. We have a political science that, by focusing so much of its attention on the competition of politics, exacerbates the largely transitory and hence mostly meaningless melodrama of elections.

This is a role like that played by the acting-out adolescent child who helps his or her parents heighten, ritualize, and neutralize the conflict stemming from their conflicted, confused relationship. Stability is gained but at a cost: Underlying issues are not addressed, and the quality of fundamental relationships cannot improve. What creates this all-too-common dynamic (it has been discovered in the relationship systems that make up formal organizations as well as families) is the fact that members prefer the predictable, though painful, distress of melodrama to the awesome uncertainties involved in facing the ambiguities, ambivalences, and conflicts attendant to attaining valid relationship (Friedman, 1985).

We see here the truth of the maxim that the macro is always contained in the micro: The conversation at the theory conference, with its acceptance of a continuing unhappy struggle over issues that are taken to be irresolvable, contains the problem of the place of public administration within political science, which in turn contains the problem of political science within American society, which in turn contains the issue of American society within its own Constitution. We suffer this distress instead of engaging in the work of becoming more aware of the relationship dynamic that produces the distress.

My purpose in this book is to address the relationship issues underlying the abiding distortions in our public administration and policy discourse. The focus for my work is the problem that expresses these relationship issues and contains all the specific conceptual questions involved—namely, the *problem of legitimacy* for the administrative role in democratic governance. It is this issue, the "bureaucracy in a democracy" problem, that summarily defines the ambivalence of America toward itself and the irresolution and incongruity in governance that flow from this ambivalence. I hope to show that by finding a way of seeing administration as a legitimate part of American government, we can (indeed must) at the same time see each other as legitimate, which is to say, as fellow members in a national community of mutual caring and understanding. Ultimately, the bureaucracy problem is simply the practical question of how we are going to live together, of the extent to which we are going to rely on the devices of cooperation in working out our national destiny.

A Word on Discourse Analysis and an Overview of the Book

To sum up the foregoing introduction: The subject of this book is the theory discourse of public administration; its focus is the issue of the legitimacy of administration as a part of democratic governance; its purpose is to help enhance the self-awareness of this dialogue—or, more accurately, of the people who carry it on. The pattern of distorted discourse surrounding the legitimacy issue in public administration has profound implications. It strikes at the center of our collective ability to encounter one another over the basic issues of how we wish to live together and what role the web of the living relationships that we think of as community will be able to play in this. Our relationships themselves are constituted in our discourse, as is our very subjectivity. A great deal is at stake.

The idea of subjectivity is very much in vogue at present. Indeed, it is perhaps the central topic of the current discourses of postmodernism (Rosenau, 1992). I take this to be a rather significant fact, in that the question of the nature of the human subject has not up to this point been engaged in quite the way it is now. In the past, discourses about "human nature" were concerned to define accurately something that was assumed to be "there," to exist in some real and present manner. In contrast, in postmodern discourse, the focus seems to be on locating or finding something (a subject) that has been decentered, lost, or alienated away into limbo (Foucault, 1970, 1979; Lacan, 1977, 1978). There is an opportunity in this. This new focus allows discourse to reframe the question in other than the economic terms that currently predominate and thereby to escape being trapped in the trivial tautological question of whether people are self-interested or altruistic and the corollary enigmas of social domination that go with it. In doing so, we can avoid a great deal of useless political and emotional baggage and the "rackets" of argument that it creates.

I mention this because I have stated that the focus of the analysis here is at bottom a question of consciousness, in which a pattern of consciousness is seen as a "stake" in some ultimate sense. I want to make clear that this consciousness does not take the form of "political interest" in the usual sense, in which those on one side of the line signified by the issue seek to exploit or dominate those on the other side. Rather, consciousness is a stake shared by all at any given moment in history, and the struggle over it is a struggle of one pattern of consciousness to overturn and replace another, in the manner of consciousness reflexing with itself. Put another way, the issue is one of *meaning* and the sense of self that various patterns of consciousness permit. This point can easily be illustrated, again, by the case of the family system. Every family system is organized around a stable pattern or equilibrium in which each member has a place, an identity, and a pattern of prescribed behaviors that together constitute the "meaning of life" in that system. A given family may be highly dysfunctional and characterized by extreme patterns of exploitation, domination, and abuse; this does not mean, however, that the dominators are better off than the others and that things should therefore be made more just and equal. Things *should* be made more just and equal, of course, but not because some members are better off than others. Indeed, *all* the members of the family are most likely to be suffering equally, in some sense, and to be equally "happy" in another sense. This is why family systems—and all human systems—are as difficult to change as they are, and why, by the way, the simplistic pleasure-pain calculus that economic theory uses to understand human motivation and behavior is so far off the mark (Rhoads, 1985).

Hence, although the usual manner of analyzing human relationships is to determine who is the "good guy" group and who is the "bad guy" group, we need another approach here. In this analysis, the good guys and bad guys are not "out there" but rather "in here," inside each of us. What the analysis will argue for is a reconfiguration of consciousness, one that produces a new and different sense of subjectivity. The way into this approach will be the specific problem of public administration discourse, which reflects a pattern of consciousness that configures people as egoistic, individual, and engaged in a mutual struggle with one another. The alternative offered will be a discourse oriented toward relationship, a mutual surrender to each other. The problem of legitimacy, it will be argued, will evaporate once this reframing of our discourse and our institutions is accomplished.

In constructing this analysis, I proceed by first recounting and commenting critically on the famous debate between Herman Finer (1940) and Carl Friedrich (1940) over the question of what is the proper relationship between the political and the administrative sectors of democratic governments. The dialogue between Finer and Friedrich is widely considered in the field of public administration to have "paradigmatically framed" the discourse on the legitimacy of administrative institutions in democratic political systems. The terms of this debate exposed the fundamental contours of the problem and showed the commitments involved in the two sides of the issue. My analysis comes at the debate from a different angle, suggesting that the most interesting thing about it is not the differences between the two positions, but what is alike in them. In my view, the two sides are grounded in a common set of assumptions and share a purpose. As a result, the debate creates a curious reverse effect by framing the problem of administrative legitimacy in such a way as to make it irresolvable—thereby, in a sense, "institutionalizing" it and making it *constitutive* of theory dialogue. The debate in turn provides a crypto-legitimation for a certain pattern of elite domination. This pattern I label the "Man of Reason" theory of governance. In other words, the persistence of the legitimacy problem makes it seem as if it is necessary that we entrust governance to a revered elite who act on the basis of "objective" empirical and "principled" moral considerations. Chapter 2 explicates how this theoretical legerdemain works. I ask the reader to heed the caveat elaborated above: Though I seem to point the finger at specific parties—namely, Men of Reason—these are not bad guys in the usual sense. They are only there because we all have come to feel, as a result of the way we talk about the legitimacy issue in governance, that we require them and must defer to them. We are victims not of Men of Reason themselves but of our own lack of insight into our very discourse, which traps us into needing them.

Having "framed" the subject of the book with the discussion of Friedrich and Finer's debate, I take up the main body of the analysis in the next four chapters, which are intended to show how the legitimacy issue developed and became institutionalized over time. I begin in Chapter 3 with a discussion of the Anti-Federalist theory of governance, the political formula that opposed the one contained in the present Constitution. The theme I develop here has a number of facets. One is that the standard interpretation of the founding era debate, the one typically passed down to us as schoolchildren, distorts the situation of American government at the time and the issues that separated the two sides. My theme will be that the Anti-Federalists held a workable and coherent theory of governance, one that visualized government as an integrated whole and as "close to the people," that, if acted on, would have obviated the legitimacy problem that Friedrich and Finer discussed. Further, I will argue that this theory of governance and the revolutionary, popular sentiment that inspired it, was and is a powerful psychological current in the American psyche, one that still seeks full expression.

In Chapter 4, I selectively analyze the course of American social and political history from the end of the Civil War through the beginning of the twentieth century. I suggest that during this period, the sociocultural-economic logic inherent in the Federalist Constitution played itself out, leading, in the process, to political ineptness and corruption, economic injustice and exploitation, environmental waste, and social domination. This story is well known; I wish only to recount enough of it to set a proper backdrop for the point I want to make about the founding of public administration. This point is that the true origins of public administration in the United States lie in the spirit of Anti-Federalism. The bursting forth of this spirit in the populist movement and the progressivism that supplanted it inspired the original idea of "good government" out of which the public administration movement germinated. My argument is that although America was developing according to the logic and dynamics established by its own Constitution, in the second half of the nineteenth century it lost coherence and identity as a nation and was seeking to find or to recreate itself at the start of the new century by radically changing its form of governance. This new form of governance was more administrative or functional than political, more participative than representative, and more oriented toward cooperative community, benevolence, and social coherence than economic enterprise. As a philosophy, this theory was called *pragmatism.* It is a complex, multithematic, distinctively American body of thought.

Of course, the new form of governance implicit in pragmatist philosophy did not develop. Indeed, it never really even got off the ground. The role that public administration played in this failure is the nominal topic of Chapters 5 and 6. These two chapters present a general overview of the literature of the field of public administration, especially the parts of this literature that to some degree might be deemed theoretical. However, there is an analytical theme in the description: The literature of the field as created by the members of the original movement quickly took administrative good government away from its populist, pragmatic sources and configured it instead as a kind of technocratic utopianism. As such, I will argue, it was in a sense innovative, and it stood in strong tension to the pattern of government that the Constitution had produced. What it did not do, though, is confront the core commitment of this form of government— namely, the pattern of consciousness that supports the regime of the Man of Reason. Indeed, despite its challenges to the Constitution, the new public administration theory simply sought to change the type of man in charge and the mode of reason used in governing. The history of the literature of the field is a story of apparent theoretical innovation, innovation that is actually a revisionism that refers consistently back to the core premise of the necessity for this new kind of Man of Reason.

As this last statement suggests, the theme around which the material in all these chapters is presented is *intellectual distortion*. Friedrich and Finer's "debate" reflects the foundational analytic distortion. That is, it *creates* the issue of how bureaucracies can be made a legitimate part of democratic governance. Similarly, our constitutional founding reveals an essential background distortion in the literature of American history and political science: the idea that the interest-based, Man of Reason pattern of governance established by the Federalist Constitution reflects the lessons of history and is validated by experience in the new American nation. The pattern of distortion that I describe in the literature of the field of public administration is more complex. It begins with an account of how the problematic social, cultural, and political conditions of the late nineteenth century produced a social and intellectual response—in the form of the social welfare movement and the creation of the philosophy of pragmatism—that recalled the Anti-Federalist tradition and hence threatened the hegemony of the Men of Reason system. This threat was met by a movement toward administrative governance based on technical expertise, which stifled the philosophy of pragmatism and its Anti-Federalist inspiration. The elaboration of this theory of public administration as a professional rather than a popular, collaborative mode of governance subsequently entailed the creation of a selective and biased—that is, distorted—discourse in organization and management theory as it applied to the public sector, a discourse that perpetuated legitimacy as its central constitutive element. The dynamic of this discourse continued to require rule by Men of Reason, since the felt need to defend public administration's role in governance led inexorably in this direction.

The reader will experience a disjunction in the concluding chapter. To ease this, I provide some continuity with the overall theme by reviewing the current crisis to which governance by Men of Reason has brought the social order of the United States and the response being mounted to this crisis. The response is a broad movement toward a "facilitative" public administration, one that involves itself with citizens not through the application of expertise as much as through efforts at collaboration. This response is entirely consistent with (indeed, it is a logical extension of) the critique I elaborate throughout the book. However, my assessment of this movement is that it will probably fail because it takes place *within* the conventional framework set by the legitimacy issue and therefore does not understand (perhaps even actively supports) the traditional pattern of governance by Men of Reason. Thus, its true effect will be conservative. It is at this point that the disjunction occurs. Given that the roots of our problem with administrative governance go so deep, any approach to it must begin at the most generic level—the idea of reason itself and the philosophical and social devices by which it is sustained. Consequently, Chapter 7 is devoted to a highly heterodox explication of the idea of reason, one that shows it to be inextricably interwoven with the issues of gender, intergroup prejudice, and the profound problem of alterity—that is, the problem of coming to terms with the implacable, immutable sense of otherness that is evoked in our social relations with our fellow human beings. Though this analysis carries the discussion onto daunting, difficult terrain, I seek to keep it cast in direct, nonphilosophical terms.

I go on, further, to make the optimistic case that although the field has followed a tightly circumscribed pattern in its development so far, there is at present a possibility that important change can occur. This case builds from the fact that we are again at a fin de siècle, and just as "everything" went into suspension at the conclusion of the last century, so a great deal seems to be up in the air at present as the twenty-first century approaches. Most significant is the development of the "postmodern" theoretical attitude, one that, at least in the United States, is grounded in the same kind of suspicion of philosophical absolutes that inspired pragmatism originally and that indeed calls up directly and in revitalized form our heritage of pragmatism as the true

American philosophy. Also, on the social and political scene, old patterns appear to be breaking up, and new challenges to change are arising, seemingly inspired by populist sentiments. I see in this situation the possibility for a refounding of the field, one grounded in its true foundation: pragmatism. The starting place for this refounding is to let go of, get over, and leave behind the pointless discourse on the legitimacy problem. We must realize that by constantly posing answers to this issue, we have institutionalized and maintained it and the structure of government that produced it. It is the continued existence of the issue itself that establishes the legitimacy of the pattern of governance we have—governance by Men of Reason. The purpose of this book is to facilitate this "letting go" and to frame the issues to be faced in bringing about fundamental change in our system of administrative governance.

A Note on the Voice of the Book

One of the most gratifying experiences in my career as an academic writer was the praise received by my essay entitled "The Phoenix Project: Raising a New Image of Public Administration From the Ashes of the Past" (White & McSwain, 1990). I believe people reacted positively because the essay offered a hopeful possibility for the future, a renewed heroic idea of the public administrator toward which we all could work. In the framing of this book, I was tempted to try to repeat the experience of the Phoenix essay on a grander scale and to marshal all the rhetorical power I could to create a romantic, heroic, even epic image of the public administrator, one capable of facing the radically different world of the future emerging as we reach the end of the twentieth century. It was not just the prospect of a positive response that motivated me but also the excitement that such work entails. Added to this was my firm belief that the public administrator is in fact going to be the hero of twenty-first-century governance.

Instead, though, I chose a different direction for this project. In this choice, I followed some of my favorite words from Carl Jung: "One does not become enlightened by imagining figures of light, but by making the darkness conscious" (Jung, 1963, p. 345). I read Jung as saying here that the goal of the human being must be not to follow normative or empirical mandates and thereby become something we *should* become, but rather to do the work of self-exploration that reveals to us the whole of what we *are*. In the end, development leads only to where it starts, with being. As T. S. Eliot's famous lines put it,

> And the end of all our exploring
> Will be to arrive where we started
> And know the place for the first time
>
> (Eliot, 1971, p. 145)

The point of this book, therefore, is to help create a certain kind of awareness, a reflexivity, in our dialogue, rather than to present directives or mandates.

On this point, I should mention again that I consider what I offer here to be merely the *template* of an argument. I wrote what was essentially the first draft of this manuscript while on sabbatical leave, living in Europe. I returned with just under 600 pages of text. During the process of developing this draft, I decided to seek to have it published in the Sage series, primarily because I felt that this series was most appropriate to the purpose of the book and the style of its discourse. This decision meant, however, that the manuscript would have to be drastically reduced in size. What I did was to redesign the idea of the project and make it into two book-length manuscripts. Still, the text had to be drastically condensed. It occurred to me in the process of doing this that actually an adumbrated argument was more consistent with the tenor of the project than a fully elaborated one. To attempt to create a completely convincing argument, one that left little or nothing to say back, would be inconsistent with the whole idea of seeking to foster a different kind of dialogue in the public administration theory community. What I hope will happen is that the template argument I present will evoke further inquiry along the lines I have laid out and that this inquiry will provide the basis for further discussion. I feel that this approach ("Don't believe me, go look for yourself") is essential to achieving the practical purpose—of getting past the legitimacy issue—being aimed at here. People's minds are seldom changed except by themselves.

Therefore, in the conclusion of the book, I will not offer an *answer* to the legitimacy question. Even if every aspect of the argument were successful, it would not support such a conclusion. My hope is that the book will succeed in setting the discourse that has surrounded the issue of legitimacy off in a different direction, and, more important, in *giving it a different texture.* In so doing, this book should relieve the distress of which I spoke earlier.

The discourse in which we are now engaged can be characterized as a tangle of what Gregory Bateson (1973) called "double binds." The way the discourse is framed creates the expectation of an answer to the problem of legitimacy, but it offers no venue for the creation of this answer and even denies such a possibility. The discourse creates a demand for responsibility, but it places all striving for responsibility in doubt. It creates a culture of fear in which every party is asked to sit in objective judgment on every other when there is no clear understanding of how to achieve objectivity. We as colleagues in this dialogue cause each other's distress, and we know it. We are truly each other's hell, and we (again, like a dysfunctional family) apparently feel that we must keep relating to each other in this way, as we fear that any alternative might be worse.

The personal angst that animates this book is thus revealed as an unhappiness with the way we in the public administration community are relating to one another as we carry out our intellectual work. Taking this as a final reference point, it seems incumbent on me to address this matter in the very manner in which I choose to make this book speak, since to write a book is a rather major act of relationship. So I have chosen a different kind of voice for the book, one that I hope at least steps in the direction of establishing more self-reflexivity in me and in my relationship with whoever might read this work. There are a number of recent illustrations of other organizational scholars with a similar intention. Two of the best are Joanne Martin in her book *Cultures in Organizations* (1992) and Barbara Czarniawska-Joerges in *Exploring Complex Organizations: A Cultural Perspective* (1992). However, because the voice I use is quite unusual, and perhaps will be disturbing to some, I want to make explicit the considerations that went into choosing it.

I begin with the most obvious anomaly of the voice—namely, that it speaks in the first-person singular. This is anomalous in that the general norm of academic writing is that any personal reference makes the writing suspect and is to be avoided. Works authored by a single person either avoid personal pronouns entirely or use the third-person singular. Coauthored works typically employ the first-person plural. Two people wrote this book, but it collapses the two authors into the singular. Of further note is that one of the two authors is male, and the other is female. Compounding these anomalies, of course, is that the book is presented as having been written by one person. The name of the author, "O. C. McSwite," is a fiction, but fittingly (or synchronously) enough, it was a name inadvertently coined for the authors at yet another public administration theory conference.

Choosing to use this name was not a frivolous or mischievous choice but the product of serious consideration. What I came to in my meditations was that the most appropriate theoretical context into which to set this choice, the context that seemed to render it most meaningful, was Michel Foucault's (1977) essay "What Is an Author?" The theme Foucault develops is suggested in the title; rather than asking "who" is an author, he poses the question of "what" constitutes the author. By this choice, he objectifies the act of writing, moving it from its conventionally attributed personal locus inside the identity of the person writing to a location outside, in social process. The author becomes, by Foucault's analysis, the result of a set of social relations that produces the writing activity. A given text, therefore, simply stands for or expresses the social relations of which it is a product. Writing in this light does not present the meaning that any given person intends.

Such thinking is quite French, quite consistent with the Durkheimian tradition. Nonetheless, it makes a great deal of sense to me as an American. It seems clear that academic writing, as a special form of discourse, gains its distinctiveness from the context within which it is produced. What is being written here simply reflects my past and present social situation, and the closer the social relations that constitute this situation are to the moment that the words of the text appear, the more immediate and powerful is the influence that the relations work on the words. Hence, I use the name that I do to signify as clearly as possible "what" is authoring these words. This text is a product of the *relationship* of the two people who constitute the first-person singular speaking through it.

Next, let me reveal my view of the book's rhetorical style. Because to my mind there is no possibility of writing without employing some type and degree of rhetorical manipulation, I want to identify my own. Basically, I shall speak from a highly personal, even intimate, position, one that seeks to let the reader inside my mind, to reveal the process by which what is being said has been formulated. Grounding the discourse of this chapter in a personal-professional anecdote as I have done here is a tactic of this rhetorical strategy. This is my intention, and I want the reader to know it full well. To the extent that I am successful in carrying out my rhetorical manipulation, the reader will be able to recognize it and be somewhat aware of its effects.

Adopting a voice of the sort I am describing is an unorthodox move, one that violates both the traditions and the current fashions of academic writing. It might even seem shocking and irresponsible, since the impersonal, objective style of conventional academic writing has been rationalized as necessary to ensure responsibility in academic discourse. Since the issue of responsibility is a grave one, especially when a book is involved, I want to state explicitly the theory of responsibility that I see myself following.

In graduate school, I came to practice writing in a highly specific way. Martin Kilduff (1993) described quite well the theory of writing that I was taught in his article on March and Simon's famous book *Organizations:*

> March and Simon's (1958) readiness to devalue the importance of style and metaphor is quite consistent with the Western metaphysical tradition, which from Plato to Heidegger, has regarded writing as merely an "unfortunate necessity" (Rorty, 1978:145). From this logocentric perspective, philosophical and scientific texts are representations of ideas. Writing, as a medium of expression, cannot add anything of value to such representations and could possibly "infect the meaning it is supposed to represent" (Culler, 1982:91). (p. 14)

To prevent my writing from "infecting the meaning" of the data-derived representations I was learning to present, I had to learn an objective, "plain style" form of writing that presented itself as purely reportorial. I was told that the attitude or value set that supported this style of writing was a kind of conservative humility; I was to believe that I had no right to demand that anyone listen to me unless I had gone out into the world and done the work of digging up hard, true facts that I could provide my readers. Theoretical opinions, were I to wish to venture any, had to be set within the context of thought that already existed in my scholarly community, and I could only offer contributions that extended or improved this body of knowledge. I thought it quite appropriate, though somehow ironic, for me that the first book on which my name appeared as an author contained no words but was simply a compilation of voting statistics that had resulted from my computer exercises (White, Waggaman, & Hofstetter, 1967).

The idea behind this pattern of socialization seemed to be to teach us to produce scholarly work from which we, as sentient (or, as Marx liked to put it, "sensuous") human beings, were distanced. The essence of being responsible was to offer your fellow scholars work that was completely objective so that the pursuit of truth could be furthered. Part of this socialization process was also, of course, that we, as scholars, were to regard research and writing as the only true work that we did. Teaching and counseling with students were simply necessary nuisances to which one deployed as little time, energy, and attention as possible. This was difficult for us, since as young people and neophyte teachers, teaching was the most challenging, exciting, and real aspect of what we were doing at the time.

I realized rather quickly that within the pattern of my graduate school socialization, there was a powerful contradiction. The objective voice that I was being taught was gained only by cutting myself off from myself and others, but the judgment that followed from the scholarly community was a *personal* judgment of me as a human being in my role. Nothing made this clearer than the repeated evaluations culminating in the process of gaining tenure. As I experienced it, I was being most responsible as a scholar when I was able to move my intellectual work process outside of myself, by becoming objective, while at the same time showing personal, necessarily subjective inspiration in my work. It seemed clear that attaining the ideal of objectivity paradoxically depended on my exhibiting an inventory of personal qualities that mirrored those of my colleagues, such as energy, diligence, intelligence, maturity, and balanced judgment.

Perhaps what sums up the picture I am seeking to draw is the standard assumption-of-responsibility clause that writers of academic books learn is supposed to be put at the end of the preface. After giving credit to others—sometimes dozens of people—who helped in the task of constructing the book (and in the process making it abundantly clear, as if it were not already, that writing a book is a social process, not really accomplished by any one person), the author "assumes full responsibility" for any errors of fact, interpretation, or whatever that the reader may find in the book. In other words, though the voice in which an academic author speaks is not his or her own personal voice, since it is a voice produced by formal rules intended to depersonalize and objectify it, each author is nonetheless personally responsible for what it (the Academic Voice for which he or she is being the venue) says.

I do not feel this way. I am confident that, read with a careful, critical eye, this book will reveal most, if not all, of my considerable personal deficiencies as a scholar—namely, that I did not work hard enough in graduate school and hence am not well enough prepared; that this tendency toward laziness was carried over into the preparation of this book itself, as there are numerous places where more work could have improved it; that, to begin with, I just am not bright enough to be up to the task of saying well what I want to say here; and that I even lack a sufficiently well-developed moral sensibility. Let me be clear about this: I confess to all these and other deficiencies of which I am not even aware. I am inadequate.

I also do not see how the pervasive sense of being judged that hangs over academic work contributes to its quality. I suspect, indeed, that the real purpose of the academic culture of judgment is to help keep academics—who might have the dangerous potential of becoming critical intellectuals—under control. In fact, I feel I must deny and thereby suspend this specter of judgment to be able to do this work at all. So I confess my rather general inadequacy and the condition of deficiency into which it puts this book. At the same time, I challenge the judgment itself. What good does it do? Why not just take whatever is worthwhile here and let the dross go? I did not have to write this book, and you do not have to read it. I am writing it as an expression of my belonging in a community that is important to me. It is a gift of sorts, inadequate no doubt, but a gift.

By bidding for this kind of *acceptance* of this work, rather than hoping for a good judgment and (I must say, condescending) tolerance of its deficiencies, I am seeking to realize the sort of reflexively aware dialogue of which the book speaks as it examines the discourse surrounding the issue of the legitimacy of public administration in a democratic system of governance. Let me conclude with a small suggestive example of what I mean.

In the introduction to her recent prize-winning book exploring the "inner life of Westerns," Jane Tompkins (1992) wrote the following about the role of Native Americans in the semiotics of the Western genre and about herself:

> The absence of Indians in Western movies, by which I mean the lack of their serious presence as individuals, is so shocking once you realize it that, even for someone acquainted with outrage, it's hard to admit. My unbelief at the travesty of native peoples that Western films afford kept me from scrutinizing what was there. I didn't want to see. I stubbornly expected the genre to be better than it was, and when it wasn't, I dropped the subject. Forgetting perpetuates itself. I never cried at anything I saw in a Western, but I cried when I realized this: that after the Indians had been decimated by disease, removal, and conquest, and after they had been caricatured and degraded in

Western movies, I had ignored them too. The human beings who populated this continent before the Europeans came and who still live here, whose image the Western traded on—where are they? Not in Western films. And not in this book, either. (p. 10)

I do not recall ever seeing such a passage in a public administration writing. I certainly would not expect it in political science, or in any of the social science and philosophical literature I read. Why? Simply because it is too honest and self-accepting, too frank about a moral injustice and a personal failure. The awareness Tompkins brings to her work has produced feeling, and she shows in her response that she is willing to suffer it. Through her suffering, in turn, she does indeed bring the Indian into her book, making of this absence a powerful and moving theme of the work.

It is the mark of the social sciences as distinct from the humanities that they seek either to ignore feeling or to act heroically on the basis of it. There is in these responses no understanding of how profoundly dynamic and productive of change the act of suffering can be and how conservative, in fact, is the heroic quest to understand scientifically or to solve social problems. Such timid heroism can be maintained only by continuing to avoid the sort of awareness that I hope this book helps to bring to the discourse of the legitimacy problem. Perhaps by working toward the model of reflexive awareness of which Tompkins affords a glimmering in the passage above, our discourse will become more meaningful and more dynamic. Enough "imagining figures of light"; it is time, with my own dim taper, to move off into the darkness.

2

The Framing of the Issue

Reason, or the ratio of all we have already known, is
not the same that it shall be when we know more.

William Blake

A FEW YEARS AGO, shortly after I moved to Washington, DC,
I was asked to attend a dinner honoring an eminent figure in
the field of public administration, a man I had known for many years.
When dinner was over and the speeches started, I reflected on how
very much he deserved the adulation he was receiving. I knew him as
a humanist (as well as a great human being) and as a person deeply
committed to the public service. Further, he had served as something
of a diplomat in that he had worked as an advisor to a number of heads
of state and other high-level officials in foreign governments. Some of
these officials came forward to speak about what a help he had been
to them personally and to their governments. Sitting next to me was a
political scientist who teaches public policy in a public administration

AUTHOR'S NOTE: The passages in this chapter from Carl Friedrich's "Public Policy
and the Nature of Administrative Responsibility" and Herman Finer's "Administrative
Responsibility in Democratic Government" are taken from *Public Policy,* edited by Carl
Friedrich. Copyright © 1940 by the President and Fellows of Harvard College. Reprinted
by permission of Harvard University Press.

program. I had worked with him on a few projects and knew he had defined me more as a political scientist than, as he would have put it, a "public administrationist." As the last of the foreign dignitaries moved through the tables to the podium to speak, the political scientist leaned over and whispered to me, "That really sums it up, doesn't it—every one of the governments he's done work in has been an authoritarian regime!"

What was "summed up" by the litany of positive testimony—at least in the view of my political scientist tablemate—was the view that public administration is an inherently antidemocratic approach to governance. My colleague assumed that I would understand the comment, and indeed I was not at all surprised. It did cause me to ponder the depth and extent of the feeling that public administration's role in democratic government evokes. The issue truly has "good guys" (the freedom-loving, democratic political scientists) and "bad guys" (the order- and efficiency-loving, crypto-fascist public adminis-trationists).

One of the more interesting aspects of this concern with the perceived antidemocratic nature of administration is the manner in which it has traditionally been framed, in terms of a pair of articles published in 1940 by the political scientists Carl Friedrich and Herman Finer. The debate focused on the need for accountability in the use of administrative discretion in the implementation of public policy. Friedrich began the debate, taking what Michael Harmon (1995) referred to as the "soft-core alternative, which relaxes strict demands for accountability in the interest of flexibility" (p. 41). Finer replied with an article delineating what Harmon described as "a hard-core defense of strict accountability" (p. 41). The list of points generated by the Friedrich-Finer debate has come to define the dimensions of the controversy over the legitimate role of administration in a democracy and has set the boundaries for virtually all subsequent discussion of it (Redford, 1969; Spicer, 1995; Waldo, 1948). The articles are distinctive in the combative way they join the issue, a distinction that may help account for the fact that reading them has become a minor tradition of graduate education in public administration. Because they have played such a central role in structuring the concept of administrative responsibility, they provide an exceptionally sharp lens for discourse analysis of the sort I want to do here. By looking into them, we can see outside of them and down the entire line of dialogue that the issue has engendered. Framing the issue in terms of this debate creates a distortion that makes it seem that administrative officials could be legitimate agents of democratic government if only the conundrum of accountability and discretion could be resolved. Since this is a false and hence impossible problem, it serves as a perpetual deflection and provides a de facto rationale for the exercise of discretion by Men of Reason.

The Carl Friedrich-Herman Finer Debate

The debate I am about to review involves not only a clash of theoretical positions but a confrontation of nationalities and political cultures. Herman Finer (1898-1969), though born of Romanian parents, was British. He was educated at the London School of Economics and subsequently served on the faculty there as a lecturer and reader in public administration. He received a Rockefeller Fellowship to the United States and then was invited by the Social Science Research Council to direct research into the Tennessee Valley Authority (TVA). He ended his career as a professor of political science at the University of Chicago. His perspective on democratic government clearly reflects his familiarity with and faith in the British parliamentary system.

By contrast, Carl J. Friedrich (1901-1984) was German, his mother being of the von Bülow family. He had been a medical student—I heard him quip once that he felt that his experience in gross anatomy class had given him an excellent sense, indeed an olfactory sense, of the nature of man—but ultimately received a doctorate in law from the University of Heidelberg. He came to the United States in 1923 as an exchange student, returning a few years later to become a naturalized citizen. He began teaching at Harvard University in 1926 and remained a professor there for 50 years. Friedrich never lost his German accent, and his perspective on administration was clearly conditioned by his background as a citizen in the German *state*, a regime that was of course quite unlike anything in Finer's experience.

These differences in personal biography are mirrored in a cultural dimension that clearly seems to run through the debate. Looking explicitly at this cultural difference helps sharpen our understanding of the more subtle aspects of the issues that Friedrich and Finer pose—issues whose magnitude tends to obscure their complexities.

Running through Friedrich's (1940) argument is an implicit theme regarding expertise. Every time I reread and then discuss his polemic, I think of an experience I had that illustrates the Friedrich position. I was carrying out research for a policy study of the development of the post-Apollo program in the National Aeronautics and Space Administration (NASA) during the late 1960s (Redford & White, 1971). During my interviews and in other, less formal interactions with NASA engineers both in field offices and at headquarters, I heard a great deal about Wernher Von Braun, the head of the rocket program at the Marshall Space Flight Center in Huntsville, Alabama. Von Braun, of course, shared a cultural heritage with Friedrich in that he was a native of Germany; he was brought over (some say "kidnapped," though he was eager to go) by our military as a member of a group of German V-2 rocket scientists whom our military wanted to put to work developing a U.S. rocket program.

Von Braun was an enormously charismatic man, a reputation verified during the interview that my coresearcher and I conducted with him, and he assumed a high profile within the NASA policy elite, not intimidated at all by his status as a former enemy of the United States. Of the many policy debates within NASA during the Apollo program and as the post-Apollo policy was being formulated, what I heard about most from NASA engineers was the position Von Braun took on an engineering problem: how to measure and document hardware reliability. The Manned Space Flight Center at Houston, staffed predominantly by American engineers, advocated and practiced a *statistical* approach to assessing reliability. They would use the statistical patterns derived from spacecraft hardware component test programs as a basis for creating a reliability number that was taken as a predictor of the success of the flight. The Houston engineers regarded this as an empirical approach and the only trustworthy one. Further, they saw it as the only *responsible* one, meaning the only one that ensured that the agency could be held accountable for carrying out a successful flight to and return from the moon.

The approach to the reliability issue of the scientists at Von Braun's Marshall Space Flight Center was quite different. According to Von Braun's "lab scientists," as they were called, the Houston approach was not empirical but rather quite abstract and hence untrustworthy. To the German engineers, the truly empirical approach was to have the people who were directly involved with the development of the various rocket components *give their considered opinion* as to how reliable these would be under actual flight conditions. This view was grounded in a sense that the rocket system was so enormously complex that no mere number could capture the possibility of success or failure. The German scientists on Von Braun's team practiced what some of the Houston engineers referred to as the "Volkswagen approach" to hardware development. They stayed with original or source design configurations; development consisted simply of uprating, or increasing the scale of original components as demanded by the requirements of the larger dimensions. This was the approach that ensured reliability according to Von Braun, and he once proudly testified before a congressional committee that the Saturn moon rocket, in effect, was only a vastly enlarged V-2 (the World War II rocket that he and his team had developed for Hitler).

The Houston center engineering staff saw Von Braun's approach as hopelessly phenomenological and approximate, and they tended to see the motive for his insistence on his subjective approach to reliability as a refusal to be held responsible for his work on the rocket. By telling Congress, the president, and the public that they assessed the reliability of the space hardware at 0.999994 (which is approximately the number they asserted for it), the American engineers were making themselves much more vulnerable to the charge that they had been misleading or otherwise irresponsible than did Von Braun when all he would say was that his staff "had judged" that the rocket was probably going to fly without failure. Consequently, we were told that a great deal of tension developed between the two centers. The tension was supposed to have come to a head (according to a story I was given to believe was not apocryphal) at a reliability assessment meeting between the two groups. After the Houston team had reported and given its latest reliability assessment numbers, attention turned to Von Braun for his report. He simply surveyed his staff: "Klaus, are you having any problems with the booster pumps?" "Nein," Klaus replied. "Eric, are you having any problems with the gyroscopes?" "Nein," Eric replied, and so on. After the survey, Von Braun reported, "There are my reliability numbers: nein, nein, nein, nein, nein."

What is most interesting about this issue, and indeed about Von Braun's role within NASA and the space program, is the ambivalence the American engineers felt about it and about Von Braun. On the one hand, Von Braun and the position he took engendered some anger—he was refusing to put himself and his staff on the line in the way that the Houston engineers believed they were doing. There was some feeling that he wanted to operate autonomously, as if he owned the rocket program. On the other hand, Von Braun was viewed with widespread, though sometimes grudging, admiration. One American at the Marshall Center described him to me as having an "incredible amount of moxie."

This reputation was spread through stories that circulated about Von Braun's capacity for bold action. One such account related that in the early days of the American rocket program, the competition between the military services had become so adversarial that President Eisenhower had ordered all the services to stop their rocket development work until he had decided on a policy for the program. Von Braun is reputed to have ignored the direct presidential order and continued his work. When inspectors came to check whether the order was being followed, Von Braun is said to have loaded the rocket components on flatbed trucks, covered them with tarpaulins, and had them driven around in the Alabama hills until the inspectors left. There were other reports, some going back to Von Braun's career in Nazi Germany. Hitler had little faith in rockets as military weapons, and at one point he, in effect, canceled Von Braun's A-4/V-2 program by demanding that it become operational within a year (an impossibility) or shut down. Albert Speer reported to Von Braun that Hitler had had a dream that had told him no rocket would ever reach England, and that he was refusing to give the program the priority status it needed. Attempts to launch the rocket had resulted in numerous disastrous failures, including one that returned to the launch site at Peenenunde and exploded, leaving a huge crater in the runway at the installation. Nonetheless, Von Braun created a film (one report was that it was pieced-together clips of failed launches, another said it was of a successful launch supplemented by animation) that created a convincing impression that technical problems had been solved and that the missile was operational. The film, along with narration by Von Braun, led Hitler to change his mind and give the program top-priority status (Piszkiewicz, 1995). At the same time that critics told such stories as evidence of Von Braun's administrative arrogance, they would admit that his actions accounted for the United States' ability to orbit a satellite in response to the Russian Sputnik as quickly as it did.

My reason for recounting these tales of Von Braun's activities in the space program is that he provides us with an actual model of administrative action against which we can reflect the Friedrich-Finer argument about the nature of administrative responsibility. Friedrich starts his argument with the premise that the *true* issue faced in governance is not to control the actions of administrators. Rather, in his words, "What is more important is to insure effective action of any sort" (Friedrich, 1940, p. 222). Friedrich's position takes for granted the positive role of governance in society and the importance of effective administration.

Friedrich emphasizes that the "complexity of modern governmental activities" renders it inevitable that there will be only an approximate understanding between the principals involved (the people and their representatives) and their agents (administrators) "concerning the action at hand or at least the end to be achieved" (p. 222). He assumes that some amount of "irresponsible conduct" is inevitable, meaning that it is certain that at some points and in some ways the agent will do something that does not square at the time it is done with the principal's idea of how things ought to proceed. Hence, "irresponsibility" is really an inevitable result of the impossibility, under conditions of complexity, that the principal and the agent will have a common understanding of what appropriate action is.

In the case of Von Braun's sensing the impossibility of explaining to Hitler the complexity of the technical details involved in developing an innovative weapon like the V-2 (and how close he and his team were to success in flying it), we can imagine that he came quite naturally to the conclusion that the responsible thing to do (for Germany, for *their* national war effort) was to create a bogus film that would dupe Hitler into continuing to fund the program.

Friedrich (1940) emphasizes that for him, responsible conduct stems from officials' taking the *initiative* necessary to achieve the goals of government. Inaction is as irresponsible as wrong action. He recognizes that the true source of wrong action is bad policy, which is to say, ill-defined and badly worked-out policy. Bad policy, however, is more the rule than the exception. Policies can never be framed clearly enough to ensure that administrators can simply "implement" without interpretation, modification, and emendation. Friedrich therefore takes the position that public policy and public administration cannot be separated but rather form "a continuous process," with the only difference between the two being that "there is probably more politics in the formation of policy, more administration in the execution of it" (p. 225).

Friedrich's central rhetorical device is an appeal to the contemporary—that is, to the emergence of modern conditions that require that action be informed by expertise. These conditions demand a bold and creative attitude toward action, one that prompts Friedrich approvingly to quote Sir Josiah Stamp in noting that the civil servant can play a role as "the mainspring of the new society, suggesting, promoting, advising at every stage" (p. 228). Under the press of coping with modernity, it is backward to worry about administrators and to hold a simplistic faith that by making them maintain the confidence of a parliament, the public interest will be protected.

In indicting legislative bodies as unable to ensure administrative responsibility, Friedrich misplays one of the more powerful cards given to his position in the debate—namely, the inherent deficiencies of democratic process as a device of ongoing governance. His major point is that legislatures can fall into rubber-stamping administrative actions out of considerations of party politics or their own political security. He could have extended this critique to well-documented problems that the democratic political process sometimes has in producing even a partially accurate image of the "will of the people" at a given time. These problems include, of course, the typically low electoral turnout rates that render electoral mandates either mysterious or nonrepresentative.

Distorted political dialogue, in turn, can skew electoral preferences; this distortion is magnified by the unrepresentativeness of the legislative process attributable to interest group pressures even in parliamentary systems (Duverger, 1955; Schattschneider, 1960). There also is the technical problem of the large minority who feel intensely about a political issue yet lose an election or legislative struggle to a slightly larger but indifferent majority (Dahl, 1956). All such deficiencies indicate that the democratic process, at least as it is carried out in representative political systems, cannot ensure accountability to popular preferences, and they highlight how simplistic it is to assume that a general popular sentiment can serve as the basis against which the actions of a government can be judged.

Some theorists have gone as far as indicting the very *principle* of democracy by pointing out that it can ground governments only on a legitimacy gained through the creation of a condition of social alienation—namely, that the losing minority, which (again) may be large and intense, is *dominated* by the majority (Thayer, 1981). Even Madison's idea of minority protection only attempts to ensure that the minority is not dominated too much—that is, past a certain point. There can be no way in the democratic process to protect minorities against losses to the majority in a vote. Voting inescapably creates alienation. I mention this point for later reference, as it indicates what I see as the major problem that Friedrich has in his side of the debate: He does not go far enough in arguing the case for a revised view of social process, a truly different one that best meets the conditions of modern society.

As it is, when Friedrich (1940) reveals his position, he is on the side of a rather commonsensical and general standard of administrative responsibility. He says that "the responsible administrator is one who is responsive to these two dominant factors: technical knowledge and popular sentiment. Any policy which violates either standard, or which fails to crystallize in spite of their urgent imperatives, renders the official responsible for it liable to the charge of irresponsible conduct" (p. 232).

It is after he defines his position that Friedrich begins to reveal that the core of his resistance to parliamentary democracy as the answer to the responsibility problem resides not only in his belief that the idea of the "will of the people" is hopelessly metaphysical but, more important, in his belief that parliaments (and legislatures in general) are incapable of embodying and representing such a thing even if it did exist. In his discussion of the role of citizen participation, he states the view that the true impact of political power is felt not through direct control—in the sense of stopping actions from being taken—but through the administrator's seeking to *anticipate* and *avoid* negative reactions on the part of both parliament and citizens.

From this point of view, then, the administrator is seen as taking the initiative in the implementation of policy. In the process, he or she reforms and refines the policy through an iterative process of antici-pating reactions from the public and political agents involved in the situation. To quote Friedrich directly on this:

> The responsible administrator today [again, under complex, *modern* conditions] works according to anticipation. Within the limits of existing laws, it is the function of the administrator to *do everything possible which will make the legislation work* [italics added]. The idea of enforcing commands yields to the idea of effectuating policy. (p. 237)

Friedrich's image of responsible governance thus relies centrally on proactive, anticipatory administration that seeks to avoid through effective planning and strategizing or, failing this, to negotiate the inevitable difficulties of policy implementation under modern condi-tions of complexity. The implication seems clear: It is only through such active, problem-solving administrative activity that the final shape of policy can be worked out at "the level of the street," so to speak. This seems to be the device that Friedrich proposes as the best or perhaps the only way that the "community at large" can be reached. Although there is no "will of the people," there is a common sense of what the community wants, a composite of the preferences, view-points, and special circumstances of various individuals and groups. The legislative process cannot comprehend or represent this composite *because the perspectives that constitute it come into existence only when the process of administering policy begins.* The ultimate nexus guaranteeing responsibility occurs at the interface of the community and the administrator, because it is only here that the thousands of negotiated transactions that ultimately define a policy can be carried out.

In the Friedrich theory of responsible governance, administration and the administrator play an *essential* role, one that cannot be replaced or even directed (in any very specific sense) by the legislative function. It is natural, then, that in concluding his essay, Friedrich bids for defining the administrator as a coactor of dignity, with full rights and citizenship. Such an administrative actor is to be seen not as someone to be controlled but rather as a trustworthy agent who seeks to make government responsive to what the community needs and wants. For example, we need not fear allowing administrators to speak on public issues because their discourse will be a scientific discourse and because where there is disagreement, it can be responded to scientifically, not politically. According government administrators the rights, dignity, and respect that their central role in governance deserves will work to *elicit* responsible behavior from them, Friedrich concludes—which is really our only choice, since such behavior cannot be ensured merely through the crude enforcement of political authority.

The Finer Reading of Friedrich

My purpose in discussing the Friedrich-Finer argument about administrative responsibility is, let us recall, to reveal how the initial *framing* of the issue, in the exchange between these two men, has distorted subsequent discourse about it. This sort of analysis can best be carried out by comparing and contrasting the two positions they take. Before getting to this, however, it is probably best to begin by simply reporting Finer's reading of Friedrich. Since reading involves a much more unconscious process than stating one's own position, such a report will yield the best descriptive account of the implicit axiology on which Finer founds his position in the debate.

Finer (1940) facilitates this project quite well by providing a straightforward condensation of his understanding of Friedrich's argument. I can begin simply by quoting it:

He [Friedrich] argues (a) that the responsibility of the official that is of any moment to us today is not political responsibility but moral responsibility; (b) that the quality of administration and policy making depends almost entirely (and justifiably so) upon the official's sense of responsibility to the standards of his profession, a sense of duty to the public that is entirely inward, and an adherence to the technological basis of his particular job or the branch of the service in which he works; (c) that the public and the political assemblies do not understand the issues of policy well enough to give him beneficial commands in terms of policy; (d) that, in fact, legislatures and the public have been obliged to allow or positively to organize more and more latitude for official policy making; (e) that there are satisfactory substitutes for the direction of officials and information as to the state of public opinion through the electorate and the legislature in the form of administratively conducted referenda, public relations contacts, etc.; and, therefore, (f) that political responsibility, i.e., the responsibility of the administrative officials to the legislature and the public, is and should only be considered as a minor term in the mechanism of democratic government, so much so, indeed, that officials may rightly state and urge policies in public to counteract those advocated by the members of the elected legislatures. (p. 261)

Let me examine each of these points and indicate how my own reading agrees or disagrees with, diverges from, or goes beyond them. To start, I agree with Finer's beginning with Friedrich's emphasis on moral rather than political responsibility. This emphasis seems consonant with the central position that this idea holds in Friedrich's argument. In the second point of his summary, there is a shading of emphasis that raises a question. Though Friedrich does give heavy weight to professionalism and a sense of public duty in his model of responsibility, I question whether he means it to be as "entirely inward" as Finer implies. I see Friedrich as arguing that public duty produces an *outward* orientation as well, an orientation that seeks to read and anticipate, as well as hear and negotiate, the wants of the public as they are expressed in the final stages of implementation of policy. Points "c" and "d" are best treated together, as "d" serves mainly in Friedrich's discourse as evidence for the validity of "c." Here I see Finer as rather substantially and substantively "off" in his presentation of Friedrich. As I read Friedrich, he is not saying that "the public and the political assemblies do not *understand* [italics added] the issues well enough" but rather that the "understanding" of a policy is something that evolves as the policy is being defined through the political and then the administrative processes (Finer, 1940, p. 261). Friedrich, in short, is saying that there is really nothing there to understand. (This is a key difference, and more will be said of this matter shortly.) Point "e," as Finer frames it, is rather incidental in Friedrich's argument, but, as Finer points out, it does play an important role in the overall structure of Friedrich's essay because it provides a basis for and leads into the concluding point "f."

Here Finer seeks to summarize Friedrich's position in its most extended form. He suggests that Friedrich's image of the administrator is that of a full-fledged political actor who, rather than feeling a responsibility to be subservient to the political arm of government, can speak out freely and even advocate for policies that "counteract" those advocated by elected officials. On the whole, Finer's assessment of this point is not, strictly speaking, an exaggeration of Friedrich's position. It does effectively obscure, however, Friedrich's persistent emphasis on the natural hesitance of administrators to assume a high-profile position in political debates (given that they see themselves above all as technical experts). Finer also highlights Friedrich's insistence on the importance of administrators' obeying all laws, policies, and directives from superiors and his assurance that administrators will always be subject to the regulating confrontation of scientific dialogue. It is, of course, the scientific process to which he sees them as primarily subject, since they should speak only on policy matters as knowledge experts. Hence, Friedrich's entire argument rests on the belief that science can provide unambiguous answers to policy questions. Science is the ultimate check on administrative power.

The Two Positions Compared, Contrasted, and Converged

Now let me examine the key points of the two positions, seeking as I do to discover especially the unstated paradigmatic assumptions that structure the debate and, consequently, the way the debate has configured discourse on the issue of administrative responsibility. We can begin with what could perhaps be characterized as the bottom line of each position: Finer's emphasis on the desirability (indeed the necessity) of "correction and punishment" of administrators so as to ensure responsibility and, by contrast, Friedrich's opposite emphasis on removing the threat of sanctions—at least to the point that responsibility can be "elicited." What is revealed by this opposition is, first, that Friedrich is willing to trust the human nature of administrators. His belief seems to be that by removing the overt threat of sanctions and the burden of direct controls, the best and most responsible side of the administrative actor will be evoked. Finer, obviously, shows no such propensity toward trust. In a most revealing passage (invoking Montesquieu), he states, "Virtue itself hath need of limits" (Finer, 1940, p. 252). Given this belief, it is not surprising that the center point of his position is oversight, control, and the threat of direct sanctions.

This difference also reveals, however, a similarity between Finer and Friedrich: They both seem to hold to a static ontology, a view that human beings do have a *nature*, that they "are" in an objective, concrete sense either trustworthy (in Friedrich's case) or not trustworthy (in Finer's case). They both end up agreeing by disagreeing with any view that would depict human nature as *dynamic* and *contingent*—for example, on styles and textures of social interaction. Their common assumption of a static ontology, which of course shapes the fundamental premise of the position each takes, transforms their discourse in all its aspects into a disagreement of fact. Even if this is only implicit at points, it is nonetheless the structuring premise of the dialogue. The effect of making the debate into a problem of fact is that the discourse is made to turn on a correct-incorrect, right-wrong, yes-no type of opposition that contains an implicit assumption that the most important point in the dialogue comes when it stops and an assessment is made through an objective device such as a vote. Dialogue is construed as a presentation of evidence that is then judged. The settlement reached can be based only on a kind of domination, whereby the losing side submits to the judgment on the grounds that it reflects reality and is by that token legitimate.

The defining point of the debate is, we can now see, conflicting sentiment. Finer is saying that people (of whom administrators are simply an instance) have to be watched; they will get out of hand if they are not held accountable through the threat of punishment. Friedrich, on the other hand, shows himself more willing to trust people. He, of course, does not generalize his position in the way that I am stating it here; he is speaking only of people who have been indoctrinated into the fellowship of science and the ranks of professional administrators. Nonetheless, I feel justified in characterizing his position in this way because he obviously feels that people have a nature that is amenable to such socialization. Finer seems to deny this—virtue itself hath need, et cetera. Their conflict of sentiment seems clear, but their shared static ontology quickly causes the issue raised by this conflict to become tangled and confused as they develop their arguments.

With respect to the logical integrity of the arguments, Finer holds the clearer and more consistent position. His objectivist ontology is congruent with the objectivist epistemology entailed by his belief (which he invokes by citing Frank Goodnow as a source and ally) in the possibility of separating politics/policy/value from administration/implementation/fact. This position enables Finer to adopt a consistently rationalist position, as he does when he argues that it is possible for elected representatives to enunciate policy as a meaningful "whole"—providing self-contained statements that can serve as the basis for effective control and accountability. Friedrich's (1940) position is less consistent in that he must deny that it is possible to separate policy from administration but at the same time claim that science and the expertise to which it gives rise are distinctive, bounded, and, by implication, separate modes of discourse from politics. Within the space of two pages, he appears either flatly to contradict himself or to shift his argument to entirely new grounds on this point when he says:

> People try to escape facing these difficulties by drawing facile distinctions, such as that officials might discuss facts but not policy. It might cogently be objected that facts and policies cannot be separated. Any presentation of facts requires a selection, and this selection is affected by views, opinions, and hence bears upon policy. (p. 244)

Then, one paragraph later, he exhorts:

> The only sound standard in a vast and technically complex government such as ours is to insist that the public statements of officials be in keeping with the highest requirements of scientific work. If a man's superiors disagree with him, let them mount the same rostrum and prove that he is wrong; before the goddess of science all men are equal. . . . Men of science inside and outside the government match their views and findings in a common effort to reach the right conclusions. (p. 245)

These two statements form a puzzling juxtaposition. The simplest way to resolve the puzzle is to conclude that by "science" Friedrich means "discourse about the facts of a matter" and thus has contradicted himself in holding on the one hand that "it might cogently be objected that facts and policies cannot be separated" and on the other hand that administrators' statements should be in keeping with "the highest standards of scientific work."

A more interesting interpretation might be that Friedrich means something entirely different in the second statement—namely, that science proceeds by a kind of discourse that conflates "views, opinions" (which is to say "values"), and facts but that nonetheless achieves a higher kind of reasoned and *objective* discourse that can lead to compelling, nonpolitical conclusions about the answers to policy questions. He seems to accord such a capacity to science in his concluding rhetorical flourish: "Before the goddess of science all men are equal. . . . Men of science inside and outside the government service match their views [values] and findings [facts] in a common effort to reach the right conclusions" (Friedrich, 1940, p. 245). If, in other words, we are speaking scientifically, it does not matter whether we are officials or politicians, inside or outside the government. Our deliberations will be regulated and directed by the process of science itself. If this interpretation is valid, Friedrich is suggesting that there are three modes of discourse, two of which are confused. First, there is "expert" discourse about facts (which implicitly and hence confusedly involves values). Second, there is "political" discourse about values (which implicitly and hence confusedly involves discourse about facts). Third, there is scientific discourse, which, through what we might appropriately call "reason," sorts and balances facts and values together to arrive at what Friedrich calls "right conclusions."

What denies this interpretation, or at least confuses it significantly, is that Friedrich makes "technical knowledge" (and hence by implication its corollary, expertise) the central part of his position. This emphasis makes it impossible to know exactly what he means by his strong insistence on the seamless connection between policy formation and policy execution. Probably Friedrich is simply ambivalent in his view on the freestanding independence of expertise. Also, he perhaps felt that denying the possibility of value-free expertise was a rhetorically weak, even impossible strategy.

It may be for this reason that Friedrich bases his case against the possibility of political control of administration on the implausibility of the idea of a "will of the state." By focusing the debate here, Friedrich strengthens his position and evokes perhaps the deepest point of disagreement between him and Finer: their assessment of the relation between community and democratic government. Finer is clear on this point: *Community* is a code word for "the state." It therefore carries all the negative connotations of authoritarianism and despotism that the Anglo-liberal democratic mind by habit attributes to this term. He wants to see the people not as a *community* but rather as an electorate, democratically expressing clear, individual preferences to representatives whom they expect to fulfill the mandates generated by a properly constituted electoral process. He is almost strident in his retort to Friedrich's position that the political process cannot yield clear policy preference—what Friedrich repeatedly and somewhat derisively refers to as the "will of the state." Finer's rebuttal is simply that the will of the people, as expressed through the political process, *does* have meaningful content. Even though the "people" may not be learned, they are wise, Finer holds, and their elected representatives can and should direct the actions of government administrators.

At bottom, then, the issue between Friedrich and Finer is exactly the one (as we will see in the next chapter when we examine the way in which the U.S. constitutional heritage bears on the legitimacy debate) that creates the primary tension that scholars of the Constitution have found within it: the tension between the *gesellschaft* principle of organizing social process around universalistic, objective corporate structures—which is to say *social institutions*—and the opposite *gemeinschaft* principle of organizing social process within more personalistic *communities*. Finer, because he no doubt defines *communities* to mean groups who share an ideology, sees them as a source of a totalitarian statism, of which public administrators are simply the agent operators. Friedrich, ironically, seems not to see communities in this way, but rather to see them as networks of relationships that make it possible to work past multiple viewpoints, preferences, misunderstandings, and disagreements. This is what he seems to mean when he says that policy is not finally defined until it has been implemented—which is to say, carried to citizens and negotiated through in specific, real-world circumstances. Indeed, it is because, in Friedrich's view, there is no ideological consensus of the sort that Finer fears that it is essential to see administration as the final phase of negotiating the meaning of policies. The generalities of policy statements, in other words, must be worked through the inevitably diverse and conflicting preferences and viewpoints that exist in the community before the policy can be said to be actually stated or known.

What this fundamental clash of sentiment and perspective reveals is that Friedrich and Finer regard human relationship in opposite ways. Friedrich sees relationship as intrinsically fraught with a tension arising out of the inevitable differences that emanate from the discrete standpoints or positions that individuals by definition occupy. At the same time, however, he sees this tension as *essentially* resolvable through the processes of discourse. Human contact can overcome human difference. Administrators who proceed with anticipation and who are sensitive to the need to work out policy rather than just implement it are not only being effective in the only way possible but also being responsible in the only way possible. Finer, on the other hand, sees relationship as somehow leading to the sort of collusive or confluent agreement that is characteristic of crowds. In a sense, the very idea of community conjures up the specter of ideology and the authoritarian statism that often accompanies ideologies. In this, he reflects to some extent the British common-law fear (even paranoia) of conspiracy. The only way, therefore, for people to govern themselves democratically is for them to express their individual preferences through the vote, preferences that he has faith can additively constitute a coherent expression of collective preference, one that elected representatives can use to hold government administrative officials accountable and to punish them when they go wrong. A corollary of this view seems to be that the community of relationship that must exist inside government organizations will produce a self-interested, conspiratorial, or ideological motive in administrators as they implement policy and will ensure the need for accountability and the potential for punishment.

The Biases Generated by the Friedrich-Finer Framing of the Issue

In my view, these reflections on the Finer-Friedrich debate reveal that the field of public administration, in taking their engagement as the frame within which the academic and practitioner communities have carried on discussion of the issue of responsibility, has limited and biased its discourse on this foundational issue of administrative theory. I see four major biases implicit in their dialogue. First, as has already been mentioned, they frame the issue of human nature, which is inevitably a part of debates on questions as generic as this one, as a matter of whether human beings are "good" (can be trusted to be responsible, etc.) or "bad" (cannot be trusted to pursue ends outside their own and be responsible to a principle or the public interest).

Finer's "virtue itself hath need of limits" position and Friedrich's reminder that political controls and rules can never work without reliance on the "good will" of administrators are just two of several indicators that this binary opposition rests on the issue of the nature of "administrative man" (sic) and, by implication, people in general. As I have already mentioned, this way of seeing the issue presumes that people *have* a nature: that is, that they *are* one way or the other, generally, either "good" or "bad." It therefore excludes the alternative assumption that human nature is not a property or an essence but a *dynamic*, emergent condition that is produced by a *process* of interaction.

A static ontology and the definition of human nature that derives from it shift the discourse over a question such as the need for control to ensure responsibility to an empirical matter of the essential traits of human beings. Because matters of fact are only resolvable when the parties involved are willing to accept each other's evidence (something that Friedrich and Finer seem unwilling to do), it becomes evident that this question is actually not resolvable empirically. In such cases, when argument within a paradigm lacks the context of a community of inquiry sufficient to resolve it at the level of fact and when alternative paradigmatic positions have not yet come into view, the argument will simply go on and on, unresolved, creating tedium and victimizing students who are compelled to study these traditional controversies as part of their socialization or education. Further, such arguments cover over the paradigmatic assumption that is configuring them and thereby hide alternative approaches from view.

The *second* bias in the debate stems from the knotted epistemological viewpoints that the two display. Both Finer and Friedrich show some degree of ambivalence with respect to a theory of *fact*. Finer is the clearer. His insistence that the political process can produce a binding statement of preference, one that is so clear and discrete that it can serve as a standard of accountability for technical implementation processes, amounts to a declaration that "facts are separate from values." At the same time, however, he states that politically set policies should guide administration to the fullest extent possible, acknowledging that at some point in the descent toward the detail of implementation there is a limit to the discreteness of policy and technique.

Friedrich is much more ambivalent. As I have noted, on the one hand, he grounds his argument in the flat assertion that the formation and execution of public policy is a "continuous process," with the one being inseparable from the other. On the other hand, he makes "technical knowledge" one of the two discrete and pivotal criteria by which administrative responsibility is to be judged, and in addition he refers to "expertise" at other points as if to denote by it a realm of purely technical knowledge.

How does one sort out such inconsistency? My view is that both men want to have it both ways, in that they wish to argue a position grounded in a theoretical pole (either the pole that facts and values are separate or the pole that they are not separable) while acknowledging the commonsense understanding that there are "matters of value" and "matters of fact." My guess is that if they were engaged in a personal conversation about the matter, they ultimately would resort to *an appeal to reason* to settle the question. They would, in other words, arrive at an agreement that facts and values are in principle distinctive from one another but that in practice they cannot be separated very far.

Given this, the Friedrich-Finer disagreement can now be seen for what it is: a matter of emphasis, a question of the point at which, in practice, policies as value statements can be separated from facts as administrative techniques. What this confluence indicates is that the two actually *share* an underlying paradigmatic commitment, one that insists on the distinction of fact and value as a matter of principle. The perspective (the one I want to argue for) that they wish to exclude denies the foundational opposition that the Friedrich-Finer paradigm requires to generate meaning. From within the paradigm that I advocate, fact and value are intrinsically conflated. Talk of values without talk of facts (or vice versa) is nonsensical and would not be allowed. This makes obvious how radical such an alternative view would be from the Friedrich-Finer orientation; it would seem inconceivable to them that intelligent discourse could be conducted without these two ideas.

However, it is not these two terms, fact and value, that ultimately are central to the Friedrich-Finer paradigm, since each of these terms, as we have just discussed, is rendered problematic by the other. Rather, what is critical is the idea of *reason,* which denotes a common viewpoint and standard that is validated simply by the fact that the participants to a discourse share a faith or belief in it. The essentially impossible fact-value problematic simply serves to create the need and the justification for the idea of reason. It is this classical idea, the idea of *reason,* that *serves as the hidden superordinate term of this discourse.* The important ideological function, the bias, of this term is to allow, yet contain, theoretical conflict while protecting an underlying para-digmatic agreement. This deception, through an implicit appeal to reason, constitutes the second major bias that the Friedrich-Finer debate injects into the discourse on administrative responsibility.

There is a further, deeply implicit agreement between the two that derives from a *third* bias: the assumption that values are at least to some extent definable outside the context of action. This is their mutual faith that *effective policies are possible*—which is to say that answers can be found to the problems at which policies are aimed. This assumption bespeaks a view of the social order as systemic, as having a patterned shape that can be discerned such that anomalies to the pattern can be identified and actions that can rectify anomalies can be framed. Friedrich and Finer both seem to hold the common belief that deliberation about society can produce meaningful, practical answers to social problems. (Friedrich's position on this point is qualified, of course, in that he insists that policies are not truly framed until they are worked out in practice, but the fact that he admits the idea of independent expertise into the picture places him on *essentially* the same ground as Finer.) The importance of this assumption is monumental: It supports the idea, which is virtually universally held at present, of defining social equity as the *efficacious program dispensing standardized outcomes*.

These two ideas, that the venue for governance is the "program" and that the meaning of fairness is "standardization," are the primary architectural principles of government action at present. They are so deeply ingrained in thinking about government that simply to raise a question about them seems odd. Nonetheless, I must raise such a question because the assumption that policy is possible completely hides the seldom considered but plausible alternative view that policy, in the sense of systematic, equitable programs, is *not* possible—that experimental, iterative *action* is the only workable alternative available for coping with social issues. Putting the alternative in this way is deliberate, because doing so gives the alternative the ring of irrationality (more accurately *nonrationality*) that is the central trait of the truly alternative. The exclusion of this alternative, along with its corollaries of situational (rather than programmatic) action and variegated (rather than standardized) outcomes as the reference point for equity, constitutes a major bias in dialogue about governance.

Related to the assumption that efficacious policy can be framed in bounded policy-making arenas is the *fourth* bias: the idea that hierarchy is the requisite structure on which government action must be built. In invoking the term *hierarchy,* I must be careful to specify that I do not mean merely that Friedrich and Finer are both committed to the idea that authority is the essential starting place for governance. Rather, I mean that they both deny the possibility that governance can proceed heuristically and collaboratively without a central source point providing guidance. This, in my view, is the *essential* commitment of those who see hierarchy as necessary and inevitable. What they mean at bottom is that, in some form, the *conscious mind* must be present and in control of a situation if effective action is to occur. Hierarchy, as I am talking about it here, is in its core meaning simply a coded way of stating the belief that only deliberate, economically calculated (opportunity costs considered, and costs and benefits balanced) action can lead to good outcomes. The fact that, in general, *hierarchy* is equated with *authority* is incidental and simply an indication that action from the conscious attitude must be taken unilaterally, since it is difficult to marshal a collaborative effort from within the ethos that it tends to create.

The position argued by Friedrich offers a good opportunity for sorting out how hierarchy in actuality means a controlling conscious attitude. His image of how the government administrator works or should work greatly *deemphasizes* the role of authority itself but at the same time asserts a strong role for a guiding consciousness. The Friedrichian administrator assumes a deferential, modest posture, obeys all rules and policies that govern his personal behavior, and then constantly seeks to avoid conflict and dissension in the implementation of policy by persistently anticipating and negotiating around and through disagreement in the political and public sectors.

Though one does not see in Friedrich's administrator the "new despot" that Finer fears, one does see an administrator who serves as a guiding, superordinate consciousness in working out the process of governance from the political level to the street. The administrator is the creative spirit who is able to anticipate and synergistically negotiate the difficulties caused by the narrow views of other parties to the process. Friedrich's administrator is thus something like the supremely deferential butler (e.g., Jeeves) who is actually in control of the narrative. (This is also the image of the professional public administrator on the BBC television series *Yes, Minister* and *Yes, Prime Minister.*) To the charge that the Jeeves character (like Wernher Von Braun) is actually not deferential, rule abiding, or subordinate at all, the retort would no doubt be that he does at least stay in his place—and he always makes things turn out for the best.

Finer's position is much less subtle on this point. Indeed, one could probably, without causing much controversy, describe him as committed to the principle of hierarchy in all of its possible meanings. He definitely demands that the public, acting through its parliamentary representatives, be placed in the position of "bossing" the administrative sector. He even insists on the necessity of punishment or the threat thereof as a validation of this authority. What interests me, however, is Finer's disagreement with Friedrich on the point of the possibility and meaningfulness of the idea of the "general will." Friedrich, of course, dismisses it as an impossibly nonsensical term. Finer, on the other hand, elevates it to the status of being an ultimate source of wisdom in governance, such that it "cannot be wrong." As we have already seen, however, his idea of general will is definitely not that it is the expression of a community (indeed, the idea seems to repel him). Rather, the general will is made up simply of *individual* voices added together. Recognizing this emphasis is important in understanding Finer's position, since it is the individual who is the natural venue for operating an economic calculus. Finer's insistence on political control of administration is at bottom an effort to ensure that what I am calling here the "conscious economic attitude" is placed in a clearly superordinate position in the process of governance.

Though Friedrich and Finer *disagree* on the locus from which initiative is to be taken and control exercised in defining the final meaning of policy, they *agree* on the mind-set or mental posture that should give shape to this initiative and control: Again, it is the conscious, rational, economic attitude. This underlying paradigmatic consensus carries the power of an almost-impossible-to-see finesse, created when a disagreement takes place as an overlay to a deeper agreement on fundamentals. What is effectively denied is the alternative view that refuses the foundational premise that the conscious, rational attitude is essential to effective, positive action. (I will suggest the model of governance and administrative action implied by this alternative mind-set in the concluding chapter.)

This preference for placing what I am calling the conscious attitude in a position of control amounts to a lack of faith in the efficacy, perhaps even the possibility, of administrative governance through creative *synergy* in the implementation of policy. Even in the picture of administration that Friedrich paints, the only potential for creativity that we see is that of the mastermind administrator (again, perhaps, like Wernher Von Braun). Since synergy entails a combination of elements, to deny its possibility is really to deny faith in relationship or, more broadly, process and, even more broadly, *community.* This fourth denial, this bias against community as a basis for a process of governance that transcends the split of preference and technique, value and fact, is the most serious distortion that their famous dialogue works on our discourse about the issue of administrative legitimacy. In a way, this bias summarizes all the others.

Finer's direct aspersions on the idea of community as a stand-in for the state make the issue explicit. Perhaps he reflects the fear of conspiracy, the group, the collective, the community that is such a deep part of the common-law tradition out of which he speaks. In making this fear as explicit as he does, he reveals that a major aspect of the problem of legitimacy—which, after all, reduces to a question of affording administrators a degree of trust for acting in governance— is the issue of social alienation. The difficulty we have in granting trust to administrators is akin to the difficulty we have, in the United States especially, in affording *each other,* as fellow citizens, a trust that we can act for the broad good of our society.

Conclusion

In concluding this discussion, let me return to the metaphor with which we began: Wernher Von Braun as public administrator. It may have seemed odd to the reader that a public administrationist like me would raise such an image in a discussion of administrative responsibility, as it plays naturally into all the usual, easy connections that critics of administration make between bureaucrats and despotism. Why did I raise it? Let me emphasize that I did so quite consciously, to give weight to what I consider the main lesson that the Friedrich-Finer debate teaches us. Now that we have reviewed the positions that Friedrich and Finer take, we can see that Von Braun does not meet the criteria set out by either one of them for being a responsible public administrator. Though the point is complicated by the fact that Hitler operated without a parliament of the sort that Finer approves—though he was appointed by one constitutionally—we can, without stretching too far, use Von Braun as a test case. Finer would, no doubt, be appalled at the idea, but it seems inescapable that Von Braun, as the neutral public servant of his political master Hitler, must be considered to some extent the epitome of the type of administrator that he advocates. On the other hand, Finer would be just as appalled at the idea that Von

Braun had deceived his political superior in the process of seeking to
be his faithful agent.

The case is the same with Friedrich. He would have to applaud Von
Braun's creative and bold initiative in doing everything possible to
make the V-2 program work out. At the same time, he would have to
be appalled at the fact that Von Braun did not seek to integrate into his
actions his views, his values, as perhaps reflective of the sentiment of
the "community of Germany" broadly speaking (rather than just the
Nazi party), and seek to resist the Hitler regime—which he could easily
have done simply by complying, in the neutral way that Finer advocates, with Hitler's order to abandon the V-2 program; the rockets were
built, after all, by concentration camp slave labor under horrific
conditions. In sum, for Von Braun to have met the approval of Finer,
he would have had to become too much like Friedrich's administrator to have gained Finer's approval, and to have met the approval
of Friedrich, he would have had to become too much like Finer's
administrator to have gained Friedrich's approval. Ultimately, neither
Friedrich nor Finer allows the public administrator a viable or workable position in the process of governance. Their debate teaches us
that if we want to find a truly legitimate place for the public administrator, we must find an alternative image of governance itself, an image
that derives from a different model of society, one grounded in community rather than in the administrator's role per se. In a sense, all the
biases I have described here as besetting the Friedrich-Finer debate
sum up to a bias against government—of this alternative sort.

What, then, *is* the kind of government they are legitimating? What
is the positive accomplishment of the dialogue they produced? Let us
recall a few of the points made above about the nature and effect of
their discourse. First, we saw that they both assume a static view of
human nature, one that sees it as fixed and centered on the key factual
question of whether people are good or bad, trustworthy or untrustworthy. Second, although at the surface level they disagree on the
point, we saw that ultimately they both waffle on the separateness of
facts and values, creating a corollary ambivalence about the separateness of politics (the realm of value) and administration (the realm of
fact). Third, though on the surface they disagree about whether and
how guidance for governance can be gained from the collective, they
agree that there is a collective mandate—for Finer, the will of the
people expressed through legislatures, and for Friedrich, the will of the
state discovered through sensitivity to popular sentiment and to
technical knowledge.

It is worthwhile to point out that these three issues provide a rather good profile of the commonsense apprehension of the issue of governance. Typically, such discussions turn on whether human beings are good or bad. Just as frequently, they revolve around tangles of fact and value questions. Also, common sense accepts the idea of an objective collective good, that what society needs can be specified rationally. We can conclude either that Finer and Friedrich started from commonsense assumptions or that their dialogue has done much to structure common sense itself. Curiously, though, this set of issues is typically employed to focus discussion about the proper nature of democratic governance, when in fact what it does is create the illusion that democratic government is impossible or, alternatively, that democratic government can only be an illusion. That is, to sum up the thrust of this chapter, the logic of the issues configured by the Finer-Friedrich debate excludes people as much as possible from the process of governance.

How this is so is rather simple. Finer and Friedrich have configured the question of the manner in which modern administrative democracies are structured in such a way that it becomes unanswerable, all the while seeming to provide the framework by which the question can be resolved. (This is no doubt why their articles have been so successful in generating discussion and term papers in graduate seminars for so many decades.) Whether people are good or bad seems a sensible question, but it is unanswerable either in principle or by fact. Likewise, whether facts can be separated from values seems quite a good question, but it too turns out to be impossible to resolve in any definite terms. That there is a definable public interest or a collective desire seems sensible, but the validity of the idea, like that of all definitions, turns out to entail answers to the very question (what is democratic government) that it seeks to address.

What Finer and Friedrich do, in effect, is establish an impossible theoretical question at the center of the practical problem of how to run democratic governments. The effect is to establish the need, indeed the absolute necessity, for a realistic resolution, one that acknowledges but nonetheless finesses the theoretical questions and "gets on with the program." This solution is what I call the Man of Reason. By making it impossible to specify conceptually the proper structure of democratic process, we are left with no alternative but to choose reasonable leaders and trust them, leaving our participation in governance ultimately to the crude devices of elections and interest groups. The problem as Finer and Friedrich frame it is a powerful engine for false answers, but even false answers, when the questions involved are taken as sensible, keep alive the illusion that an answer is possible.

In the meantime, at least in the field of public administration, we become content to let Men of Reason rule. Indeed, we even appreciate that they take on the burden, in making public policy, of deciding how far people can be trusted, of untangling factual questions from value questions and then sorting out the best of each. Most of all, we admire and respect them for seeking to define what is best for all of us, our collective good, even though this seems impossible. What we never stop to think about is that perhaps if we looked at the question in a different way, through a different frame, we could see valid possibilities for doing our own governance, with no need for Men of Reason to decide for us. The bias that Finer and Friedrich perpetuate in us is just this. It prevents us from thinking in ways that would put people generally, rather than politicians and administrators, in control of the everyday business of governance.

The reason we do not readily notice this rather pervasive bias in Friedrich and Finer's dialogue is that it is one that we as Americans tend to share with them. This bias has its roots in the struggle during the founding of our nation, especially in the writing of its generic political formula. It was here that the struggle between the opposing principles of republican institution and communitarian process was first joined in our history. The settling of this issue at the time of the founding, as we shall see shortly, was not complete by any means, but it did decide the issue, at least officially, in the terms that Friedrich and Finer reflect. It is not inaccurate to say that the biases that the structure of their debate injected into the dialogue about legitimacy are mostly *reflections* of the fundamental bias against community that can be found in our constitutional heritage. Marking out how this bias was produced at the period of the striking of the U.S. Constitution is the project of the next chapter.

3

The Political Background
of the Issue

But the framers were also, as they loved to say about all
men, self-interested. To justify their radical change from
anything that had gone before . . . they argued that
conditions under the previous form of government, the
Articles of Confederation, were considerably worse than
they appear to have been. Without denying the genius of
Alexander Hamilton . . . or the extraordinary creativity of
James Madison . . . the question remains whether
Americans might have developed differently, and perhaps
in some respects better, if they had continued to be ruled
by the totally noncentralized political system organized
under the Articles of Confederation. . . . It is a failure of
imagination as well as historical perspective to believe that
the federal system that began with the Constitution was the
only political structure that Americans might have had, or
that, as different as it was from other forms of government
at the time, Americans might not have governed
themselves in an even more radical manner.

Wildavsky, "On the Articles of Confederation"

AUTHOR'S NOTE: Several passages in this chapter by Anti-Federalist writers (Agrippa,
1966; John De Witt, 1966; Henry, 1966; Lee, 1966; Mason, 1966; Smith, 1966; A Republican Federalist, 1966) are excerpted from *The Antifederalists,* edited by C. Kenyon,
1966, New York: Bobbs-Merrill. Copyright 1966 by Simon & Schuster. Reprinted by
permission.

◆ VIRTUALLY EVERY CITIZEN of the United States who has attained a high school education is familiar with the story I want to document in this chapter, although few think of it as distorted. I became aware of the type of distortion embedded in it in an indirect way when I began studying government as a child in Texas. We were required by law to take courses in Texas history and government before, in fact, studying U.S. government. The battle of the Alamo, of course, loomed large in our young minds. Santa Anna was a vivid villain and Sam Houston a powerful avenger. Even with these tales of glory, I remember being worried about how Texas came to be in the first place. It seemed to me that early American settlers had simply moved into Mexico and, after living there a bit, declared a substantial portion of it to be their new country—the Republic of Texas. Perhaps I had early "postcolonial" sentiments, but my teacher's response proved to be both prophetic and unsettling. She was not interested in pursuing this line of discussion and urged me to "trust the textbook" and the heroic pioneers/soldiers who gave their lives for my freedom.

The prophetic aspect of her answer was revealed in my later university work. In those days, higher education in the social sciences was crashingly dull—or at least it seemed so to me. Every scrap of intellectual controversy that one came across in texts was treasured as material for discussion. Since the intellectual venue of the day was the study of institutional structure, most of the issues in the literature involved were rather bloodless (e.g., do the traditional boundaries of the states still make sense, or should they be redrawn so as to create more efficient government?).

The most striking exception was the debate surrounding the progressive writer Charles A. Beard's *An Economic Interpretation of the Constitution* (1913), which, because it was so interesting, was brought up in a wide variety of courses, from introductory to advanced. What Beard argued was that the framers of the Constitution represented a specific class of privileged economic interests. His research showed that, disproportionately, they were wealthy land and slave owners, manufacturers and shippers, moneylenders, and bond holders who had a direct interest in establishing a government that protected such holdings and investments. What was exciting about this material was that it was critical, suggesting as it did that the founding fathers, whom we had all been taught to revere, might have been narrowly self-interested in framing the Constitution. It seemed to me that this kind of thinking was what going to university was supposed to be all about.

Debate in class on the topic was always lively, and, as is typical in cases involving a large and ultimately undecidable issue, students looked for cues as to how to feel about it, where to come down on it, what, in short, to think. The signals that professors sent were remarkably consistent: (a) These are interesting, well-stated ideas that must be seriously entertained even if they are different and challenging; (b) the critical attitude of mind, though, has difficulty maintaining its objectivity (the ultimate trait of the thinking, educated person); and (c) these ideas are controversial in the sense that the evidence for them is not completely conclusive, and many disagree with Beard's interpretation of his research data. Much was made of the point that (as Beard himself took pains to point out) he was not claiming that the founders wrote the Constitution to benefit themselves personally, only that they sought to benefit the commercial classes and, by implication, the development of commerce generally in the new nation.

For the most part, we students came away from this discussion with an image of the founders as incredibly brilliant young men (the absence of women was not lost on me) who had embarked on a project of nation building and had hammered out, through struggle and debate, probably the most perfect instrument of government ever devised by *man* (we were not told how easily they came to agreement on the key provisions affecting commerce). We were told that the genius of the Constitution lay in its adaptability, its power to comprehend the enormous changes that the nation quickly underwent (we were not told of the rather widespread critical reaction during the time of the populists and progressives—I did not even discover that Beard was a progressive until much later in my educational career). We were told that the moral compromises in the Constitution—the way it treats the slavery issue, women, and the principle of democracy itself—were necessary, temporary artifacts of its construction, like ugly scaffolding that everyone knows from the start is never really intended to be part of a beautiful new building (McWilliams, 1979; Storing, 1979).

Most of all, though, we were told that the founders had saved the young American nation from the failure of the Articles of Confederation, which was the first constitution of the United States. The message was that the writing and ratification of the Constitution were a reflection of the immediate lessons of history and experience under the malfunctioning, inept Articles. This coup was made to seem all the more brilliant because it was done with a certain degree of secrecy and manipulation. It was a credit to the rhetorical power of our teachers that we came away feeling that our founding fathers were great democratic republicans even while they deceived and manipulated the citizenry of their day. It was somehow a testimony to democracy that the people of the day did not realize they needed a new government, whereas the founders did, and gave them one, in one sense, regardless of their wishes.

This picture of the founders and the Constitution is the background distortion that supports the legitimacy issue and hence the regime of Men of Reason. My project in this chapter is to reveal this distortion by suggesting what it obscures. What the distortion hides is an alternative ethos and way for democratic governance, one that was present at the founding of the Constitutional regime under which we currently live but obscured by the way the story of the founding has been handed down to us.

A number of intellectual distortions have provided a "cover" for Men of Reason, one that hides their effective control of our administrative institutions even though these institutions appear open and democratic. The framing of the legitimacy issue in the Friedrich-Finer debate accomplishes such cover at a surface level. This technical level of cover is not sufficient, however. Indeed, it can be made to seem plausible only by setting it against a backdrop that depicts government as necessarily involving agents and that highlights the issue of how to control these agents.

"Deep cover" is thus provided by a distortion in the way the history surrounding our political formula—set out in the Constitution—is presented and taught. Since the case I want to make is essentially historical, it should be clear that arguing it conclusively is, for all intents and purposes, impossible. History is the most plastic of arts; my hope is that the account I want to give is so simple, familiar, and standard that it will seem plausible. My interest is not in countering one set of "facts" with another but rather with recounting a tale that emphasizes different aspects of a well-known story. By doing so, I want to open a line of discourse about American political origins that has the potential to reframe our understanding of the role of public administration. I want to suggest what alternative was present at our founding, take another look at the experience of governance under the Articles so as to indicate the legitimacy of this alternative ethos, and then offer an adumbrated, but slightly more formal, statement of it through the lens of the Anti-Federalist theory of government.

Governance as the
Creation of a Peaceable Kingdom

There is, at present, rather broad consensus across the political spectrum that a serious disconnection has developed between American citizens, their government, and political processes (Barber, 1984; Drucker, 1995; Hall, 1995; Maurer, 1996; Olasky, 1992; Putnam, 1993; Sandel, 1996; Toffler & Toffler, 1995). It seems fair to say that the situation has reached crisis proportions. This problem will serve as the central focus of the last chapter of this book, and it will frequently be a key point of reference for the analysis that leads to that concluding discussion.

A great deal of research is aimed at the question of what has caused citizens to fall away from their traditional political identifications, political activity, and even interest in political matters (Naisbitt, 1982; Yankelovitch, 1991). Some of the more interesting research has been conducted by the Harwood Group (1995, 1996), a consulting organization that works with communities on civil society projects aimed at revitalizing citizen involvement. The specific question orienting their research was: What do people want to happen when they talk to each other about civic matters? The answer emerging to this question fits something like the following image. They definitely do not want conflict to occur but rather seek to use conversation as a way of strengthening relationships with their conversation partners. They see social issues as complex and highly interconnected "webs" of concerns that are best approached as wholes. Rather than declaring what the problems are, they want to use the conversation as an opportunity to sort out their perceptions, to make sense of them in collaboration with others so that a shared view of the matter is developed. They want the expression of feelings and emotions to be a legitimate part of the process. Although they do not demand that decisions immediately result from the talking, they want action decisions based on their perceptions to occur and to be carried out as the direction for action becomes clear (The Harwood Group, 1991).

In general, people as citizens see the process of civic discussion properly proceeding when it is grounded in human relationships with each other and when the discussions emanating from these relationships are heuristic and full, such that a shared context for viewing the situation under consideration is developed. Once this context is achieved, priorities will be clear, decisions can be made, and actions can be taken. The emphasis clearly is on the process of human interaction and its foundation, human relationship. If this is politics, it is a politics of the heart and the human connection.

Two things stand out as striking about this image of discourse and the model of governance that it implies. The first is how thoroughly *different* it is from the economic interest, expertise-based idea of politics and governance that we actually have developed in the United States, and the second is how *similar* it is to what seems to have been the original ethos of social life that developed in the new American nation as its ties with the British empire were eroding. Even though the colonists wanted a different kind of life from that they had left behind, they had little choice but to replicate much of the European social pattern from which they came (Wood, 1993). In addition, the isolated and rather primitive living conditions they were forced to endure gave the ethos they developed a distinctive twist.

The general cultural pattern may be described as an anomalous combination of social intimacy and separation. Life was lived in what would appear to the contemporary eye to be an extremely personal way. As Wood (1993) put it:

> In such a small scale society, privacy as we know it did not exist, and our sharp modern distinction between private and public was as yet scarcely visible. Living quarters were crowded, and people who were not formally related—servants, hired laborers, nurses and other lodg-ers—were often jammed together with family members in the same room or even in the same bed. (1993, p. 59)

People watched (indeed, spied on) each other continuously and felt free to turn each other in for infractions against community norms. Regulation of behavior was accomplished primarily through face-to-face relationship. There was little sense of individual freedom of the modern sort. Social relationships constituted a kind of mutual paternalism, a web of interwoven dependencies. Again, as Wood (1993) put it:

> No relationship could be exclusive or absolute; each was relative, reciprocal, and complementary. "Every service or help which one man affords another, requires its corresponding return." These "re-turns . . . due from one person to another" were in fact "the bands of society, by which families, neighborhoods, and nations are knit together." Society was held together by intricate networks of personal loyalties, obligations, and quasi-dependencies. These personal loyal-

ties were not the same as the legal bondage of the unfree; they were
not like the explicit subjection of the landless; and they were not even
precise reproductions of the many subserviencies of patronage-
ridden England. (p. 57)

Although the colonists reproduced European paternalism, they gave
it a distinctively mutual and personalistic cast. They were fond of
invoking the famous passage from 1 Corinthians (12:25) that calls for
social caring: "that there should be no Schism in the Body; but that
the Members should have the Same Care one for another" (Williams,
1983, p. 3). Selfishness was condemned, as was "anything that dissolved in a moment the solidest friendship" (Wood, 1993, p. 20).
Indeed, the mutual dependencies that constituted the social bond
were referred to as "friendships," "the only term universal and affective
enough to describe them," as the idea of formal dependencies became
anathema (p. 58).

Government and politics were also construed in personalistic,
immediate terms. Officials were familiar persons who might call
parties to their homes to work out solutions to issues. Public money
might be used for private purposes, and magistrates might live from
the fines they levied; on the other hand, officials might use personal
money to supply troops or pay taxes owed by the citizenry. Courts were
more interested in relationships than in the specifics of the law, and
out-of-court settlements were greatly preferred over litigation.
Breaches of mutual trust were regarded as more serious than violence,
and the punishments of the day reflected the fact that society was seen
as a skein of social relationships (Zuckerman, 1970). The nomination
and election process was often simply a rubber-stamping of decisions
that had been reached through informal conversation and negotiation.
Zuckerman (1970), in his landmark study of the Massachusetts colonies, described the politics of the day elegantly:

The reality of local politics rested in a hundred humble conversations,
across fences and tavern tables, quietly allusive, subtly suggestive,
endlessly tactful. If all went well, an almost silently shared understanding would be reached among the inhabitants, and there would
be no contest at all for the office at issue; more often than not, the
"sense of the meeting" would be set before the meeting met. (p. 182)

Similarly, law was not seen as a venue for positive social purpose.
Indeed, "Government was regarded essentially as the enlisting and

mobilizing of the power of private persons to carry out private ends"
(Wood, 1993, p. 82). It certainly was not widely regarded as a device
for redistributing wealth and power. Society was seen as arising from
a pattern of organic, private relationships. Government was simply a
closely related adjunct, mostly a device through which questions
could be answered such as whether people should be allowed to let
their hogs run free.

Another, and in a sense more revealing, pattern can be seen in the
way that economic relations were construed in the colonial period.
The conditioning factor was the concreteness of the colonists' sense
of life and the corresponding style of mind that it produced. There was
little sympathy with abstractions such as market processes. When
something like rational market dynamics developed, for example, the
populace maintained, by force, customary prices and traditional ways
of distributing goods against the manipulations wrought through
impersonal market relationships (Wood, 1993, p. 90). The economy
was conceived of as analogous to the private relationships characteristic of a family household, where providing for the needs of all was
the focus of decision making. There was little comprehension of the
abstract idea of money, and often there was no circulating currency.
Wood (1993) summarized the economic picture this way:

> Merchants, shopkeepers, and craftsmen all tended to regard their
> businesses as a series of personal transactions with familiar persons.
> . . . Often they treated their economic activities simply as extensions
> of their personal life: they mingled their domestic and business
> accounts to the point where they had little or no awareness at any
> one moment of the profitability of their enterprises. (p. 67)

Even debt between two people was regarded as something of a social
bond (p. 68).

In sum, the sense of life in the colonies stressed organic connection.
It seems fair to say that at least implicitly, and without realizing it,
people saw themselves as part of one another, as creating each other.
Conformity, and in one sense the suppression of individuality, was a
part of this. Strangers and vagabonds were "warned out" and sent away
from communities until, in principle, they landed back where they
belonged (Zuckerman, 1970, pp. 62-63). There was a premium on
social serenity, and the colonists created as much of it as they could,
given that they necessarily had to import the only patterns of social
organization they knew—namely, those of Europe (Ver Steeg, 1964).

One metaphor for this ethos is the "Peaceable Kingdom" of the famous American painting by Edward Hicks. This painting depicts children and wild beasts as friendly companions in a tranquil village setting, symbolizing, above all, a distinctive psychological condition of serenity between the conscious mind (the human beings in the picture) and the unconscious world (the wild animals). Purposeful—that is, commercial—activity is absent from the picture and hence rendered derivative. Valid relationship, the painting implies, is primary and precedes all else. In this sense, the famous mural in the city of Sienna, Italy, *The Benefits of Good Government*, provides a wonderful coda to the Hicks painting. The mural depicts the active, prosperous commercial life of the city; its message seems to be that general physical well-being is dependent on the collective psychological health that must underpin good government.

The significance of the relationships that constitute community is the powerful image created by Zuckerman's book, itself entitled *Peaceable Kingdoms* (1970). As Zuckerman summarized the importance of the colonial experience to American history, he argued that it is "not to be found in its democracy, and assuredly not in its regard for the individual, but rather in the emergence there of a broadly diffused desire for consensual communalism as the operative premise of group life in America" (p. 4). What the colonists seemed to want, or at least what they *came* to want, was an organic form of social life that emphasized mutual caring for the whole, the social body itself, as a means of ensuring harmony and prosperity. Nonconformity typically resulted in intensified efforts to bring the straying individual back into the group. Excommunication meant that the community was going to make *certain* that the member in question was going to appear at meeting the next Sunday (p. 63). However, if these efforts failed, separation was the ultimate remedy, designed to preserve the sanctity of the peaceful community. Dissent and difference that could not be resolved were seen as destructive, so they were segregated. It is important to note that the maintenance of harmonious relationships "took precedence over more mundane matters of material advantage and even, on occasion, over the apparent imperatives of nature itself" (p. 142). "Men lived together in agreement or they did not live together at all" (p. 124). The separation that resulted over unreconcilable disagreement was not seen as *negative* but as the positive consequence of valuing the good of the whole; disparate cultural and religious communities lived amicably in distinct but proximate communities.

The Articles of Confederation

I sketched above a rough picture of the social and political ethos of the colonial period as a context for describing the type of government that the American revolutionaries wanted to have, and to counter the common idea that the government they established after winning the war with Britain was defective. The theme in this part of my story is that the popular historical account of the new American nation's experience under the Articles of Confederation is a distortion, one that sets the stage for an overvalorization of the virtues of the government established by the Constitution. This popular history not only casts government under the Articles in a negative light but also suppresses the genuine political theory, represented by the Anti-Federalists, that opposed the Constitution. The point is that the formula of governance implicit in the Articles and made more explicit in the pronouncements of the Anti-Federalists is one that denies a place for Men of Reason, suggests an entirely different basis for the legitimacy of government action, and entails an idea of administration's role in governance radically at odds with our contemporary one.

The story we have all been told by our secondary school American history textbooks about the Articles of Confederation is, first, that they were biased by the American nation's recent emergence from a revolution, in that this experience produced an irrational or extreme distrust of central government authority. This bias in turn, as the story goes, led the Continental Congress, the body that wrote the Articles, to create an excessively decentralized, weak, and ineffective government. It was a government reputed to be incapable of acting to carry out the work of producing and maintaining ordered social, political, and commercial relationships. Typically, emphasis is placed on the point that the government could not create a standard, stable currency (this is a problem that is understandable and suitably frightening even to schoolchildren) or effectively carry out trade relations. In short, this story says, the Articles *failed,* and necessity *required* a new government (Bragdon, McCutchen, & Ritchie, 1994; Burns, Peltason, & Cronin, 1984; Hardy, 1992; Jordan, Greenblatt, & Bowes, 1985; Kownslar & Smart, 1983; Remy, Elowitz, & Berlin, 1984).

The powers accorded the national government are typically listed in the negative, as if to underscore the limitations of the structure from the beginning. The authors of a popular text describe the strengths and weaknesses of the Articles in this way:

> The Articles of Confederation had *one strong point* [italics added]:
> They formed a new nation—the United States of America. . . . But the
> Articles were too weak to form the basis of a lasting government. The
> new nation was poor. Soldiers in rags begged to be paid for their
> service during the Revolution. People who had loaned money to the
> struggling government wanted it paid back. Congress had asked the
> states for money. But the states pinched their pennies. Congress could
> not even pay interest on the money it had borrowed. The thing that
> was the most damaging to the nation was the lack of any way of
> enforcing the laws. There were no national courts—only state courts.
> If a state did not approve of a law passed by Congress, it just ignored
> the law. By 1787, many people in the United States were deeply
> worried about the future of their new nation. (Kownslar & Smart,
> 1983, p. 75)

Is this not the story you were told in elementary school, in high school,
and even at college or university? The question is, however: Is such a
description the whole story?

The world in which the Articles of Confederation were proposed
in 1777 was a world of intimate communities, linked together into state
governmental units. These governments were taken for granted by
citizens as the legitimate loci of sovereignty. The entire thrust of the
state constitutions had been to *guarantee* citizen involvement directly
in the conduct of government through a process that occurred as
closely as possible to the source of sovereignty, the people (Morris,
1987, p. 55). The central government as defined by the Articles of
Confederation was intended primarily as a forum for broader discussion of issues that crossed state lines. The issue of sovereignty was
never in question; Congress under the Articles held power only via a
direct authorization from the people through the state governments.
Thus, to argue, as the Federalists later did, that state governments
became the captive of popular wrangling and that a structure to
embody popular sovereignty would be more effective at one remove
from the people reveals how far they disagreed with the principle itself.

The desire for a delicate balance between centralization and decentralization was the guiding force behind the structure of the Articles. Although the number of delegates to the national Congress was
proportional to state populations, ranging from not fewer than two to
no more than seven, each state had only one vote, regardless of its
number of delegates. Responding to concern that an aristocracy of
delegates might develop, a provision required that any delegate might

serve only three out of any six years. Delegates were perforce required to develop a process whereby they might discuss and decide about issues as a group in order to cast a single vote. If any group of delegates divided equally on a question, the state's vote was lost. Within the Congress, approval of any issue required two thirds of the states. Overall, the Congress under the Articles is often said to have resembled a group of diplomats assembled to discuss and consider common concerns. The overwhelming emphasis was on the process of discourse and the development of agreement in virtually consensus terms (Hicks & Mowry, 1956, p. 96).

Social and economic conditions under the Articles did become difficult. Immediately following the war, conditions within the states improved as people spent money accumulated from war sales on imported goods. This period of prosperity began to end in 1784 as hard currency ran out, and a two-year depression ensued. Massive social changes were also underway as the democratic thrust of the Revolution combined with the potential for prosperity that existed in the postrevolutionary era to raise expectations among average citizens. Concomitantly, it became apparent that dependence on foreign trade was dangerous. Difficulties in trade relations with Great Britain were exacerbated by Britain's unwillingness to withdraw from the Northwest, American inability to guarantee repayment of citizens' war debts, and the failure of the new government to restore Loyalist property. Despite the Treaty of 1783 and the assignment of John Adams as delegate to Britain, relations remained strained. Trade with Spain was also problematic, hinging on the American desire to maintain open navigation of the mouth of the Mississippi River, which lay within Spanish dominion. Overall, foreign trade was insufficient to provide the markets necessary to fuel anticipated growth. As a result, it became necessary quickly to develop internal markets within and among the states to foster the exchange of goods in interstate commerce. This required internal coordination and, perhaps more important, a stable mechanism of exchange—that is, currency (Ferguson, 1979, pp. 1-14; Hicks & Mowry, 1956, pp. 103-105; Morris, 1987, pp. 130-161; G. S. Wood, 1987, pp. 69-109).

During the Revolution, the issuance of paper money had allowed the government to pay for goods and services in an expedient manner. The government's ability to continue this currency was, however, curtailed under conditions of indebtedness following the war. America had incurred more than $40 million of debt during the war. A portion was owed to France and other foreign sources, but about $32 million was owed to American citizens as back pay for soldiers and certificates of indebtedness to citizens who had provided supplies for the war effort (Hicks & Mowry, 1956, p. 193).

The central government under the Articles was limited in its efforts to generate revenue. Further borrowing was possible but only if sources of credit were found. Public land sales and the post office brought in small amounts annually, but the government was primarily dependent on the process of requisitioning funds from the states. States, suffering similar financial situations, acceded to the requisitions from Congress only occasionally and at will, resulting in payment of about 10% of the sums requested (Hicks & Mowry, 1956, p. 103). State governments were suffering a similar fate. They had the power to levy tariffs that the Congress lacked, but the variability of tariff policy and implementation among the states resulted in confusion, competition-causing friction, and limitation on internal trading (Morris, 1987, pp. 148-150).

With the conclusion of the war and the establishment of the Articles of Confederation, debt was used to fund growth and expansion (Riesman, 1987). The depression that followed the decline of available currency meant lowered standards of living, overextension, and an expanding cycle of indebtedness. Calls for the printing of more paper money reached a crescendo in the 1780s as the merchant and emerging middle classes as well as the agricultural sector demanded continuation of the opportunities and expectations that had been set during wartime. Once allowed participation in a more egalitarian, expanding market society, the nongentry were unwilling to return to their prewar state of dependency (G. S. Wood, 1987, pp. 77-81; Wood, 1993, p. 316).

This desire for the printing of currency was directly symbolic of the new spirit of equality that was created after the war and was also, perhaps, a reflection of the colonial ethos—one in which debt was seen in personal terms and was secondary to the maintenance of relationships and social well-being. In addition, the people of this day had little appreciation or understanding of the abstractions embodied in money. Average citizens wanted a larger role in the economy and also in the government that sustained and regulated that economy. *In short, the average citizen wanted to participate in the conduct of public affairs.* It was this shift in self-conscious activism that alarmed the "ruling class," the landed gentry (G. S. Wood, 1987, p. 81). This alarm began to take a more dramatic and violent turn by the 1780s with the outbreak of civil conflicts throughout the states, most notably in Rhode Island and in Massachusetts.

In Rhode Island, the traditional bonds of paternal dependency were particularly weak, and the need for trading was especially high. This combined to allow merchants and paper money advocates to dominate state politics. Paper money was issued continuously and in such quantities and lent to debtors on such easy terms that by 1760 it had become, in effect, worthless. Creditors and merchants began to refuse to accept it. The legislature, in response, passed a law making it illegal to refuse to accept the paper money and even allowing conviction and imprisonment for this offense without a jury trial. Enforcement resulted in a precedent-setting case, *Trevett vs. Weeden* (1786), in which the Supreme Court overturned the law as contrary to the charter of the state. The legislature, unhappy with this decision, simply voted it as unsatisfactory and replaced the judges at the next election. The legal precedent survived, but the threat of direct action against those who did not support the expansion of currency was not lost on the gentry in Rhode Island and in other states (Hicks & Mowry, 1956, p. 104).

Massachusetts experienced an even more dramatic outbreak of economically inspired civil violence, one that deeply affected the critics of the Confederation. The Massachusetts conflict originated in the split between the fairly wealthy coastal towns and the agricultural interior. The farmers found themselves caught in a predictable cycle of indebtedness. The problems of farmers were widespread throughout the states, and by the 1780s, prisons were filled with debtors. There were several instances of riots and conflict at foreclosure sales, property seizures, and courts (Parenti, 1974, p. 43; Wood, 1993, p. 307). Throughout the summer of 1786 and the winter of 1787, open rebellion erupted in Massachusetts, with bands of debtors marching on courthouses to prevent the hearing of debtor cases. Led by the western Massachusetts farmer Daniel Shays, these groups took up arms, and the uprising became known as Shays' Rebellion. It was ultimately put down during the winter by the state's militia funded through a "loan to which well-to-do citizens, fearful that a wholesale attack upon property rights was imminent, subscribed generously" (Hicks & Mowry, 1956, p. 104).

Although Shays' Rebellion was short-lived, its demonstration of underclass power appeared as an ominous portent of the future (Brown, 1987; Zinn, 1995, pp. 90-94). At the next Massachusetts state election, Governor Bowdoin, whose administration had suppressed the rebellion, was roundly defeated by John Hancock, a hero to the rebels. The majority of the voting populace was obviously sympathetic to the concerns of the farmers, an alarming point to the local gentry. In fact, the violent outbreak of Shays' Rebellion and its political aftermath had a profound effect on the gentry throughout the states.

Although the issue of a stable currency and basis for credit had become acute, it was actually the fear of the emergence of the traditional underclass as a potent political force that created the greater political furor (Morris, 1987, p. 264).

Although this situation might appear difficult or even dire to the contemporary eye, it must be emphasized that its primary source was economic—the emerging pattern in the distribution of wealth—rather than governmental. Most of the circumstances creating the problems of this period were not as related to the structure of the Confederation as its critics sought to allege. "Recent research . . . indicates that the adverse conditions were overdrawn by representatives of the more conservative classes to emphasize their demand for a stronger national government" (Hicks & Mowry, 1956, p. 105). By the zenith of the discontent in 1786, with Shays' Rebellion, the Confederation government had already had a number of important successes in governing, and the general circumstances within the country were improving. As Aaron Wildavsky (1993) noted:

> It will not be difficult to show that the government under the Articles of Confederation, though imperfect in many respects, was quite satisfactory in others, and the condition of the people recovering from a lengthy and debilitating war was about as good as might be expected. The management of the Revolutionary War by the Continental Congress, also a noncentralized political system, left much to be desired, especially in the financial realm. Yet it is easy to forget that the war was won by this noncentralized system and that it triumphed over a highly centralized opponent. (p. 13)

The postwar depression was lifting, and international trade as well as domestic productivity was growing. The financial condition of the Confederation government was never as bad as its critics have depicted (G. S. Wood, 1987, p. 80). The Congress had been able to borrow money from the Dutch to begin repayment of the war debt and had been able to keep up with interest payments on the Dutch loan. Foreign investors were emerging, willing to further extend credit. Though conditions in Massachusetts were problematic, in other states, such as Virginia, economic circumstances were rapidly becoming prosperous and stable. Virginia had been able to issue paper money and keep its value constant. She had also funded and was quickly retiring her war debt. The Confederation had even had some success in dealing with foreign governments. Wartime treaties with France and

Holland were maintained and renewed, and a few other trade treaties were signed, most significantly with Sweden and Prussia. Internally throughout the states, conditions overall were improving. Even in the troublesome area of interstate commerce and cooperation, the government was developing some successes (Hicks & Mowry, 1956, pp. 102-103).

Perhaps the greatest area of effectiveness under the Articles, and the one that held the most promise for the future, was the management of the western lands (Hicks & Mowry, 1956, pp. 56-102; Morris, 1987, pp. 220-244). In the settlement of the West, the Confederation government displayed unprecedented ability to coordinate interstate relationships and to manage expansion and development. With the approval of the Articles, it became apparent that the central government would deal with the question of how to expand the western lands, and almost all claims by states to western properties were ceded to the national government by 1781. (Georgia held out until 1802.)

Rights to local self-government were ensured under the Articles, and the passage of a series of "Northwest Ordinances" protected the rights of citizens to move into the West and establish states with the same guarantees of autonomy that obtained in the East. The Ordinance of 1784, introduced by Thomas Jefferson, organized the West into a set of potential states. As initially proposed, this ordinance eliminated slavery from western territories, although this provision was dropped before passage. The Ordinance of 1785 created the system of rectilinear surveying that established the pattern of township grids, ranges, and sections that still characterizes most of the western United States. These surveying activities produced the Ohio and Scioto Company schemes by which the Congress enabled some war veterans to buy land with the effectively worthless certificates of indebtedness that had been issued to them in lieu of pay. This ordinance also provided for the sale of western lands, in the hope that through a series of state competitive auctions, a source of national government revenue would be generated.

The most famous of all the western ordinances was the Ordinance of 1787, which provided for the development and government of the territories northwest of the Ohio River. This created a staged process through which territories might be settled and moved ultimately to statehood. In addition to protecting freedom of religion, freedom from unfair imprisonment, right to trial by jury, and guarantees of public education, the ordinance prohibited slavery throughout the Northwest, revitalizing the aim of the original Ordinance of 1784.

Ironically, one of the successful efforts at interstate cooperation under the Confederation structure gave inadvertent momentum to the overthrow of the Articles themselves (Hicks & Mowry, 1956, p. 105; G. S. Wood, 1987, p. 70). In 1786, Maryland and Virginia delegates met in Alexandria, Virginia, to negotiate conflicting regulations concerning the Chesapeake Bay and the Potomac. They were successful in resolving differences and reconciling their regulatory structure. This very success in interstate negotiation spurred the participants to call for a general conference to discuss overall matters of interstate commerce. The Virginia legislature thus invited all states to send representatives to a conference in Annapolis in September 1786 with this task as its mandate. The Annapolis conference, attended by only five states and dominated by Alexander Hamilton, adopted a report calling for another convention to address, not an interstate negotiation process, but rather a general consideration of the limitations of the Confederation itself. The result was the Constitutional Convention in Philadelphia in 1787.

For my purpose, there is no need here to recount again the debate that produced the Constitution. I do want to emphasize two aspects of it, however. First, the government of the Articles of Confederation was broadly legitimate at the time, had successfully accomplished a number of acts of governance, and was in the process of developing—learning—how to expand its capacity to govern in the inclusive manner that was its central principle. As G. S. Wood (1987) wrote:

> The 1780's were, after all, a time of great release and expansion: the population grew as never before, or since, and more Americans than ever before were off in pursuit of prosperity and happiness. . . . The general mood was high, expectant, and far from bleak. . . . Why did some men, members of the elite, think America was in a crisis? Certainly it was not the Articles of Confederation that were causing this sense of crisis. These defects of the Confederation were remediable and were scarcely capable of eliciting horror and despair. (pp. 70-72)

Michael Lienesch (1980) also noted the general contentment:

> It must have come as a surprise to Americans of the time to learn how bad the Confederation had been. In the years from 1783 to 1787 numerous writers had shown dissatisfaction with the course of American affairs. But in the public pronouncements of the day there

had been no suggestion of desperation, contemporary writers speaking of the Confederation period not with despair but uncertainty.
(p. 13)

Second, the Federalists, the architects of the Constitution, can only be
considered, in fairness, to have brought about a coup d'état, one that,
typical of such coups generally, involved secrecy, some violence, and
much rhetorical manipulation.

The Federalists and the Constitution Convention

The Federalist reform movement was actually tantamount to a second
revolution, animated this time by growing suspicion that the Revolutionary War had created too much democracy at the expense of
economic stability. Men of education and property, those who formed
the gentry, saw themselves losing control of the state governments,
which were increasingly dominated by the debtor classes. As Hicks
and Mowry (1956) put it:

> Some of the demand for a new government was clearly activated by
> an aristocratic dislike of the new social and political position of the
> masses. The Society of Cincinnati, an organization of Revolutionary
> War officers, was repeatedly charged with desiring a change in
> government so that *the lower classes* [italics added] could be put in
> their place. Many other aristocratic elements in the states undoubt-
> edly agreed with the Society. (p. 105)

(As a footnote to this statement, it is interesting to note that pay in the
Revolutionary Army was $6.66 per month for enlisted soldiers and
$75.00 per month at the rank of colonel—just under the current ratio
of pay between industrial workers and corporate CEOs; Zinn, 1995,
p. 84.) The gentry thus turned to a central government, distant from
the erratic demands of the people, to serve as the stabilizing
mechanism that would ensure the appropriate order of things necessary to prosperity.

The question of paper money was the central issue and was
symbolic of the overarching fear of involvement in the regulation of
public affairs by the common person. For the gentry, a strong central
government could protect the value of their securities and regulate
money and commerce not only because of its direct empowerment

under a new form of constituting legislation but also because it would inevitably and predictably be controlled by propertied men of the gentry who would serve as disinterested parties (Wood, 1993, p. 253).

These are precisely the kinds of figures I would call Men of Reason. If, at the end of the twentieth century, after years of observing the interplay of interests that followed the Federalists' triumph, it is difficult for us to believe that such Men of Reason truly wield disinterested power, then it is unsurprising that the Anti-Federalists and the bulk of the population at the time were suspicious as well. The events of the Constitutional Convention in Philadelphia and the subsequent ratification of the Constitution seem from a contemporary vantage point to be nothing less than an amazingly successful coup d'état.

The very convening of the Philadelphia Convention occurred under conflicted auspices. The successful Chesapeake Bay/Potomac River gathering resulted in the Annapolis Convention, dedicated to a general discussion of interstate commerce. This group, heavily influenced by Alexander Hamilton, issued a document specifying a number of defects of the Articles of Confederation and calling for a convention in Philadelphia in May 1787 to revise the Articles. This call was sent to state legislatures and to Congress, and in February 1787, Congress endorsed the meeting. The explicit purpose of the meeting in Philadelphia as stated in the official call was *to propose amendments to the Articles of Confederation* (Mason, 1979, p. 39). Though it was clear to most that some change was necessary, few citizens felt that wholesale reform was called for, and suspicions ran high as to the purposes of the convention. A number of Anti-Federalists refused even to attend. Patrick Henry, for example, declined, saying he "smelt a rat" (quoted in Morris, 1987, p. 269). The delegates to the convention came from twelve states; Rhode Island refused to send a delegate.

It was obvious from the outset that reform of the Articles was never the intention of many of the delegates, and nothing makes this clearer than the rule of secrecy they adopted from the start. To ensure that deliberations inside the convention were not stifled by the threat of delegates' remarks being leaked back to the states and to the people whom they represented, the members of the convention decided to have the windows of the hall nailed shut and the entrances continually guarded. Although there was the occasional leak, reputedly traced to Benjamin Franklin, in general, secrecy obtained (Morris, 1987, p. 276). The resulting document has been called "an open covenant secretly arrived at" (Morris, 1987, p. 277). It seems clear that the cabal-like nature of the convention was critical to its success: Madison himself remarked that "no Constitution would ever have been adopted by the convention if the debates had been public" (quoted in Morris, 1987, p. 277).

Although the debates inside the convention, insofar as we can reconstruct them, were often heated, the outcomes were easily predictable. The final Constitution remarkably resembles Madison's original Virginia Plan, which had been circulated among the Virginia and Pennsylvania delegates before the convention opened. The strongest opposition to this plan, submitted to the convention by Edmund J. Randolph, came from the small states in the form of the New Jersey Plan, which, despite several nods toward increased national power, was in effect a redesign of the Articles of Confederation with a unicameral legislature in which each state had one vote. John Dickinson of Delaware was even less attracted by reform and proposed that both the New Jersey and Virginia Plans be tabled and that a more moderate reform of the Articles, in keeping with the instructions issued by Congress, be undertaken.

In what turned out to be a brilliant political maneuver, Alexander Hamilton rescued the Virginia Plan from the already-voted-on postponement, sponsored by Dickinson, when he took the floor to criticize the Articles for their obvious deficiencies. He castigated both alternative plans as overly democratic and offered a radically centralized, virtually monarchical alternative. This had the intended effect of making the Articles seem woefully inadequate and Madison's Virginia Plan seem a moderate, reasoned response (Mason, 1979, pp. 37-55); the next day, the convention defeated a series of proposals that, in effect, "amounted to a complete rejection of the Confederation form of government" (Morris, 1987, p. 281). It became quickly apparent that the Anti-Federalists' fears were well grounded, and the few Anti-Federalist delegates became even fewer as several notables, such as Luther Martin from Maryland and the New Yorkers, Robert Yates and John Lansing, Jr., left the convention in disgust.

What is most apparent in retrospect is the degree to which the intention of overturning the Articles was present from the beginning of the "reform" movement. Madison and his colleagues had already decided on the need for a different form of government, one in which individual economic interest was made the central constituting unit. Madison (1952) viewed the inevitable downfall of "pure" democratic governments to be directly linked to the unfolding of factionalism based on passion, which undermined rationality and destroyed stability (p. 50). Passion also fostered the emergence of charismatic leaders

by whom the people were easily swayed. The cause of such factionalism was "sown into the nature of man" and was thus intractable (p. 50).
The effects of factionalism, however, could be controlled. What Madison envisioned was a republic based on a different kind of factionalism, factionalism grounded in individual economic interests derived
not from the "inequality of property" but from the "variety of property"
(Diamond, 1979, p. 54). Thus,

> If Americans can be made to divide themselves according to their
> narrow and particularized economic interests, they will avoid the
> fatal factionalism that opinion and passion generate. By contrast, the
> relatively tranquil kind of factionalism resulting from economic
> interests makes possible a stable and decent democracy. (Diamond,
> 1979, p. 54)

It would seem an irony that, given this attempt to soften, if not
eliminate, the power of individual passion and reduce it to economic
interest neutralized by the overall production of a wide range of
property, much of the debate at the Constitutional Convention was
taken up with whether the process of ratification would have an
individual- or state-based nature, with the Federalists demanding an
individual citizen-centered process. This seemingly contradictory
assertion of, on the one hand, the individual as the essential validating
basis of any democratic republic and, on the other, the individual as
an easily swayed, passion-driven, unpredictable element requiring
overall structural control is, however, quite understandable when one
considers the political expediencies involved.

Indeed, the entire debate over the process of ratification is an
illustration of the political acumen of the Federalists and the force of
political expediency. The demand that ratification be based on popular
vote rather than state legislative approval was couched as an issue of
sovereignty: Were the people or the states sovereign units? This debate
pervaded the convention. In the end, the Federalists triumphed in their
demand for popular ratification through the submission of the proposed Constitution to state assemblies directly elected by the people
solely for this purpose. The ratification provision was adopted finally
on July 23. The degree to which this approved ratification process
actually reflected any genuine Federalist sentiment about the importance of popular support is questionable (Mason, 1979, p. 53). Given
the dominance of standing state legislatures by local political concerns
and Anti-Federalists, avoidance of them was perceived to be vital to
the success of the Federalists' program. The choice of popularly elected

ratification conventions was an astute political manipulation, particularly because, as became apparent during ratification, broad popular support for the new Constitution was actually quite limited. The convention closed with a landmark decision that the ratification process would require the approval of only nine states out of the thirteen. This amounted to "a revolutionary course," dramatically disregarding the provision requiring unanimous agreement among the states for changes under the Articles (Morris, 1987, p. 298).

The Ratification Process

On September 28, 1787, the ratification process officially began. The traditional story suggests that there was widespread agreement and that a fairly rapid and uneventful process of ratification ensued. Such was hardly the case. In fact, as Richard Ellis (1987) noted, "It is undeniable that the Constitution was not very popular when it was first adopted" (p. 297). The first state to take action was Pennsylvania, and the Federalists moved rapidly there to attempt to ensure passage. In fact, on September 28, before the standing national Congress had completed its review, George Clymer, a Federalist, pushed legislation through the Pennsylvania assembly, calling for an immediate ratifying convention. Aware of this potential coup, the opposing Anti-Federalist legislators stayed away from the assembly, thus preventing formation of the required quorum of two thirds of the members. Opposition to a centralized government and thus to the proposed Constitution was widespread in Pennsylvania, particularly in the western regions. The Federalists in Congress, aware of this resistance, had the Congressional resolution sent by express rider overnight from New York to Philadelphia, but it did not arrive until the morning of September 29. Still without a quorum, however, the assembly could not act on the formation of a ratifying convention. On the afternoon of September 29, therefore, the members present instructed the sergeant-at-arms to bring in *by force* the members who were not present. "With the assistance of a mob, two Anti-Federalists were dragged out of their lodgings and forcibly returned to the assembly. A quorum was then declared present and the delegates voted that afternoon for the election of delegates for the convention to meet in Philadelphia on November 20" (Morris, 1987, p. 302).

This was only the beginning of the strife in Pennsylvania. On November 20, a Philadelphia mob attacked the homes or lodgings of several assemblymen who were known opponents of the new

Constitution. Although they then lost the November election, Anti-Federalists argued that the larger proportion of the state had not been represented, excluded by threat and geography from participation. When the expected approval of the new Constitution came, reaction in the western portion of the state was predictably violent, epitomized by the actions of a mob in Carlisle that burned in effigy "James the Caledonian," as Constitutional delegate James Wilson was called (Morris, 1987, p. 302).

Although the motion to consider amendments was vetoed at the ratifying convention, the campaign to amend the Constitution gained momentum after its approval. Petitions bearing more than 6,000 signatures from citizens in the western counties were sent to Philadelphia, censuring the Pennsylvania delegates to the Constitutional Convention for exceeding their authority and demanding that the assembly consider amendments in favor of states' rights and constraints on the powers of the national government. These were ignored by the assembly through the use of procedural devices.

As one of the more populous states, Pennsylvania's difficulties with ratification illustrate a curious aspect of the Federalists' position. The Federalists repeatedly expressed concern that the government of the United States needed to be accountable not to intervening units (i.e., the states) but directly to the individual citizens themselves. This was a cornerstone of the Federalist position and was the declared rationale for their proposed process of ratifying conventions in each state rather than approval by the state legislatures. Federalists argued that ratifying conventions would link citizens directly to the proposed central government without the mediating influence of the states. It is instructive that the actual result of the ratification process was that the *least* populous states, such as Delaware, New Jersey, Georgia, and Connecticut, approved the document quickly; the states with far more citizens, such as Pennsylvania, were riddled with disagreements, often erupting into violence. The ratification by small states was used effectively to suggest broader public consensus than events indicated. The process was hardly the kind of broad democratic approval that the Federalist delegates argued was required for a republic answerable directly to its citizens. It was, however, a clever political strategy rendered somewhat ironic in retrospect by the careful argument by Publius (1952) in "The Federalist Papers," in which he specifically warned against

> reference of constitutional questions to the decision of the whole society. . . . The danger of disturbing the public tranquillity by interesting too strongly the public passions, is a still more serious objection

against a frequent reference of constitutional questions to the decision
of the whole society. Notwithstanding the success which has attended
the revisions of our established forms of government, it must be
confessed that the experiments are of too ticklish a nature to be
unnecessarily multiplied. (p. 160)

Rather than use the state legislatures, where actual statewide
citizen participation had been fostered and, importantly, where ratification would have required approval by *two* houses, the Federalists,
shrewdly aware of the degree of disagreement that existed throughout
the country, argued for and won approval of a model of ratification
that, given their national clout and urban dominance, could gain
swift passage of the new Constitution by excluding the consideration of large numbers of citizens. In fact, ratification by the required
nine states was accomplished on June 21, 1788, without the approval
of powerful and populous Virginia and New York. It is testimony to
the political acumen of the Federalists that the ratification process
they instituted made it possible to install a radically new form of
government without the assent of the majority of citizens in whose
name the reform had initially been proposed. Even when approval
occurred in the large states, the bitterness of the battles indicates that
there was hardly the happy general agreement that our textbooks
suggest preceded the adoption of the Constitution (Morris, 1987,
p. 305).
    Support for the Federalist cause in the states came, as might be
expected, from the commercial, urban seaboard and professional
interests, whereas the opposition drew its strength from the much less
influential, poorly funded and organized farmers, states' righters,
debtors, and all of the other interests not represented at the convention
(Morris, 1987, p. 305). In the end, the opposition's lack of resources
and polish was telling, nowhere more so than in Virginia and New
York. Noted Anti-Federalists such as Richard Henry Lee in his "Letters
From the Federal Farmer" (1966), James Winthrop in his "Agrippa"
letters (Agrippa, 1966), George Mason in his "Objections to the Proposed Federal Constitution" (1966), and Melancton Smith in "An
Address to the People of the State of New York" (1966) argued their
cause eloquently, but none were as persuasive as the powerful Hamilton, Madison, and Jay in "The Federalist Papers" (Publius, 1952).
Writing as "Publius," these authors set out to influence the debate over
the Constitution primarily in New York and secondarily in Virginia,
the two states whose inclusion seemed key to the success of the new
republic, if not to its formal approval.

The debates in populous Virginia and New York took place that June and brought together some of the most powerful leaders of the time. In Virginia, James Madison himself led the Federalist debate with Patrick Henry on the side of the Anti-Federalists. Hamilton was at work in New York, and he and Madison had special courier arrangements to follow the debates not only in their respective conventions but also in that of New Hampshire—expected to become the ninth officially ratifying state before the debates in either Virginia or New York ended. Although it was estimated that three fourths of the people of Virginia were opposed to the new Constitution, and despite the oratorical power of Patrick Henry, the well-organized, well-funded, and prestigious Federalist leadership of Virginia carried the day. Virginia approved the Constitution on June 25, 1788.

Although New Hampshire had ratified four days earlier than Virginia, putting the Constitution officially into effect, the inclusion of New York seemed crucial to the success of the Union. Opposition to the Constitution in New York was quite strong; Anti-Federalist delegates to the ratifying convention outnumbered Federalists by more than two to one (Morris, 1987, p. 312). The split inside the state followed predictable lines, with the interior supporting the Anti-Federalists, led by Governor Clinton, and New York City squarely behind the Federalist cause.

The Federalists triumphed in New York State through effective political maneuvering. Rumors spread that New York City, provisional capital of the republic and its major commercial center, might secede from the state and join the newly formed Union if the convention did not ratify the Constitution. This was a serious threat and created a frightening image of the remainder of the state left landlocked. As a demonstration of the power of the Anti-Federalist cause, the result of the election for delegates was particularly significant. New York had the most democratic criteria for delegate selection of any state-ratifying convention—any free male citizen over twenty-one was eligible to vote (Morris, 1987, p. 312). The Federalists had supported this open suffrage, much to the surprise of the Anti-Federalists. Anti-Federalists were also taken aback by the opening Federalist motion, quickly approved by the Convention, in which delegates decided to consider the Constitution clause by clause. This move, often proposed in other state-ratifying conventions and defeated by Federalists themselves, bought the New York Federalists the time needed to ensure their victory, as the news of New Hampshire's and then, more tellingly, of Virginia's ratification reached New York City. It became apparent that the passage of the Constitution by ten other states and the ardent support of New York City rendered the question of New York State's approval or disapproval virtually moot. With the inclusion of a letter calling for a second convention to consider amendments, New York State ratified the Constitution on July 26, 1788, by the small margin of 30 to 27.

It remained only for North Carolina, an Anti-Federalist stronghold, to ratify on August 2, making Rhode Island the lone holdout. Rhode Island, dominated by Anti-Federalists, had refused to send a delegate to Philadelphia, and now it refused to call a ratifying convention. It is interesting to note that Rhode Island had the most liberal law for suffrage of any of the thirteen states and was perhaps the most ardent states' rights stronghold. The commercial seaports of Providence and Newport, supporting the Constitution, considered seceding to join the Union, but when the newly formed Congress began to consider economic sanctions and even a total embargo against the entire state, the Rhode Island assembly conceded defeat, called a ratifying convention, and, after a fractious series of defaults, ratified the Constitution by a vote of 34 to 32 on May 29, 1790 (Morris, 1987, p. 316).

On careful examination, the ratification process hardly appears to be one of straightforward "rubber-stamping" by a population that, despite its internal differences, was united by relief at its rescue from the impotent government of the Articles of Confederation by a heroic group of selfless nation builders. Indeed, the Articles were staunchly defended as representative of the spirit of the Revolution, and the founding fathers were suspected of being less than purely altruistic saviors. The existing government had weathered several major national crises, and overall conditions throughout the Confederation were improving. There had been important administrative and policy successes under the Articles, and despite widespread sentiment that some reform was necessary, many, if not most, citizens were comfortable with the orientation of their governmental arrangements. State governments had become the vehicles for genuine democratic participation with all of its attendant dilemmas and conflicts, and, as the ratification process all too clearly demonstrated, most citizens were loath to give up state supremacy in favor of a distant national government. The process of ratification itself excluded many from participation in the actual decision to replace the Articles; support could at best be described as uneven.

By March 1789, when the first Congress under the new Constitution met, there was certainly widespread relief that the period of uncertainty was over, and most Anti-Federalists moved to support and participate in the new government (Kaminski, 1983, pp. 30-37). This may have been more a reflection of the underlying revolutionary spirit of community than a matter of a broad and sudden conversion to the principles of the Constitution. They and their Federalist opponents honored the pledges made in five states during ratification to create a Bill of Rights; on September 25, 1989, the first ten amendments to the Constitution were adopted as the Bill of Rights by the Congress (Morris, 1987, p. 230). But the sentiments that animated Anti-Federalism, although overcome by the force of the Federalists' arguments for centralizing power and promoting commercial activity, were not to disappear.

Anti-Federalists as Theorists of the Peaceable Kingdom

I have argued so far in this chapter that, first, a distinctive ethos of organic social connection developed during the prerevolutionary period in America, an ethos that was both fostered and contradicted by patterns of social life that the colonists brought with them from Europe. Second, this ethos was extended by the experience of the Revolution and became, to some extent, institutionalized in the Articles of Confederation. Government under the Articles functioned predictably, given the principles of its design, but economic unrest so threatened the gentry classes that they mounted a sort of coup against the government, resulting in the adoption of the present Constitution through a process of ratification emblematic of the fact that it was a coup. Third, this account implies that the accepted history of this period has cast a distorted backdrop against which to consider the strengths, weaknesses, and possibilities of our present form of government, especially the legitimate role of administration within it, by making the Federalist strategy seem laudatory and indeed inevitable.

The Anti-Federalists were the clear losers in the founding debate and so have been overshadowed to virtual exclusion from the subsequent official account (Lienesch, 1983, 1988). The story of their defeat is not, however, simply one of certain institutional arrangements being chosen and others rejected in the creation of a new republic. What was debated during the founding of the United States was really two images of collective social life, each sustaining a distinctive political and administrative arrangement. With the Federalists' victory came not simply the triumph of a governmental structure but the assertion of a social ideology, the implications of which are more profound than

surface-level decisions and agreements about the particulars of organizing a state.

The true power of constitutions is that they do much more than
create structures, procedures, and loci of sovereign power. As Rousseau noted, "He who dares to undertake the making of a people's
institutions ought to feel himself capable, so to speak, of changing
human nature" (quoted in Jacobson, 1963, p. 568). The way we constitute our collective life constitutes us as the subjects within that life.
We write our constitutions, and they, in turn, write us and the generations to follow. It is this aspect of constitutions, the manner in which
they profoundly create us, to which Robert Goldwin (1979) is referring
when he writes:

> Thus, considering how long Americans were on this continent before
> 1787, it is perfectly intelligible to speak of what the American
> constitution was before the Constitution of the United States was
> written, as well as to speak of the formative influence the Constitution
> of the United States had, subsequently, on the American constitution.
> (p. 8)

What I have been focusing attention on here, then, is how the American constitution was altered by the American Constitution. I want to
proceed now to a fuller description of the Anti-Federalist viewpoint,
taking it as an expression of the colonial ethos I described earlier. In
so doing, I hope to suggest that what was lost or hidden from view by
the vanquishing of the Anti-Federalist perspective was an alternative
vision of social life and the process of governance that goes with it,
one that would have rendered the issue of legitimacy moot.

I want to show that the result of the Federalist/Anti-Federalist
debates was the creation of an American political and governmental
life that is very narrow in its commitments. The Federalist triumph
established strongly centralized government, dedicated to ensuring
the stability and order required for the large, commercial empire that
was at the core of the Federalist vision of America. The dream of the
Federalist founders centered on economic prosperity, and the engine
of this dream was an implacably self-interested human nature. Endlessly acquisitive and self-absorbed, human beings could be counted
on to pursue their individual interests. The role of government was to
control, structure, and direct these predictable energies into channels
that would enhance and support the public interest as a corollary
benefit of private gain.

Thus, the constitutional formulation drafted by our Federalist forefathers was one oriented to balance and control. It was a structure of government designed to ensure that all interests competing against each other would produce a moderated, reasoned response to political issues. This response, fully satisfactory to none, would be *acceptable*, at least, to all—the measured mean. This is the thrust of the famous statement by Publius (1952) in "The Federalist Papers": "Ambition must be made to counteract ambition. . . . What is government itself but the greatest of all reflections on human nature? . . . If men were angels, no government would be necessary" (p. 163). Obviously "interest," the source of human motivation, must be, in some sense, fettered; at a minimum, differing interests must be coordinated and channeled, offsetting each other. Since people cannot govern themselves directly, government must be carried out by the agents of reasoned control. This is the specific genesis in our political culture of what I am calling the requirement for Men of Reason to be in charge.

The Constitution was written out of a world of patriarchal order. The Federalists were its gentry, and many of them saw themselves and others whose material prosperity was already guaranteed as capable of serving government as disinterested officials whose eyes could be turned to public benefit. This original elite, the first Men of Reason, imagined the objects of their fear to be the masses, who might refuse to accept the pattern of gain and loss that the pursuit of self-interest through free commerce produces. However, it seemed then, as it seems now, that if we must fear the power of unlimited self-interest, then we must constrain both our leaders and ourselves by institutional arrangements equal to a vast and growing nation. The result of such a vision is a strictly limited set of governmental and civic relations, the primary orientation of which is toward checking popular passion with reason. As Publius (1952) argued in "The Federalist Papers," "But it is the reason alone of the public that ought to control and regulate the government. The passions ought to be controlled and regulated by the government" (p. 161).

The founders sought to constitute the American character as devoted to moderation, even in its loftiest moral aims, and as deferential to the institutional leadership that guarantees that extremism will be controlled. This is essential, given that in society one can expect only a cacophony of individual interests in need of restraint, management, and accommodation. What this orientation trades away, however, is the capacity to generate and sustain a *collective* moral will, the ability for a people to set a normative frame for their lives together. The negative (even mean) idea of avoiding extremism becomes the highest principle possible. Even Robert Goldwin (1979), in an article that ultimately venerated the Federalists' sentiments, acknowledged the limited, unappealing nature of moderate morality:

> If that is the American constitution, the morality most characteristic of America, then and now, is what might be called a measured, or a restrained, or a moderated, or even a mean morality. . . . There is something drab and unsatisfying in moral moderation. There is natural yearning for something higher and purer. All that aiming lower has to recommend it is that it works, but that leaves many of the best of men and women restless and dissatisfied. (p. 15)

The Federalists, afraid of men's self-interested passions, aimed high in rhetoric only; their practical target was much lower, leaving the higher reaches of human life to the realm of the private self.

It should be clear that the emphasis on moral moderation and control through counterbalancing limits was not representative of how we were constituted as a people prior to our constitutional founding. Rather, it represents a wrenching *reconstitution* of the American social and political character away from its revolutionary origins and Anti-Federalist sentiments. The Anti-Federalists offered a different vision. They shared with the Federalists an awareness of the dark and selfish side of human beings. Unlike their counterparts, however, they did not see human beings as isolated individuals but rather as living in relationship to each other. They saw the regulatory power of human relationship as deriving from community, from lived interaction, rather than from formal institutions.

The Anti-Federalists were even less sanguine than their Federalist colleagues about the ability of governments to control human passion, and for this they are often charged with being undemocratic, of mistrusting citizens' abilities to judge in their own collective behalf. This is a dangerous half-truth. They distrusted the isolated, rational individual, the self-interested hero of seventeenth- and eighteenth-century liberalism that so enthralled the Federalists. They were liberals, to be sure, but of a sort closer to Rousseau than to Locke. "How is the will of the community to be expressed?" asked Melancton Smith (1966). "Individuals entering into society become one body, and that body ought to be animated by one mind; and every form of government should have that complexion" (pp. 376-377). For the Anti-Federalists, the proper limits of human action were created out of the processes of communities that were networks of relationships, not simply associations of mutual convenience.

The Anti-Federalists saw . . . the insufficiency of a community of mere interest. They saw that the American polity had to be a moral community if it was to be anything, and they saw that the seat of that community must be the hearts of the people. (Storing, 1981b, p. 76)

Human beings and human virtue were the consequences not of individual rationality but of participation and engagement in a process of discourse. It was in discourse that human actors and actions were constituted; discourse was the only viable source of the civic virtue that protected freedom. "Civil liberty, in all countries, hath been promoted by free discussion of publick measures, and the conduct of publick men" (John De Witt, 1966, p. 102). The further discussion by John De Witt on the nature of legal contracts gives us a sense of how vital human interaction was to social stability in the eyes of the Anti-Federalists: "All contracts are to be construed according to the meaning of the parties at the time of making them. By which is meant, that mutual communications shall take place, and each shall explain to the other their ideas of the contract before them" (p. 104). Anything more abstract than concrete relationships was viewed as unreliable or even foolish as a potential restraint on human action. Patrick Henry (1966) derided the Federalist dependence on legal/structural checks that resulted from "consolidation . . . into a powerful and mighty empire," calling them "specious, imaginary balances, your rope-dancing, chain-rattling, ridiculous ideal checks and contrivances" (p. 251).

Today, we believe in the necessity for structures and rules because we are the creations of our Constitution. We believe in checks and restraints because we are afraid of each other, of our own natures, characterized as they have been in terms of selfish interests. David Schuman (1973) has called the process created by the Constitution "politics as mistrust" (p. 28). We do not believe in our own ability to resolve conflict through relationship and talk. Consequently, we do not trust the process of human interaction in intimate communities. Rather, we see social process as driven by the pursuit of self-interest and as incapable of producing workable regulation of our common actions. If the paramount function of any constitution is the education of its citizens, then in our case, our Constitution teaches us the necessity of government that checks those who govern, making it difficult, if not impossible, for us as a people to govern ourselves. Thus, ironically, we come to require our Men of Reason. This is the consequence of the Federalist Constitution.

The Anti-Federalists saw clearly the interdependent relation between a form of government and its people. They wanted a government born out of its citizens' active agency on behalf of their own freedom and dedicated to the continued production of civic virtue in subsequent generations of citizens. According to Melancton Smith (1966), "Government operates upon the spirit of the people, as well as the spirit of the people operates upon it. . . . Our duty is to frame a government friendly to liberty and the rights of mankind, which will tend to cherish and cultivate a love of liberty among our citizens" (p. 388). The Anti-Federalists realized that the aim of the Federalists was to check human passion not with virtue but with reason through structural controls. As "A Republican Federalist" (a staunch Anti-Federalist whose identity is not known) put it, this creates "a government which substitutes *fear* for *virtue*" (A Republican Federalist, 1966, p. 125).

Judged by the people living at the time, government under the Articles of Confederation was not a failure. Nor were the Anti-Federalists who argued the Confederation's case simply untutored provincials pleading a local cause. Numerous Anti-Federalist accounts document this:

> The country is in profound peace, and we are not threatened by invasions from any quarter. The governments of the respective states are in the full exercise of their powers; and the lives, the liberty, and property of individuals are protected. All present exigencies are answered by them. . . . Individuals are just recovering from the losses and embarrassment sustained by the late war. Industry and frugality are taking their station, and banishing from the community, idleness and prodigality. Individuals are lessening their private debts, and several millions of the public debt is discharged by the sale of the western territory. (Brutus Junior, 1965, p. 103)

> Our people are like a man just recovering from a severe fit of sickness. It was the war that disturbed the course of commerce, introduced floods of paper money, the stagnation of credit, and threw many valuable men out of steady business. From these sources our greatest evils arise. . . . But then, have we not done more in three or four years past, in repairing the injuries of the war, by repairing houses and estates, restoring industry, frugality, the fisheries, manufactures, etc., and thereby laying the foundation of good government, and of individual and political happiness, than any people ever did in a like time? (The Federal Farmer, 1965, p. 113)

> Consider our situation, sir: go to the poor man, and ask him what he does. He will inform you that he enjoys the fruits of his labor, under

his own fig-tree, with his wife and children around him, in peace and security. Go to every other member of society,—you will find the same tranquil ease and content; you will find no alarms or disturbances. Why, then, tell us of danger, to terrify us into an adoption of this new form of government? (Henry, 1966, p. 251)

[The Articles of Confederation were] a most excellent constitution— one that had stood the test of time, and carried us through difficulties generally supposed to be insurmountable. (Lowndes, 1981, p. 149)

I do not wish to suggest that the Anti-Federalists were heroic figures filled with love and trust in an altruistic human nature, but rather that in their ideas, we can find an alternative role for government, one grounded in an understanding of human behavior as regulated organically rather than mechanically and as capable of development. We have been denied an opportunity truly to consider this alternative by the dominance of the Federalists' rendering of the tale of our founding. Yet now it is opportune to reconsider the Anti-Federalists; they have distinctive applicability to contemporary conditions. As Lienesch (1983) aptly observed:

In our time, their [Anti-Federalist] example seems particularly important. Many today have reluctantly come to consider the faith in progress that inspired so many nineteenth and twentieth century scholars to be increasingly illusory. . . . Thus as philosophers and politicians look ahead in search of a political theory that does not so blithely assume the inevitability of progress, they might look back to Antifederalist principles. In much-maligned Antifederalism, they may well find a model of political reform appropriate to these post-progressive times. (p. 87)

Among academic historians and political scientists, the discussion of our founding is, of course, fraught with long-standing intellectual disputes. Even within academic writing, however, the lot of the Anti-Federalists has not been a happy one.

The Anti-Federalists, like most of history's losers, have not been treated very kindly. Until fairly recently, the tendency has been either to ignore them or simply to dismiss them as "men of little faith," who have only a peripheral place in the American political or constitutional tradition. (Ellis, 1987, p. 295)

Indeed, it is not even easy to identify who the Anti-Federalists were. Even their name was given them by their adversaries. As Mason (1979) noted, they might more accurately have been called the "antinationalists," as the focus of their objections was not "federalism," which they in fact staunchly advocated in its original form, but rather what they perceived to be the threat of an overly powerful national government (p. 37). Supporters of the new Constitution attached the term *Anti-Federalist* to their opponents during the ratification battles of 1787 and 1788, appropriating the popular term *Federalist* to themselves in a strategic public relations coup (Ellis, 1987, p. 302).

The Anti-Federalists were a diverse group. They came from widely differing backgrounds but shared a state-based political orientation and local focus, together with a fear and suspicion of the wealthier, gentleman class to which most Federalists belonged. They were, in the main, newly made men who had been thrust into leadership. They found themselves unprepared for public debates, without the social skills of presentation and articulation that defined traditional leadership behavior (Wood, 1979b). Though personal shortcomings may have caused them personal anguish, they heightened Anti-Federalist suspicions that the move toward more centralized government was an aristocratic plot to thwart the equality and independence that were the legacy of the Revolution.

In the American context of the 1700s, the Anti-Federalists could see all around them the power of the traditional social order, the upper ranks of which the Federalists populated (Wood, 1993). At every turn, the Anti-Federalists found themselves to be the local, the country, the uneducated, the "ungentlemanly." The Anti-Federalists were the inheritors of the Revolution; they had become politicians and leaders through the egalitarianism that the Revolution released (Wood, 1979b). They were self-made men, and they naturally distrusted the gentry. They were suspicious of the Federalist plan because they saw the social and economic advantages that produced it. The Anti-Federalists saw the movement toward centralized government as a turning away from the gains of the Revolution and suspected the Federalists who proposed it to be usurping government from the common man in the name of a hidden aristocracy.

What then are we to think of the motives and designs of those men who are urging the implicit and immediate adoption of the proposed government; are they fearful, that if you exercise your good sense and discernment, you will discover the masqued aristocracy, that they are

attempting to smuggle upon you under the suspicious garb of repub-
licanism? (Centinel, 1966, p. 110)

They also saw the natural tendency of the lower classes to defer to
elites and their willingness to be overawed by their "betters" and to
believe in the eighteenth-century order of things in which it was the
aristocracy's given ability and responsibility to discern and act in the
best interests of the whole.

The Articles of Confederation had embodied the ideals of the Revolution in a loose alliance of states whose authority rested on the small,
homogeneous localities that were the communities of eighteenth-
century America. What little central government existed was entirely
dependent on the agreement of the states, whose sovereignty was
paramount. The Anti-Federalists approached changing this form of
government with great trepidation. They experienced the Federalist
assertions of crisis with concern.

It is natural for men, who wish to hasten the adoption of a measure,
to tell us, now is the crisis—now is the critical moment which must
be seized or all will be lost; and to shut the door against free enquiry,
whenever conscious the thing presented has defects in it, which time
and investigation will probably discover. This has been the custom
of tyrants, and their dependants [sic] in all ages. (Lee, 1966, p. 201)

Uniting the various Anti-Federalists' positions with respect to reform
was a theory of social change that was inherently conservative. They
believed that institutions had stabilizing and protective merit and
feared that radical change might threaten liberty rather than enhance
it. The structure of the American government had been carefully
constructed to maximize the benefits of the Revolution, namely
freedom; injudicious tampering with these arrangements might well
open an opportunity for supplanting these protections with less appropriate and effective mechanisms. Change itself was to be regarded
as suspect. Customs, rituals, and cultural norms reflected the true
spirit of communities, and the stability of these institutions was the
greatest source of individual freedom. The Anti-Federalists recognized
the somewhat ironic aspect of their conservatism, oriented toward
protecting the gains of a revolution. They were aware of the threat that
revolutionary change poses, breaking connections among people and,
as Edmund Burke would later write about the French Revolution,
creating the chaos that opens the door for oppression. They were

deeply concerned to keep the gains of the Revolution alive by resisting the inevitable tendency of governments to decline into tyrannies over time. They were aware that the American Revolution had already loosed critical bonds and that the current institutions were as yet too new to be even marginally effective in containing further efforts at change. Centinel (1966), either the author or the son of the author of Pennsylvania's Constitution, wrote:

> If it were not for the stability and attachment which time and habit gives to forms of government, it would be in the power of the enlightened and aspiring few, if they should combine, at any time to destroy the best establishments, and even make the people the instruments of their own subjugation. The late revolution having effaced in a great measure all former habits, and the present institutions are so recent, that there exists not that great reluctance to innovation, so remarkable in old communities, and which accords with reason, for the most comprehensive mind cannot foresee the full operation of material changes on civil polity; it is the genius of the common law to resist innovation. (p. 4)

The Anti-Federalists saw firsthand the extent to which the Revolution had fundamentally altered civic relations and bonds. The Revolution had altered far more than simply the source of political power.

> The Revolution not only radically changed the personal and social relationships of people, including the position of women, but also destroyed aristocracy as it had been understood in the Western world for at least two millennia. The Revolution brought respectability and even dominance to ordinary people long held in contempt and gave dignity to their menial labor in a manner unprecedented in history and to a degree not equaled elsewhere in the world. The Revolution did not just eliminate monarchy and create republics; it actually reconstituted what Americans meant by public or state power and brought about an entirely new kind of popular politics and a new kind of democratic officeholder. . . . Most important, it made the interests and prosperity of ordinary people—their pursuits of happiness—the goal of society and government. (Wood, 1993, p. 8)

For the Anti-Federalists, this was a primary accomplishment, the recognition of the significance and power of the common person in articulating his or her own interests and governing in light of them. It was this acknowledgment that founded the Articles of Confederation and established a new social order that needed time and stability to develop the average citizen. This is a subtle and delicate point. The Anti-Federalists were far more optimistic than were their Federalist opponents about the potential of the common person to be educated or developed so as to perceive his or her own interest as well as the interest of the larger community. Active political participation was the vehicle for accomplishing this development of civic virtue.

> The great object of a free people must be so to form their government and laws, and so to administer them, as to create a confidence in, respect for the laws; and thereby induce the sensible and virtuous part of the community to declare in favor of the laws, and to support them without an expensive military force. (Lee, 1966, p. 215)

As Storing (1981b) noted, the Anti-Federalists "saw civil society as a teacher, as a molder of character, rather than as a regulator of conduct" (p. 47).

The Articles of Confederation rested government on smaller communities of similar citizens in which political participation was based on lived association with others rather than on education or class. Surely representation of any sort would dilute direct involvement of citizens in governance, but it was less likely to create a fatal distortion when the representatives were *of* the people and communities that they represented.

> The idea that naturally suggests itself to our minds, when we speak of representatives, is that they resemble those they represent. They should be a true picture of the people, possess a knowledge of their circumstances and their wants, sympathize in all their distresses, and be disposed to seek their true interests. (Smith, 1966, p. 382)

> To promote the happiness of the people it is necessary that there should be local laws; and it is necessary that those laws should be made by the representatives of those who are immediately subject to the want of them. (Agrippa, 1966, p. 133)

In these more local arrangements, the will of the majority could emerge, and the citizens themselves could be educated as to the importance of their own interests and to those of the larger community as well. This created, as Jennifer Nedelsky (1982) defined it, "a close and active relation between the citizen and his government. . . . The Anti-Federalists wanted a government in which the people would take an active, responsible part" (pp. 343-344).

The Anti-Federalists were egalitarians and communitarians with "warm sentiments of esteem and respect, of mutual friendship, fraternity, and independence"—hardly naive or simple in their understanding of human nature, however (Jacobson, 1963, p. 562). Human beings were no less grasping and self-interested to the Anti-Federalists than they were to the Federalists; the possibility for right action on the part of the large proportion of individuals was always the central problematic for them. It was the regulation of the inherently selfish nature of human beings that concerned both sides in the debate and that was the basis for the governmental arrangements that each favored. The Anti-Federalists believed that the only genuine curb on the passions that swayed men into choices that did not reflect the public good or even their own individual long-term good was the possibility of civic virtue and fellow feeling that could be developed and nurtured only in local communities. The *process* of individuals' association, their lived experience, formed them into citizens, *created* their common values, and regulated their actions in ways that the Anti-Federalists could not imagine a distant, disconnected governmental structure ever accomplishing. "A republican, or free government, can only exist where the body of the people are virtuous, and where property is pretty equally divided. In such a government the people are the sovereign and their sense of opinion is the criterion of every public measure" (Centinel, 1965, p. 134).

These interlocking ideas of community, civic virtue, and citizenship are usually seen as the core of the Anti-Federalists' position, and they have frequently been targets of misunderstanding and criticism. The idea that citizens have responsibility for the control, regulation, indeed governance, of their own individual and collective lives had intrinsic merit to the Anti-Federalists, apart from the correlative purpose it served in regulating society. The Anti-Federalists believed in active citizen involvement for its own sake. This sentiment is echoed throughout Anti-Federalist writings, especially as it serves as a guard against the encroachment of social divisions based on class and material advantage. This was the heart of the Revolution, self-determination and freedom for self-government, and the Anti-Federalists zealously wanted to protect it against the deterioration that they correctly perceived the Federalists to accept, indeed desire. "Beyond basic prudence lay a strong Anti-Federalist belief that truly free men control their own destiny and govern their own affairs, both public and private. The Anti-Federalists were committed to the protection of rights, but they were also interested in the potential of genuine self-government" (Nedelsky, 1982, p. 345).

They had few illusions that average eighteenth-century Americans were necessarily ready for this responsibility. Community life was *developmental*; active involvement in the affairs of day-to-day life developed individuals and groups. This was possible only if the setting was intimate enough to allow for such active involvement. For the Anti-Federalists, the Constitution's centralization of power in the name of safety and prosperity was elitist and inevitably aristocratic. It diminished the possibility of citizenship, it created divisions, and thus it fragmented a sense of the public good. Ultimately, it threatened liberty and equality.

The role of community in the formation of civic virtue is a central target of one of the most famous of the critiques leveled at the Anti-Federalists, by the noted historian Cecelia Kenyon (1955/1979). For her, the Anti-Federalists leave two key questions unanswered: (a) How much and what kind of unity is necessary? (b) Absent perfect homogeneity, how are differences to be resolved? Such questions are typical of the difficulties that most scholars have with the Anti-Federalist perspective (Beeman, 1987; Schambra, 1982; Storing, 1981a; Wood, 1979a). This is, in large measure, testimony to the triumph of the Federalist worldview and conception of human nature. Because we have come to see individuals through primarily Madisonian eyes, we can imagine ourselves only as bundles of self-directed interests, approaching social and collective questions through a calculative posture in which our already-formed interests are traded in an economic exchange. This is the vision that renders Kenyon's questions sensible. Under such conditions, it is necessary to know how much commonality is required for exchange of interests or congealing of interests to take place. How much must we have in common to create a sort of social "lingua franca" that is the prior condition required of collective life? If we do not have enough interest in common to allow for our collaborative exchange, it is then sensible to wonder, who will mediate? How will conflicts and differences be resolved?

The Anti-Federalists were less concerned with these questions because they approached the idea of human nature and association from another vantage point. They harbored (although they would not have expressed it in these terms) the core of a concept of developmental process. They had the intuition that we human beings are not isolated individuals, carefully (and perhaps even sympathetically) calculating our private interests to produce an acceptable product; rather, *we are the products, the results of processes of social interaction.* We are formed by our relationships. Unity of purpose or agreement about action is created as an outcome of living together, of face-to-face, intimate conversations. This process of living together is how citizens are formed because it is how our very human subjectivity is formed. It is also how differences, which are inevitable, are resolved. Civic virtue and freedom are meaningful only in such a context, and they are maintained in the way they are created, through the vigilance of living together.

The Anti-Federalist genius was in appreciating the regulatory, generative power of the process of interaction. Kenyon does not see this as sufficient because she and her colleagues are, in the main, good Federalists who do not believe that it is ever fully sufficient simply to trust a *process* to function as a regulatory mechanism. There must be agents (Men of Reason) with sufficient authority to adjudicate differences in light of abiding principles, rules, or values. In fact, this is the limitation of many contemporary communitarians who see communities as essentially constructed agreements on how groups will live together, based on articulated values. The Anti-Federalists also saw communities as requiring agreement and homogeneity; however, their sense was that a community was *implicitly* generative in nature. Though similarity in values was important for community cohesion, the source of this homogeneity was not reason but relationship. By living together, genuine agreement emerged; this was what shaped people and created in them the sense of connection and general weal that was the soul of civic virtue. The Anti-Federalists certainly feared individuals' selfishness, but they saw that the only viable means of controlling it lay in the relationships of each to the other, in the image of one reflected daily in the eyes of the other.

Kenyon identifies this but does not see its potential implications. She emphasizes the problematics of representation—the large numbers and the dilemma of sufficient inclusiveness. She also sees "one of the basic fears of the Anti-Federalists: loss of personal, direct contact with and knowledge of their representatives" (Kenyon, 1955/1979, p. 62). However, she interprets this fear in light of traditional allocative politics: "that the immediate, individual *influence* [emphasis mine] of each voter over his representative would be lessened" (p. 62). This is rather like a reduction in lobbying capacity, which makes sense only in a politics of interest. For the Anti-Federalists, the loss was rather one of intimacy and connectedness, a lessening of the ability to constitute each other mutually through the repeated interactions of living together.

Kenyon's (1955/1979) conclusion is that the Anti-Federalists were "men of little faith." They were antidemocratic, fearing human nature and thus human capacity for self-government. They even chided their Federalist opponents for "optimism" in trusting in the virtue of elected officials (p. 64). What she fails to see is that their fear was of individuals disconnected from the communities or human groupings that constitute and regulate them as subjects, to use contemporary language. Whereas the Anti-Federalists were dedicated to broad protection of self-government through the creation of a virtuous public citizenry, the Federalists were concerned to protect individual ability to pursue private interests from the ill-conceived dictates of a democratic majority. It is here that we can most clearly see the source of the ideology that has so distorted the foundations of our discourse on governance.

Jennifer Nedelsky's (1982) prescient comment is pertinent: "The debate between the Federalists and the Anti-Federalists suggests that the Constitution was designed to substitute effective administration for political participation and to rely on private interest rather than public virtue" (p. 342). This is administration through Men of Reason. They protect us from each other. We need them because we are unable to cooperate with each other. The Federalist state was dedicated to the idea that a growing commercial empire, based on human beings' naturally selfish, acquisitive natures, would provide the attachment through prosperity and security that the small, Anti-Federalist communities had offered through involvement and the processes of interaction. In short, the Anti-Federalists wanted to create peaceable kingdoms, whereas the Federalists wanted prosperous markets.

The Aftermath and the Legacy of the Second Founding

In retrospect, the social and economic conditions in the years immediately following the approval of the new Constitution were eerily indicative of the future, and the Federalists themselves became disenchanted with what they had wrought (Wood, 1993, p. 366). "Especially following ratification, however, as American politics began to degenerate into partisanship and violence, supporters were forced to reconsider Constitutional theory, admitting that good laws alone would not create good government. . . . Laws, as Peres Forbes would remark, 'cannot reach the heart' " (Lienesch, 1980, p. 7).

Perhaps the most influential man of this period, in terms of the implementation of the Federalist program, was Alexander Hamilton in his role as Secretary of the Treasury. His avowed purpose during the first years under the Constitution was to create a stable fiscal state characterized by a close connection between existing commercial interests and the government. This connection was designed to link directly the business elite with the government, largely through the management of the national debt and the creation of "hierarchies of patronage and dependency" (Wood, 1993, p. 263). As Federalist Christopher Gore remarked, "What other chain is so binding as that involving the interests of the men of property in the prosperity of the government" (Pinkney, 1969, p. 37). The Federalist agenda had been largely economic, and insofar as the masses of Americans were to benefit from a centralized, national government, it was to be as a result of that government's ability to protect and control the continued growth and prosperity of the economic elite.

While economic consolidation and nationalization were going on officially under the new government, conditions among average citizens were increasingly difficult in unanticipated ways. The America of the end of the eighteenth century was a violent and troubled place. "Everything seemed to be coming apart, and murder, suicide, theft, and mobbing became increasingly common responses to the burdens that liberty and the expectation of gain were placing on people" (Wood, 1993, p. 306). Alcoholism was rampant; by the second decade of the nineteenth century, consumption of alcohol was almost three times the rate that existed 170 years later in 1990. Rioting in the cities became commonplace, tied to racial and ethnic strife, labor tensions, and general resentment on the part of the common people. Violence within families also rose in tragic fashion. For example, ten of the twelve multiple family murders that were reported in the United States between the seventeenth century and 1900 happened in the years 1780 to 1825. Use of security guards and watchmen increased dramatically, and professional police forces were created by the second decade of the nineteenth century (Wood, 1993, p. 307). In all, the people of the new republic seemed alienated from each other and from their communities to a degree never before experienced.

This disconnection from any containing community was also characteristic, of course, of the elite whom the Federalists appointed to positions of power in the new government. Predicating their government entirely on a conception of the self-interested and privately concerned individual, the Federalists had sacrificed any basis for leadership grounded in civic virtue and the public interest. Far from being men of disinterested virtue, the new government officials had private economic concerns and interests to serve, and they began to exploit their offices for economic gain. Momentum developed to pay and then to increase salaries for government officials to prevent them from such exploitation.

The combination of these conditions both inside and outside the government became a source of disillusionment and despair to many of the Federalist leaders who, ironically, had been responsible for setting in motion the vectors that produced them. The Federalists' response was often to reinvigorate controls on suffrage and participation in government, attributing the cause of this social and political deterioration to an excess of freedom and democracy. "They found it difficult to accept the democratic fact that their fate now rested on the opinions and votes of small-souled and largely unreflective ordinary people" (Wood, 1993, p. 367). There was, however, no turning back from the individually based, self-interest-directed, economic state that had been set in motion.

The irony was, of course, that it was not democratic participation and individualism as such that were at the core of the appalling circumstances of the times but, as the Anti-Federalists had cautioned, participation, democracy, and individualism *disconnected from any process of community or relationship.* It was the alienated, ungrounded nature of the new democracy, set free from the container of lived relationship and discourse, that the Anti-Federalists had feared. As one Anti-Federalist in the newly formed Republican party wondered in 1820, did the Federalists not know that "our community is an association of persons—of human beings—not a partnership founded on property?" (quoted in Wood, 1993, p. 270).

The Anti-Federalists are often charged with being "men of little faith" in human nature, of being antidemocratic—for example, by Kenyon. Oddly enough, they were antidemocratic if we take democracy to be the alienated variant of late twentieth-century America. They saw what the Federalists then, and we today, call democracy to be a kind of disconnected, disembodied denial of the human subject—of the citizen. That citizen, distant and only related to "his" fellows through the indirect vehicle of the satisfaction of self-interest, is hardly the outcome of the Anti-Federalists' community.

The Federalists saw relationship as too inefficient a basis for commercial empire they viewed as vital to American prosperity. Maintenance of such a dream required stronger control at a broader level. So they created our Constitution as the foundation for this experiment in nation building. However, perhaps we have come to the limits of their dream (indeed, it was already fading by the time of their own deaths), and the current crisis of government in America is an indicator of the need to come to terms with the repressed and unresolved Anti-Federalist part of our heritage. We have continued to tell the traditional story as a way of justifying our founding, a way of spawning a receptivity of mind, a way of constituting our people with a nature in concert with the underlying premises of our dominant Federalist heritage. Correspondingly, we have denied the parts of ourselves that belonged to the Anti-Federalist alternative. As David Schuman (1973) so eloquently wrote:

> We are structured not for cooperative acts but for private ones; we are given a form of government that calls not for the best in man but only for the minimum in him. What we must realize is that we are living a self-fulfilling prophecy: that by founding a government geared to selfishness, we can maintain it only by being selfish. (p. 26)

We have been condemned to "an autistic public life" (p. 26).

It is in the constitution of this Federalist citizen and the autism of his public life that I see the source of public administration's crisis of legitimacy. The great Federalist/Anti-Federalist debate of our founding prefigures the issue; the central elements of it can be seen clearly here. The subsequent American discourse of governance has stuck on the issue of the source and hence the possibility of human cooperation. This is the central concern of the framing Friedrich and Finer debate, as we saw in the previous chapter. In the shadow of the Federalist triumph, we have defined ourselves as "autistic," unable to relate to and communicate with each other. This inevitably requires that our processes of governance be once removed from us and handed over to cooler, wiser heads (i.e., literally those who will work with their "heads," their *reason*) to come to the measured mean through considered decision. Yet regularly in the history of our country, the Anti-Federalist image of life has resurfaced, perhaps most interestingly at the time of public administration's founding as a self-conscious field.

Conclusion

The information in the historical accounts presented in this chapter is not only not arcane or obscure, but so well known and easily available as to be almost popular. These are facts that one can consult in sources ready to hand. All I have done here, in a sense, is reformat them and set them within a different, heterodox interpretive context. Yet the intellectual distortion that has been generated around the constitutional founding of the United States is so powerful and widespread that when the history is presented in the way it is here (as I have presented it many times before in the classes I teach and to professional colleagues), strong negative reactions ensue, even when the subsequent dialogue results (as it frequently has) in critics' taking the final defensive position that what I am calling the "distorted" version is necessary to the proper socialization of young Americans, as they must be taught to revere their founding fathers, the institutions they created, and the traditions that have arisen under them.

My response to such attacks is dismay—not so much at being attacked as over what I see to be the devastating implications of the critics' position. What our teachers tell us is that our founding fathers—namely, the Federalists—were wiser than the people of their day. We are told that the government that resulted from the Revolution (one that I and others such as Norman Jacobson believe reflected a high faith in humankind and the possibilities of human relationship) was wrong, inadequate, incorrect. We are asked to honor those heroic men who could recognize this, imagine a remedy, and lead a sufficient number of the right people of the day (albeit with a bit of violence) to conclude that the new Constitution should be supported. We are even taught not only to smile knowingly but even to admire the rhetorical and other maneuvers that it took to bring off this founding coup. I am, of course, representing the feelings of some of those who were "left out" at the time of the founding—those who were finessed out of the ratification—and suggesting that from the point of view of such parties, the "genius" of the Constitution might not seem to justify the moral compromises and antipopular designs built into the Federalist plan of government. Arguments that these were only the ugly scaffolding necessary to the construction of a great and beautiful governmental edifice or that time has vindicated the founders are simply not persuasive. At best, the evidence is not yet in on the Federalist idea of government (our whole national history amounts to only a couple of minutes relative to the history of other regimes), and it seems clear that all present-day Americans are receiving mixed results from the governmental system we have developed.

The worst of my dismay, though, is over the fact that in being taught to accept the orthodox story and to reject the alternative ethos represented by the Anti-Federalists, we are being taught a subtle kind of self-hatred. The subtext of the story of our founding is that people cannot trust themselves to make their own governments and to make them work, that people need privileged and superior elites like our founding fathers to plan and operate our governments for us. Constitutions are the most powerful teachers, and it is dismaying that ours has taught us this. It is all the more dismaying that the venue for this lesson has been the notion that the United States as it currently operates is the very epitome of what it is possible for democracy to be. This is the most pernicious dimension of the distortion.

The Anti-Federalists had another idea, and their ideas did not simply go away after the founding but rather persisted as a counter-subtheme to Constitutional government. This subtheme erupted in an especially relevant and critical way at the time of the founding of the field of public administration, resulting in yet another intellectual distortion. It is to this history that I now want to turn.

4

The Misfounding of the Field

The White Man is strange—he would own a hundred
horses and let his brother walk.

Chief Sitting Bull

The years between the nationwide railroad strike of 1877
and the Spanish-American War define an era of labor
violence unparalleled in any other industrial nation.

Stephen Skowronek

The point is that the discoveries of the nineteenth century
were in the direction of professionalism, so that we are left
with no expansion of wisdom and with greater need of it.

Alfred North Whitehead

A FEW HOURS' DRIVE from where I live, there is a rather
famous Atlantic Ocean beach. It has been a vacation spot for
many decades; it was discovered by the rich of the eastern seaboard
in the previous century. Originally, it was used mostly by millionaire
hunters who came there to shoot waterfowl during the annual migra-
tion south from Canada. It is said that the birds used to descend on

the area by the millions, darkening the sky as they approached in their airborne flocks. This is no longer the case. The hunters devastated the birds, shooting them by the thousands. Sometimes, when I am visiting there in the late summer and am thinking about the approach of the fall season, I try to imagine what it must have been like to see all those waterfowl traveling at once. Mostly, though, I wonder what motivated the hunters to kill the birds to the extent that they did. Since they obviously did not, in any sense I can imagine, "need" to kill them, what rendered such an act sensible? Against what social backdrop could their wholesale slaughter be considered a rational, even a sane, thing to do?

The same question can be raised, of course, about the elimination of the buffalo herds on the Great Plains. There was some incidental commercial value in the buffaloes' hides and bones, and there was the idea that the slaughter of the herds would help "starve out" the Native Americans who inhabited the region, but it seems that by any stretch this was a case of the end not justifying the means.

It is a widely recounted story among Jungians that once when Carl Jung visited the United States, he had a conversation with an American Indian chief. The man regaled Jung with an account of how Indians perceived the white race. What stood out to the Indians, the chief said, was that with the white man, there was no "right way." The whites, he said, were continually smiling and lying. They seemed to be obsessed with owning things and had no sense of respect for the Earth. He concluded by telling Jung, "We think they're crazy."

Although the purpose of this book is to pursue a theme of intellectual distortion, it is not entirely inappropriate to use the chief's remark as a benchmark for the turn that the theme takes in this chapter. There was indeed a great deal of craziness in America during the period of the founding of public administration, from after the Civil War through the turn of the twentieth century. This era's history itself is well known; all I want to do is cast aspects of it in a somewhat different light. I want to retell the story, suggesting a new interpretation as a basis for a new set of conversations about the origins of our field. The profile I seek to draw suggests that America did become crazy, in a way, and then sought to heal itself. One key result of this curative effort was the founding of the field of public administration. This is of special moment to us as we move toward the close of the twentieth century. The social, political, and economic conditions we currently face are often compared to those that obtained in America at the end of the nineteenth century. There seems to be a powerful comparison to be made between these fin de siècle periods. Perhaps we are again entering an era in which the possibility for seeing our field in a new light may be available to us.

I begin where the previous chapter ended. My characterization of the ethos that developed in the colonies suggests that America was originally organized around an impulse toward cooperation. This cooperative impulse inspired the Articles of Confederation. The colonists were, however, also products of the competitive, exploitative patterns of social organization they had lived under in Britain. The collective psyche they produced was, in effect, split between their egalitarian, communal, Revolutionary War experience and their European, class-dominated, exploitative inheritance (Wood, 1993; Zinn, 1995). These two oppositional ideas of social life came to be expressed in the debate between the Federalists and the Anti-Federalists over the ratification of the American Constitution. The legacy of this debate stretched far beyond the Federalist victory. In fact, echoes of the Anti-Federalist theme of community remained as a persistent counter-theme to the powerful Federalist theme of commercialism that dominated the early development of the United States (Ellis, 1987). The changes wrought during the post-Civil War period proceeded at such an unbridled pace, however, and in so many directions at once that the Federalist constitutional formula could not sufficiently comprehend them. By the end of the nineteenth century, these motifs surfaced again as social conditions in America plunged the country into social and political limbo and engendered a public debate curiously analogous to that of the founding period a century before. It was in this context that public administration emerged as a field.

In developing this chapter, I first recall several elements of the economic and political history of the United States from 1870 through the beginning of the twentieth century. I argue that it was during this period that the logic of the Federalist Constitution was played out to such an extent that its full implications for social life could be seen and felt. As the outlines of this new America took shape, a reaction set in that was inspired by what I will describe as a renewed, philosophically refurbished, and, in a sense, more sophisticated version of the Anti-Federalist sense of life. The reaction began producing social and cultural changes that suggested a new kind of government, one grounded in a common sense of life and operating through the principle of social and political cooperation. These changes could have served as the founding conceptual frame and ethos for a radically new kind of administratively grounded governmental process, one that

would have cast public administrators in a central and wholly legitimate role. However, this did not happen. Instead, the field became
established on another foundation, one consistent with the Federalist
idea of society as an arena of commercial enterprise and government
as the purview of Men of Reason. Accounting for how this happened
renders, in effect, a description of the powerful intellectual distortion
that was built into the founding of the field of public administration
in the United States.

The Economic and Political Background

During the roughly thirty-year period between the end of the War
Between the States and the beginning of the twentieth century, America underwent a fundamental and amazing transformation. It is a
familiar story of the realization of an American national identity. This
identity that America achieved as it entered the twentieth century was
hardly novel; it was the identity of the commercial giant that had been
implanted in the genetic code set for the embryonic nation by the
Federalist Constitution. Had Madison, Hamilton, and Jay been alive to
witness the panorama of this period, they might well have exclaimed,
"Yes, yes, this is what we had in mind."

Since the logic of the Constitution was essentially economic, it is
in the area of economic development that we can best see the dynamic
by which the heroic image of America as a vast commercial empire
came to be fulfilled. The hallmark of this development was the *rapid
increase in scale* of national economic institutions (Fainsod, Gordon,
& Palamountain, 1959). The economic demands of the War Between
the States are frequently credited with increasing exponentially the
rate of economic growth of mid-nineteenth-century America; the
validity of this claim seems undeniable. A brief retrospective reveals,
however, that although America would, under any conditions, eventually have become a society of vast economic institutions, the rapidity
of the development of the American commercial empire was not
accomplished without significant societal and personal costs.

The primary structural factor that stimulated such growth in
American business in the post-Civil War period was, of course, the
integration of the economy through national transportation and communication linkages, developments that were accomplished with a
degree of private profiteering that boggles even the contemporary

mind. The social impact of these essentially technological changes was monumental and worked consistently in the direction of breaking the organic relationships that had been the grounding of American community. These were replaced with abstract mechanisms connecting large-scale systems into a whole (Wiebe, 1967). The most obvious effects were in patterns of commerce. As the political scientist V. O. Key (1959) noted, "The transportation network sucked the life out of little businesses in villages and hamlets over the land" (p. 186). Other, more profound changes occurred at the personal level. For example, with four fifths of the population living in rural areas, people's sense of daily life had been tied directly to natural rhythms. The condition of "being late" barely existed, and people had little idea of time as a device for standardized coordination. The advent of the railroads changed this. People began to conform to railroad schedules; it became critical for farmers to mesh their personal sense of time with railroad time; knowing "what time it was" became a commercial necessity. It was no accident that it was the railroads, in 1884, that pressured the federal government to establish time zones (Ventura, 1995).

People also discovered that the new "necessities" of life—sugar, kerosene, matches, and so forth—were now under the control of a new institutional form, corporations and trusts. These were of unimaginable size and made decisions that affected everyone on the basis of the entirely alien and abstract calculus of business accounting. The size of these new corporate structures had given industrialists a kind of power that went beyond market theory, into even the realm of social coercion (Hofstadter, 1955, pp. 231-234). The exploitative pricing that resulted became a central reference point for the new commercial ethos of America.

This was further supported by the tariff protectionism of the day, which worked along regional and class lines, disadvantaging the South and the West, lower-income groups, and the agricultural sector. Reconstruction psychology, in which the South was viewed as a conquered people who had lost because they had an unjust cause and thus "deserved" to be exploited, helped to provide a rationale for the continuation of high tariffs (Hicks & Mowry, 1956). Anti-inflationary monetary policies, benefiting the wealthy, exacerbated the already pervasive sense that distant, unknown agents were manipulating and controlling the economics of day-to-day life in ways that had invidious consequences for specific groups.

These psychologically critical changes uprooted the rural, traditional mind, unsettled the American people, and produced a general-

ized paranoia that began to surface in the politics of the day (Hofstadter, 1955). This political paranoia had roots deep in the American
psyche and went back to the distinctively concrete and communal
sense of life that developed in the colonies, a sense of life that saw
social relationships rather than official institutions as the primary
working bases for social order. The following remark of Henry Adams
implicitly acknowledged this:

> The great object of terror and suspicion to the people of the thirteen
> provinces was power; not merely power in the hands of a president
> or a prince, of one assembly or several, of many citizens or few, but
> *power in the abstract* [italics added], wherever it existed and under
> whatever form it was known. (quoted in McConnell, 1966, p. 33)

It was this kind of fear that generated the powerful populist
movement. As McConnell (1966) noted about populism and the other
political orientations of the times, "All of these movements were
symptoms of a deep and widespread sense of exploitation and disor-
der. . . . The sense of an evil turn in national development was
pervasive; the public's preoccupation with corruption was the most
certain symptom" (p. 33). What populism sought to do was to engage
in open battle with the exercise of abstract power that its adherents so
dreaded. Although the Populist Party was minimally successful in the
politics of the times, populism as a broader political orientation
opened a vent for the reappearance of the suppressed Anti-Federalist
cultural countertheme. In its dimension as a social movement, one
grounded significantly in the actual cooperative activities by which
agricultural communities sustained themselves, populism appeared
as a remarkable reincarnation of the Anti-Federalist spirit (McMath,
1993). People saw in it the possibility for realizing a collaborative
approach to governance, one that they would attain by direct involvement. On the other hand, the movement also evoked the darker aspect
that resides within all forms of communalism: the paranoid fear of all
impersonal social relations. Specifically, the rapid development of a
national market and the new reality of abstract power that it created
was precisely the correct agent for attracting the shadow side of
Anti-Federalism. In this shadow side, there was fear of the abstract
power by which ambition commonly seeks to further itself (and for
which it constructs the devices of large-scale, impersonal institutions)
and the corresponding fear of the elite conspiracies that controlled
these institutions. These, the Anti-Federalists felt, would always work

to the detriment of common people and society generally. This dark aspect of Anti-Federalism also energized the populists (Goodwyn, 1976).

The question that populism and the major political issues of the times did raise anew, however, was the appropriate role of government (not politics) in dealing with social and economic circumstances. It is difficult to appreciate fully from a contemporary point of view how disconnected *government* was from the social and economic life of the country during the period of time I am discussing. The idea of government "programs" aimed positively at social purposes simply did not exist. Government administrations, both Democrat and Republican, did not see even conditions of rather severe economic depression as any of their "business." Rather, they were something that should be left alone to play themselves out in the private sector (Hicks & Mowry, 1956). There was, of course, the idea that law could be used to curb specific abusive behaviors, in much the same way that we think about criminal laws. This idea of law was all that existed in the way of a theory of "positive government," and generally, "law" was left up to the courts to interpret (Skowronek, 1982). Acting on the logic of the Federalists and the Constitution that they wrote, nineteenth-century national governments simply set the structural conditions and the ground rules for commerce and then let the market and the patterns of social life it produced take care of themselves. During this period, the nation experienced probably the widest, most serious economic and social turbulence it had ever undergone; however, there was little basis for understanding how anything could be done about it through government. Early attempts at compensatory reaction to the heroic overreachings of the late nineteenth-century American "robber barons" were challenged at every turn, but these efforts remained largely unsuccessful until the initial decades of the twentieth century (Redford, 1965).

Such uses of policy to structure social life appeared first in the areas of regulation of work life and the control of immigration through quotas, literacy tests, and the like (Hicks & Mowry, 1956). By far the most important such attempt, of course, was the move to regulate railroads. The history of railroad regulation reveals the size of the tear in the fabric of American political culture that the economic expansion and turbulence of the post-Civil War years had caused. The range of political opinion during this period was perhaps the broadest ever seen in the United States. Proposals were made to solve the railroad problem by having the government take over the railroads and operate them outright or by establishing government rail companies that would hold rates down by competing with the privately owned lines (Fainsod et al., 1959; Hicks & Mowry, 1956; Redford, 1965). Opposition to such ideas was pervasive, of course, and regulation seemed the only acceptable alternative. However, there was ambivalence even about minimal regulation. The Interstate Commerce Commission (ICC) was given power only to investigate complaints and seek remedy to abuses through court action. It was not until the period of reform, in the Theodore Roosevelt administration, that the ICC became a real player in the game of interstate commerce (Fainsod et al., 1959).

We can see a history similar to the ICC's in the struggle of the nation to bring the abuses of the new corporate monopolies and oligopolies—the "trusts"—under control. In the social-government context that developed after the Civil War, these new large corporate entities held a decidedly advantaged position. They were an entirely new creation, something beyond the conceptual frame of reference of the general public and even of those in government. The public tended simply to feel fearful (again, "paranoid") about them and to send out a general demand to their political representatives to do something to restrain them. The institutions of government strained to place them within the conceptual frame of the Constitution, which, though it did envision and provide the conditions for exactly the sort of economic expansion that produced them, in fact did not provide a ready frame for comprehending their place, their role, and the relation of government to them. The states, in principle, had ample power to act toward them, but they were limited by their geographically determined jurisdictional constraints—they could not act in ways that affected interstate commerce.

Common-law traditions did, however, legitimate regulation of businesses that were "public in nature," and these traditions also sanctioned government action against conspiracy in restraint of trade (Hartz, 1948; Lippmann, 1937; Skowronek, 1982). These were the grounds for most of the state actions against the trusts, and they provided the rationale for Congress ultimately to pass the Sherman Anti-Trust Act in 1890. The trusts fought the act in court and invented the device of the "holding company" as a way of evading it. The Supreme Court at this point took positions that were highly favorable to the trusts (e.g., that restraining trade through the purchase of property alone was allowable and that manufacture and production in themselves were not part of interstate commerce), and of the first eight attempts to invoke penalties under the Sherman Act, the result was seven lost cases (Fainsod et al., 1959; Hicks & Mowry, 1956). Even with the Sherman Act on the books, private monopoly became de facto legal in the United States. The underlying transformation in the collective identity of the nation represented by the impulse to regulate had not proceeded to a point that it could serve as a guide to effective governmental action. As was the case with the ICC, it was not until things had changed further at this level that, under Theodore Roosevelt, the Sherman Act could be enforced with enough sense of direction to be partially effective against the new giant organizations of American commerce (Fainsod et al., 1959; Hicks & Mowry, 1956).

It was in the area of civil service reform that the impulse toward regulation had the most impact. The Pendleton Act establishing a second Civil Service Commission (the first was never fully funded) passed in 1883. Initially, the commission had jurisdiction over about 12% of low-level government offices. Aided by the motive of successive Democrat and Republican presidents to protect their respective appointees, however, and by President Harrison's appointment of Theodore Roosevelt to the Civil Service Commission, the number of jobs covered rose to 45,000 by 1893, 100,000 by 1900, and then, within another decade, to half a million (Hicks & Mowry, 1956).

As I mentioned earlier, the idea of government's intervention in the affairs of the economy simply did not seem to be within the mainstream "operating frame of reference" for the political system at the end of the nineteenth century. This is not to say, however, that the idea of government regulation is alien to the American political culture. Ancient common-law traditions brought over from England were very much a part of our initial legal frame of reference and ultimately (in the twentieth century) provided the legal basis for regulation under our Constitution. These same traditions were operative during the colonial period, and, as we have seen, governments of that day were, even by current criteria, quite active in the economy—setting standards, rates, and rules for business practice and even specifying wages in some areas (Hartz, 1948). Recalling this helps reveal the symbolic meaning of regulation as an aspect of political community. Criminal law tends to be oriented largely toward reducing or eliminating activities that disrupt the stable life of the community. Regulation, on the other hand, is more in the direction of a positive expression of the community's sense of itself. Regulations state positive norms—norms that, taken collectively, define how the people in the community *want to live together.* The fact that the American nation had as much difficulty as it did in resuscitating its regulatory traditions during the

[margin note: Criminal law vs. regulation]

key nineteenth-century period of economic expansion, and thereby expressing itself as a political community, is indicative of the extent to which this tradition had been suppressed by the operating form our government had taken. For a potentially more positive role of government to emerge, a new and more supportive social ethos had to develop. Transformations in the social and cultural conditions of the times ultimately began to provide this foundation.

Social and Cultural Transformations

On April 12, 1891, President Benjamin F. Harrison, at Sutro Heights, had the following items for his lunch:

> oysters and beef tea with California Riesling, Rudesheimer and Sauterne; cold turkey, goose, ham, tongue, goose liver, sardines, sardelles, caviar, asparagus and artichokes with Zinfandel; sweetbreads with mushrooms (an intermediate course) with Chateau La Rose; roast chicken and duck with Chateau Lafite; followed by sponge cake, wine jelly, ice-cream, macaroons and strawberries with Sauterne, Champagne, Cognac, and Chartreuse. (Bayley, 1991, p. 205)

This meal is emblematic of the dialectic that energized the transformation of American culture in the time between the end of the Civil War and the beginning of the twentieth century. The end of the nineteenth century was characterized by the interplay of extremes. At the time that such lunches as Harrison's were being consumed (and we can imagine that in the private dining rooms of the rich, they were even more opulent), it was not uncommon for other Americans literally to be dying of starvation. Such contrasts of fate typically are the engines driving history through periods of turbulence, and it is testimony to the distinctive commitment to the value of stability in the American character that they produced a cultural rather than a violent political revolution—though there were smatterings of even this.

    This contrast of extremes, in playing itself out, energized a middle perspective, a point of view that sought to represent what is *between* people rather than what is inside each discrete individual. Faced with social conditions that seemed to portend either the complete bifurcation of society into an exploiting and an exploited group or, perhaps even worse, degradation into a kind of suppressed cultural anarchy, a new collective spirit seemed to well up spontaneously, one that sought to produce a shared formula for social, economic, and political life. In general, this was an adapted version of the social sentiment that underlay the government of the Articles of Confederation and that the Anti-Federalists sought to express.

As the Civil War ended and America moved down the short path to the new century and a national economy, social and cultural conditions were characterized by chaotic and rapid change. An emerging business class was juxtaposed as exploiter to a rapidly growing (largely by reason of immigration) and increasingly vulnerable underclass. The period was one of severe economic ups and downs. The war had created prosperity, but then, in 1873 and again in 1893, panic and depression hit. In contrast to the general condition of deprivation and mood of disaster that had begun to set in, America had developed an entire class of *arriviste* rich that met the lowest standards of taste in lifestyle and personal behavior and that had no compunction whatever against flaunting its largesse with the utmost vulgarity. As C. E. Norton, a prominent social commentator of the day, put it, "The lack of intellectual elevation and of moral discrimination is a source of national weakness. The prevalence of vulgarity is a national disgrace" (quoted in Damrosch, 1995, p. 57). Profiteering and speculation had produced much of the wealth. The formula that the newly emerging exploiter class followed in amassing its power and wealth was simple. In the case of railroads, the exploiter class used the protection and support provided by state and federal aid to fund vast, rapidly executed construction projects, which were then followed by equally rapid consolidations into huge rail network empires (Hicks & Mowry, 1956). Individuals and tight, small, selfish groups sought to consolidate small enterprises into large ones and, as they grew, to use economies of scale to drive down prices, eliminating small companies and creating market power that in turn could be used to gain other concessions and advantages. As one thoughtful commentator surveying the new American power elite put it:

> If our civilization is destroyed, it will not be by . . . barbarians from below. Our barbarians come from above. Our great money makers have sprung in one generation into seats of power kings do not know. . . . Without restraint of culture, experience, the pride or even the inherited caution of class or rank, these intoxicated men think they are the wave instead of the float. To them, science is but a never ending repertoire of investments stored up by nature for the syndicates,

government but a fountain of franchises, the nations but customers in squads. (Henry Demarest Lloyd, quoted in Hicks & Mowry, 1956, p. 416)

It seems clear that this pattern of economic development was directly implied in the logic of the Federalist theory of the Constitution. Unfortunately, the Federalist framework did *not* elaborate how the practical legal structures that were required to make this new system work effectively were to be put in place without destroying the social infrastructure on which every economy depends. Indeed, the Federalists' theory was not at all well considered on this point. It left the problem of attaining and maintaining community to the informal, "unofficial" realms outside government and in doing so assumed that the cleverly designed mechanisms of its political institutions (checks and balances, etc.) would protect the government from the potentially negative consequences of the freewheeling entrepreneurship that the founders envisioned (Diamond, 1979).

What they did not see was the powerfully corrosive effect that free enterprise would have on social relations, political processes, and even the belief in free enterprise itself when truly large *scale* came into the picture. In the smaller business arena—capped at most by some regional monopolies—that existed before the development of a national market system, binding norms and standards of business conduct existed for commercial relations. Being a "good business man" meant first maintaining the goodwill of the customer by respecting this informal code. It was the face-to-face relation, the more or less personal connection that occurred in commerce on a small and medium scale, that made this system of norms real and operative (Wood, 1993). With the advent of large-scale enterprises, this critically important connection was broken, there were no rules to replace it, and no conceptual frame was available that could contain or even render sensible the corporate pirating that had taken over the economy.

Opposition was just as extreme, especially by the new laboring classes, who were the most direct victims of the emerging economic order. The wave of immigrants who began during this period to move into America's cities brought not only new ways of living, strange languages, and different foods but also what were, for the American political scene, radical political theories of the left and the tradition of violence in politics that had characterized European history. America had a labor movement, with organized unions, from the beginning of the 1800s. However, the unions did not have the strength of organization required to contain the reactive feelings created in workers by the exploitative work conditions that were the policies of the new large corporations (Hicks & Mowry, 1956).

Throughout this period, the government, state and federal, consistently intervened on the side of the owners, and it seemed clear that America did not want to follow the path of radical change. Nonetheless, it became increasingly obvious that "something was going to have to give." The social conditions produced by the economic struggle being acted out between business and labor were no less than horrendous. The absence of ethics in the conduct of business, the excess and decadence that were expressed in the vulgar ostentation of the lifestyles of many of the new rich, and the attitude of disdain and self-righteousness that they openly held and theoretically justified by espousing social Darwinism were matched by urban poverty of the most tragic proportions, including outright starvation (Olasky, 1992).

Living conditions in the cities were abysmal at the lower end of the economic scale. The luckier ones resided in practically unmaintained tenements that offered few sanitary facilities; the less fortunate were relegated to disease-breeding cellars. Because the poor lacked knowledge of prophylactic hygiene practices made necessary by urban living and no one cared to teach them, preventable diseases such as typhoid, typhus, and others spread in waves, especially through the new immigrant groups (Hicks & Mowry, 1956). A huge population increase in Europe beginning in the mid-eighteenth century provided the base for the expansion of America's population, but it was as much the explicit campaign mounted on numerous fronts to recruit cheap labor as it was the pressure to leave Europe that actually made it happen. These campaigns, along with the extremely cheap fares for passage that were offered (e.g., port-to-port passage across the Atlantic for $12, including meals), were effective in achieving their purposes of providing a supply of cheap labor and new population for the western states. The worst of this was the concomitant exploitation of children and women as labor (Hicks & Mowry, 1956).

The horrendous conditions that developed in American cities were unprecedented. They grew out of an open motive to exploit immigrants as labor and a lack of concern for them as human beings. In addition to such exploitation, immigrants encountered widespread prejudice. It is no surprise, then, that other social problems began to spin off from these urban conditions. Alcoholism, which had soared during the Civil War, continued to increase alarmingly. Crime grew at what seemed to be an exponential rate, with murder rates doubling and prison populations growing by as much as 50% within one decade.

It looked as if American cities were destined to become among the meanest and lowest places on the earth (Vidal, 1976).

This destructive pattern of change was not limited to the cities, however. Farmers also underwent a kind of degradation. From being proudly individualistic men who, with their families, "lived on the land" and helped their neighbors do the same, they became users of machines who sought only to produce as much as they could in order to do as well as they could in the market, then massing together to seek collective advantage through politics. The deterioration of agricultural community was especially acute in the South. Although the industrial revolution increased production significantly, few benefited, because the huge majority of farmers were tenants. The practice of going in debt to merchants until crops were harvested drove these small farmers further and further into a kind of indentured servitude (Hicks & Mowry, 1956). The national political system, as exemplified in two-party competition, offered little or no hope for coming to terms with these problematic conditions. Neither of the parties was able to articulate an agenda of issues that spoke to the social crisis the nation was experiencing, and instead, politics degenerated into "dirty tricks," propaganda, and personality assassination. The scandals of Reconstruction government and the Grant administration set the moral tone of the day, and the Tweed Ring in New York provided the organizational model for corrupt urban machine politics. No line of political rhetoric or arena of dialogue emerged to address the mess America was making of itself (Hicks & Mowry, 1956). The fabric of American community was not able to withstand the stresses of these postwar decades, probably because it was sewn into a patchwork quilt pattern by the history of the nation. Community had always existed, but it was supremely local in nature and highly diverse. As I have mentioned already, when the era of urban industrialization hit, it quickly outstripped the dimensions of this patchwork quilt, leaving Americans without any framework for making social choices about the form of the new society that was emerging.

Indeed, in addition to social crisis, political fecklessness, and economic turbulence, there was intellectual disorientation and confusion, making it all the more difficult for a sense-making perspective to emerge. First, there was the problem simply of diversity. Immigration had brought with it a degree of diversity unknown to the United States. Although the alien political and social theories that immigrants introduced did not overcome the basic American commitment to social stability, the religious heterodoxy that the immigrants constituted by their presence alone had a significant impact in refracting the collective moral mind of the American people into a number of divergent directions (Hicks & Mowry, 1956).

Second, the rising importance of science in the popular mind played an even larger role. By some accounts, science in effect became the working religion of the America of the new century, unsettling the foundational beliefs of traditional religious points of view. Darwin's doctrine of "evolution" (or natural selection) had an especially devastating impact in this respect. The new statistical theories developing in the field of physics seemed to add to what seemed to be a spreading ethos of relativism. Churches were rent with strife as "modernist" ministers, challenging doctrines of infallibility, were driven from their pulpits. It seemed that some new point of view, a perspective that could weave the various threads of the unraveling American culture, was desperately needed (Hicks & Mowry, 1956).

The Emergence of a Healing Tendency

The structural conditions for the development of this new American culture were laid by the national transportation and communication system and the new national economy. Americans were drawn together by their dependence on the new large-scale producers and markets of the goods they used in daily life. As Hicks and Mowry (1956) summarized this development:

> Americans everywhere became accustomed to the same "makes" of washing machines, farm implements, bicycles, wagons and buggies; wore the same styles of readymade clothes; painted their houses with nationally known brands of house paint; purchased quantities of breakfast foods, toothpowder, and liniment. . . . Mail order houses . . . did a thriving business. Retail prices . . . varied little from one section to another, and even the methods of doing business became standardized. (pp. 539-540)

The population also began to move from one section of the country to another, fusing and homogenizing further in the process.

Public education had become virtually universal and by happenstance had taken on a highly similar pattern, both in institutional form and in educational content. New theories of education were arising and were aided in implementation by the establishment in 1867 of a U.S. Commissioner of Education, new tax-supported teacher-training schools, and the creation of free public high schools. Even the South, though it lagged, shared in such developments. Even more remarkable was the rapid rise of the American university. The Morrill Act of 1862 established the land grant college system, which required that each state establish at least one college under the system within five years. Aided by philanthropy and a new generation of educational leaders familiar with European institutions but intent on fashioning a new, American variety of higher education, the university system grew rapidly. The widening of educational opportunity at the college level even included women and black people. A few women's colleges opened their doors after the war, but the true mass entry of women into higher education came with the acceptance of the principle of coeducation. Howard, Fisk, and Shaw Universities, and the Hampton Normal and Agricultural Institute in Virginia, opened in rapid order at the end of the war, making possible higher education for blacks in the South (Hicks & Mowry, 1956).

With this sort of boost, education became what one might call the central artifact or analogue of the new theme developing in the collective mind of America. Indicative of this is the astonishing growth of graduate education after the Civil War. More and more, the average American citizen saw learned people, the expert knowledge they carried, and the scientific process they represented as a kind of a universal curative for social problems and the venue by which they and their children could better their lot in life.

A parallel development was the mushrooming growth of professional societies, associations, and other organizations on a national basis. With better transportation available, members of such groups from all parts of the country could gather in one place to hear the same presentations and engage in common dialogue from which they garnered ideas that they could carry back to their colleagues in the localities. The new availability of transportation also facilitated lecturers and entertainers traveling on "chautauqua circuits" that covered the country. This had the effect of providing common intellectual and artistic experiences to the entire American population. Road and local "stock" companies were quick to form and take popular New York entertainments to the towns of the "provinces," so that even before radio or motion pictures, the entire nation could be singing the same songs. A single newspaper story could now be transmitted nationally through news-gathering agencies such as the Associated Press, and newspapers and magazines quickly imitated the copy-selling sensationalist style that seemed to work best in capturing the new national market. Through this new venue, baseball quickly became a *national* pastime, one linked structurally to the localities through the "farm" system, thus making it all the more powerful in knitting the nation together into one identity. Football added to this as it came to be adopted as the sport of colleges and universities, and professional boxing came on the scene as one more sports entertainment on which the nation as a whole could focus its attention (Hicks & Mowry, 1956).

More and more, Americans came to see themselves reflected in consumer products, activities, entertainments, and ideas as one people, with one identity, one fate, and, by implication, one responsibility for how they lived together and dealt with one another. The same surging, at times chaotic, economic development that put so much strain on the social fabric of the country in the post-Civil War decades also laid the basis for a healing reaction to the destructive turbulence that it created. This mix of factors produced, overall, a distinctively American ethos by the beginning of the twentieth century. It was distinctively American in the sense that its origins were in a resurgent Anti-Federalist temperament. What might be called "ecological factors" intermixed with the general economic and political situation to form a collective ethos from which arose an impulse toward administrative governance consistent with Anti-Federalism.

What was required was a new relationship between society and community, a new grounding for economic and political activity in a new form of social relationship. What emerged to meet this requirement was a different kind of American community, community on a *national* scale. Indeed, it was through the quiet but deep processes of reforming community that a healing compensation arose for the destructive struggles going on in the political and economic arenas. The elements in the situation produced a *practical communitarianism,* a motive energizing social action. Practical communitarianism expressed itself as an impulse toward *reform,* aimed directly at the offending condition and implemented through cooperative organization and activity. One example is the problem of alcoholism, which was addressed through policies such as raising liquor license fees and local and state alcohol exclusion options (Hicks & Mowry, 1956).

Other examples can be seen in the charity boards that were set up in numerous states to deal with the problems of poor relief, the deaf and blind, and juvenile delinquency. What characterized these activities was their desire to find guidance in addressing social problems through association and practical action at the level of the problem itself (Olasky, 1992). Practical cooperation came to have the power of a legitimating ideology, and this, in fact, was the ideology that provided inspiration for the founding of the profession of public administration.

The Rise of Progressivism

Though the new sense of national identity developed implicitly and hence was nothing like the sort of national ideology that results from explicit, *political* change, America's emerging sense of itself did provide the basis for a kind of political revolution, complete with its own ideology of sorts, in the form of the creed of progressivism. To understand this ideology, we must first understand how it was a theory generated from the middle. One sense in which this is so has to do with the aforementioned dialectic of the capitalists versus the populists.

The new American industrialists sincerely believed that there was a kind of divine logic, a social Darwinism, in the market and the way that it sorted some people into positions of ownership and economic power; everyone was better off if this process of "letting the cream find its way to the top" was left undisturbed by government (Lux, 1990). Their overall position, not unlike that of their Federalist forerunners, was to let the game (for them, the *economic* struggle) play out as it would. The needed protection from government interference could be ensured, they felt, by their having extraordinary influence within government through their political party activities and associations. The populists, on the other hand, felt that government should be controlled by the people generally (McMath, 1993). The majority could and should simply demand that government adopt policies that protected the masses from economic tides set in motion by the market. The politics of this period was thus one that counterposed elite use of abstract power and mass use of abstract power. The two sides were actually playing the same game; hence, neither represented a new or positive alternative, one that could move the country out of the turmoil in which it had become embroiled (Key, 1959).

The progressives stood between these views. To a certain extent, they represented interests, especially small-scale business enterprises and their owners, who were endangered by both; the capitalists threatened to swallow up small business with their huge corporate organizations, and the populist movement seemed all too close to (and hence likely to mutate into) socialism, which presented a threat from the other side. The essence of the progressive creed, however, was not inspired by economic interest of this sort as much as it was by a new sensibility about how society should express itself through government. The foundation for this was emerging in an inchoate manner far beneath the surface level of the economic and political struggle. This process was drawing together what might be called the positive aspects of the Anti-Federalist sense of social life: the sense of connection between people; the sense of community that such a connection produced; and the resulting sense of direction for collective life. This foundation served as the initial basis for the progressive movement (Noble, 1981).

Progressives believed, first, that private power over government, exercised at the time mainly through party politics, had to be broken. Rather than majority rule setting broad policies that made brute-force alterations in the course and outcomes of the market, government should establish within itself the capacity to *regulate* the economic sphere on an ongoing basis. They were able to see the basis for such regulatory actions in the emerging professional, educated, scientific, technical "consciousness" that so many of them possessed. This new mind-set entailed another possibility: Government could act positively to realize values and ideals. This is seen best in the progressives' desire to protect women and children from victimization by the market. To some elements in the movement, government could succeed even in setting a "good" lifestyle—one without alcohol or gambling, for example. On any specific policy question, of course—as in what to do about trusts—one was likely to find a wide range of opinion among the progressives. On the whole, they can best be characterized as a movement that was seeking to establish a new kind of government in America, a government that would reflect and maintain a sense of *national* community that both evoked talent and material progress by reliance on market processes and at the same time provided for the human protection and support that characterizes a moral community. Initially, progressivism marked the emergence in America of a theory of government based on the attainment of social virtue through positive, practical action.

Viewed in this light, the progressive movement could have been a modernized version of Anti-Federalism. By the turn of the century, conditions in the country had rendered the original Anti-Federalist vision of social and political life anachronistic and impossible. Aspects of the program of progressivism, however, as well as broader patterns of political change, can be seen as the updating and upscaling of the Anti-Federalist constitution for America. Rejecting the results of the official Constitution's reliance on the private realm, the progressives sought reforms that struck in the direction of creating community in America on a grand scale, a national community. In this sense, as other commentators have said, what we see in the progressive period is the beginning of the project that was given an official launching in Roosevelt's New Deal and that was to continue for the following half-century, coming to a failed conclusion in Lyndon Johnson's Great Society program (Schambra, 1982).

The field of public administration was founded during this period, and the ethos of this time played a crucial role in its history. In fact, because the history of twentieth-century America is the history of the American administrative state, it is no exaggeration to say that public administration is the formula for the new constitution by which America came to be governed during this era. Is the theme of my story, then, that the history of public administration is the history of Anti-Federalism playing itself out in modern times? No. Although the positive side of Anti-Federalism did indeed provide the inspiration for the founding of public administration, this founding was soon aborted, in something like the way that Federalism overwhelmed Anti-Federalism during the writing of the official Constitution. This distortion of the true founding ethos of public administration led to the mutation and failure of the progressive project and has, in turn, led to the legitimacy problem that is the main subject of this book.

To see how this happened, we must look at the history of the progressive reforms, seeking to see their underlying animus. Then we must look at the dynamics of the social ethos that provided the context for, and thereby guided, these reforms, with an eye to understanding how the abortion, the distortion, and the denial of the Anti-Federalist spirit once again occurred.

The Meaning of the Progressive Reforms

It is difficult for contemporary Americans, as accustomed as we have become to modern centrist politics, to appreciate fully the transformation that occurred in the United States political system during the early part of the twentieth century. I have found that contemporary American students become almost incredulous when they are presented with the line of critique that provided inspiration to the reforms—focused, as much as it was, on the validity of the Constitution as a political formula. What took place was no less than a revolution, a fundamental alteration in the methods by which government functioned and the aims that government pursued.

One of the most obvious places that this change could be seen is in municipal government, where it took the form of a concerted campaign to break the hold of party machines on governmental processes. The New York Tammany Hall machine was not an aberration but rather a highly visible example of a widespread pattern in local government and politics. Payoffs by organized crime for protection from prosecution, and graft and corruption in the granting of contracts, were the privileges to which the urban machines gained access by obligating voters through neighborhood "casework" to needy individuals and by stuffing ballot boxes, altering reports on election returns, and employing hundreds of other corrupt political practices (Mosher, 1980; Waldo, 1955).

The movement for reform initially focused singularly on the idea of separating politics completely from the operation of the city government. This conceptual focus was largely due to the fact that at the turn of the century, the city services that were among the most important to the urban citizen—gas, electricity, transportation, and water utilities—were privately owned concerns carrying out business under franchises granted by the city. It seemed logical to conclude, therefore, that there was no need to have a political element involved at all in the picture. The only purpose politicians appeared to serve was that of receiving graft in the awarding of the utility contracts. It seemed obvious that the way to get better service and lower rates was to let the city own and operate the utilities, thereby cleaning up the government by cutting the politicians out of the picture completely. Government at the local level was most like a business. Why did it need to involve a party politics modeled after the national government (Mosher, 1980; Waldo, 1955)?

This government-as-business mind-set was given impetus by the disastrous flooding of Galveston, Texas, in 1900 and the struggle of the city to come to terms effectively with the disaster. The recovery program was turned over to a commission of five city department heads, each with a designated functional responsibility (Uveges & Keller, 1989, p. 6). Other cities soon experimented with this commissioner idea, and by the early 1900s it had inspired the idea of a city manager for local governments (Mosher, 1980; Waldo, 1955). Hundreds of mostly smaller cities adopted the new concept, enough to at least establish the notion that there was a workable and a "better" alternative for urban government than sole reliance on the political process. Although the rational city manager model of government movement did not immediately sweep the nation and displace "poli-

tics as usual" in urban governments throughout, it did proceed quickly
and widely enough to gain a kind of moral high ground.

This was significant because it indicated that a *common sense* was
developing (or had developed) about how government could and
should function—a sense that rejected the freewheeling competitive
market process of politics. Corollary to this was the notion, implicit in
the idea of improving services, that the citizen was to be considered as
a *discretionary* consumer of city government services, not as a victim
who was simply to be manipulated through casework and provided
with whatever service at whatever price the providers wanted to make
available. The rationalization of city services marks a move away from
the market ethos that had begun to emerge as the trusts developed, an
ethos within which the private citizen was seen as a cipher, with no
discretion and not enough of a connection to other citizens to be able
to develop a basis for asserting preferences against the huge organizations that were coming to dominate the scene.

The widespread pattern of corrupt government at the city level, of
course, was duplicated at the state level, since it was here that reforms
took their most ideological and politically radical form. Wisconsin and
Robert La Follette were pioneers in the changes that took place at the
state level—increased taxation of corporations (especially railroads),
political reforms, and a new emphasis on conservation. La Follette was
matched in Missouri by Joseph W. Folk, in New York by Charles Evans
Hughes, in Iowa by A. B. Cummins, in Minnesota by John A. Johnson,
and in California by Hiram Johnson, to list only the most prominent
(Hicks & Mowry, 1956).

The pattern of political reforms at the state level was quite definite:
the Australian (secret) ballot and improved voter registration laws;
the abolition of the convention process for nominating candidates and
replacement of it with the open primary system; the initiative and ref-
erendum (whereby citizens could propose legislation and/or express
specific opinions on proposed legislation); and the recall (whereby
officials can be put out of office during their term) (Hicks & Mowry,
1956). Within this political context, too, the Seventeenth Amendment
to the national Constitution was passed, providing for the direct
election of U.S. senators. Such a change had been resisted for decades
by the Senate, even though the House had presented it with such an
amendment on four occasions. In the ethos of popular control that
developed as the twentieth century opened, however, the pressure
became inexorable. Preferential primaries, in which voters could

inform state legislatures of the popular choice for the senatorial posts, were adopted in more than half the states (Hicks & Mowry, 1956).

The changes in state government are most revealing of the subtextual meaning of the reform movement. As I noted above, although municipal reform proceeded under the nominal idea of making city government like private business, the intent was really more to provide a venue by which an emerging sense of popular discretion could be acknowledged. This theme is even more visible in the changes at the state level. After all, business was seen as corrupt and exploitative and as big an enemy of society as the political parties, machines, and bosses. The "Wisconsin idea," which was emblematic of the state reform movement, was centered primarily on releasing state government from domination by big businesses through severing its connections to corrupt party bosses.

The nominal idea was that every avenue for the expression of the popular will should be opened. In the final analysis, however, these devices of presumed citizen involvement were actually intended to lead to the installation in office of officials who would govern through the counsel of experts, people "who were only free to do what was right" (Hicks & Mowry, 1956, p. 599). This concept that there was a "right way" had to be supported, again, by a "common sense" or a generally shared view of social life. The growing acceptance of the idea that commonly held standards could be asserted through politics marked a shift away from the market orientation that had dominated economic and, as a consequence, political and social life in the latter half of the nineteenth century.

Although the progressives' concept of government by technical experts has come to be seen as a denial of the role of the citizen, what is missed by this characterization is the radical notion of community that preceded the turn toward expertise (Noble, 1981). The early progressives had to create a basis for the faith in expertise; they had to energize the formation of a sufficiently strong and active community to sustain a commonly held idea of appropriate governmental action. Even though this common sense might actually have been closer to "rational like-mindedness" than a shared popular sentiment, the denial of the validity of such a common sense and the "standards" for choice that it implies distinguishes microeconomics as a social theory, even today.

This same theme can be found in the area of social reforms. The new state-level workmen's compensation legislation of the day is a good example in that it explicitly overturned the traditional principle in common law—consistent with market theory—of placing the assumption of responsibility for job injuries on the worker and his or her fellows (who freely chose to contract to do the work) rather than the employer. The new laws asserted a principle of "fairness." Essentially, if the occupation were hazardous, then workers hired into it deserved to be compensated under any circumstances when and if they were injured doing the work (Hicks & Mowry, 1956).

Though the record on other labor legislation by the states was uneven and at best fell far short of that of Europe, what must be called significant progress was made. Legislation limiting the number of work hours per day for women and children and prohibiting their employment in certain types of jobs was passed, and it was complemented by laws for compulsory school attendance. A few states even passed minimum-wage laws (Hicks & Mowry, 1956).

Such legislation as this marked the development of a widening sense that law could justifiably reflect collective norms, that people had the right to create a social environment for themselves through government. The most visible thrust in this direction, perhaps, was the movement to bring alcohol under social control. With the formation of the Anti-Saloon League in 1893, this movement gained great momentum as the new century opened. The brewers and distillers were among the most deserving of the title of "corruptionists," because they had long been involved in the process of using politics to further their business objectives. Mainly through an unflagging wearing away at the opposition and winning small battles at the local level for the dry option (the antialcohol movement created "dry" ground under nearly half of the population of the country by the time of World War I), the reformers culminated their campaign in victory with the ratification of the Prohibition Amendment in 1919 (Hicks & Mowry, 1956). Whether we favor the policy or not, Prohibition was evidence that America was seeking for the first time in its history to use government to define the style of life it wanted to live.

This was also evident in the increasingly rational approach to urban life that emerged. Codes were enacted ensuring that buildings were safe and hygienic, parks and playgrounds were planned and constructed, and programs were mounted to remove gambling and prostitution from the streets and to curb juvenile delinquency (Hicks & Mowry, 1956).

At the national level, these local innovations were mirrored in the movement for labor legislation, mainly in the protection of women and children, the establishment of the principle in the railroad industry of employer liability for workers, and limitations on the use of injunctions against labor. The importance of the progressives' reforms at the national level, for purposes of my argument, can perhaps be seen most clearly in the conservation movement. The best of America's public lands had been exploited, 80% of its forests had been cut down with no program for replacement, and mineral resources of all types had been mined with utter wastefulness. The Reclamation Act of 1902 and the establishment of the Inland Waterways Commission in 1907 marked at least the commitment to a new way of thought about how America as a community was relating to its environment (Hicks & Mowry, 1956). Though it is difficult to see from a contemporary perspective, such programs were extremely controversial in the context of their times because they confronted in a direct and unprecedented manner the reigning ethos of individualism and personal freedom and rejected the principle that politics and the market (through their de facto results) were to constitute social policy. Rather, the people, through their government, were to configure the structure and process of social life.

This dimension of the changes is vividly apparent in the posture that the great reform president Theodore Roosevelt took toward business. In some ways, Roosevelt embodied—probably as far as any man of the day could—the emerging ethos I am describing. Though it is probably not accurate to see him as holding a vision of America as one community, he was extremely nationalistic and romantic about "America" as an idea (Corwin, 1957; Hicks & Mowry, 1956). Further, oddly for a man of his background, he empathized with the plight of the dispossessed and made no effort to hide his disdain for men of commerce. He respected culture, but as the venue for human fructification, not as a device for invidious status distinctions. He had a sense that the American people should share and participate in cultural symbols and artifacts. He was the president who, one evening while having dinner with his family, reportedly asked an aide to pull the dining room curtain back so that the people could see the president eat (Corwin, 1957).

He also saw the president as an active agent of the people. In this he drew from a definition of the office first set by Andrew Jackson, another president who could plausibly be said to have embodied an outcropping of the Anti-Federalist constitutional theme in the American political psyche. Roosevelt felt that the ruthless market process should not be allowed to set social policy; the president should take an active role in designing and proposing legislation that would protect the public from the consequences of competition. The most interesting aspect of his developing theory of the presidency, however, was the idea that there was a basis for the exercise of judgment that reflected commonly held norms in the use of governmental power.

This is clearest in Roosevelt's struggle to breathe life into the virtually stillborn Sherman Anti-Trust Act. With the Supreme Court's granting them the status of persons under the Fourteenth Amendment, corporate organizations had grown, at an almost exponential rate, to gigantic proportions by the turn of the century—from a total capitalization of $170 million in 1897, to $5 billion in 1900, to $20.5 billion in 1904. Worse still was the fact that these organizations had come to control not just such basic industries as steel and transportation but even the "minor" consumer products and commodities on which people depended in everyday life. Roosevelt initiated twenty-five actions against these trusts during his administration, and in some cases, such as railroads and meat packing, he scored dramatic successes. In this arena, Roosevelt could, in a sense, be said to have led the Supreme Court. He persuaded it to reverse the protective Knight Sugar Trust decision, but, more important, he provided the basis for the distinction (which the Court came to accept) between "good" and "bad" trusts, which rested on the idea that some trusts took account of the interests of the public in their business practices, whereas others did business with an eye only to their own selfishly defined interests. The Court came to employ the same distinction in the form of its "unreasonableness" standard, by which it was willing to accept monopoly in an industry as long as it did not interfere unreasonably with interstate commerce (Fainsod et al., 1959; Hicks & Mowry, 1956; Leonard, 1969; Mund, 1965; Redford, 1965).

The importance of these conceptual innovations for the formula of American governance cannot be overestimated. They offered no less than the potential for synthesizing the dialectic of the Federalist and Anti-Federalist themes into a new mode of governance. We can see how this is so by examining briefly the "problem" of the Sherman Act in light of the Federalist theory of government. In many ways, the Sherman Act is a perfect example of the Federalist perspective and consequently of the dilemma implicit in it. The Federalist idea was that government should simply put "objective" bounds on the exercise of private activity such that individuals and their liberties would be protected. In principle, this gives free rein to human initiative, but at the same time it provides protections against it. The problem is that it sends the message, for example, in the arena of the economy: "Freely compete, and win as well and as much as you can, but (as in the Sherman Act) do not win *entirely*, because if you do, you will be punished." An objective rule, such as limitations on size, punishes winning (Redford, 1965). What seems necessary to resolve this dilemma is a rule that assesses *consequences* rather than outcomes, such that players can be allowed to win (become large) as long as their size does not end the game of competitive interstate commerce. This is exactly what Roosevelt proposed to do with his distinction between good and bad trusts and the Court's criterion of reasonableness. At the symbolic level, these new standards amounted to the idea that the nation, as a community speaking through its government, could set "substantive" rather than "objective" limits on the actions of persons—in this case, firms as persons. This innovation, as subsequent history of course shows, did not work. It failed for the same reason that the resurgent Anti-Federalism on which it was based failed, and the founding of public administration as a key part of a new form of governance was aborted. My purpose here is only to point to Roosevelt's antitrust policy as an illustration of the Anti-Federalist spirit expressing itself.

Another excellent example is money. The money issue as it was played out during the era of populism embodied abstract power; thus, it became perhaps the most volatile "policy area" with which the government had to cope, as it was (and is) so closely tied to the ephemeral realm of the psychology of paranoia and collective confidence. The second of Theodore Roosevelt's administrations provides textbook case material of this phenomenon. His "trustbusting," proregulation, prolabor, and conservation policies, the business community claimed, served to undermine the climate of confidence needed for healthy economic growth. Such charges were given emphasis by a business panic that hit in 1907. Though stock manipulations clearly were a significant causal agent in creating the panic, the dynamic of monetary policy also came into play. Because the money supply at that time, which was composed of gold, silver, and national bank and Treasury notes, was fixed, any psychological perturbation that led to the hoarding of money would quickly produce a shortage. The situation was exacerbated by the fact that the supply of credit was set, for all intents and purposes, by the lending discretion of a few large banks in New York who used this power to control virtually the entire national banking network. When the panic hit, runs against the major banks began to multiply, forcing the Treasury to do what it could by depositing funds. During the panic, J. P. Morgan used the specter of impending disaster to convince Roosevelt that U.S. Steel should be granted immunity from antitrust prosecution so that it could absorb another large but vulnerable steel firm (Hicks & Mowry, 1956).

Roosevelt came out of the experience convinced that business itself had caused most or all of the problem, perhaps as a way of validating its claim that his policies were undermining economic confidence. The experience seemed to leave no doubt, however, that the U.S. monetary system needed to be brought under some sort of governmental control so that discretion rather than collective psychology might govern it. This led to the planting of the seeds that grew ultimately into the Federal Reserve system, established during the administration of Woodrow Wilson; the Aldrich Vreeland Act of 1908, empowering the national banks to issue currency to meet emergencies; and a National Monetary Commission, designed to study the world currency system and set plans for redoing the U.S. system (Hicks & Mowry, 1956).

The most immediate effects of the move toward economic reform, however, came in the area of regulation rather than in the more "structural" reforms of the sort of which the Sherman Act was an example. With the passage of the Hepburn Act of 1906 especially, Roosevelt made a great stride in giving the ICC the sort of regulatory punch that critics of the railroads had wanted it to have. Now the carrier had to take the initiative, by going to court, if it did not want to accept the rates set by the commission. In addition, ICC jurisdiction was broadened to include other common carriers (even pipelines and bridges). The granting of free passes was forbidden, the carrying of commodities (except those for their own use) that companies had produced themselves was proscribed, and, most important, the power to mandate a uniform bookkeeping system was granted. As a result, rates were significantly reduced, and the prestige and acceptance of the commission soared; more and more, its decisions came to be accepted without comment by the railroads (Fainsod et al., 1959; Hicks & Mowry, 1956).

Despite the attention given to them by journalists and social critics, the food and drug industries were not brought so quickly or so well into a sphere of effective governmental influence. Existing inspection laws were extended to cover domestic as well as imported meats, and the Pure Food and Drug Act, in 1906, placed some controls on prepared foods and patent medicines. A 1911 amendment attacked the problem of fraudulent or absent labeling, but it did nothing about the problem of misleading advertising. Still, such actions gave evidence that the government did have a valid basis for applying standards based on common discretion to the process of commerce (Fainsod et al., 1959; Hicks & Mowry, 1956).

In sum, the transformation of municipal government and the reform of state governments, the restructuring of the political process, and the developments in social legislation and in economic regulation reflect the emergence of the idea that something like "principles" that mirrored a common sensibility could be brought to bear on the affairs of the public world. Again, it is difficult for us as contemporary Americans to appreciate the profundity of this conceptual change. For it to happen, movements deep within the emotional substructure of American society had to occur. These structural dynamics constitute our next topic. By examining them, we will be able to see more clearly just how fundamentally the ethos of America was shifting during this period, what the dimensions of the shift were, and why there was such a powerful and pervasive reaction to it, a reaction that split and muddied the foundation on which public administration was to be grounded.

The Emergence of a Collective
Sensibility and the Pragmatic Attitude

As I have stressed above, the truly paradigmatic aspect of the changes that began to take place was not the social, economic, and political reforms themselves but rather the underlying changes in the direction of developing a societal capacity for the expression of a common sensibility. The reforms of the period were but a reflection of these deeper changes. One of the best markers of change at this level is that America began to attain a truly widespread and collective sense of *taste.* The nouveau riche behavior of the American millionaire class was a reflection of the fact that for all intents and purposes, such a sensibility had been lacking in the United States. As Charles Perkins, a social commentator of the period, put it:

> Nowhere is modern sterility in the invention of form so marked as in America. . . . We borrowed at second hand and do not pretend to have a national taste. We take our architectural forms from England, our fashions from Paris, the patterns of our manufacturers from all parts of the world, and make nothing really original. (quoted in Bayley, 1991, p. 122)

This situation began to change as a woman named Elsie de Wolfe established a career, and in so doing established *the* career, of interior decoration in America. Although the problem of *bad* taste had been attacked persistently by social critics, it was not until de Wolfe published her book *The House in Good Taste* that the term *good taste* entered American social discourse (Bayley, 1991, p. 124). (This is an interesting fact in itself in that it suggests that the very idea of positive standards was novel in the turn-of-the-century context.)

The starting place for her theory of good taste was rejection of the monied extravagance of the new American entrepreneur:

> It is no longer possible, even to people of only faintly aesthetic tastes, to buy chairs merely to sit upon or a clock merely that it should tell the time. Home-makers are determined to have their houses, outside and in, correct according to the best standards. But what are the best standards? Certainly not those of the useless, overcharged house of the average American millionaire. (Bayley, 1991, p. 124)

Further, her orientation toward taste was universalistic, democratic, and popular rather than elitist. Her doctrine held that "there has never been a house so bad that it couldn't be made over into something worthwhile" (Bayley, 1991, p. 125). She simply emphasized a considered respect for the past, utility, creative self-expression, and authenticity. Good taste was in her view simply the exercise of good sense; "common sense" could decide suitability. Her book was popular, successful, and influential, going through numerous editions. She extended this influence in many magazine articles and a second book, *Recipes for Successful Dining*, in which, again, she emphasized the values of good judgment, simplicity, and authenticity. She spoke the voice of an emerging sentiment in America—that people could exercise discretion in the way they lived and that this discretion could be shared and provide a basis for common action. As a "culture leader," she helped consolidate and thereby furthered a critically important transformation in the American psyche.

The significance of a shared sense of taste for the development of a mutual social commitment that could serve as a foundation for collective action can be seen in one of the most remarkable cultural episodes in American history. It does not seem an exaggeration to say that, during this era, the nation was in nothing less than a ferment over the question of how to find an identity for itself as a community. Emblematic of this was the extraordinary history of the book *In His*

Steps (Sheldon, 1984). Essentially a parable of practical Christianity, the story it told was of a minister and church congregation in 1896 who were challenged by a homeless, out-of-work stranger shortly before he died of hunger and exposure. The man entered the church during Sunday meeting and asked to speak about the dreadful social and economic conditions that had become prevalent in America and about the widespread suffering these were causing. He asked the congregation to consider what Jesus would do about the men and women dying of drunkenness and hunger in the tenements. The man then fell over in a faint, and although the minister took him home and cared for him, he died within the week. The minister and the congregation, transformed by the encounter with the dying man, embarked on a program of remedying the social conditions around them. They followed a "social gospel" in which they were guided by struggling to define situationally specific answers to moral questions, in much the way that Jesus had taught through the device of parables. In doing so, they moved the abstractions of their religion into the real social world and used them as a basis for action, forging in the process a shared identity for themselves as a body of caring human beings.

The response to this book must be counted as one of the more astounding cultural phenomena that has occurred in America. By one account, the book sold more than 8 million copies in America by 1925, but Jane Tompkins' (1992) assessment is that it is probably not possible to calculate except very approximately how many were bought. Because of an error on the part of the publisher, the book was not copyrighted, and it was immediately pirated by at least sixteen publishers in the United States alone. It subsequently was translated into twenty-one languages and "bootlegged" by fifty other publishers in Europe and Australia. The book was stupendously popular, selling, ultimately, more copies than any other book except the Bible, according to *Publisher's Weekly* (Tompkins, 1992).

The enormous success of the book marks a change in the social context that is critical for understanding the transforming American ethos. The term that captures this change is the word *practical*. This was the core of the response to the ideology of Spencerian social Darwinism. Turn-of-the-century theologians saw that the way to save the Christian humanist sentiment from the onslaught of evolutionary theory was to turn Darwin's theory against itself by stressing its own emphasis on the importance of environment in the development of the organism. By changing the circumstances surrounding people's bodies, the material circumstances of society, one could transform their minds and souls also. This conceptual shift drew theological emphasis away from the mystical dimensions of religion to the "street-level" problem of social action, resulting in an enormous outpouring of popular support for the temperance movement, the settlement house movement, the inspirational lecture programs, and even Christian Science, which, by preaching the primacy of spirit over body, give religion an exceptionally practical turn (Olasky, 1992; Stivers, 1993).

As this ideology of practicality spread, doctrinal differences among church creeds began to ameliorate and disappear; churches focused attention on the matter of social reform and came together around specific objectives. Reflecting such changes, novelists moved toward the "naturalist" style, with its sharp implication of social criticism, and writers such as Edward Bellamy, William Dean Howells, H. H. Boyeson, and Paul L. Ford wrote influential books that exposed and criticized existing social conditions and painted pictures of a kind of "Christian Socialist utopia." Social clubs inspired by these images formed all across the country for the purpose of furthering such idealistic projections of the American future. Although these developments began before the turn of the century, they formed a sociocultural context that surged forward and was influential well into the first decades of the 1900s (Hicks & Mowry, 1956).

The ethos of "practical Christian action" that I have just been describing can be connected directly to the intellectual environment that developed through the period of transition into the new century. The intellectual turn that America took in this period came about largely as a response to the same sort of turbulence and disorientation that produced the move away from a "mystical" to a social action-oriented religious attitude. The traditional frame of reference on which people had relied for comprehending and bringing order to their perceptions of the human condition seemed to be inadequate when held up against external developments. A massive conceptual refurbishing seemed to be called for, social developments supported it, and it occurred nowhere more visibly than in the way intellectuals began to interpret American history.

I have already discussed the progressive intellectual Charles Beard's *An Economic Interpretation of the Constitution of the United States* (1913), wherein the revered founding fathers were depicted as ambitious young men of advantage who were seeking to further the economic interests of the social class that they represented. No less than Theodore Roosevelt, as president of the United States, came to believe it, and when looked at in the context of the times in which it appeared, it was more a balanced analysis than an ideological polemic (Hicks & Mowry, 1956).

If we compare Beard's analysis to the one that foreshadowed his, for example, we can see this clearly enough. J. Allen Smith's *The Spirit of American Government* (1907) *was* polemical. In Smith's perspective, the Constitution was inherently opposed to democracy. Much of his argument relied on an analysis very much like the one presented in Chapter 3 of this book. Because the Articles of Confederation had expressed the faith in democracy that was at the core of the revolutionary spirit on which the country was founded, the Constitution itself, the work of wealthy conservatives, was a "reactionary document." The political formula embedded in the Constitution is one that at every point—the amendment process, the independence of the judiciary and its power to review legislation, checks and balances, separation of powers—is designed to thwart the expression of the popular will. Exactly the points of design so frequently held up as the indicators of the framers' genius are to Smith indicators of a conspiracy of aristocrats that began in the Philadelphia convention and that remained in continuous struggle with the principle of democracy and its constituency, the common people (McConnell, 1966).

The attack on the Constitution by writers such as Smith and Beard formed an effective backdrop against which the pragmatist sentiment could be expressed as a theory of politics. This was done best by the journalist/social critic Herbert Croly, a student of William James and the main founder of the *New Republic* magazine. Croly stood at the boundary between pragmatism as a philosophy and pragmatism as a theory of social and political organization, and as such, his work provides an excellent venue for understanding the connection of pragmatism to the issue of government. Although pragmatism the philosophy was central to the intellectual ethos of the day, it was pragmatism the theory of social action that constituted the "theory that was coming into use" as the progressive movement proceeded.

Croly drew directly from Beard's analysis, citing his evidence that the Constitution was supported and ratified by a tiny minority of privileged men. The constitutional problem had now transcended the Federalists, and just as it had in Croly's view produced slavery, it was responsible for the social and economic mess that the country had been experiencing for the past few decades. At the most general level, his complaint was the patently undemocratic nature of the Constitution, its denial to the people of the possibility for acting in their own name. By structurally concentrating power, the Constitution had perpetuated the elite it had created. He went on to say that the populists were the same type of people as the Anti-Federalists (Noble, 1981; Safford, 1987).

At the level of philosophy, American pragmatism took the form of social critique. Pragmatism formed the core of the intellectual ethos of early twentieth-century America. I include in this school of thought— in alphabetical order—such thinkers and actors as Arthur Bentley, Herbert Croly, John Dewey, Mary Parker Follett, Sidney Hook, William James, C. I. Lewis, Walter Lippmann, George Herbert Mead, C. Wright Mills, C. S. Peirce, Theodore Roosevelt (in his role as historian-intellectual), Thorstein Veblen, and Woodrow Wilson (in his role as political scientist). The development of the pragmatist school in American thought is an episode in American history remarkable both for its degree of radicalism and for its real impact in the political and social arena. Seldom in America does one see an ideology or theoretical system having anything more than a remote connection to events. Further, at no other point in American history has the structure of government been so severely questioned as it was under the scrutiny of some of the pragmatists and their fellow intellectual travelers. What was the intellectual mood, tone, and general ideological direction of the pragmatist movement?

First and above all, pragmatism is an *attitude* toward reality and human experience. Its distinctiveness can best be seen at this level. If one looks only at methodology, for example, pragmatism looks similar to a number of other philosophical positions. Its attitude can be described as a *commitment to continuous experimentation* (in the broadest sense), grounded in the view that reality is best apprehended through action. This commitment implies that everything that is "known" by human beings must be regarded as tentative and held in suspense as a hypothesis until the next action experiment, ad infinitum. Although one can say that this attitude confronts philosophical realism (Croly certainly did), the opposition of realism and idealism is actually rendered moot. In fact, virtually all the typical epistemological oppositions are finessed by the pragmatic attitude. The fact-value dichotomy, the foundationalist-relativist dichotomy, and the phenomenology-positivism dichotomy are collapsed by the pragmatic commitment to continual testing of hypotheses (West, 1989).

The only opposition that it does challenge is elite rational choice versus collaborative action. The essence of the rational choice model of action is the concept of the correct or best choice. Even if constraints are acknowledged, the idea is that, "all things considered," there is one correct or best way of understanding a situation and hence one correct or best line of action toward it. According to the rational choice model, decision makers must arrive at this correct understanding, take the indicated choice, and then act. Those who dissent are not simply in disagreement but must be judged to be "wrong." The pragmatic model, by contrast, collapses knowing and acting into one process. If one makes everything an experiment—which presumes that nothing is ever known reliably enough to make it a *conclusive* basis for action— the judgment that some perceivers of a situation are right and others are wrong never has to be made. Action under conditions of disagreement thus becomes possible, since even parties in contention can collaborate in further experiment.

Pragmatism challenges and denies the prerequisites of rational choice at every point. It pictures social relationships as collaborative, as grounded in joint project and joint action. As a fellow collaborator, I can engage in dialogue with my partners without having to "prove" anything to them, without their suspecting me of making a claim for a motive of my own (i.e., of manipulating them), without, in a word, being "objective." Anything that I have to say may be relevant to our project, whether I am butcher, baker, candlestick maker, planner, preacher, philosopher, scientist, or engineer (Schmidt, 1993). Any procedure for experimentation that we decide to follow is, therefore, a matter of efficiency or convenience rather than a basis for coming to an authoritative conclusion independent of our collaborative dialogue. Finally, the very reason that we are committed to experimentation is that we consider, as pragmatists, that "reality" is overdetermined and dynamic; what is important is to go as far as possible toward making the world the way we want it to be through our actions instead of trying to "know" it.

Just as pragmatism collapses traditional philosophical oppositions, it also denies traditional political ones such as individual and group, freedom and responsibility, and efficiency and democracy. Democracy as collaborative action, when the philosophical frame for it is pragmatic, is synonymous with efficiency. What the collective, the group, decides to do is, perforce, the best, most efficient thing that could be done in the situation. The agent-principal relationship, which is the basis for objective assessments of efficiency, is eliminated.

Croly's analysis of American political and social life reflected the essence of the pragmatic perspective, though not explicitly. The starting place for his position was a critique of government restricted by law. He saw the idea of law as restraint—for example, in the principle

of judicial review—as obstructing the process of social experimentation. American democracy must be emancipated from "the continued
allegiance to any specific formulation of the Law" so as to provide
"increasing ability to act upon its [society's] collective purposes." He
emphasized that "freedom to experiment is more valuable than limiting the possible abuses of power" (Croly, 1963, p. 400).

This critique of law is grounded in the pragmatic denial of any
standing idea of Truth, any tendency to act *conclusively* in the present
situation on the basis of "knowledge" or principle gained from past
situations. The idea of deferring to law by regarding it as an unques-
tioned constraint is synonymous with the rationalist idea of correct
process and cumulative, situation-transcendent understanding. To
accept this scheme denies the core pragmatic idea that truth is known
through outcomes in real, present situations.

An essential corollary to the rejection of law as binding constraint
is the social theory of the self. Croly attacked the traditional American
myth of the individual and the theory of natural rights that went with
it. Such an idea denied the pragmatic concept of the human person as
emerging from action and implied that there was a basis for grounding
judgments in a place outside the action situation, a Truth to which
results could be referred. The social idea of the self, the self as emergent
from social action and the interaction that surrounds it, is essential to
the pragmatic belief in dynamic progress, progress that moves toward
a future that people responsibly choose rather than toward a future
that simply fulfills a somehow preordained "human destiny" or realizes a fixed or given "human nature," both of which are mythic ideas
that must be based in an individualistic theory of the self as fixed or
given. Croly's idea was the pragmatic one that people become themselves through realizing a collective purpose; they create themselves
through such actions, and at the same time, they create others and
others create them. Collective action thus becomes a kind of school in
which people find themselves as they are and "teach" others who they
are, and others do the same for them (Croly, 1963).

The American system of government seemed to Croly and other
progressives such as Wilson to be rather completely out of mesh with
this view of the person, society, and government. It needed to be
uprooted and redone to allow for the degree of association and experimentation demanded by the pragmatic vision of progress. The basic
rules of the game needed to be rewritten because the old rules (stemming from the principles of the Constitution) presumed antagonistic
social relationships grounded in self-interest. In this view of the social

world, government necessarily became a dangerous prize that could be captured by the most ambitious and successful interests and used for their own purposes. Government was thus to be feared and should be put under limits to prevent its capture and/or abuse.

From this vantage point, the history of American government had validated the pragmatic theory of the self. It seemed that the Constitution, as the most powerful teacher in the school of society, had constituted people as self-interested individuals, some of whom had captured government and put it to their own uses, with rather disastrous results for America as a society. What Croly and the progressives were seeking to do was, literally, to constitute the American citizenry in a different manner from that in which the Constitution had constituted it. Progressivism was a movement toward nothing less than "constitutional reform" of the most basic sort (Eisenach, 1994). (Woodrow Wilson's call for parliamentary government and the idea that grew out of this period of redrawing state lines so as to form more sensible regional governments are symptomatic of this mood.) The progressive movement, insofar as it was pragmatic, sought to reconstitute America as one large community where social cooperation was the baseline of relations between citizens. This is how fundamentally different the pragmatic ethos was in the American context.

No less than this was called for. Any intellectual ethos that fell short of this level of approach to the situation in America at the time would have seemed superficial. In a sense, the Federalist theory of government, and the Constitution it framed, had failed. It was natural that the Anti-Federalist ethos would reassert itself, but although its mood and tone fitted the new conditions, its theory of government could not. A new worldview with a new guiding principle was needed. Pragmatism, articulated as an approach to government by such spokesmen as Croly, provided the required philosophical inspiration.

At bottom, the genius of the pragmatic commitment is the theory of scientific method that it contained. By assuming the posture of permanent doubt, placing experimentation in a collaborative context, and making results the operational definition of truth, pragmatism maintained the highest aspect of the scientific spirit (i.e., the principle of open exploration) while at the same time giving it a shape that could fit the drastically new context faced by government. Pragmatic citizens, politicians, and administrators—which is to say, pragmatic scientists—*saw no inconsistency or tension between democracy and efficiency or between democracy and freedom.* A pragmatic government could not dominate or become tyrannical. Government administration would by this light serve as an expression of popular will, not as a means for denying it.

When Croly argued, "The administrative commissions are really free only to do right. Just as they go astray the bonds tighten on them. They derive their authority from their knowledge, and from their peculiar relation to public opinion" (quoted in McConnell, 1966, p. 43), he seems to be saying not only that "scientific objectivity" or expertise would serve as an external force to limit the decisions and actions of the officials on the commissions but that, in addition, the attitude of judging the truth of actions by their results as defined by citizens would ensure that commissions would govern by a permanent process of self-correction. Expertise in this light does not become "knowledge" that bestows power and the privilege to decide for others; rather, it bestows the skill that makes possible the design of clear experiments that yield understandable results that can be popularly assessed.

As part of an intellectual ethos, the progressives' attack on the traditional system coupled with the pragmatic worldview constituted a powerful formula for change. If, as some argue, the period of progressive reform and the ethos that went with it found its culmination in the New Deal, and the New Deal fixed the course of American politics and government until 1980, it appears that the power of this formula is given full testimony. The New Deal and the history it produced, however, are not fully consistent with the ethos I have been describing. What progressivism actually ended up producing was a version of regulatory welfare government that relied heavily on an instrumental, rationalistic form of public administration. This form of government has been substantially rejected, and public administration has become progressively less legitimate, as its present low status testifies. To understand what happened, how the intellectual frame of this period and the social ethos in which it was grounded were put off course, we need to look at how this progressive-pragmatic idea was actually expressed in government and at what interpretation and reaction this expression evoked.

The Expression of the New Ethos

The story above portrays America as attempting to heal itself from the ravages of a period of socially unmediated individualistic *competition* by finding a way of institutionalizing social *cooperation* as its official way of life. This meant no less than the overturning of the Federalist constitutional tradition. But what evidence is there that any such change even *began* to take place in America? Is it actually the case that by the first decades of the twentieth century, significant movements toward an ethos of cooperation had begun to be visible at a national level?

I have already mentioned, in describing the social changes of the turn-of-the-century period, the growth of professionalization, as manifested in the formation of new associations, the holding of conventions and other meetings, and the dissemination of new ideas and information. This was the period in which a new, professional, "white-collar" middle class developed, complete with its own distinctive class interest (Hofstadter, 1955; Merkle, 1968; Wiebe, 1967). If there was an explicit ideology to this development, it was the theory of scientific management formulated by Frederick Taylor (1947). Although Taylor's system is most widely known as a methodology for maximizing work procedures and relationships, the aspect of it on which I wish to focus at this point is its utopianism—one of its more neglected dimensions. As the Taylor movement grew to worldwide scope, it was articulated ultimately as a full-scale utopian vision of a future world in which conflict could be eliminated from human affairs. Taylor himself had a morbid aversion to conflict, and it was this personality trait that no doubt drove the approach to organization and work that he originated (Copley, 1923; Habor, 1964; Kakar, 1970; Nelson, 1980). Although his theory has been billed in the contemporary world as a technology for dominating and exploiting workers (March & Simon, 1958), his intention, in fact, was to finesse the issue of domination by finding a place and way for everyone to be properly fitted together into one harmonious system. His theory prescribed professionalization, and it was professionalization on a democratic basis. He made much of the point that a person's background should have no bearing on his or her prospects for becoming a new scientific manager. What counted was how well the person could perform. The only domination involved was that which came from submitting to the requirements of the system itself, the well-being of which, of course, was in everyone's collective interest. There was no idea that the organizational system benefited some and exploited others. Scientific management was a theory thoroughly grounded in the principle of cooperation, and it, in effect, served as part of the ideology for the movement toward progressive change. In saying this, I do not want to be misunderstood as being overly sanguine about the possibilities of this kind of utopianism. An intellectual tension, if not contradiction, that afflicted Taylor also affected the progressive movement generally. This was a profound ambivalence toward "the common man" (Cross, 1993). This was and is a major issue for American intellectuals, one that produces not only a crypto-intellectual elitism but an incomplete, often incoherent idea of how "expert knowledge" can be integrated with the knowledge held by lay people. Although this is not a problem for the core pragmatists, progressivism—as a not entirely pragmatic approach—was afflicted in this way.

It is in this context that we must place the movement to develop a new organizational type, the *trade association*. Formation of such groups became a social cause complete with a theory and a spokesman, a lawyer named Arthur Jerome Eddy (McConnell, 1966). As Eddy stated it, the advent of trade associations constituted "a radical change . . . in the commercial and industrial world—the change from a *competitive to a cooperative basis*" (quoted in McConnell, 1966, p. 58). The new organizational pattern would allow America to transcend the evils of its commercial past, involving as it did conspiracy and cutthroat behavior. The associations would be a step toward a more civilized form of government and social life. Explicitly rejecting the Spencerian idea of the fittest eliminating the weak, Eddy's notion was that "the human law should be not the survival of the strong, but the *survival of all*, of the best there is in all, and, oftentimes, there is more of good, more of real value to humanity in the weak than in the strong" (quoted in McConnell, 1966, p. 58).

The device that would supplant cutthroat competition was the "open-price trade association." Though the Federal Trade Commission investigated such organizations in 1929, its finding was that they should be licensed. This specific organizational form, however, was not the essence of the broader shift that was occurring in American political culture. As one account put it, Eddy's advocacy of such associations was based on a general perception of this shift, and "he was quite correct in seeing a widespread turning from the idea of competition in business and the seeking of a series of organic societies within the large society" (quoted in McConnell, 1966, p. 58).

The wider cultural sea change began to manifest itself officially in 1912, when Charles Nagel, Secretary of Commerce and Labor under President Taft, called a meeting of representatives of the Chambers of Commerce and other business associations. This meeting was held in Nagel's offices, and during its course, the group drafted a blueprint for a national organization of business groups. Subsequently, a conference was organized to which thousands of commercial organizations were invited. Taft and Nagel both spoke to the meeting, and the conferees' subsequent work sessions produced the founding of the Chamber of Commerce of the United States.

The extent to which Nagel, with Taft's approval, envisioned the creation of a structural linkage for cooperation between business and government is indicated by the fact that he went so far as to suggest that the chamber be given a "National Charter" that would authorize it to develop and submit a "common commercial opinion" to government. Government officials would, in turn, acknowledge such opinions as coming from "the recognized representative of commerce and industry in the United States" (McConnell, 1966, pp. 59-60). Though neither apprehended it, Taft and Nagel were tampering at the constitutional level with the institutions of American government. However, probably because their actions were consistent with the general direction of change in American society and government, there was no noticeable reaction.

Vastly more remarkable in both concept and scale was the reliance on cooperation between government and the domain of commercial enterprise during the mobilization for World War I (Skowronek, 1982). America had, of course, never undergone this type of total collective effort. To carry it out, a large network of industrial leaders became involved in government. At least for a short time, the idea of private-public cooperation became the operating principle of governance in the United States. The intricate coordination and compliance problems posed by the mobilization "were solved brilliantly and in a manner that relied heavily upon . . . [the development of an ideological commitment to government-private sector cooperation]" (McConnell, 1966, p. 60). Significant power had to be conferred on industrial executives, and because trade associations were so helpful in the coordinative process, the government followed an official policy of encouraging their development. The principle of cooperation worked to blur the line between government and the private sector.

This cooperative system, operated mainly through the War Industries Board and the Food Administration, was hugely successful in turning out a process of "cooperative, democratic, self control with industry for national purposes" (McConnell, 1966, p. 61). Not only was it successful in the sense of fulfilling its purposes, but it did so in a manner that was "scientifically" efficient and that led to enhanced conservation as a result of the overturning of many traditionally wasteful practices of industry. Freedom, efficiency, and conservation were viewed as completely compatible values.

This form of governance existed as an operating system only momentarily in the historical sense during the war effort; however, the experience itself had a large and lasting impact. This was carried, to a significant extent, by one man: President Herbert Hoover. Hoover was an engineer and a man whose significance for the field of public administration has been seriously neglected. (Indeed, he has been given credit for creating the neologism *administrator*; McConnell, 1966, p. 65.) As the wartime national food administrator, he extended the application of the principle of cooperation even further than it had been used in the mobilization of industries, moving it down to the level of the individual household.

If the war had continued and if America's involvement in it had truly begun to tax its resources, the shift to a process of governance by voluntary cooperation might have gone so far as to alter permanently the working constitutional formula by which America was governed. Hoover's experience in the mobilization, set as it was in the context of an (albeit implicit) ideological ferment, inspired in him a complete theory of how governance could be fitted compatibly into a democratic and individualistic society. The main tenets of this theory were keeping the individual free of as much governmental coercion as possible; relying on voluntary action to the greatest extent possible in marshalling and deploying collective resources toward social goals; fostering "moral development" not through law but rather through having associations adopt and promulgate ethical codes of practice; using the principle of conservation (especially avoiding waste) as a way of inducing cooperation and voluntarism; and decentralizing social-political decision making as far as possible through reliance on voluntary agreement and self-regulation via the trade association mechanism (McConnell, 1966). (Note how Anti-Federalist in orientation these tenets are—as if Anti-Federalism had been "fast-forwarded" 100 years.)

Hoover held this theory with an intense moral passion, and it had the kind of powerful influence on the milieu in which he pronounced and practiced it that is only possessed by theories that are closely in accord with the cultural, social, and intellectual ambience of their historical moment. In choosing to act from such a conceptual base, Hoover took up an operating methodology that was in mesh with pragmatic social-political theory as articulated by a spokesperson such as Herbert Croly. Like Theodore Roosevelt with his "discretionary" antitrust policy, Hoover adopted a pragmatic test for the possession and use of private power: If use of the power resulted in a good effect, it was legitimate and acceptable; if it resulted in a bad effect, it was an evil against which government could act. This position committed Hoover to a kind of experimentalism, again pragmatic in spirit, that meant a rejection of law as a device for social action. The war effort provided a context within which the idea of legal methods as a device for effecting social programs seemed rigid, cumbersome, and unworkable. Everyone knew what the purpose of the mobilization was, and society could more easily move iteratively toward that purpose through decentralized, voluntary action than it could through obeying legally enshrined commands issued from a central authority.

As with many historical moments, it would have been fascinating to see what sort of formula for governance might have resulted eventually if Hoover had not had the misfortune to be president when the Depression hit and instead had reigned over a protracted period of prosperity. Even as it was, it seems obvious that the second Roosevelt and the New Deal were heavily influenced, if not by Hoover's example directly, then by the general power of the ideology of cooperation that was then in the air (Himmelberg, 1976; McConnell, 1966). As any student of constitutional law can testify, the National Recovery Administration (NRA) policies seem directly inspired by Hoover's theory of governance, though they took the idea of ignoring legal constraints to facilitate cooperation at least one step too far. Why should this not be the case, given that the NRA's first administrator was a veteran of the war mobilization effort? Roosevelt also extended Hoover's logic in his encouragement of new labor organizations and in his policies toward agriculture.

I need not recount these stories, also well documented and well known, to meet the purpose at hand, however. The central claim I wish to establish is just that the ethos that resulted from the reaction to America's period of chaotic economic growth was one of cooperation grounded in an emerging common sense of the public good. The structural device for realizing this ethos in the process of governance was the private, voluntary action association—in business, labor, and agriculture working with and through government. Government's role was to provide a public space within which such cooperation could take place. This space was created by encouragement, facilitation, and legitimation of the actions of such networks. Central to the successful operation of this scheme was the belief that democracy and what was referred to as "efficiency" were not only compatible with but complementary to and symbiotic with each other.

The distorted discourse on the question of the legitimacy of administration in democracy makes this belief appear profoundly puzzling, if not absurd. To the mind-set shaped by the discourse of legitimacy, democracy evokes images of politics and political choice making through processes that are grounded in and reflect sentiment, preference, interest, and stakes. In a democracy, no one tells anyone what to do, or so the belief goes—the only boss is the "people." The institutions of "efficiency," on the other hand, are seen as cold, bloodless enemies of sentiment that overwhelm and dominate it by determining objectively what must be done, thus becoming the de facto "boss experts" of the social order.

Both aspects of this contemporary and prevalent view are, of course, right and at the same time wrong. They are correct in the way they construct the issue as long as one assumes a positivistic view of science. They are wrong in that in democracy, the majority dominates or bosses the minority (even though the minority may be protected from domination past a certain point), and experts are not bosses in the usual sense of the term, given that they must subordinate themselves to their method. If one assumes the pragmatic perspective on science that was in the air surrounding Taft, Hoover, and their contemporaries, however, this view appears off the point of the issue. To reiterate the characterization I made earlier: Pragmatism collapses sentiment, value, objectivity, and fact into the crucible of experimental action.

It was quite possible, in such a context, to have founded a public administration without seeing its role in democratic governance as problematic. This would have been a public administration unencumbered by the "legitimacy problem." Why did this not happen? Why do we have a legitimacy problem in American public administration? From where did it come? My view is that its origins are to be found in a profound intellectual distortion that took place at its founding and that has continued to work its prejudices into public administration discourse ever since, making the problem of legitimacy worse and worse. What is this distortion? How did it occur? Who were its agents? What motivated these agents—or were they unaware of their distorting prejudices? To such questions we can now turn.

The Hidden Agenda in the Founding of American Public Administration

Answering entirely the questions that have just been posed will require a review of the entire intellectual history of public administration. Before setting out on this task (in the next chapters), I want to state the central thesis around which the answers are oriented. Put schematically, this thesis is that *there was a hidden, undisclosed, perhaps even unconscious interest at work during the period of the founding of the field.* Conceptualizing administration (or, by its other name, bureaucracy) as standing in a tense, inconsistent relation to democracy was essential to the furthering of this interest. The existence of this hidden interest explains how the "legitimacy problem" developed in the field. I will sketch out this theme in a preliminary manner by critically reviewing two interpretations of the founding period, both of which bear directly, though unintentionally, on my thesis.

The analysis I turn to first, because it takes the broader perspective, is John Lugton Safford's study *Pragmatism and the Progressive Movement in the United States* (1987). My reason for choosing this work is that it provides an excellent illustration of the effects of the distortions on the legitimacy discourse. In my view, Safford's assessment of pragmatism is prejudiced in precisely the way that one would predict, given the biased framework for thinking about democratic governance that has been established by the discourse on legitimacy. I shall focus only on that part of his analysis that bears directly on the issue at hand here—a part to which he refers as his "secondary thesis" and that he states as "that the American philosophy of pragmatism has worked to the detriment of a true science of society" (p. x). The standard of a "true science of society" against which Safford measures pragmatism is that the social scientist should function as a kind of physician of social health—that is, "A social scientist, like a biologist, should be able to distinguish without bias a healthy from an unhealthy . . . society or a nation" (p. x). To play this role, a social science approach needs to be able to function along two related dimensions. It must have a capacity to identify the normative standards that define a "healthy" society, and it must have the capacity to test empirically whether actual social conditions conform to the dictates of these standards.

Pragmatism failed, Safford says, because it split these dimensions and because its method of empirical assessment is flawed. This split forces those interested in providing a normative framework into the role of romantic mythmakers who set out visions of society that it is impossible to test empirically except by rather positive, non-nominalist methods. This last point introduces pragmatism's other problem: its method of empirical testing. Grounded as it is in a nominalist epistemology and the operationalism that this approach implies, pragmatism is, by Safford's light, too practitioner oriented, so that it produced a picture of the social world that was murky, indistinct, and far removed from commonsense understanding. The best exemplars of this problem are pragmatists who sought to combine mythmaking with the practical; their failed attempts to integrate the two halves of the pragmatic method prove all the more that the basic theory is framed so as to make these two halves incompatible. One such is B. F. Skinner (who assumed William James's chair at Harvard), with his strange utopian vision of Walden II and "weird" glass boxes for raising infants—an unlikable "normative" myth attached to an unworkable technology for realizing it.

Safford's answer to this problem is to use natural law as a guide for generating specific normative hypotheses that can then be tested empirically using a more rigorous and strictly positive science methodology. This solution, and what I see to be the serious problems that beset it, need not concern us here, because we are interested only in understanding the process by which the ethos of the time became distorted. How, in a social context where cooperation and pragmatic action had the potential to become so prevalent and legitimate, did pragmatism and the principle of cooperation that it entails become lost? What Safford's analysis points to is that there must have been a countertheme coexisting in this context that resisted the full expression of the developing ethos of cooperation. We can see this countertheme, indeed, in Safford himself. Figures who embody the answer he suggests are people such as Sidney Hook and Walter Lippmann, men whom he sees as having the grand scope of intellect that gives them access to natural law but who are open to being taught by the social facts of the day whether or not the hypotheses derived from natural law are keeping the promises they made. Note, though, what is involved here: The design and testing of social experiments are to be done by an intellectual elite.

What is noteworthy about the solution Safford proposes is what he resists and denies: namely, the easily at hand, truly *pragmatic* solution to the problem he identifies. What I am referring to, of course, is the pragmatic notion, exemplified in the action experiment approach of Dewey, of resolving the split of the normative from the practical through *collective collaborative action.* Safford rejects Dewey as overcommitted to collectivism, leading him to ignore or deny social facts.

However, even in his rejection of Dewey, Safford assumes that the key question is *what approach yields the best intellectual leadership* for society. He rejects, out of hand, any notion that "social facts" are judged not by an elite but by the people involved in creating, through their own actions, the social conditions that the facts describe. Safford seems unwilling to accord collective assessment of social experiments the same prima facie validity that he gives to assessment done by intellectual leaders. What makes collective assessment the lesser alternative? Safford has grounded his analysis on an undisclosed premise, namely the preeminence of positivist science, and in doing so, he serves as an exemplar of the line of thought that framed the identity of public administration at its founding. What Safford does not seem to consider is a kind of social science that is carried out as actual social experimentation—that is, pragmatic *action research.*

Action research is defined by the very fact that the normative premises, the identification of variables, the design of the experiment, and the assessment of results are all done by the actors themselves. The role of the professional social scientist is simply to facilitate the process. Why is this alternative not considered as an answer to the fact-value disabling of the traditional social sciences? Why was it not considered as the social sciences developed and public administration was founded and drew from them? Or was it considered but then ignored by public administration? (I cannot resist jumping ahead here: The answer is "yes.") What is the stake, interest, or prejudice driving this rejection? I leave such questions standing for now to gain further perspective on this issue by reviewing another analysis of the history of the impact left by the progressive movement on the founding of public administration. After this second review, I will return to these questions.

The interpretation of the founding to which I now wish to turn to gain additional perspective on the "hidden agenda" is Camilla Stivers' book *Gender Images in Public Administration: Legitimacy and the Administrative State* (1993). Written from what I judge to be a "moderate" feminist perspective, the imaginative analysis that she carries out is, nonetheless, radical in its implications for understanding the present identity of public administration and how this identity was established.

The central theme of her interpretation, as I reconstruct it, is that the "conceptual symbols" that public administration has venerated as constituting the rationale for its legitimate role in democratic governance have, each and every one, been defined in essentially masculine terms. Among these symbols are the ideas of objective, anonymous expertise; professional autonomy; hierarchy; brotherhood; and leadership—all of which, according to the contemporary gender-sensitive psychological understandings that Stivers invokes, are highly male in orientation. The consequence of defining these core terms as the foundation of a legitimate identity is that public administration has become, conceptually, symbolically, and actually, an alien, if not hostile, place to women. This is despite the fact that, as Stivers documents, women played an important role in the founding of the field and have historically made a tremendous contribution to the social well-being of the nation.

Stivers then argues that in the founding days of public administration, probably the central issue of the struggle to define a legitimate place for administration in American government was based in the contrast between politicians (who on the whole had proven to be corrupt, greedy, and self-serving) and the new *administrator*, who was objective, neutral, and, above all, virtuous in representing not his own but the broad, common, public interest. Some of the most interesting and telling critical material that Stivers presents addresses the image of the administrator as virtuous. She points out that in America, the idea of virtue has historically been very much attached to women. What has been done in public administration, however, is to develop a masculinized concept of the virtuous administrator.

In the concluding section of her argument, Stivers examines the role of women in the reform movement that spawned public administration. Generally, her theme here is that "women reformers played a significant role in establishing the terms and symbols by which proponents would promote and later defend positive administrative government," but that "gender dilemmas and paradoxes . . . came to inhabit these key ideas" (p. 104). By "key ideas," she means such concepts as morality, science, facts, positive government, business, leadership, and efficiency.

Most interesting, however, is that the benevolent activities of women formed the embryo of American social science. Stivers quotes the secretary of the American Social Science Association as writing, in 1874, that "the work of social science is literally women's work" and going on to say that social science is the "feminine side" of political economy (p. 110). As Stivers and her sources interpret it, what happened was that social science underwent a gender transformation as the reform movement gained momentum and the progressive idea of completely reforming society became the dominant agenda of the day. As such, the traditional culture of politics came into direct conflict with the agenda that the events of the day were presenting to the political process.

Politics had always been a definitely *masculine* activity. Politics "provided entertainment, a definition of manhood, and the basis for a male ritual. . . . Party leaders commonly used imagery drawn from the experience of war . . . [and] commented approvingly on candidates who waged many campaigns" (p. 111). Stivers points out that party politicians demeaned reformers as impotent people who constituted a "third sex" of American politics and called them "Miss Nancy's" and "man-milliners" (p. 112). Another dimension of the emerging situation was that women began to take initiative in using and developing a complex, comprehensive, and sophisticated social scientific perspective on social issues.

The situation faced by the nascent public administration movement was how to present itself as the centerpiece of the movement toward social improvement without appearing to be "merely" an aspect of the women's movement or nothing more than the women's movement itself. It needed to separate itself from politics, but the nonpublic, nonpolitical sphere had been designated by male tradition as female. It needed to attach itself to "science" as a key, legitimate social symbol, but *social* science had, again, developed as a female activity. It needed to present itself as legitimate by reason of its orientation toward the public interest, the "good," but virtue was a quality that had been relegated to the realm of the home and women.

As Stivers puts it, the pressure was this:

> Male Progressives felt a need to make reform appear more muscular. Accused of being sissies by people they thought of as party hacks and rascals . . . the men of public administration responded by attempting to purge reform of any taint of sentimentality—of femininity—by making sure that it was seen as tough-minded, rational, effective, and businesslike. (p. 117)

The key symbol in the effort to give public administration a more "muscular," male identity was the idea of *efficiency.* Indeed, efficiency was cast as virtually synonymous with progress itself:

> The efficiency movement in cities . . . began . . . in an effort to capture the great forces of city government for harnessing to the work of social betterment. It was not a tax-saving incentive nor desire for economy

that inspired this first effort . . . but the conviction that only through
efficient government could progressive social welfare be achieved.
(Bruere, quoted in Stivers, 1993, p. 117)

Like all symbols, the specific meaning to which it was supposed to
point was never entirely clear. What was clear, though, was that being
male helped one understand the idea and achieve it in fact.

As I mentioned in passing earlier, Stivers' analysis is very much
consistent with the argument I want to make here. Indeed, in sub-
stance, and omitting my interest in the role that pragmatism as a
philosophy played in this history, Stivers' analysis overlaps this one a
great deal. This is especially true of what she suggests in the concluding chapter of her book as a new feminist way of thinking about the
legitimacy question. She stops short of the point to which I finally
want to come, however. This is because, it seems to me, in her effort
not to "support what she opposes by opposing it" (an admonition that
she takes from Ursula Le Guin), she is more conservative in her
analysis than she is in her conclusions. Though she presents truly
paradigmatically different suggestions for a changed way of thinking
about public administration legitimacy, in her analysis she employs a
frame of thought that seems to accept the key distinctions and assumptions of traditional thinking.

We can see this at the critical place in her analysis where she argues
that to take the initiative and ownership of the social reform movement
away from women, men instituted a campaign of ideology holding that
reform programs should be made maximally *efficient* by being
grounded in science and objective, rational knowledge. This move,
she goes on, was intended to and did have the effect of giving the
reforms a more masculine cast, allowing men to take up ownership of
them and to provide the "leadership" necessary to make them "efficient."

What happened in the process, though, is not just that men took
the reform movement away from women. That is, the transformation
of reform into a movement for administrative efficiency was not based
solely and simply on the opposition of masculine to feminine. Just as
important was the fact that it posed "good" men (the administrative
reformers) versus "bad" men (politicians). Here we see the kernel of
the legitimacy problem and the distortion that created it. Administration and politics, bureaucracy and democracy, were counterposed.
Further, an opposition of power was established. Opposing democracy
and efficiency meant opposing politics and administration. Within the

terms of this opposition, one form for the gaining and exercise of power (politics) was posed against another way of gaining and exercising power (the expertise on which efficiency is founded). The legitimacy problem as we have come to know it stems directly from this clash; this, indeed, is the opposition that establishes it. Public administration was cast as bidding to become a power actor on the scene of governance. It is natural that the question of its legitimacy would inevitably arise.

This helps explain why the field has always turned to the famous Wilson essay of 1887 as its founding document. Wilson argued that public administration must be imbued with "large powers" and not be a "mere passive instrument" (Wilson, 1887/1978, p. 12). Further, his idea of using techniques for good purposes has the effect of establishing not only the assumption that means and ends are separate but the assumption that purposes can be taken as givens, making their realization a matter of the correct use of instrumental power. Wilson's was an idea of public administration worthy of the notion of an "administrative state." What it really was arguing for was governance by a new kind of elite: not a political elite—the traditional version of the Man of Reason—but a modern, scientifically enlightened "Man of Reason."

Making, as Stivers does, the opposite role to politics a model of efficiency that is merely male makes it seem as if, as I noted, the distortion we are facing is one of gender-role stakes, and it obscures the fact that at the deepest level there was an additional opposition energizing the situation. This opposition poses, on the one hand, *instrumental action effected through the use of power* (whether political or administrative) and, on the other hand, *collaborative action* (of the sort envisioned within the spirit of pragmatic philosophy).

Going one step further, we can see that what this opposition poses is elite leadership—government by "Men of Reason"—versus a government of process, involving groups. This latter kind of government avoids the traps of the conventional model of democratic participation because it closes the fissures that make the conventional model impossible. Whereas traditional participation founders on the question of fitting means to ends, which demands that ends be defined and judged as "good" in both a moral and a practical sense, collaborative action, by denying the validity of abstractions, combines ends and means into the same question—"What do we want to do?"—addressed iteratively, continuously, and permanently. The question of efficiency is entirely finessed, since it is contained in the one summary question that is to be collectively addressed. Most important, the question of legitimacy is avoided completely because there is no agent or leader acting on behalf of others.

The real issue, in other words, was a constitutional one, the same issue I described the nation facing at its founding in the debate between the Federalists and the Anti-Federalists. In turn, the distortion of the dialogue of the founding of public administration came not primarily from an attempt to make the reform movement more masculine as much as from an attempt to make it more consistent with the Federalist way of thinking that has dominated American thought about governance since the ratification of the Constitution.

The issue of power/politics versus collaborative action does fall along gender lines quite substantially, of course, and to the extent that it does, Stivers' analysis and this one are coterminous. Beneath the stakes of gender, however, are the stakes of a pattern of consciousness, which is the ultimate grounding of all stakes and all politics. On the face of it, what an analysis like Stivers' does not explain is why pragmatism, mostly written by men, was not taken up more explicitly and thoroughly by the public administration movement. Looking beneath this level, though, we can find that Stivers' analysis does suggest an answer to this question: The consciousness reflected in pragmatism carried a feminine gender identity (most obvious, of course, in the work of Mary Follett), and it was for this reason that it was not taken up by public administration. I shall return to this matter in the concluding chapter.

Conclusion

To sum up, the distortion in the dialogue surrounding the founding of public administration was essentially this: No point of view, such as pragmatism, that went outside the assumptions of the founding Federalist worldview could be incorporated into the theory of public administration, no matter how pertinent it might be to the situation faced by the field. The implicit but paramount project pursued by the founders of the field was to revise the political formula of government in the direction of administration while at the same time preserving the central principles and the worldview on which it was based, namely that of the Federalist Constitution. It is a worldview that justifies the ratification process the Constitution had, which even Madison acknowledged was undemocratic. The Federalists felt that the well-being of the nation required their installing the new Constitution irrespective of what a fair vote would have allowed. The nation needed leadership to exercise extrademocratic power in a judicious way. The model of administration that resulted from the founding period of public administration fitted this idea quite well at the paradigmatic level. The only question was how to justify the use of power so obviously removed from popular sanction.

What never was given full and fair consideration was an Anti-Federalist, pragmatic model of administration, one grounded in the principles of decentralization and collaborative action. What would the *structure* of such a system be? The pragmatist, Mary Parker Follett, outlined it in her book *The New State* (1918). What would its *process* be? Dewey and Follett both had a great deal to say about that. What would its inspiring ideology be? James's work was eloquent as a call to an inspired search for progress. What happened was something like what occurred when cancer came onto the national agenda as an issue of health policy: We launched a campaign against it, vowing to root out its cause and find a means of destroying it, a cure. We did not consider that what we ought to have done was to bend research toward finding mechanisms for boosting the human body's immune response to cancer cells, developing behavioral strategies oriented to prevention, or exploring environmental responses to reduce carcinogenic risks. We were trapped within a way of thinking about disease, and this way set our course.

Earlier, in discussing Safford's study of pragmatism, I posed a concern as to why the pragmatic answer to the fact-value question was not taken up in the legitimacy discourse of public administration. This issue is part of the broader one of why pragmatic process theory was refused on its own terms and transmuted into behavioralism and/or mythic social evangelizing. My answer is that pragmatism was "unconstitutional" in the Federalist sense of the term. Pragmatism's central idea of the tentative, experimental fact, determined through collaborative action, leaves no place for power and the Men of Reason who exercise it. Pragmatism's communitarian idea of science, therefore, had to be changed into a hierarchical idea of science, one in which some facts are judged to be better than other facts by leaders who then put the "best" facts together with their judgment to launch programs to achieve goals that have been judged to be morally good. Social relationship, the heart of the Anti-Federalist idea of governance, had to be denied by those working from the Federalist perspective. The methodology of this denial was applied throughout the intellectual history of the field of public administration. What this history reveals is that at every point, as the literature of the field developed, the pragmatist process approach has been downplayed and distorted, with the effect of keeping the discourse about legitimacy within the "power" framework—and, I would argue, keeping it unsolved and indeed unsolvable. It is this part of the story that forms the next topic: the legitimacy dialogue in the history of the literature of public administration.

5

A Selected Intellectual
History of the Field I

The Founding Through
Simon's Modernism

Democracy is a way of government in which the common
man is the final judge of what is good for him. Efficiency is
one of the things that is good for him.

Luther Gulick

Professors back from secret missions
Resume their proper eruditions,
    Though some regret it;
They liked their dictaphones a lot,
They met some big wheels, and do not
    Let you forget it.

W. H. Auden

AUTHOR'S NOTE: The lines from the Auden poem that serve as an epigraph to this
chapter are from *W. H. Auden: Collected Poems* by W. H. Auden, edited by Edward
Mendelson. Copyright 1976 by Edward Mendelson, William Meredith, and Monroe K.
Spears, Executors of the Estate of W. H. Auden. Reprinted by permission of Random
House, Inc.

◆ I BECAME A UNIVERSITY PROFESSOR in 1964 at the age of
twenty-seven. My original intention had been to obtain an MPA
degree and pursue a career in the public service, but as my encounter
with the field of public administration deepened, I became interested
in it as an intellectual enterprise. As was typical for those studying
public administration then, my main identity in graduate school was
as a political scientist. I even started, and wrote about a hundred pages
on, a political science dissertation on American political behavior. I
self-consciously shifted my topic and my identity, though, when I
came to the view that the central issues of human life in the future
were going to involve the organizational rather than the political
world. In this, I was following a large number of writers of that day
who were concerned about the problem of bureaucracy in modern
society. Having grown up in a small town, I could see rather clearly,
against the backdrop of my bucolic naïveté, how the rational organizational world had an alien and problematic cast to it.

Pursuit of this interest led me to make connections with others who
shared it, most notably the great urban sociologist Gideon Sjoberg, who
was famous for his groundbreaking book *The Preindustrial City* (1960).
Gideon was unique to my experience of academics (Sjoberg, 1989). He
took seriously the problem of ideology and, following an inspiration
from Karl Mannheim, had decided that the only way one could hope
to escape the social forces making intellectual work ideological was to
place oneself in a marginal social position.

As he and I began to collaborate in our research and writing, I, at
least partly, moved into his "marginal position" and began to see the
social world from this new viewpoint. The main structural change that
Gideon had made in his living pattern to achieve marginality was to
reverse his diurnal cycle so that he slept during the day and stayed
awake and worked during the night. He scheduled all his classes for
the late afternoon and early evening, just after he awoke and had
"breakfast." Because I had a family with young children at the time, I
could not duplicate his pattern, but I did find myself many times
working through the night with him, our sessions punctuated with
long coffee breaks at the Night Hawk coffee shop.

Gideon pointed out to me that one could better see the outlines of
social dynamics from this nocturnal perspective. "There are so many
fewer bosses around at night," he said. By contrasting what you see
then with what you see in the daytime, "you can get a glimpse of how
people's relationships are dominated." He introduced me to the *critical*
perspective, the perspective of the intellectual. This was something

that I had not really encountered in graduate school, at least in the form of a living model. There were professors on my graduate school faculty who were critical or even controversial to the point of outrageousness, but their discourses were contained within conventional categories. They did not *see* things differently; it became increasingly clear to me that Gideon did. As we sat and chatted over coffee, he consistently pointed out to me how two powerful, hidden limitations or controls worked to shape and contain the intellectual processes of the academic world. The most frequently invoked of these limitations was the "discourse of common sense." This entered when academics talked about "real" matters of business involving one's personal life or departmental issues. Any viewpoint that went outside the assumptions of a commonsense understanding (that people are egoistic and rational, for example) was acceptable in the classroom but was nonsense in the "real world." Also, one learned not to invoke findings from research studies when discussing real issues. Even when such findings seemed definite and pertinent, they were discounted ("That is controversial, and more research is needed"). The second limitation was the "discourse of the institution or of authority." When things were not decided on the basis of "common sense," they were decided by the dictates of institutional necessity. This meant that it was best not to say or do anything that raised doubts about present institutional arrangements or the viewpoints of those in positions of institutional power. The way things are and the opinions of the current leadership were to be taken for granted. The idea was that change must be either initiated from or proposed by those above.

What Gideon pointed out to me was that I, too, was unconsciously taking these controlling discourses for granted and was letting them structure the way I saw and thought about the world. I was discounting my own intellectual work, not taking it seriously, letting it be trumped by common sense and the presumption of the status quo. I was becoming not an intellectual but rather, in the words of a radical student I knew at the time, "a petty academic; a bourgeois working-stiff faculty member." In the terms of my analysis here, I was becoming an apologist for Men of Reason.

I recount this personal history to suggest a perspective from which to engage the story of the literature of public administration that I am about to narrate. This is not a complete review of the literature; I am concerned here only with considering and discussing the field as it has developed around and bears on the issue of legitimacy. Typically, historical accounts of academic literatures suggest that they develop as a patterned but partly random configuration of mutual intellectual influences. Such histories usually find overlooked issues and blind spots that occur in the literatures as a result of the only partly systematic manner in which they progress. Public administration's concern with legitimacy is different. Its main problem, I believe, is that it is a "bent" body of theory. We saw in the preceding chapter how the public administration twig was bent at its sprouting. In this chapter, we shall examine the direction and angle of lean that the tree took as it grew. I use this metaphor to suggest that public administration theory about legitimacy is exceptionally ideological. It is singularly slanted toward the purpose of providing a rationale for governance by Men of Reason by defining administration in such a way as to render it incompatible in principle with democracy. To see this clearly, though, one must suspend disbelief for the moment and assume that, as Gideon saw in the nighttime world, life can go on quite acceptably even when Men of Reason are not there.

I will trace the literature of public administration through three overlapping historical periods. In this chapter, I will discuss an *Orthodox* (or classical) period lasting from the founding of the field through the first few decades of the twentieth century; a brief *Traditionalist* period that took place during the administrations of President Franklin Roosevelt and after the end of World War II; and a *Modernist* period beginning at the end of that war and lasting to the height of the Vietnam War, around 1968. In Chapter 6, I will present the first part of a *Contemporary* period beginning in the late 1960s and continuing through the 1980s. A discussion of the most current literature of the Contemporary period is reserved for Chapter 7. The story that these periods constitute has a conservative and a progressive aspect. On the one hand, the Man of Reason ideology had to work persistently to maintain itself against internal problems and external attack; on the other hand, the ideology moved consistently forward into an increasingly powerful position of hegemony.

The Literature of the (Mis)Founding of Public Administration: The Orthodox Period

The historical review in the previous chapter indicated the extent to which the free-market ethos eroded the foundations of American society. This process proceeded so far, and corrupted governance to such an extent, that the need for change become obvious. As a context for intellectual development, turn-of-the-century American culture demanded little or nothing in the way of theoretical guidance. The problems were obvious; their seriousness and what had caused them were clear enough. Further, there was little need for normative guidance. The outlines of bad and good were clear. Civil service reform, for example, was not seen as a technical change to bring about "systematic personnel administration" as much as it was seen as a morally *good* reform. The context demanded *action* much more than it did theory or moral ideology.

It was natural, then, for public administration to develop a founding literature that was more grounded in practical action than in theoretical, scientific, or technical understanding. It was also natural that the focus of this early literature was the governance of *cities*. The early movement at the end of the nineteenth century toward "good government" began with citizen groups organizing to reform city governments, where problems of corruption and ineffectiveness were most directly visible. It was a national convention of the original eighty-four such groups formed by the mid-1890s that led to the founding of the National Municipal League (Caiden, 1971, p. 35; Stewart, 1950). The first lesson this movement learned, however, was that morality was not enough. Reformers found they could not simply "vote the rascals out" to bring about improvements in the way local governments functioned. As a result, political machines and "bossism" experienced periodic resurgences—for example, Tammany Hall was back in control of New York within three years of the eviction of Boss Tweed by reformers in 1871 (Stone & Stone, 1975b, p. 19). What was needed was expertise (Caiden, 1971, pp. 30-35).

The turn-of-the-century American sociocultural scene was doubtless the most radical period of "normal politics"—that is, nonviolent social conflict—in the nation's history. Politics came into disrepute, and a new form of governance was sought that could supplant it. Public administration was born into a tension with politics. The establishment of the New York Bureau of Municipal Research in New York (funded by Carnegie and Rockefeller) in 1906 illustrates this well, as it marked a turning point in the reform movement toward a new methodology of governance. Refused access to official records by Tammany Hall, researchers went into the streets to assess their condition, comparing their actual state with what it should have been if the funds allocated to them had been used effectively. The resulting report, distinctive for its use of facts and figures, provoked a libel lawsuit against the bureau by Manhattan Borough president Ahearn that ultimately vindicated the bureau and led to the first formal ouster of a local government official. Ahearn was removed by New York governor Charles Evans Hughes for incompetence (Stone & Stone, 1975b, p. 20).

This incident, based on the Manhattan Street Survey, brought the research term *survey* into widespread use. Soon, other cities, learning of the successful work of the New York Bureau, sought its assistance and launched similar "surveys" into the areas of budgeting, purchasing and accounting, public works, public health, and reorganization. Though the bureau movement had its origins in voluntary, grassroots citizen sponsorship, ultimately local governments—originally Los Angeles and Toledo—decided to install such units within the administrative institution of government itself. The establishment of the Bureau of the Budget at the national level in 1921 can perhaps be considered the culmination of this trend, and in fact, the New York Bureau leader Frederick Cleveland headed the Taft Commission that recommended its establishment (Caiden, 1971, p. 35).

The strategy the new movement followed in establishing itself was different from the traditional mode of pursuing political goals. It sought to be as decidedly *unpolitical* as possible, working through the channels of education, citizen influence, and self-enlightenment. At the same time, it avoided negative publicity, unconstructive muckraking or personal attacks, and political campaigns. It made its program narrowly technical, focusing on the message that what it sought to do was to carry out the public's business in accord with the effective principles of private business. As Caiden (1971) summed up the programmatic orientation of the early bureau movement:

> If irresponsible political bosses and invisible government were removed, government could be reconstructed as if it were a private business. Government [therefore] should contain a strong executive with full administrative powers, a watchdog legislature, an independent auditor, unifunctional administrative units, a standard all-inclusive budget, and a merit civil service. Mastery of the scientific laws on which these proposals were based was to constitute the discipline of public administration. . . . The political environment of public administration was not overlooked, merely glossed over. (p. 35)

These innovative, action-oriented "survey reports" constituted the original literature of the field of public administration in the United States. One could characterize this founding literature as "pragmatic" in that it was tied closely to real-world conditions and pursued the purpose of developing action alternatives for addressing them. The processes of governments were documented, and policies, procedures, and alternative forms of administrative structure were evaluated for effectiveness. Such an approach was pragmatic as long as it was grounded directly in citizen involvement. What happened, however, was that the bureaus began to develop principles, doctrines, and other abstract forms of recommendation that purported to transcend specific situations and to be beyond modification through processes of popular involvement. As this occurred, the movement became less and less pragmatic and more and more one that reflected an institutional (and, necessarily, an ideological) interest. The outline of this ideology—a deemphasis on politics coupled with an emphasis on building administrative institutions—can be seen in the recommendations themselves: elimination of overhead governing boards for agencies, the short ballot for elections, centralization of agencies under executive leadership with legislative oversight, the executive budget, rationalization of personnel and processes, and, above all, analysis of policy and administrative problems and the creation of alternative solutions for them by professional experts. The founders of the fledgling movement sought to tie themselves to the symbol of science and to link the scientific method to the idea of efficiency. The Bureau of Municipal Research published the journal *Municipal Research* with the express purpose "to promote the application of scientific principles to government," and a number of its trustees founded the Efficiency Society of New York (Caiden, 1971, p. 35).

A main vehicle used for the purpose of conflating the symbol of science with the idea of efficiency was Taylor's scientific management movement, discussed briefly in the previous chapter (Waldo, 1955, pp. 18-19). Taylor, who felt that his principles could be applied universally, supported those who wanted to bring his theory to government administration. A major success came when the Taft Commission on Economy and Efficiency, headed by some of the founding fathers of the public administration movement (e.g., Frederick Cleveland), used the scientific management approach in carrying out a broad study of national administrative agencies (Caiden, 1971, p. 35). Although the study did not produce significant change, it did promulgate the idea that government could be better run like a private business enterprise.

The motive of making the locus of reform an expert elite led quickly to the development of a professional research network. This was initially created by bureau personnel who moved across the country conducting surveys. Next, the Governmental Research Association sponsored an annual conference of bureau staffs for the sharing of research and experience. At the same time, professional and public interest associations then began to form; public works officials, city managers, police chiefs, fire chiefs, municipal finance officers, and civil service officials all became organized in the first decade and a half of the 1900s. This development was capped by the formation of the National League of Cities (Stone & Stone, 1975b).

The vigor and impetus of the movement is difficult to appreciate from a contemporary perspective, in which so little consensus or sense of direction about issues of governance exists. It was exemplified, however, in the formation of the Public Administration Clearing House in Chicago in 1929. Directed by Louis Brownlow, this organization acted to centralize and extend the movement toward a fully professionalized public administration. It brought together under one roof the associations of city managers (International City Managers Association), civil service officials (Civil Service Assembly), finance officers (Municipal Finance Officers Association), municipal researchers (American Municipal Association), state legislators (American Legislators Association), public works administrators (American Public Works Association), welfare professionals (American Public Welfare Association), and others. The Council of State Governments, the Governor's Conference, and the Public Administration Service (an agency providing consulting services, research, and publications) were established under the same auspices. These organizations, housed at 1313 East 60th Street, became known as the "1313" public administration center (Stone & Stone, 1975b, p. 23). They constituted, in effect, a national center devoted to the reformation of American governmental institutions, primarily at the local and state levels, but with major implications for the national government as well. They had a clear sense of purpose, an ideology, and a body of technique, and they enjoyed legitimacy not only within the arena of government itself but with the American middle-class public. The development of such an institution today, one having the power and influence that it was able to garner, scarcely seems imaginable.

This no-less-than-remarkable spurt toward professionalization was accompanied by a corollary surge in educational innovations designed to train new public administration professionals. The first of these was the Training School for Public Service, begun by the New York Bureau of Municipal Research in 1911. It provided university-level education and was transformed in 1921, along with the rest of

the bureau, into the Institute of Public Administration—an organization more congruent with the seriousness and quality of the teaching
mission it was pursuing. Universities did not respond to the developing need for education for the public service until the 1920s. Then, in
the period preceding the inauguration of Roosevelt's New Deal in 1933,
thirty to forty university public administration training programs were
established. Only a few of these attained true shape as professional
curricula, and many failed to survive (Stone & Stone, 1975a, pp. 268-
290). Those that succeeded relied heavily on the Training School
model and taught from the literature of surveys, reports, and comparative studies that was being produced by the bureaus (e.g., Buck, 1921;
Heer, 1926; McCombs, 1927; Smith, 1925; Studensky, 1920).

The first true "school" of public administration was formed with
the transfer of much of the program of the Training School for Public
Service to Syracuse University in 1924. Other important programs
were soon established at the University of Cincinnati, the University
of Southern California, the University of Minnesota, Columbia University, the University of Chicago, and the Brookings Institution in
Washington, DC. In addition, several important universities formed
public administration research bureaus, and educational programs for
specialized public administrators such as police, highway and sanitary
engineers, and public health officials were instituted (Stone & Stone,
1975a).

These programs provided the vehicle for public administration
education, but what did they teach? As noted earlier, descriptive,
reform-minded research bureau reports constituted the first true literature of the field. However, the core of actual courses was political
science literature—largely historical, descriptive studies or works of
political philosophy with an overlay of public administration. Only
the New York Training School (later transferred to Syracuse University), the University of Southern California, and the Brookings curricula were designed wholly as public administration courses of study
(Stone & Stone, 1975a).

In its founding phase, then, the field's intellectual content was the
bureau survey oriented toward practical reform of specific problems
of governance and social life that had not been handled effectively
through the political process. The conclusion seems inescapable that
from the beginning, the field of public administration signified a
critique, even a rejection, of republican political institutions and
processes as they had developed under the U.S. Constitution. Although the field avowed a strong devotion to the principle of democ-

racy, the literature clearly wanted to present public administration as offering a different form of democratic governance than what had emerged to date.

The founding literature and teaching of the field must be judged as uneven at best and as rather naive or primitive at worst. It is remarkable that it developed as rapidly and as well as it did, because the movement represented a major shift in the American social and political scene. It also met with the hostility and lack of support from established intellectual and political circles that such changes typically engender. Stone and Stone (1975b) provided an excellent summary glimpse of the initial thrust during this founding period:

> In the absence of textbooks, much of the course work was inductive. Students worked problems, examined surveys and reports, and sought ways to improve administration and performance. There may have been too much emphasis on "pat" solutions and techniques, and on personnel and fiscal procedures. Perhaps what the curricula lacked in administrative theory, organization behavior, decision models, and analytical methods was partly compensated by their emphasis upon pragmatic skill in improving the conduct of public service. . . . The best curricula in the 1920's and early 1930's provided the graduate with a lot of operative mileage, both immediately and for a lifetime. They generated a sense of mission, ethical standards, and confidence that the public service could be advantaged by better management. (pp. 45-46)

This overview provides a focus for reflection on the key issue posed in the founding of public administration: the relation of politics to administration. I noted that the field itself initially represented a critique of politics as it had developed in the United States (at all levels, but especially in the cities) and that the public administrative form of governance really signified a different form of democracy. Yet Stone and Stone's account reveals an idea of public administration that falls far short of its original radical inspiration.

The conservatism of public administration is made explicit in perhaps the founding book of the field, Frank Goodnow's *Politics and Administration* (1900). Although the symbolic birth is typically traced to the 1887 Woodrow Wilson essay "The Study of Public Administration" (Wilson, 1887/1978), it was Goodnow, in this early text, who had the greater impact in establishing the paradigmatic frame for the new field (Dahlberg, 1966). Goodnow argued that the functions of politics and administration are concretely separate; the political function expresses the will of the state, and the administrative function attends to the scientific, technical, and commercial activities involved in governance. Because the U.S. Constitution considered the executive and the legislative functions as discrete, it was not impossible for suitable control of politics over administration to develop within the formal governmental system. However, such control was developed by the system of political parties as a necessary supplement to the design of the Constitution. Goodnow saw no problem with defining administration as separate from politics but necessarily under the control of the political process.

In saying this, however, he was not bowing to the political sector. Rather, as a progressive who had inherited the populist spirit of disdain for politics, he felt that the United States did not have democratic politics so much as it had political control by partisan interests. Goodnow advocated political reforms that would create more direct democracy. In his view, it was possible for the proper spheres of politics and administration to be clearly and discretely delineated, and he saw increased political activity as a device for enhancing administrative efficiency. It was only *partisan* politics, expressed through legislative controls of and interference in administration, that hampered efficiency. He denigrated "politicians" as professionals who sought to usurp the rights of the people to define the path they wanted government to take and argued for a strong executive who could protect the administrative branch from improper political interference so that it could function like the nonpartisan bureaucracies in Germany that he had studied (Caiden, 1971, p. 34).

This argument is fraught with implications for the identity of public administration. Goodnow's definitions of *proper* political control and of *proper* administration seal administrators off from *involvement* with both the policy processes "above" and the citizenry "below," making administration into a neutral tool to be left alone except for being given purposes to implement. It was an insulated administration that called for respect as an "objective" process. This concept of administration demands a legitimacy independent of what it might actually do or not do in carrying on the processes of governance. Revealed here is an overlooked aspect of the legitimacy issue: *What the traditional call for legitimacy is demanding is that administration be protected from being called into question at all.* By invoking the symbols of science and technique, Goodnow was bootlegging into his argument the idea that because it was grounded in science, administration should be considered beyond controversy, or even inadver-

tent question. Administration, defined as scientifically based efficiency, provides the ultimate device for finessing the possibility of
criticism or "interference": criticism can only be about *what* is being
done, not *how* it is being done—namely, efficiently.

The literature of the Orthodox period, which emerged directly from
the founding and the paradigm that Goodnow set, represented the field
as a kind of "public sector scientific management" that, though it was
crude, pretended explicitly to the status of basic science. An exemplar
of this literature was Leonard White's (1926) text. Other authors of this
era were Luther Gulick (Gulick & Urwick, 1937), William Willoughby
(1927), William Mosher (1937), John Pfiffner (1935), and Fritz Morstein-Marx (1946). No doubt the most widely read and cited example
of the work of the Orthodox period is Gulick and Urwick's *Papers on
the Science of Administration* (1937). In a sense, this volume is a
showcase for the primary kinds of organizational wisdom of the day:
Lower-level, "working" concepts, such as span of control and unity of
command, and generalizations built out of the basic logic of laying out
organizational structures and formatting lines of supervision are elaborated. The notable exception to the writing of this time period is the
contribution by Mary Follett (1918, 1940).

What is the distortion, the slant, that is revealed by adopting this
identity for public administration? I have written in the past (White &
McSwain, 1990) that eschewing politics and defining public administration as a democratically sensitive science of efficient implementation seems a perfectly natural response to the sociological vectors of
the day—a sensible move that maximized the likelihood that the
movement would gain acceptance and influence. What this assessment does not account for, however, is the alternative possibility—
present, for example, in the work of Follett—of a genuinely democratic
administration. On this point, let me invoke the sketch of the sociopoli-
tical context drawn in the preceding chapter. At the most general level,
there was the *popular* reform spirit that inspired the resurgence of the
spirit of Anti-Federalism—that is, the ethos of practical benevolence
embodied in the *In His Steps* book discussed in Chapter 4 of this
volume (Tompkins, 1992). The nation had come to a crossroads in its
development. What the populist and social benevolence movements
and the *In His Steps* mood stood for (and that was even an impulse
among the Progressives) was a rejection of the commercial nonidentity
that America had developed. Americans were looking for an identity
as a community of people, as a nation with its own distinctive ethos.

At the level of institutional change, these were also peak years of
wartime cooperation. They allowed the nation to experience the

possibility of collective expression and action on such matters as conservation—avoidance of waste and protection of natural resources and ecological balance. Herbert Hoover and the virtual army of those he enlisted as public-spirited leaders found in the ethos of the times inspiration for formulating a theory of neocorporativist associational-ism (Himmelberg, 1994). The progressive movement intersected with Hoover's efforts to some extent, and the possibility arose for forming a joint movement centered on an idea of an associationalist public administration pursuing the mission of fostering popular cooperation. Enthusiastic support came from both sides of the industrial aisle, as department store magnate E. A. Filene claimed that "the modern business system, despised and derided by innumerable reformers, will be both the inspiration and the instrument of the social progress of the future" (quoted in Dumenil, 1995, p. 33), and as feisty labor leader John L. Lewis of the United Mine Workers (who voted for both Coolidge and Hoover) pronounced that "distrust and hostility toward the busi-ness system wanes as it is becoming better understood how the general prosperity and individual and family welfare of modern society has been usurped by the use of capital in production to multiply the productive power of man's labor" (quoted in Dumenil, 1995, p. 34).

Most important of all, Mary Follett published *The New State* in 1918. In it, she laid out both the problem of the day ("Our political life is stagnating. . . . The twentieth century must find a new principle of association" [p. 3]) and the solution ("Group organization is to be the new method in politics" [p. 3] such that political parties and ballot box democracy are replaced by direct citizen involvement) with a compre-hensiveness and cogency that is today, three quarters of a century later, still remarkable. Other pragmatist writers such as Dewey and James had become famous, popular, and influential, providing a legitimate philosophical base for reorienting our ideas of political and social process toward a vision of widescale involvement of citizens with their institutions. Yet the public administrationists paid little or no serious consideration to Follett's visionary scheme and only selective attention and lip service to the pragmatists (Waldo, 1948).

One path from the crossroads configured at the opening of the twentieth century headed toward a new form of popularly controlled, community-based governance. Realization of this alternative would have meant that a cooperative politics, based on increased social integration and the linking together, in the form of corporativism, of the realms of private, voluntary association with public institutions would have replaced party politics and ballot box democracy. Govern-ance would necessarily have been radically decentralized, and politics would have been grounded in collective dialogue rather than in the rhetoric of party competition and elections. The function of elites would have been the facilitative one of arranging, representing, and protecting the centrally important process of public dialogue. In such a system, there would have been neither "politics" nor "administration" in the traditional sense. The vehicle for traveling down this path was public administration, and the field could have been founded with an identity as the structural core of such a new form of governance (Stivers, 1995).

Given this possibility, it seems that the most sensible and appropriate intellectual strategy for the founders, especially given that public administration began as a movement at the local government level, would have been to write an idea of administration that defined it as an *integration* of generic policy and implementation processes, defined as the *direct citizen linkage into and involvement with governance as one pragmatic process of deciding and doing.* Would this not have been a better device for differentiating the field from the bankrupt and out-of-favor system of party politics? Both Dewey and Follett had showed explicitly how the claim to scientific expertise (in pragmatic terms, everyone equally can be an expert) was perfectly compatible with this idea of administration and governance. Why did the founders not choose this theoretical option? One answer is that this alternative denied a place for Men of Reason. Public administration as separate from politics but controlled by it from above preserved the need for Men of Reason in positions of political control. It also accomplished a place for a new kind of Man of Reason: the expert public administrator.

The destination of the path that the founders of public administration chose was the refurbishment of the traditional system, adjusting into it a sensitivity for citizen dislike of the corrupt manipulations of political elites and giving it the capacity to promise a venue for the formation of a national identity. This identity made public administration an adjunct of the existing Federalist system. As such, it was in principle a competitor with the democratic political process, but it came to function, in fact, as an instrument of and scapegoat for it.

In founding the field on the idea of politics and administration as separate, Goodnow expressed and set in place the strategy of finding a rationale for Men of Reason under the changed social and political conditions that emerged in the new century. The key move was to employ the contemporary abstraction "efficiency" as an orienting concept. Now there would be two kinds of Men of Reason—one to set policy, one to decide on the best way to effect it—all in service of the *idea* of popular control of government.

World War II and the Traditionalists

As the youthful field of public administration gained a foothold and grew, the social and political conditions that had produced it were eclipsed by the larger changes that the new century introduced. The industrialization of the economy proceeded, and the nation's contemplation of a way of life for itself faced a new and overwhelming question: whether to organize life around time and leisure or money and consumption. The issue was decided by default, as intellectuals, business, labor, and other institutional leaders all failed to theorize the question clearly and to frame a paradigmatic idea that would answer it (Cross, 1993). As a result, America made the transition into a fully industrial society as one driven centrally by production and consumption. (An exemplar of this transition is Henry Ford, who went from seeing himself as a socially concerned innovator and leader—the inventor of the five-dollar day, which more than doubled wages at the time—to being a labor-hating "capitalist.") A period of turbulent economic growth and social change extended through the 1920s, culminating in the presidency of Herbert Hoover, whose high expectations on entering office—and the dashed hopes he carried away as he left it—capture the sense of missed possibility that this brief historical moment held. Though the economic distress that brought down Hoover's presidency was probably beyond all control, Hoover's failure to be reelected meant that the potential raised by populism and the social, cultural, and political movements that followed it now was lost.

Franklin Roosevelt's presidency, however, serves as a kind of testimony to the strength of Hoover's idea of cooperative government, since the core of his approach to the Depression and the social problems that accompanied it showed considerable continuity with Hoover's associationalist philosophy (Hawley, 1994; Himmelberg, 1976). Nonetheless, Roosevelt's vision for the country was different and, curiously perhaps, was judged to be quite consistent with the mind-set of the emerging field of public administration as it began to enter a new stage. This might be described as a mix containing 30% Hooverism and 70% Rooseveltism. Roosevelt set the nation on the project of becoming one big community, and he was willing to devolve policy-making discretion to agencies and private groups to further this goal. In this sense, his program showed continuity with the turn-of-the-century movement toward finding a national identity. Where he differed, however, was in the belief—in a sense, the emblematic idea of the New Deal—that the national community should be organized around standard, centrally promulgated norms. His idea of community was the traditional one that saw communities as defined by a core of normative agreement. Roosevelt's famous fireside chats are a direct metaphor for what he saw himself as doing—drawing the national family around the feet of the father to hear how he wanted their lives to be. This was by no means the notion of community that had emerged in the turn-of-the-century social context and that was expressed in the writings of the pragmatists (most notably Mary Follett) and in Hoover's associationalism. The alternative theory of community is defined by stable relationships that enable a group or a society to resolve its issues and make choices on an ongoing basis. Such a theory assumes conflict of viewpoint as a baseline. Roosevelt wanted to build a foundational consensus around a "liberal" or humanistic image of society.

This is the sense in which Roosevelt represented a break with the Hoover administration. Given the right conditions, the Hoover presidency might have produced a different "New Deal," of the same magnitude as Roosevelt's, that would have eventually transformed into Mary Follett's "New State." Roosevelt's approach to government was more consistent with the philosophy that progressivism ultimately embodied. This philosophy was grounded in a kind of Frederick Taylor engineering vision of the good society, where the right way to live was understood and everything had been put into place so that this way could be effected. H. G. Wells's novel *Things to Come* (1935/1975) and the popular movie based on it and directed by William Cameron Menzies captured this sensibility precisely. It depicted a postapocalyptic society of chaos. The population was afflicted with a strange malady—"wandering disease"—that caused people to stray about aimlessly, like zombies in the night. (This served nicely as a metaphor for what the engineering mentality consistently sees as the requisite issue for attaining effective action: having a clear goal.) By contrast, a subsector of people, led by engineers, used the advent of the apocalypse as a beginning point for building a highly advanced, utopian society that saw even exploration of space as a possibility.

The implication of this shift in social mood for the emerging identity of the field of public administration was fundamental. Public administrators began to see themselves as centrally involved in the process of making the major normative choices that were to give shape to the new national community coming into being under Roosevelt. They began to move away from the founding concept that administration and politics are separate and to see administrators as inevitably involved in policy making. This was the beginning of the school of public administrative thought that I have referred to in other writings as Traditionalist (White & McSwain, 1990). I gave it this name to indicate, first, that it showed continuity with the "Orthodox" school developing out of the founding period in that the Traditionalists continued to have faith in the utility of the "approximate scientific principles" (rules of thumb) espoused and taught through the founding period. Second, the Traditionalists were distinguished by a concern to make explicit a normatively grounded framework that could guide administrative action. They called this the "theory of the public interest" and sought to base it on a foundation of expert utilitarianism and broadly shared social norms. These norms were "traditionalist" in the sense that they were to be found in the constitutional and cultural heritage of the nation.

The essence of public administration's new identity was epitomized in the Tennessee Valley project, the legislation for which was passed in 1933. This was a large-scale engineering project designed to bring rural Tennessee into permanent prosperity by electrifying it and modernizing its farming practices. It was a policy decided on and implemented from the top, one that met considerable resistance at the grassroots level because it permanently disrupted the way of life of the people in the region. To the Traditionalists, such resistance was not ultimately important, because the general good implicit in the program was seen as outweighing any personal disruptions it might create. Further, in carrying out the project, the administrators found it necessary to make serious compromises of program goals with local interest groups to gain the legitimacy they needed. Here, then, was the Traditionalist approach to administration exemplified in a single case: The design of the program was inspired by a vision of the public interest; it furthered the project of bringing the whole nation into a common way of life; it required independent expertise of the highest order; and it required judicious accommodation of political realities and immediately affected interests.

During this period, public administration burgeoned. The American Federation of Government Employees was founded in 1932, and the state and municipal employees organized an association in 1936.

Public administrators were seen as savior-knights rescuing American society from the Depression as one program innovation followed another, involving government in both commercial activity and social life to an unprecedented degree. Roosevelt attempted to bring the nation back to a condition of economic and social health and security, and the New Deal program, as conservative as it was, had the effect of reconstellating and sharpening the traditional lines of political battle and party identity. The brief moment in which the impetus and opportunity for Americans to think about themselves as a society evaporated as the identities of "labor" and "business" hardened into their roles as the central contending interests under a fully developed capitalist economy. Agriculture, too, began to see itself as an industrial political interest.

What was distinctive about this was the new idea that the public interest was best seen as the outcome of the interest group struggle. This notion entered public administration theory as the concept of "administrative institutionalism." The political scientist Richard Neustadt, in a groundbreaking study of presidential power, came to the conclusion that what was good for the president was good for the country—an idea that had become a working principle for adminis-trators of the Roosevelt administrations (Neustadt, 1960). Everything an administrator could do to further the "program" and the "agency" was going to be in the public interest. The hope and possibility for a social order produced through ongoing discourse was transformed into the notion that an agreed-on floor, a baseline of protections and norms, was all that was required of government. Beyond this, the social good would be determined through economic and political competi-tion.

As the nation mobilized for and moved into World War II, a generation of public administration academics were drawn directly into the practice of government. When they returned, they began to theorize their experience into a full-blown "philosophy" of public administration. Dwight Waldo, himself a member of the returning wartime corps of academics turned administrators, provided a key foundation stone for this effort with his book *The Administrative State* (1948). Waldo carried out a direct assault on the theoretical tensions that clearly afflicted the new field. These tensions originated with the Orthodox idea that administration could be separated from politics. Waldo's analysis made clear that the "administration-politics dichot-omy," as it was called, was not a philosophically tenable idea.

The Traditionalists' main break with the founding orthodoxy of the field was to agree with Waldo's critique and state explicitly that politics and administration were not discrete processes in fact or concept. Writers such as Paul Appleby (1945) laid down a new theoretical frame by stating this explicitly and with enthusiasm. At the same time, the Traditionalist writers designated the presidency as the point of reference for their new concept of the public administrator, thereby finessing the issue of legitimacy by subordinating the administrator to the electorally validated discretion of the president. Administrators were involved in policy making, but under the purview of the top executive. They further tempered the new discretion they allowed themselves by articulating a perspective, a way of structuring one's attention, that would reveal the public interest to them as a normative guide in policy making. Their theory of knowledge was "structuralist" in the sense that they believed that administrative situations took a limited number of generic shapes, each of which posed specific issues, and for which there was a "rule-of-thumb" right way to decide. (An example: Generally, when a question arises as to whether to act so as to fulfill a professional principle or to do what the boss says, doing what the boss says is the right thing.) These were to be learned by studying descriptive case studies—historical narratives of actual public administration problems, actions, and consequences.

Although he can be classified as a Traditionalist only in this specific sense, Charles Lindblom's (1959) influential idea of "disjointed incrementalism" epitomizes the Traditionalists' methodology of administrative decision making. Described in the title of a famous article in the *Public Administration Review* as "the science of muddling through," this was an idea in great good currency with Traditionalists. Lindblom's argument was that values and actions designed to achieve them must be defined incrementally and iteratively, in response to concrete results. As such, it appears to be close to the ideal of pragmatic action. Actually, though, it is more accurate to characterize it as an operationalization of Friedrich's approach to policy making that is grounded in Popper's concept of an open, disconfirmative idea of scientific method (Braybrooke & Lindblom, 1963). It is Traditionalist only in this sense: It assumes that the ambiguities of fact and value are just that—ambiguities rather than fundamental mysteries—and can be *resolved* through tentative, reasoned discourse that is informed by a continuing assessment of experience. Just as Popper's approach to science is not completely open in that it presumes an implicit accretion of agreed-on truth that has not been disconfirmed (Lieberson, 1982a, 1982b), Lindblom's is not at all an argument for radically decentralized choice because it presumes that the orienting framework guiding the muddling through is "scientific"—which is to say, grounded in a foundation of at least implicitly accepted values and empirical knowledge.

Although the Traditionalist period is rather brief—fifteen years at best—it offers the most fully articulated statement of a working theory for the Man of Reason that one can find in the literature. The Traditionalist orientation reveals that the Man of Reason's legitimacy is grounded in an identification with other Men of Reason, an elite group whose authority is sustained by homage to the president. Further, although the Man of Reason considers the conclusions of expertise, these will typically conflict with one another; thus, he cannot decide merely as an expert. Although he considers the public interest aspect, the normative dimension of decisions is never entirely clear, and he cannot decide on the basis of value considerations alone either. Finally, although he considers political exigencies, these will certainly pull in different directions, and he cannot be controlled by them. As a result, the ultimate choice point for the Man of Reason's decisions is *his own reasoned judgment.* Indeed, the very denial of all singular points of reference for decision and the amalgamation of these into a whole context for choice is depicted as the rationale, the legitimation, for the exercise of this personal discretion—precisely the point at which Finer and Friedrich's "debate" leaves us.

The new Traditionalist identity of the public administrator was captured well in one of the original case studies of the Traditionalist literature: "The Disposal of the Aluminum Plants" (Stein, 1952a). The issue was how "government officials" decided what to do with the government aluminum plants built as part of the war effort. The government's aluminum production expansion program had cost $750 million in all, and its plants represented half the nation's aluminum production capacity. The question immediately presenting itself was whether to dispose of the plants to Alcoa, thereby solidifying Alcoa's position as the dominant producer in the aluminum market, or to allocate the plants in such a way as to foster competition in the industry. The case involved complex legal, patent, technical, and political issues at the presidential level and obviously posed a question of major economic dimensions. It depicted the public administrator as a major actor in the policy arena of government. This is what the Traditionalists meant in saying that the public administrator is one who helps to make the normative choices by which the shape of American society is set. Students were taught to see how involvement in a case of this magnitude had structural similarities with what administrators faced in even the most trivial of issues—how letters were written, data disposed of, and survey questionnaires designed

(Henry, 1987; Stein & Arnow, 1948-1951). The lesson was, in short, that administrators at all levels of the governmental administrative hierarchy and in every jurisdiction were to see themselves as part of the leadership elite of government. They were different from others in this elite only in degree.

The Traditionalist idea of public administration was, in a number of senses, a wonderful and heroic one. It was also a brilliant theoretical strategy for resolving the populist critique of the Federalist pattern of government. It preserved the integrity of the Man of Reason elite structure set in place by the Constitution but gave it balance, perspective, and broad social concern (Redford, 1958). Nonetheless, the Traditionalists became little more than a Camelot-like moment in the history of the field. As the postwar period proceeded, an entirely new social mood took hold. The Roosevelt programs and the war experience, naturally and predictably, had produced a new deference toward and legitimacy for political leadership and a new emphasis on personal life. Americans were weary of participating in large-scale collective events. They wanted normalcy, and they thought they knew what that was. The questions involved in attaining it were largely technical and could be technically solved by such things as building planned places to live, inventing new home appliances, and improving the performance of automobiles. A concern with social issues and, implicitly, the public interest, persisted into the 1950s, but the new modernist, technical mood was growing, and along with it emerged still another idea of what public administration should be. The harbinger of this new identity was a man named Herbert Simon.

Simon's Modernist Revolution

To understand fully the nature of the change that Herbert Simon's work brought about in public administration, we must contrast it at the level of ontology with the perspective of the Traditionalists; the difference is fundamental. As the debate between the two camps developed, it became difficult to see what was at issue because the change was not as much in ideology as in regime. The Man of Reason ideology remained the dominant theory underlying governance; Simon simply wrote a new set of qualifications for admission to its ranks.

The image of the Man of Reason that the Traditionalists produced was grounded in the ontological presupposition that institutions possess a certain kind of facticity. Institutions were seen by the Traditionalists to be *real* in a way that was not entirely metaphysical. The administrators who led the institutions of governance were seen as acknowledging and validating this realness by following the traditions of policy and process that defined the institutions. They felt, for example, that an organization such as the Federal Trade Commission attains a reality beyond its component parts by virtue of the general policy framework—that is, the set of principles—that it incrementally develops for settling issues of commerce, by the procedures that it sets in place and legitimates, and by the ethos—that is, the ethical culture—that it establishes over time. To use a sports analogy: After a sport has become officially established and comes to be regulated by officials, it takes on the status of being a "GAME" in the grand sense of the term. People begin to love "the game," and owners and players are evaluated in terms of whether their behavior is helping or hurting it. Most germane to our consideration is that the officials who referee the sport are seen to represent the game, and ultimately their role becomes much more than simply enforcing the rules; rather, they manage the play according to the circumstances of a specific event in a way that furthers the best interests of the game. Like the members of a community surrounding a sport, the Traditionalists saw administrators, and everyone surrounding them, as participating in a reality that was greater than themselves. In the words of the British anthropologist Mary Douglas (1986), this is "how institutions think"—the people who compose them act out the institutional definition of reality and the logic that this definition entails.

What legitimated the Traditionalist version of the Man of Reason was that he participated in this larger reality and that it existed under the broad sanction of the top political executive. The primary symbol of this dimension of the institutions of governance was the idea of the public interest. Although within the Traditionalist theory the public interest could not be defined in any positive way, it was nonetheless quite real. Indeed, this quality of mysteriousness gave the idea all the more power as a legitimator for administrative leaders. The message seemed to be that the best and primary access to the public interest lay in the public administrator himself and his seasoned judgment.

Simon's technical vision of institutional reality confronted the Traditionalist's romantic vision in the most fundamental way. However, it did not confront it in a manner that challenged the idea that Men of Reason are essential. What Simon did was call into question the "reality" that the Traditionalists had attributed to institutions. The beginning place for his doing this was his reduction of institutions to "organizations"—which is to say, his claim that they were nothing more than arenas of an activity that was carried out according to the results of rational calculations based on information. The frame of the calculation was fixed. It was efficiency as measured by the ratio of resource inputs to outputs of product. What varied was the information that went into the calculation, the *decision premises* that formed its substantive content.

At bottom, Simon's image of the institution evacuates it completely, reducing it to nothing more than an organized dynamic of intersecting flows of information carried by decision premises. The metaphor he uses for describing this image is a river looked at from a point high in the air. From this perspective, one can see that the main line of action in the river—its central flow—results from hundreds of tributaries of all sizes flowing into the main channel from myriad source points and directions. The entire system is dynamic; its movement is constant, and it is changing at every moment. The person best suited to "manage" an organization seen through the frame of this metaphor is not the romantic administrative leader depicted in the Traditionalist literature but an engineer, the person who can comprehend the whole "hydraulic system" of the river, someone who has the specific technical knowledge required to site strategically and to build the dams, spillways, and redirected channels needed to efficiently turn the power of the river to good purpose.

What I consider in 1997 to be the most admirable and impressive aspect of Simon's key book *Administrative Behavior* (1976) is the power of the rhetorical strategy he employed and the skill and finesse with which he carried it out. For a book whose origins were a PhD dissertation, it is something of a marvel in this regard. The sociological conditions in which Simon was writing were ripe for the introduction of a new image of the administrative leader, and Simon seems somehow to have intuited precisely the outlines of the image that best fits this newly configuring ethos.

America as it emerged from World War II was ready to get on with the business of pursuing happiness, and happiness was embodied in innovations such as the Levittown housing development, where a veteran could move with his family and find clothes and dishwashing machines already installed (the machines were in the home physically, and their prices were in the mortgage contract, so that they were paid for over twenty or twenty-five years) and ready to implement the American dream. The Marshall Plan, devised and led by a prominent military figure, captured the idea of the work at hand after the war

much better than did the social programs of Roosevelt's New Deal.
Truman's Fair Deal, a significant aspect of which was to help veterans
and to broaden access to the American dream of good jobs, education,
and homes, was more to the point. The deprivations of the war period
produced a broad consensus about what the good life was. This shared
image, plus the goodwill toward the returning young soldiers, created
a context in which it seemed that the only question at hand was the
technical one of how to get people installed in the good life. Simon's
administrator-manager fitted this context precisely.

The rhetorical strategy Simon adopted was to parody theories that
had preceded his as wishy-washy and ambiguous. He did this through
the tactical masterstroke of drawing a critical analogy between the
prescriptions of Traditionalist management theory and the nonspecific
and contradictory guidance of proverbs. Proverbs, he said, speak in
both directions, and hence provide no true guidance at all—as in "Look
before you leap" (Proverb 1) and "He who hesitates is lost" (Proverb
2). Similarly, management principles such as "span of control" advised, at the same time, "Do not place too many subordinates under
one supervisor" and "Do not place too few subordinates under one
supervisor." Simon seemingly reduced Traditionalist management
principles to absurdity.

The wonder is that Simon gets away with his critique, effectively
labels the Traditionalists as vague and indefinite, and brings off a
convincing presentation of himself as providing precise guidance to
working managers. This is the baseline of his strategy: He poses
himself as holding to a balanced viewpoint, one that stands between
two extremes. His theory of authority (which he borrows substantially
from Chester Barnard, 1938/1968), for example, follows this line.
Managers should not see themselves as having absolute authority over
the employee once he or she enters the organization, nor should the
manager feel that the role holds no authority and that everything must
be negotiated with subordinates—the organization does pay them,
after all. Rather, the "truth" is that authority operates within a "zone
of acceptance" in the middle of these two extremes. Simon seems to
be implying that this qualified or "balanced" view of authority settles
the old, silly debate between the view that all authority resides in the
manager and the view that all authority emanates upward from the
employees.

Another example of how Simon seizes the high middle ground is
in his adoption of a "behavioralist" analytical stance toward organizational phenomena or activity. Though he does not fully elaborate this

aspect of his position until later, in his coauthored public administration textbook (Simon, Smithburg, & Thompson, 1950) and in his
organization theory book with James March (March & Simon, 1958),
it is clearly implicit in *Administrative Behavior* (Simon, 1976). He
denies, and in the process roundly denounces, the "mechanistic" view
of the human being that he claims is the foundation of Taylor's
scientific management movement and other similar efficiency-ori-
ented theories. The Traditionalists, of course, put a good deal of stock
in such approaches. The mechanistic view depicts the human being
as a kind of automaton who can be programmed by the manager once
optimal production routines are identified. It is clearly simplistic and
insensitive to the complex emotional-motivational dimension of human psychology.

However, Simon implies that the romantic, humanistic notion of
the human person as idiosyncratically creative or spontaneous is
incorrect as well. Human motivation and behavior follow stable patterns, patterns that can be understood and reduced to lawlike generalizations. These generalizations, in turn, can be used by the manager
and *applied* to the organizational context such that optimum motivation and productivity are attained. Simon again presents himself as
rejecting the extremes and adopting the middle, reasonable position.
In so doing, he gives his theory the powerful appeal of the "balanced
mean." This, when accompanied by the convincingly put claim that
he is going to provide more specific and practical guidance about
administering organizations than those who have gone before him,
accords his argument unstoppable momentum.

I have pointed out that Simon's theory posits an information
process rather than an institutional view of organizations and that his
central focus is efficiency in the strict sense. He also assumes a
rhetorically powerful position with his idea of rationality as a concern
for the optimal ratio of input to output. This carries great prima facie
plausibility. Simon points out, however, that the idea is in fact beset
with a difficulty—namely, that to be efficient, the decision maker must
possess a valid comprehension of how the elements in a situation (the
independent variables) bear on and produce the effect or product being
sought (the dependent variable). The problem is that in a situation of
any complexity, the array of independent variables that can be considered continues virtually into infinity. The information-processing
costs of rational decision making can therefore quickly escalate to an
unacceptably high level; "rational decision making" begins to look like
a not-so-rational way to proceed.

The way this problem must be solved, Simon indicates, is through adopting a model of rationality as *bounded*—which is to say, limited to only those variables that are clearly important to achieving the intended goal. He uses an example of the problem of understanding the factors affecting the production of honey in the English beehive industry to illustrate this. He speculates that a correlation might be found between the number of "old maids" living in the countryside and the level of honey production. He theorizes that the "reason" for this correlation is that old maids, presumably out of loneliness, have a proclivity toward keeping cats as pets. Cats, in turn, like to hunt and kill honeybees, which, of course, diminishes the amount of honey that the hives from which the bees work can produce. He concludes that such a way of understanding a situation is obviously not necessary to a rational process of decision. To avoid falling into the ludicrous condition of thinking in such a manner, one should bound or limit the process of rational analysis to the key *proximate* variables affecting the situation. Again, the idea of "bounded rationality" carries the powerful ring of balance and reasonableness. Simon begins with a position that seems valid on its face, problematizes it, solves the problem with an appeal to "reason," and strengthens the appeal of the concept he is offering.

Simon's remarkable explicitness about his epistemological position functions in the same manner. By declaring himself a devotee of logical positivism, he may fling himself into academic thickets of philosophical controversy, but the reverse is true in the case of the general reader, who may not be a positivist but who believes in a deeply implicit way in the idea of right and wrong. To the general reader, deciding right and wrong is not the same thing as deciding matters of fact. By adopting the positivist position that values can be and indeed are separate from facts, Simon places his argument on the side of common sense and on the field's founding belief in the separateness of politics (values) from administration (facts). His position becomes at once radically critical and conservative—a powerfully persuasive position from which to issue a theoretical polemic.

Successfully treating the fact-value problem is central to Simon's effort to establish the plausibility of his approach. It is the issue on which, in one form or another, he was most frequently "taken on" by his critics in the debates that his book engendered, the most famous of which was an exchange between Simon (1952) and Waldo (1952) in the *American Political Science Review*. The line of attack that he correctly saw as most likely to be raised against him was that his concept of efficiency would appear amoral and antihumanistic. The key to his strategy in meeting this class of objections was to relativize the problem by insisting that the choices involved in achieving efficiency were always "in relation to" other choices and not to be held against any absolute standard. He opens this part of his argument by asserting a qualitative difference between the world of human activity and the "physical world." In the physical world, he notes, all attempts to achieve efficiency are governed by the law of conservation of energy, which holds that outputs can never exceed inputs. This law makes possible an absolute standard of "perfect efficiency," defined as the case in which outputs and inputs are precisely equal. In the realm that the social sciences seek to understand, Simon says, there is no law of conservation of energy. Having freed managers from any absolute standard, Simon can then argue that questions of efficiency are to be *situationally* decided. With this premise, he is able to argue, again with great plausibility, that all relevant value and factual considerations can be taken into account and all irrelevant ones ignored.

Simon's denial of the idea of conservation of energy as applicable to the social world is supremely important to the general foundation of his argument—much more so than is indicated by his brief mention of it in dealing with potential objections to the idea of social efficiency. The final rationale of his idea of organizations is that effective management action can improve the ratio of outputs to inputs. Managers, he is saying, can "beat the system," meaning the structure of laws that constitute the social world, if they are good enough to see what variables to manipulate and are able to control them. In making this implicit promise, Simon is asserting not only that there is no law of conservation of energy in the social world but also that managers can take actions freely (i.e., independent of determination) that will turn the dynamics of the social world to the purposes that they seek to implement. They can do this because they understand the laws of the social world and can use these laws to attain relative increases in the efficiency of the organizations they manage. The manager's relation to the social world is seen as just like his or her relation to the physical world. Managers are engineers, able to take their understandings of the laws of physical mechanics and use them to design and build efficient techniques, procedures, and machines. Simon ignores the critical issue of self-referentiality. That is, he does not explain how the manager is exempt from determinative social laws such that he or she is *able* rationally to apply management techniques to others.

What could better fit the frame of common sense than such an assertion? Simon has accomplished the clever feat of offering a new theory that is critical of what has gone before but that fits perfectly the way that people already think about the subject it seeks to explain. It is a remarkable performance, one that deserves the accolades and the place in history that it has received. On the other hand, there is no escaping the judgment that the book is more a masterpiece of rhetoric than the innovative theoretical tour de force it has been made out to be.

Critical assessment of his work shows it as beset with a series of ambiguities, tensions, and contradictions. In saying this, I am not reflecting the several critiques that have been leveled at Simon when his work was having its initial and most visible impact. In the main, these critiques were issued from positions within the Man of Reason ideology and did not focus on its problems at what might be called the "paradigmatic" level. It is only recently that critique at this level has appeared (Davis, 1996; Dennard, 1995; Harmon, 1995; Harmon & Mayer, 1986; Little, 1994; Marshall, 1996).

The problems with Simon's model of organization and management have gone largely unremarked, however. His rhetoric carried the day and wrought an enormous influence. The acceptance of his theory was greatly facilitated by the configuration of sociological forces that was present at the time of the publication of *Administrative Behavior* and by the fact that it did not present a true challenge to existing approaches to administrative process. In making this judgment, I take as given that an essential requirement for a theory's being considered fundamentally new is that it implies a restructuring of power relationships. Simon's did not do this. The practical implication of his theory is that one type of Man of Reason—the "man made wise by experience and the gift of a transcendental judgment" of the Traditionalists—was to be replaced by a new type of Man of Reason—the rational decision-making, scientifically informed, ethically sensitive but primarily concerned-with-efficiency administrative engineer. Simon must be given credit for the capacity he showed for leadership in the arena of intellectual politics. He demonstrated a truly exceptional instinct for choosing conceptual symbols appropriate to the sociological setting within which he worked, and his theoretical rhetoric proved to be invincible in the context of his time.

The perspective that he brought to the field addressed a major problem besetting the Traditionalist school, one that it did not even admit to itself but that was obvious to those working outside it. This problem was the *moralism* that infused Traditionalist thinking about administration. The Traditionalist concern with the public interest functioned as an emblem of the field's moral purpose and its idealism. In this, public administration was like all fields of study that support a body of practice and a community of practitioners. Most fields of practice are either clinical or technical, however, and the ambiguity that is inherent in the application of moral principles is contained by relatively clear professional codes of ethics and even more by the specifics of law regulating such practices. Some ambiguities occur in the day-to-day situations of practice, and no doubt conflicts occur between the practitioner's sense of the "right thing to do" and governing ethical or legal restrictions. In general, however, the education and training of practitioners is not greatly impaired by this kind of conflict; practitioners can be schooled rather definitely to follow procedures, codes, and laws, and for the most part such training will fit the experience they subsequently encounter.

Such is not the case in public administration. The situations faced by the public administration practitioner are vastly more open, complex, and varied than those in most other applied fields. Many are nonrecurring, so it is difficult to develop a context around them and identify "acceptable" responses for them. The source of the most difficult complications arising for the public administrator is the fact that public administrative organizations interface with the political arena, where the compromise of principle in the name of what is possible is a matter of everyday business. Public administration has struggled with the problem stemming from its connection to politics from its inception. As the field began to embrace openly its role in policy formation, it necessarily took a moralistic posture. The clearest manifestation of this was in the city manager movement, in which a tradition quickly developed that the expectation should be given to would-be city managers that they would sooner or later find themselves in a deadlocked conflict with their mayor and council. In this conflict, they would be representing the side of the public interest, and the politicians would be representing some narrower, shorter range and specific interest. As city managers, they were to hold their ground, and the result of this was that they would be fired.

This expectation formed the central concept of the city manager ethos up until quite recently. As a result, the city manager community created an informal support network providing information and help in finding new employment for fired city managers. The issues over which conflicts arose were rather standard: They usually involved favoritism on the part of the council or a preference for a policy alternative that violated professional judgment. The public interest during this time functioned as a legitimate symbol by which a city manager could stand unshakably in the name of the greater good.

In other roles, however, this proposition was more problematic. At the level of state and federal bureaucracies, beginning public administrators did not hold jobs that interfaced directly with the roles of political decision makers. They seldom experienced the tension between politics and administration. It seemed, rather, that the administrative roles they occupied primarily involved pleasing the boss by doing a good job at the specific, usually rather mundane, tasks they were given. The idea of the public interest could serve as a kind of secondary inspiration for doing one's work well, but it seemed to hold no direct relevance to the day-to-day activities of the working bureaucrat.

The Traditionalist viewpoint acknowledged this situation of the beginning administrator, but it had little to offer by way of response to it. Grounded as it was in the field of political science and government, its research and teaching interest lay in the broad pattern of institutional dynamics by which top-level policies were formulated. It saw its teaching mission to be educating future public administrators by providing them with an understanding of the "governmental and political context" within which policy making took place so that, as administrators, they could understand the forces that would be at work in the settings into which they would eventually climb.

Coupled with this kind of perspective was training in specific skills such as budgeting and financial management, personnel administration, and organization and management techniques. As to the immediate organizational context, the fledgling administrators were sent the message that they should "go along to get along"—work hard, do a good job, issue no complaints, cause no trouble, please their boss. The idea seemed to be that a work style like this would enable the career administrator to learn from experience how senior administrators operated in the arena of administration and politics.

Given this, the Traditionalist educational message to the student never had to address the messy reality of day-to-day organizational life and reveal the human complexities, ambiguities, moral and ethical quandaries, and dilemmas that are routine there. As an educational program purporting to train people to cope with these, it would have had to tell students something about what to do in them. Given the strongly prescriptive theme in its literature, these would have taken the form of instructive working principles. The problem was that Traditionalism had no way of doing this. It had no research literature that could guide it in formulating such instructions, and even if it had such a literature, the "realistic" prescriptions indicated by it would probably have been unacceptable within the moralistic ethos of Traditionalist teaching.

I can mention two Modernist period works that help illustrate this point. One is Peter Blau's *Dynamics of Bureaucracy* (1965), in which a case is discussed of a government inspector who, as a practical tactic, overlooked some infractions of the law as a way of gaining leverage for enforcement of other aspects of it. One could scarcely imagine this behavior being discussed and assessed positively in a Traditionalist classroom. The second example is cast at a more general level: Aaron Wildavsky's famous book *The Politics of the Budgetary Process* (1984), which was met with the reaction, "Everyone knew all this already, yet Wildavsky's book became famous because he wrote it down!" The point here is that in the Traditionalist discourse that preceded Wildavsky, the fact that budgeting involves politics was best not acknowledged in writing!

Simon's rather easy victory over the Traditionalists reveals, then, a number of things about the "revolution" that his modern approach brought about in the field. I have already noted the first of these, that the change from Traditionalism to Simonian Modernism is actually a shift *within* the Man of Reason ideology. Second, this shift occurred partly as a result of Simon's genius at theoretical rhetoric and partly by reason of sociological factors and the deficiencies of Traditionalism in providing an approach to *organizational management*. This last point suggests the largest factor at work: that the new elite role that Simon defined better fitted the postwar situation. During the war, politics had been eclipsed—presidential leadership was everything. The war was won by managers and experts, and the rather bumbling reign of heroic Dwight Eisenhower in the postwar period marked the fact that America had moved into a new condition of emphasis on social and economic progress driven by rational expertise. Simon's idea of the Man of Reason was thus much more contemporary than the Traditionalist's romantic, moralistic idea of him.

The presenting issue was that Traditionalism left out the middle level of administrative reality, the reality of organizational process. Its strategy was to substitute the rule-of-thumb generalizations that had formed the core of classical public administration and management studies, the principles that Simon found so easy to parody. What was needed, then, was a more descriptive approach, one that could be used to look at what actually went on in public administrative organizations and to suggest ways of coping with this reality that were based on how the people who worked in them were already doing it. This is exactly what Simon brought to the field. By breaking with the moralism of the Traditionalists and the domination of the political science and governance disciplinary perspective on which it was based, Simon showed the way for a new generation of public administrationists to incorporate into the field research and theories from a variety of related academic disciplines. A number of separate but related lines of study developed within public administration, each taking a different focus but all sharing the commitment to the tenets of rationalism and behavioralism that underpinned Simon's *Administrative Behavior.* The next stage in the literature, after the Simon revolution, saw a proliferation and incorporation of subfields into the study and teaching of public administration.

Simon and the myriad of organizational specialties that followed Simon make up what I am calling the Modernist period in the literature of public administration. The pattern of distortion that characterized this era was the *selectiveness* with which each subfield was incorporated into public administration research and teaching. Those aspects that were inconsistent with Man of Reason ideology were glossed over or ignored, whereas those aspects that supported the principle of legitimate elite discretion were made explicit and emphasized.

Organizational Sociology in Public Administration

The most important in the array of subfields developing in public administration was the sociological study of organizations and bureaucracy. Simon opened the way for the incorporation of this perspective into the field with the publication of his coauthored textbook *Public Administration* (Simon et al., 1950) and then in the book *Organizations* (March & Simon, 1958). The Traditionalists had incorporated some of the "institutionalist" sociological perspective into their framework, but they showed no interest in the dynamic aspects of the sociological way of understanding. The literature of organizational sociology covered a wide spectrum of research approaches and organizational types. Max Weber's work on bureaucracy was studied, but it seems fair to say that in general, his "ideal type" of bureaucracy was misconstrued within the field as primarily providing an argument for not only the inevitability but the desirability of bureaucracy as an organizational form. Other sociologists who were influential were Peter Blau (Blau, 1965; Blau & Scott, 1963), Michel Crozier (1964),

Amitai Etzioni (1961, 1964), Charles Perrow (1961, 1972), and, more generally, Talcott Parsons (1951) and Robert Merton (1936, 1940, 1949).

What sociology brought to public administration was an awareness of the importance of system and structure to understanding how things turn out as they do in institutions. The core unit of structural analysis is the *role*, defined as the sets of stabilized expectations that organizations comprise. Human beings are seen as role players who simply respond to "role senders" who transfer expectations to them. "Personality" is defined out of the picture. From this perspective, given persons will take on whatever "personality"—defined as pattern of attitudes and behavior—the structural setting in which they find themselves induces.

The other major focus of sociological analysis is *system*. The idea of system refers to a number of related concepts. The first is the notion that social "entities" such as organizations have a discrete reality and an existence independent of the people who compose them. This view sees an organization as more than the sum of its parts, analogous to an organism that seeks to survive and prosper in its environment. Second, a defining aspect of system is that a change in one part will affect all the other parts. The components of a system are all to some degree interdependently linked. Third, systems are characterized by a set of "functional requisites." These are categories of activity that must be performed if the system is to survive: defining and seeking to attain goals, inputting and transforming resources into usable values, obtaining and socializing new members, and coordinating and managing tensions among and between components (Parsons, 1951). Of special note is that all these requisites are *essential* or of equal importance. Failure to attend sufficiently to any of them will cause the system to "die."

It seems clear that the systems perspective provided substantial enhancement to the Man of Reason ideology. Human collectivities could now be regarded as beyond their parts and hence, by implication, not comprehensible except from a superordinate perspective. Further, because systems were seen to operate in lawlike patterns, such a perspective would need to be grounded in scientific expertise. The Man of Reason could now assume the posture of system manager and attend to it as if he were a physician and the system a human body. Rather than viewing dissent or any other heterodox behavior in political terms, to be resisted in the open (and capricious) political arena or with risky shows of authority, one could now "professionally" judge such behaviors as "dysfunctional"—that is, as impairing the ability of the system to perform its functional requisites. In sum, systems theory provided the basis for a new kind of legitimation for Men of Reason: Because human behavior and social life were now going to be seen in technical terms, politics could be forfeited in favor of social management or, in its "proactive" form, engineering.

Turning systems theory to such an ideological purpose required, as noted earlier, a highly selective reading of it, however. In fact, rather than showing how Men of Reason could now technically lead organizational systems, the summary conclusion to be drawn from organizational sociology was that *the intentional control of social systems in the manner presumed by the organization and management theorists of the postwar period is impossible.* How is this so? What was typically left out or deemphasized in the representation of systems theory to the field of public administration?

First, I return to the point discussed earlier regarding Simon's denial of the applicability of the principle of conservation of energy to the world of social systems. An axiological premise of systems theory is that all functional requisites are essential. Therefore, organizations, as systems that emphasize goal attainment over all else (this is their defining characteristic), are by definition going to be beset with irrational "compensatory" behavior patterns. This means simply that because organizations are oriented toward goal productivity, other functional requisites have to be subordinated. This subordination sets off implicit strains in the system that induce members to behave in ways that compensate for the deemphasis on essential functions (Etzioni, 1960). The project of organizational sociology could be said to be to document the pattern of such strains and how it produces an "informal organization" working to relieve them. Empirical studies show that a law closely analogous to the principle of conservation of energy operates in the social world just as it does in the physical world. The best that managers can do is constantly "chase the tail" of the informal organization, monitor it, and reactively seek to ameliorate its effects on the formal system (Homans, 1950).

Second, organizational sociology has documented that the "double-edged sword effect," seen at the level of the functional requisites, operates through all aspects of the structure of organizations. Condensed to its essence, the idea here is that every attempt formally to specify goals and other aspects of structure creates not only clarity and a singular sense of purpose but also ambiguity and a diversion of purpose. Robert Merton (1936, 1940) showed, for example, that formal rules not only achieve their intended purpose of providing clear guidance to workers about what they must do in their roles—thereby *lessening* the need for close and punitive supervision and making goal attainment more effective—but also provide information about the *minimum* that workers can do in their roles and escape sanction. This allows workers, in order to be safe, to retreat behind the rule and do only what it says they must, thus lessening goal attainment and *increasing* the need for close and punitive supervision. Every aspect of Weber's ideal type of bureaucracy has been analyzed in this fashion (Etzioni, 1961; Gouldner, 1954). Again, this leaves managers— inevitably—(as Men of Reason) with only the possibility of "chasing the tails" of such unintended effects. March and Simon discount this implication, however, by claiming that it is merely a conclusion drawn from an unnecessarily narrow "machine model" of organizational behavior. Yet in doing this, they are in effect issuing a blanket refusal of sociological systems theory itself. The sociological picture of managers certainly does not show them as able to control the organization from their leadership positions.

A last aspect of the sociological perspective that was effectively left out of its incorporation into the field of public administration is the problem of scientific objectivity in the study of social systems. This is the issue of the sociology of knowledge to which I alluded at the opening of this chapter in recounting my relationship with Gideon Sjoberg and the self-referentiality problem that I discussed in Simon's approach to managerial control. Because sociology is the study of the effect of social vectors on people, the doing of sociology itself must be affected by the social context in which it is carried out. Objectivity in the study of social systems is problematic when viewed with this awareness; the possibility of objective, intentional, managerial control is also a virtual impossibility (MacIntyre, 1984). Because I have already discussed this matter as it applies to Simon, I want here to carry it one step further. An extension of the logic of self-referentiality implicit in social analysis carries one to the view that social role performances are simply dramaturgical enactments and not at all the "rational" responses to the expectations of role senders that standard sociological analysis makes them out to be. This perspective on social life was developed and carried forward by the school of sociology known as ethnomethodology and interpretivism (Garfinkel, 1967; Heritage, 1984). It is a recent addition to organization and management theory, I think for the obvious reason that it depicts the Man of Reason as a kind of Wizard of Oz: A little character masquerading as an all-powerful godlike figure who pretends to control everything but actually has no real control.

I hope that these few comments suggest the dimension of the distortion that was entailed in bringing organizational sociology into the field of public administration. The sociological perspective was employed as an extension of and support for the idea that Men of Reason, as managers, can intentionally and rationally direct the affairs of organizations. It was ill suited, if not entirely inappropriate, for this task, but it had the required effect. It worked partly because of the plausibility of the systems metaphor itself. There was a general desire to see social life as merely entailing technical questions that could be managed, and despite its many conceptual problems, systems theory provided a seemingly plausible way of thinking in such terms. The other reason organizational sociology worked as a support to management as control was that the hegemony of the Man of Reason ideology itself legitimated the selective reading that came into public administration. The conceptual tensions were overlooked because the war effort had given such a large boost to the belief in rational leadership. As a result, March and Simon (1958) could attack Frederick Taylor for being insensitive and mechanistic and set out Merton's analysis of the unintended effects of rules (recounted above) and other aspects of organizational structure—all of which they did in *Organizations*—yet deny the ironies entailed in this.

More Organizational Sociology: The Subfield of Interorganizational Relationships

One of the most remarkable aspects of the Traditionalist literature is the dearth of research and theory on the politics of administration. Because the Traditionalist school was founded on the idea that administration involves policy making, it seems that many would have followed Paul Appleby's lead and studied administrative politics. This did not happen, however, and the Traditionalists largely taught the political aspects of administration through examples documented in the Inter-University Case Program (ICP) studies.

Of course, the Traditionalists were "atheoretical conceptualists" who believed that administrative reality was too complex to be comprehended by the linear causal mode of thought. Also, they were primarily interested in educating future practicing administrators, and as I have noted, they felt it best to teach the topic of politics purely through examples. The connection of administration to the political world was not formally acknowledged, and the moralistic bent of the Traditionalists disposed them to go along with this official appearance. It seemed enough to expose students only to case illustrations of administrative politics, without theoretical editorializing. The grounding for a theoretical understanding of the politics of public administration had to come, therefore, from outside the field. Again, the source was sociology—specifically the sociology of interorganizational relations—and the venue again was the work of Herbert Simon and his collaborators.

The hallmark study of interorganizational relationships, also known as the study of organization-environment relations, was the aforementioned Philip Selznick's *T.V.A. and the Grass Roots* (1949). What Selznick discovered was that the Tennessee Valley Authority, facing the task of legitimating itself in a local political setting that was hostile to it, found it necessary to surrender a significant amount of its policy-making discretion to powerful elements in its environment to gain their good opinion and cooperation. In the case of less powerful elements, the organization found ways of *appearing* to grant access to its policy processes while in fact it was simply using these environmental units as sources of information. Selznick provided the field with an idea and a jargon term that has served as a key point of reference for understanding the political aspects of administration—*cooptation*—in the two forms I just described: informal (real power sharing) and formal (sham power sharing).

The notable exception to the dearth of research into administrative politics is Leiper Freeman's (1955) study of the legislative relations of the Bureau of Indian Affairs in the U.S. Department of the Interior. Freeman found that this agency's orientation toward its mission oscillated in a regular pattern, shifting from a policy of containment of Indians on reservations to one of seeking to promote their integration into mainstream American society. The oscillation was driven by the waxing and waning of the political fortunes, in the larger political arena, of the two sets of interests behind these opposite policies.

The Inter-University Case Program series contained a number of excellent studies of agency-environment relationships. These atheoretical, historical narratives depicted instances of agencies failing completely to cope with political conditions and being "killed off" by politics (The Grazing Fee Dilemma; Foss, 1960) as well as instances in which agencies were successful in fending off even severe assaults by

political forces (The Battery Additive Controversy; Lawrence, 1962).
The understandings that study of these stories produced, however,
were left largely implicit.

It was Herbert Simon and his collaborators, in two chapters of their
innovative 1950 textbook *Public Administration* (Simon et al., 1950),
who offered a theoretic framework for understanding administrative
politics. This perspective, following organizational sociology, viewed
the agency as a discrete entity that had to "look out for itself" in the
political jungle surrounding it. Although the Traditionalists well understood the fragmented pattern of political power in the U.S. system
and acknowledged that agencies had to fend for themselves by managing their public images and building alliances with interest groups
and congressional committees, they cast this understanding within
the frame of a commitment to presidential leadership. There was
deference to the notion that the presidency was the locus of a coherent,
coordinated sense of policy direction. Agencies were depicted as
fending for themselves in their own "whirlpools of political activity"
but at the same time following the president's lead.

Simon et al. (1950), in *Public Administration*, diverged from this
view. Though continuing—as in Simon's *Administrative Behavior*—to
take as their main inspiration Barnard's inducements-contributions
model of organizational commitment, they depicted the agency-
environment situation in explicitly sociological systems theory terms.
Agencies were led by executives who compromised agency goals in
return for the resources they needed. Notably absent was the idea that
the agency was part of a larger, containing institution of governance to
which it showed a normative commitment and deference. The focus
was on the managing executive and his or her manipulation of the
environment to further the interests of the organization. The main
issue was the attachment of the organization's personnel to its goals
and identity and ways in which this attachment restricted the ability
of the executive to adapt.

At first glance, it appeared that Simon had agreed through his
collaborators to back away from the positivist epistemological commitment he had staked out in *Administrative Behavior.* Citing the
Traditionalist hero, Paul Appleby, *Public Administration* states flatly
that administration involves policy making and is always to some
extent political. However, the way the perspective is framed leaves the
legislative arm of government in final control of policy, and contending
groups in the agency's environment are shown to hold not differing
value positions but different ideas of how efficient agencies are in

implementing the goals they have been given. Administrative politics is thus still a politics of instrumentalism and a rational process whereby the political executive makes calculations as to how much the goals of the agency can be compromised while still maintaining a sufficient level of employee commitment to meet the executive's idea of the essential mission. This is not politics as the term is usually meant, but simply another version of value-free rationalism, now reduced to the essential schema of deciding *what* one wants to do and then *how* one wants to do it. Any doubt about this can be resolved by consulting the invectives that Victor Thompson (one of Simon's collaborators on the text under discussion) issues in his book *Without Sympathy or Enthusiasm* (1975) against the idea of a normatively concerned, truly political public administration.

The path set by Simon et al. (1950) thus laid the foundation for a newly enhanced image of the Man of Reason. It helped set a context in which Wildavsky's *Politics of the Budgetary Process* (1984) could be written, creating a new image of the administrator as a political player (a "budgeteer") in the funding process. Wildavsky's study, after all, must be counted as a key work in the literature of organization/environment relations. Politics itself (as policy making), now transformed into a rational process of environmental adaptation, came under the purview of the Man of Reason as organizational scientist-executive. The movement in this direction was given a strong boost by research publications coming from the new Center for the Study of Administrative Science at the University of Pittsburgh (Thompson, 1959). The sociologist James D. Thompson, working from the center and later the School of Business at Indiana University, made major theoretical and research contributions to the new "technical" understanding of organization/environment relations (Thompson, 1967; Thompson & McEwen, 1958). Thompson's work was influential in stimulating the development of other work on the organization/environment interface, both in the business school organization theory community and in the field of public administration (Kronenberg, 1977; Lawrence & Lorsch, 1969; Terreberry, 1968; White, 1973a). Gary Wamsley and Mayer Zald's *The Political Economy of Public Organizations* (1973) was a key work in providing a needed theoretic frame for understanding the environmental situation of public agencies.

The Administrative Science Center, however, brought a perspective to organization studies that sought to comprehend the entire spectrum of factors affecting organizational life, from general culture to the specifics of production technologies. Harold J. Leavitt, at one time president of the University of Pittsburgh during a period of major organizational innovation, was the inaugurating editor of a new journal, *The Administrative Science Quarterly*, committed to the idea of a "generic" organizational science that sought to construct generalizations valid for all organizations—public, private, or voluntary. The new image of the executive as organizational scientist was given another boost through the implication that organization studies could be a "basic" science.

But what about the relationship of the organization/environment focus to the Man of Reason ideology in the field of public administration? I have already noted that incorporating this perspective gave the Man of Reason administrator role an additional dimension. He could now be seen as legitimately involved in the politics of policy making under the label of managing the environmental relations of the organization. This activity was rendered consistent with the technical role orientation—not being involved in questions of value. The distortion involved in this (a kind of linguistic sublimation) seems obvious.

In addition, the idea of the agency executive as manager of "interorganizational" or environmental relations begged the question of what point of reference was to be used for such maneuverings. The agency leader was left in the position of acting on the basis of "what is good for my organization is good for everybody" (like the CEO of General Motors). This was an interesting congruence with the Traditionalist notion of institutionalism; however, the Traditionalists saw the presidency as a superordinate check on the agency's motive to further its programs. To the environmental manager, the overhead executive was simply another unit in the environment to be managed. Hence, in the context of public administration, interorganizational relations provided a venue for moving the interest group pluralist idea of doing the business of governance inside the boundaries of the administrative system. The Man of Reason as agency executive could now truly be a power player in the elite game of policy making.

Organizational Psychology and Social Psychology

I mentioned earlier Simon's book with James March, *Organizations* (March & Simon, 1958) and his attack on Frederick Taylor's insensitivity to human psychology. March and Simon also presented in this key work the best and most relevant of what was known at the time about the social psychology of organizational life. In doing so, they opened the way for the incorporation of this material into the field of public administration. Simon and his collaborators laid a general basis for this change in their textbook, but the schematic, "scientific-looking" presentation of such material in *Organizations* gave it a compelling legitimacy and sense of currency.

The core of the social psychological approach to understanding organizations as it came into public administration was again the idea of role, and Katz and Kahn's *The Social Psychology of Organizations* (1966) became required reading for students in the field. There are close ties in this analysis to the structural understanding employed by sociology generally. The psychological emphasis carried structural analysis of the connection between the person and the role to a more intimate level. Where sociology provided a way of doing a gross vector analysis of behavior, in which the force and direction of role expectations were seen to produce "resultant" behaviors, social psychology carried the vector analysis deeper, inside the "black box of the role" to the person in the role, showing the microdynamics of role vectors and their effect on behavior.

With this and the other incorporations of social science approaches into the field, the perspective of the Man of Reason was drastically revised in the direction of becoming more mechanical and detailed. Where the Traditionalists saw administrative events in the large, general, and rather vague, indeterminate terms of institutions and timeless archetypal patterns, the Modernists theorized in terms of determinately interacting variables that could be identified, understood, and manipulated by those in managerial positions. Again, the manager was depicted as the operator of a sophisticated technology of human control.

This new emphasis carried over into a movement to direct organizational change. For the most part, the primary tools were improvements in work routines and economic incentives. With awareness of "human relations," however, beginning with the famous Hawthorne studies and enhanced by psychological research, knowledge reached the state at which it could be applied programmatically.

This came mainly in the shape of the organization development movement. The earliest forms of such change efforts were "programmed" leadership training. The Blake and Mouton grid approach is an example of this approach (Blake & Mouton, 1964). The basic format was, first, to refer the change effort to an ideal leadership style in which maximum emphasis on task was combined with maximum emphasis on people or relationship. Using this model as a goal, the consultants carried out a diagnostic activity that indicated how the organization's leaders were operating at present. Then training and team-building activities were applied for bringing the organization's leadership styles closer to the ideal.

In this, of course, we can see all the more vividly how Taylor's scientific management idea of the "one best way" was raised to new heights. It is also obvious that March and Simon's (1958) critique of Taylor was a blatant instance of projection. In the context of the late 1950s, however, this was not so clear. The scientistic-technical mood of the postwar period made it seem that scientific analysis and the identification of optimum techniques could generate a superconscious perspective on the social world. In the world emerging in the 1950s, this reached a degree of intensity that gave it a qualitatively different texture. The Man of Reason as culture figure reached an unprecedented degree of power and legitimacy. Dwight Eisenhower's warning against the dangers of the increasing hegemony of a "military-industrial complex" is one striking testimony to this fact.

The Transformation of Traditionalism

The profound change taking place in the field during this time marked what was, in essence, the demise of Traditionalism as a school of thought. Although sales of the ICP case studies as teaching materials continued to grow steadily, they were used more and more as illustrations for theories than, as they were intended, to suggest to students the ultimately unfathomable reality of administration situations, a reality that made "various conclusions" the only possible mode of generalization. Modernism had triumphed. As a result, Traditionalism itself started a process of self-transformation. Accepting Simon's "decision-making schema" as at least a nominal frame, those identified with Traditionalism began conducting studies of policy decision making with a gesture toward using cases as the basis for theoretic generalization. The ICP program initiated a series of such studies with funding from the National Aeronautics and Space Agency's universities program. The title of one of these studies, *What Manned Space Program After Reaching the Moon: Government Attempts to Decide* (Redford & White, 1971), suggests the new, amalgamated orientation that Traditionalist researchers were seeking to forge. This perspective had roots in political science, in the proposals of Harold Lasswell (1971) that the study of government be framed as a policy science. Developments that I will discuss shortly, however, indicate the difficulty of identifying an unambiguous place for the study of policy once the Traditionalist's institutionalist conceptual frame was rendered anachronistic. In addition to the turn toward policy decision making, some Traditionalists issued meditations on the development of the field and reflective assessments of the institutional apparatus of government in the United States. Though many of these works—notably E. S. Redford's *Democracy in the Administrative State* (1969)—have attained the status of classic literature in the field and teach timeless lessons about the nature and functioning of American bureaucracy, in the setting of the day they marked the "tailing off" of Traditionalism rather than its rejuvenation in a new direction.

The Comparative Administration Movement

In addition to the demise of Traditionalism and the distillation from various social science sources of a new scientific decision-making/ environment-managing model of the agency executive, elaboration of the Man of Reason ideology proceeded on a broader front—as developer of nations. The backdrop for this was provided in part by the success of the Marshall Plan for European recovery after World War II. The end of the war marked also the beginning of the end of classical colonialism, and newly liberated nations began to proliferate.

Sensing the possibility for the development of new markets, U.S. foundations funded studies of how to modernize these new countries and other existing "underdeveloped" societies as well. In the field of political science, this initiative led to an interest in constitution framing, especially the nexus of cultural patterns and the development/functioning of governmental institutions (Beer, Ulam, Spiro, Wahl, & Eckstein, 1958; Spiro, 1959). In the field of public administration, it produced the Comparative Administration Group (CAG), led by Fred Riggs (1965, 1991, 1994), a brilliant theoretician who found initial inspiration in Simon's work. This group of scholars embarked on a dazzlingly ambitious research program: to theorize government from the outside in, from culture through social institutions to political and administrative process (Guess, 1989; Heady, 1989).

A wide array of "area studies" of specific nations was produced, as well as theoretic speculations of the highest order—on such topics as the nature of space, time, and, in Riggs's case, the "diffraction" of social institutions (Braibanti, 1969; Esman, 1972; Heady, 1966; Lapolambara, 1963; Montgomery & Siffin, 1966; Riggs, 1965; Siffin, 1957, 1966a, 1966b). The ostensible point was to build social institutions and bring about broad national development so that these emerging countries could become strong trading partners in the world economy. Because America had emerged from the war as the only standing modern industrial system, it was seen as the source point for knowledge and models of how to achieve social development in other contexts. Although CAG produced much fine research and writing, disillusionment grew over the question of whether the goal of generating practical and effective development strategies would ever be attained through the work of the group. When CAG's funding eventually ran out, the movement officially ended at a conference at Syracuse University in 1971, where Warren Illchman, a political scientist then at the University of California at Berkeley, read a final plenary session paper in which he bluntly raised questions about the integrity and validity of the entire enterprise (Henry, 1987). CAG marked an important point in the maturation of the field of public administration, a radical opening up and out of its intellectual perspective. The study of comparative government cast the Man of Reason in the heroic role of affecting the destiny of whole societies, and it sought, at least, to provide a knowledge base that went far beyond the expertise of rationalism that Simon initiated. Entailed in doing this, of course, were all the normative tensions and contradictions that afflict the enterprise of colonialism generally. These were only overlaid, not resolved or diminished, by the free-market brand of American colonialism that superceded the traditional cultural usurpation and political domination of the European variety.

What the United States in this period introduced was a curious reverse colonialism epitomized in the epithet of the day, drawn from the title of a widely read book, *The Ugly American* (Lederer, 1958). Although the term was generally taken to refer to Americans who engaged in the kind of snobbishness and condescension characteristic of traditional colonialism, the actual ugly American was one who was not "beautiful," who pitched in with the natives, developed relationships with them, and worked side by side with them to help them improve their lot. The critique that the book made was that there were so *few* ugly Americans on the development scene. The United States, as a colonial power, became distinctive for wanting to have nothing to do with underdeveloped countries except to come in, sell them something, and leave. This attitude was consistent with the new techno-cratic identity of the Man of Reason: The utopia that he offered was to be gained through objective manipulation that produced immediate tangible gains.

The New Man of Reason in the New America

The intellectual transformations I have been describing here took place and were probably only possible in a supportive sociocultural context. I alluded to a few such conditions that were conducive to Simon's introduction of the rationalist mode of thought in the postwar period. Other developments supported the elaboration of his approach in public administration. The war experience had created a great deal of military interest in the phenomenon of group leadership. After the war ended, money poured into universities to fund studies of small group leadership and aspects of social life related to it. The Korean War—giving America its first experience of what seemed to be broad disaffection in its military forces—created an awareness of the phe-nomenon of mind control. The term *brainwashing,* partly as a result of a popular movie of the time *The Manchurian Candidate,* entered the vernacular. The rapid growth of the industrial sector of the economy during these years, and the labor strife that accompanied it, increased a concern with management and worker relations. The public gener-ally became aware of management as a category of social life, and the issues involved in the move to humanize and optimize it were pre-sented to mass audiences in stage plays and movies such as *The Pajama Game* and television dramas such as *Playhouse 90.* The conceptual tensions entailed by the new rationalistic identity of the Man of Reason derive from the generic issues that Simon's rhetoric finessed. These distortions were required so that the other social science approaches I have described could be added to Simon's generic model. Taken as a whole, they create a remarkable picture of social ideology. Just as social conditions make ideology possible, however, so can they work toward undoing it. This is the next part of the story of American public administration literature.

6

A Selected Intellectual History of the Field II

From Minnowbrook to the Present

> To be in a Passion you Good may do,
> But no Good if a Passion is in you.
>   *William Blake*

The Social and Intellectual Context
of the Minnowbrook Conference

In the fall of 1968, at a remote conference center outside Syracuse, New York, a group of public administration professionals held a conference that marked a turning point in the intellectual history of American public administration. Whether something happened at the meeting that *caused* a turning point to occur or whether the meeting was simply a marker of a shift in the intellectual terrain of the field, there seems no disputing that it was the beginning of the end of an era. To understand this, it is useful to look at some key social and intellectual conditions that surrounded the meeting itself.

The most important of these, perhaps, was the disarray into which the field of political science began to fall at the end of the 1960s. Throughout the 1950s and early 1960s, the social sciences had become, through research grants, more integrated into the institutional structure of American society. Increasingly, this research was based on the methodology of behavioralism and its theoretical frame, functionalism.

In political science, functionalism/behavioralism operated not only as an explicit research orientation but also as an implicit value orientation that infused a variety of research, from "logical theory exercises" such as Robert Dahl's famous *Preface to Democratic Theory* (1956) to the equally famous *American Voter* (Campbell, Converse, Miller, & Stokes, 1960) series. Although uncharitable observers had already begun to call mainstream political science an apology for the American brand of political domination, on the whole, a normative consensus existed among political scientists that the American political system was working well as a democracy.

The model that reflected this view saw the American political process as "democratic pluralism," in which citizens participated through groups organized around specific economic, ideological, or policy interests. Through such groups, citizens could have at least a *negative* impact on the policy-making process so that no one group would be able unilaterally to control outcomes; each group had the ability to stop policy initiatives that damaged its interests. Even at the local level, pluralism prevented the emergence of a single dominating elite group (Dahl, 1961).

The model depicted policy making as an essentially conservative process, benignly suppressing extremes. Stability was ensured because the system never produced severe threats to any group. Also, citizens belonged to a multiplicity of overlapping groups, and these overlapping interests and memberships worked to mitigate the development of extreme opinions and positions. The summary judgment that political science passed on the U.S. political system was quite favorable. No one was left out, the system did not allow anyone to get hurt, and tendencies to extremism were blunted. Some political scientists even went so far as to judge that voter apathy was a positive sign that average citizens were so happy with the way the system was operating they did not feel the need to participate (Dahl, 1967).

This rosy picture was believable because America was still living under the "Let's all pull together—we're all in it together" ethos of the war, and the postwar economic boom had reinvigorated the American belief that "anybody can make it big here." No one acknowledged any visible evidence of serious social problems either. In the minds of most Americans at the time, poverty, and certainly hunger and starvation, did not exist in America—nor did brutality in prisons, environmental pollution, sexism, family dysfunction, child abuse, and so on. Even the obvious racism had not yet configured active opposition; despite *Brown vs. Board of Education* in 1954, segregated "equality" was still widely viewed (at least by whites) as a plausible idea. It seemed that no one was protesting or complaining except the labor unions, who caused problems by striking or threatening strikes. These typically occurred over the issue of higher wages, however, and were "understandable" as a demand that had its source in human nature, not in the arrangement of social or economic institutions.

Americans were rudely awakened from this dreamlike state with the Watts riots of 1964. Though America had had a long history of often-violent civil protest, the masses of people had always experienced it at one remove, through after-the-fact media and historical accounts. With the trouble in Watts, Americans were astounded to witness live television coverage showing, to mention only one example, National Guard soldiers spraying a black woman's car with bullets from a jeep-mounted machine gun as she attempted to drive through a street barricade. Clearly, things were not as they had been thought to be, and they became progressively and inescapably worse as the civil rights movement matured, the war in Vietnam threw thousands of protesters into the streets, and body counts moved onto the televised evening news. America haltingly began to acknowledge the harsh physical, social, and economic realities that existed within its borders.

Intellectual leadership of the country passed to writers who were either nonacademic or defiantly marginal to the academic arena. Writers such as Rachel Carson (1962) paved the way in this respect and were followed by social critics such as Michael Harrington (1962). They were initially seen as radical (in Carson's case, "hysterical"), but their books became popular texts in college and university courses, implicitly drawing into question the utility and "relevance" for social life of a traditional academic perspective (Jamison & Eyerman, 1994). Ralph Nader's work had a special impact in that he exposed the irresponsible attitudes of corporate leaders toward the public welfare. This impact was solidified and strengthened when it was revealed that Nader had been the object of a calculated program of spying, threats, and entrapment designed and authorized by top corporate leaders.

All institutional sectors of American society, including the universities, similarly began to be called into question. Clark Kerr (1967), a university leader himself, described universities as stodgy, intellectually reactionary, and failing both students and society. Student movements for wide-ranging reforms exploded on campuses and included demands for the evaluation of teaching and the reexamination of curricula. Most interesting for my discussion, however, is that the social sciences in particular became objects of controversy to the general public. Black Americans complained that they had been ignored, or worse, denigrated, by research instruments based on biased indicators such as IQ and standardized test scores. Native Americans began issuing similar complaints about the way that anthropologists had defined them as "culturally marginal peoples" prone to high levels of social problems such as alcoholism. A newly invigorated feminist movement surged forward to expose the distortions and prejudices that social science had institutionalized under its "objective" methodologies. The controversy surrounding social science heightened during the late 1960s with the publication of the Moynihan Report, which blamed the black poverty cycle on the matriarchal structure of the black family (U.S. Department of Labor, 1965).

Similar developments occurred in other fields, including movements to establish "new" studies in history, economics, psychology, and sociology. The writings of the Frankfurt School critical theorists, especially Herbert Marcuse and Jürgen Habermas, were widely read and discussed. Entire academic literatures developed critiquing the Enlightenment, technology and technicism, interest-group/pluralist democracy, liberalism, and rationalism across the social sciences (Catron & Harmon, 1981; Connolly, 1969; Dolbeare, 1974; Ferkiss, 1974; Lockhard, 1976; Lowi, 1969; Marini, 1971; McConnell, 1966; Playford & McCoy, 1967; Schuman, 1973; Stanley, 1972; Waldo, 1971; Walker, 1966; Wills, 1971; Wolff, 1968).

Political science did not escape the firestorm. Its positive interpretation of American politics was called into question in the popular press. An editorial in a major magazine attacked Robert Dahl's work not only for not predicting events such as the Watts riot but for presenting a picture of community politics that tended to blind citizens to the possibility of such occurrences. Inside the universities, student protest leaders and their junior faculty sponsors often came from political science departments. Lines of radical theoretical and philosophical critique emerged in all subfields of the discipline. Almost all of these had as their point of orientation the liberalist/pluralist political order that had so charmed the political science elite.

By the late 1960s, social and political events in America were providing contemporary fuel for these critiques (O'Neill, 1971). Wide-

spread questioning of American institutions followed the turbulent
events of 1968: the assassinations of Robert Kennedy and Martin
Luther King Jr., urban rioting that accompanied the King assassination,
daily televised images of violence and tragedy in Vietnam, and the
disastrous 1968 Democratic presidential nominating convention, during which television brought to American living rooms pictures of
vicious police attacks on mostly middle-class youth carrying out what
were largely nonviolent political demonstrations. Most aspects of
American life became politically charged, as reflected in the feminist
slogan, "The personal is the political." Despite these critiques and
continuing student protests, university political science departments
were still dominated by an elite whose funding ties to the military-industrial (-university) complex remained intact. The rationalist systems
orthodoxy remained the paradigmatic baseline of political science.

In addition to these dramatic external events, there were developments within the field of public administration that implicitly but
significantly influenced what happened at Minnowbrook. Three of the
most notable were (a) the hiring of Alberto Guereirro Ramos, a Brazil-
ian exile, at the University of Southern California (USC); (b) the work
of Neely Gardner in organization behavior; and (c) the establishment
of the Federal Executive Institute in Charlottesville, Virginia. Ramos
(1981) had been educated in Husserlian phenomenology, existential-
ism, and dialectics, and his work at USC, through graduate student
teaching conference presentations and manuscripts, exposed a large
portion of the field to "subjectivist" perspectives, which had been
excluded by the dominant orthodoxy of analytical philosophy. Neely
Gardner (1963, 1965, 1974) was steeped in the client-centered psychology of Carl Rogers, and his very "applied" approach brought a
blatantly psychological and social-psychological focus into the field.

These new (to public administration) intellectual orientations were
seen in practice at the Federal Executive Institute (FEI) under the
direction of Frank Sherwood. The FEI was the flagship training program for federal government executives. It was important to public
administration in a number of ways. First and probably most important, its philosophy of executive development was innovative and
challenging, aimed at producing (or at least providing the opportunity
for) significant personal transformation in the managers who attended
it. The central concept was that content material—new ideas about
how to organize and to manage more effectively—could and would
only be put into practice when it was assimilated in the learning
executive through a process of personal development. The kind of

change in perspective that the experience often produced can be seen in the heterodox writing that some FEI alumni produced, such as Anders Richter's (1970) article, "The Existentialist Executive," published in the *Public Administration Review.* New ideas required new personal capacities for their implementation; thus, the training staff at FEI were oriented toward andragogical teaching methodologies that were more personalistic and psychological than usual. The idea of grounding the educational process in personal development marked a major departure from learning as cognitive assimilation of information and mastery of "impersonal" techniques. At the structural level, the traditional academic idea was consistent with the epistemological belief that information and learning could be regarded as neutral because the "life world" of learners could be assumed to be standard. The FEI idea supported an alternative epistemology: that the life worlds of learners were, to a significant extent, idiosyncratic and variable and that true learning could only take place when the learner was provided the opportunity to reconstruct the learning personally, through an essentially affective process, into a form that was appropriate to the mental world in which he or she was living.

The intellectual setting that had developed by the time that the Minnowbrook meeting took place was one where the hold of some of the strongest intellectual traditions in the social sciences generally and in political science and public administration specifically had been substantially loosened. Major institutional challenges coupled with intellectual critiques and the undermining of the standard cognitive approach to education created the possibility for a considerably different public administration to emerge. It appeared that the "Man of Reason system" had failed and that something different might arise to replace it.

I do not want to exaggerate the picture I am drawing. Awareness of the unacknowledged ideological dimensions in the social sciences provided only a *possibility* for heterodoxy to develop in the field. The most likely outcome in a case in which the ruling elite is grounded in the legitimacy of technique is that it will not only acknowledge problems but embrace them as a renewal of the rationale for control—namely, that someone needs to solve the problems. Critique in an only putatively democratic context, where an elite is actually in control, produces a conservative effect. The existence of critique is essential to maintaining the appearance of democratic ethos that masks the fact that power is actually being wielded by the elite. Critique can produce change only when it focuses on the deeply hidden commitments that sustain a social reality, such as assumptions that rationalize power as arising from human nature or the natural order. What a "democratic" elite such as that constituted by Men of Reason must do is to ensure (a) that dissent and critique occur and (b) that they do not go to the level of the foundational sustaining principles of the existing social world. Minnowbrook and subsequent events produced this type of critique; their initial impact was to help preserve governance by Men of Reason.

Because truly alternative viewpoints did not arise at Minnow-brook, people in the field struggled to render the new intellectual perspectives consistent with traditional ways of thinking by employing a two-way process of assimilation and modification. The result was a great deal of confusion and miscommunication and a period of intellectual disorientation to which Dwight Waldo (1971) referred on numerous occasions (invoking a commonly cited old Chinese curse) as an "interesting time."

The Minnowbrook Meeting and Subsequent Professional Developments

The Minnowbrook meeting itself has been well described by Frank Marini (1971) in the introduction to his edited volume of papers from the conference. In brief, the participants "revolted" against the standard conference format and resolved into a more open and informal forum. Intellectually, perspectives in the group ranged from the most orthodox (positivist and behavioralist) to highly heterodox (phenomenological and psychoanalytical). The clearest common theme was that the field of public administration, intellectually and practically, needed to change. The most important outcome of the meeting was the formation of new intellectual networks that later served to support and sustain the heterodoxy that had existed at the meeting. Representatives of each point of view at the meeting found enough support to go away feeling that each perspective had some legitimacy and relevance to the field.

The meeting also generated considerable professional momentum. Within the next few years, other meetings of the same type were held. These involved people from the original Minnowbrook and others who represented new points of view and who were seeking to change the field. The first of these was organized at a retreat site at Sonoma, California, by Todd La Porte and Robert Biller, both of whom were then at the University of California at Berkeley. A third "Minnowbrook" group meeting was convened at a conference site outside Austin, Texas, the following year. It was organized by Orion White and sponsored by the newly founded Lyndon B. Johnson School of Public Affairs.

It became clear from Minnowbrook and subsequent meetings that no generally agreed-on image of the "new public administration"—or the society it should seek to achieve—was going to emerge. What did develop was the "Minnowbrook sense" of intellectual heterodoxy and dissatisfaction with the status quo in the field. Repeated meetings of roughly the same core group of people also began to create a sense of momentum behind a "New PA" (perforce suggesting a certain tension with those who represented the "Old PA"). Though the idea of the New PA as a movement had been discussed at one follow-up meeting, no clear answer had arisen to such key questions as membership eligibility and common purpose. The group could not even agree that it would be worthwhile to have someone write a sociology-of-knowledge dissertation to explain the forces producing the change in intellectual direction.

Nonetheless, the "movement" gained strength, and it came to a head at the 1970 meeting of the American Society for Public Administration (ASPA), held in Philadelphia, where a rather amazing and unprecedented event occurred. Led by H. George Frederickson, some members identified with the New PA group called a plenary session, renounced the official program of the conference as irrelevant and anachronistic, and announced the formation of an alternative, rump conference of panel sessions on topics that the group considered contemporaneous and socially relevant. The rump panel sessions were well attended, and discussions were lively. In the months following this meeting, whether owing to it or not, top leadership at ASPA changed, and the structure and processes of the organization were opened to a more democratic venue. A revolution of sorts had taken place. As later events demonstrated, however, it was a case of "the more things change, the more they stay the same."

The General Intellectual Orientation
of the New PA Period

Questions of epistemology and ontology formed the focus for the discourse of the New PA. This was only natural, given that the traditional identity of the field of public administration was grounded in neutral scientific expertise. Any *new* public administration, if it were to live up to its name, had to transcend the idea that the bureaucrat was an expert whose only involvement beyond the application of technique was to resolve analytically the ambiguities of policy issues. The idea of positive fact as it had developed in behavioral social science—even as "soft" and probabilistic as it was—could not be left to stand. If there were facts, the application of them through expertise would appear, ultimately, to be the only legitimate idea of the bureaucrat's role.

Tied directly to this issue was the question of human nature. If human beings were no more than rational calculators seeking to reduce their drive-based needs, they could be understood in causal terms, behaving in response to stimuli from their environment. The only question was whether their needs could best be met through centralized, explicitly rational strategies such as planning, or through decentralized, implicitly rational devices such as the market. The sentiment inspiring the New PA was that there was more to people, as both clients of government and agents of their own governance, than this. People as citizen-clients were seen as bringing more than interest-based needs to government; bureaucrats were seen as being more than their ability to calculate rationally. Those who wanted to write a New PA had to find and establish not only an epistemology that undercut the idea of positive fact but also an ontology that showed the human being to be more than just drives, needs, and the capacity to reduce them.

Alberto Guereirro Ramos and Neely Gardner were important in just this respect. Ramos introduced his students to the phenomenological mode of thought as it applied to the study of organizations, and Gardner represented a view of the human being that transcended the economic rationality and sociological "black box" models prevalent at the time. Their influence, working on the New PA group both personally and through their students, was aided greatly by several key books published during this period: Thomas Kuhn's *The Structure of Scientific Revolutions* (1962), Abraham Maslow's *Toward a Psychology of Being* (1968), Michael Polanyi's *Personal Knowledge* (1958), and Peter Berger and Thomas Luckmann's *The Social Construction of Reality* (1966), all of which legitimated the idea of contextual rather than positive fact and a transrational image of human nature.

There were other supporting developments. Among these was the publication of David Silverman's *A Theory of Organizations* (1970), which catalogued the anomalies of the functionalist understanding of

organization life and advocated an interpretivist or social constructionist approach (specifically drawn from Peter Berger) that could
comprehend these anomalies. There was a burst of renewed interest
in the theory of democracy, evidenced in such books as Carole Pateman's *Participation and Democratic Theory* (1970), one point of which
was a reminder that a classical requisite as well as rationale for
democracy was the development of citizens as human beings and not
the satisfaction of interests. A variety of humanistic psychologies came
onto the scene, some of which, such as gestalt, transactional analysis,
and existential psychotherapy, were grounded in heterodox philosophical positions (Berne, 1970, 1972, 1976; Fagas & Shepherd, 1971;
Hatcher & Himmelstein, 1976; Herman & Korenich, 1977; May, 1953;
May, Angel, & Ellenberger, 1958; Perls, Herfferline, & Goodman, 1951;
Smith, 1977). In addition, an interest arose in applying the work of
Carl Jung to the study of organizations. In 1976, John Ingalls, an
organization development consultant, published *Human Energy,* an
application of aspects of Jung's work to understanding organizational
dynamics. By 1974, when the Association for Psychological Type was
established, the Myers-Briggs Types Indicator, based on Jungian theory, had become very popular (as it continues to be today) and was
widely used in management training (Keirsey & Bates, 1978).

　　These multiple opportunities, however, did not produce a coherent
and productive reconsideration of the foundational issues. Indeed,
distortion, misunderstanding, and confusion were the dominant conditions in the discourse. This was most visible in conference discussions. Debates took shape as polarizations. Typically, on one side were
those who held the still-prevailing behavioralist-empiricist view; on
the other were the wide-ranging oppositional perspectives. The old
characterized the new as relativistic, humanistic, nonempirical; the
new saw the old as reactionary and dominative. It seemed that it was
not possible to articulate a coherent middle position (White, 1983).

　　The distortion that this produced can be illustrated in a number of
ways. In the debate focusing on humanistic psychology, for example,
people were seen as either for or against Maslow's view of the human
being. One either believed in self-actualization or not. Middle-of-the-
road perspectives, written, for example, from the Jungian point of view
and holding that Maslow's idea of what human development meant
was off the mark, even containing elements of sexism, racism, and
national chauvinism, were ignored or misunderstood (White, 1973b).
Herbert Shepard (1965), hoping to argue a perspective on human
nature that showed cooperation as natural, pointed out that Maslow's

humanistic theory was actually reactionary in that it showed development as a *need* (and one that could be reversed) rather than as a positive
potential. The debate often seemed to be framed methodologically as
a battle between the "number crunchers" and the "touchy feelies."

The misunderstanding was even more serious with regard to
interpretivism or the social-construction-of-reality perspective. Again,
because the debate was polarized, those working from the social
constructionist position were cast as relativistic nonempiricists who
did not believe in the idea of compelling fact and thought that people
could make reality any way they wanted it. The empiricists were seen,
conversely, as arguing that there was, by necessity, only one true
representation of reality. These distortions had implications for human
intentionality and social change. Despite empiricist fears, the interpretivist view, rather than depicting social reality as open-ended and
up for choice, holds that intentional social change is not possible.
Thus, interpretivism cannot properly be a foundation for programs of
planned social change and indeed must oppose them. This was clearly
spelled out in Berger, Berger, and Kellner's book *The Homeless Mind*
(1974). To argue, therefore, over the question of whether social reality
can be constructed in any way one likes is completely off the point.

Perhaps the oddest aspect of the intellectual scene at this time,
however, was the reaction to Kuhn's *Structure of Scientific Revolutions*
(1962). Kuhn's idea of the incommensurability or mutual exclusivity
of scientific paradigms seemed to pose a dire threat to the reigning
empiricist orthodoxy and, of course, to the Man of Reason ideology.
Obviously, if all knowledge is paradigm dependent, then there is no
way either to ground the exercise of authority in expertise or, correla-
tively, to discount or disregard ideas that are being proposed from
alternative paradigms. Kuhn's opponents first attacked the idea of
paradigm itself as ill defined (as if any term can be defined against all
ambiguity!) and simply read him as not really meaning to say that
paradigms are incommensurable. The debate quickly reached stale-
mate and has remained there, even in the face of Kuhn's subsequent
statements and many well-informed interpretations of him (Astley,
1985; Barnes, 1982; Guba, 1990; Rorty, 1979).

Irrespective of such blockages, innovative work did proceed within
the field of public administration, work that sought to lay the foundation for a fundamentally new definition of the administrator's role.
Leading the movement to bring a new philosophical orientation to the
field, Michael Harmon published *Action Theory for Public Administration* in 1981. Attempting to extend interpretivism, he argued that

administrators and citizens were not limited to behaving as a result of causal determinants but were capable of acting in ways that could "dereify" organizational realities that had been taken as immutably fixed. Robert Denhardt struck a similarly innovative blow for an alternative perspective in his book *In the Shadow of Organization* (1981). Basing his analysis primarily on Jungian psychology, he described much of organizational life as pathological and came to the profoundly heterodox conclusion that the best way to achieve organizational goals was to focus first on the development of the people who staff the organization. This recommendation stood as a direct retort to those who argued against the New PA and the change movement on the grounds that organizations are set up for the purpose of attaining goals, not for the growth of the people in them.

Another line of development working to bring a new philosophical perspective to the field was the incorporation of phenomenology into the study of administration, initially through the work of Jong Jun and Richard VrMeer, both graduates of the USC program and students of Guereirro Ramos (Jun, 1986, 1994). They established a curriculum grounded in phenomenology in the public administration department at the California State University, Hayward beginning in 1968, a program that must be considered one of the most intellectually innovative in the field. Ralph Hummel was also a leader in extending phenomenological understanding, particularly in his 1977 text, *The Bureaucratic Experience*. Although this book engendered a fair degree of controversy, it was very popular, is now in its fourth edition, and was recently appreciated in a review essay in *Public Administration Review* (Ventriss, 1995b).

By far the most the most controversial book of this period in public administration was Frederick Thayer's *An End to Hierarchy! An End to Competition!*, which in subsequent editions had the title of *An End to Hierarchy and Competition* (1981). This was also the book that probably had the greatest impact on discussion in the field. Thayer, as a retired air force colonel, was in a strong position to write such a critique; it seemed that it could not be said (as it typically was about critics of hierarchy) that he did not know how the "real world" worked and why hierarchy was necessary. His argument, however, was misconstrued by the majority of his readers. Given the polarization of the debate surrounding the New PA, Thayer was relegated to the "left" pole and interpreted as arguing for participation or even, some thought, outright anarchy. How competition came into play as a device of domination, and hence an aspect of the hierarchy issue, simply baffled most readers. What he was actually advocating was not "participation" but the creation of structures that would foster a specific kind of contactful, unalienated dialogue among people in organizations and institutions (White, 1990). His agenda in this book was precisely congruent with Mary Follett's. Without this quality of discussion or empowerment, getting rid of hierarchy was not only pointless but a case of going from "the frying pan into the fire." Thayer argued against competitive economic markets precisely because they were too close to the alienated, dominative relations that typically occur under conditions of hierarchy. The widespread misunderstanding of his argument is one of the more revealing instances of how an ideological orthodoxy can structure discourse so as to close off effective challenge.

This is not to say that Thayer proffered an alternative to the field and had it rejected. He did not specify precisely enough what the new kind of dialogue would be like or how the change in consciousness it entailed could be brought about. He suggested that the dialogue would be "something like" what went on in the "T Groups" or "sensitivity labs" of the day but stated that only some worldwide disaster or crisis could bring about the needed change (Heilbroner, 1974). The lack of a better or more positive change strategy was actually the limit to Thayer's otherwise imaginative and highly innovative line of thought.

The intellectual evolution in the field in the 1970s was marked by the type of confusion and miscommunication that surrounded Thayer's work. Despite this, a thematic line of development did begin to appear. The importance of the 1970s as a period of change in America has been underestimated. I believe that subsequent histories will show that the beginning of the end of the Cold War occurred at the demise of the Nixon presidency and that the facile characterization of this ten years as a narcissistic "Me Decade" covers over a much more troubling reality. Underlying the narcissism of the period, and probably producing it, was a social disorientation at the personal level of the most profound sort, the feeling that resulted when traditional institutions had been challenged and critiqued and a president had fallen but when no significant workable idea had emerged as to what or how to do anything differently. This social condition validated Lyndon Johnson's defensive warning, issued at the height of the attacks on his presidency: "Remember, I am the only President you've got." America was facing the classical problem of revolutionaries: tearing down more than can be replaced.

The irony was that there had been no revolution. Even the downfall of Nixon had proceeded in an orderly way. Underneath, Nixon and

Watergate symbolized a general fall from innocence, one that only a young nation such as the United States could have undergone at this stage of world history. What we must remember is that it is the fall from innocence, the encounter with the realities of adult life, that shocks the adolescent into a more balanced assessment of the routines of living that parents model in the hope that the child will adopt them. The net result is usually that the child becomes a contemporized version of the parents. This is what happened to public administration. The field fragmented into a number of approaches, each of which was a reaction to a specific aspect of the various branches of the Modernist school described in the preceding chapter, yet each retained some form of strong continuity with it.

There was a fairly unified response on the part of the "Old PA"—the Traditionalists and the Modernists—to the dissenting presence of the New PA. Their reaction is summarized most vividly in Victor Thompson's *Without Sympathy or Enthusiasm* (1975), a head-on rebuttal to what many of the older members of the field saw as the main point of the New PA critique: The Old PA had become irrelevant because it was so doggedly holding to the "neutral bureaucrat" model of the public administrator. This was not simply a reiteration of Finer's theory of bureaucracy in a democratic government. Members of the Old PA read the New PA as going past even Friedrich's notion (to which many of the Old PA school subscribed) of bureaucratic discretion and advocating that bureaucrats take the initiative to work actively for the realization of certain principles of social justice that transcended any specific policy. This idea seemed to go far beyond any prior concept of the administrator's role, and it was opposed by partisans of both the Finer and the Friedrich side of that debate.

Varieties of the New PA

The aspect of New PA thought that most directly engaged this reaction, and the one that in a sense was the most "conservative," was the definition of the New PA as "equity" set forth by George Frederickson (1980). Frederickson, as a "founding member" of the New PA (he was one of the organizers of the original Minnowbrook meeting), was sensitive to the growing critique that it had no coherent intellectual identity or program. His response was to declare that *social equity* was the grounding of the New PA identity. His position was that "equity" could serve as an operational definition of the public interest for administrators. They could work actively to realize equity in whatever way they wished, given their particular roles. Dvorin and Simmons also espoused this idea in their book *From Amoral to Humane Bureaucracy* (1972), which advocated a humanistically concerned, activist stance for public administrators. In a sense, the argument for equity-oriented activism could be seen as radical; as an intellectual position, however, it was the most conservative or traditional of the emergent New PA responses because it did not reach the level of ontology and epistemology.

[handwritten margin note: New PA focused not ontology on ontology.]

This definition of the New PA was highly influential in the mainstream of the field, however. Many took it to be a definitive statement of the New PA. It was given force and legitimacy by its congruence with John Rawls's influential book *A Theory of Justice* (1971), which argued in an imaginative new way for a utilitarian idea of distributive justice. Rawls's argument was widely read, drew much attention and comment, and had great influence on social thought at the time.

To the left of the equity position was a point of view that can be termed "neoconservative anti-administrationism." The precursor or backdrop for this perspective was provided by Vincent Ostrom's *The Intellectual Crisis in Public Administration* (1973). Ostrom argued from what was to emerge as a standard "American conservative" position: The founders had not envisioned a hierarchical pattern of government, especially one under an overarching presidential leader. Rather, the political formula of America called for decentralized government that provided services as closely as possible along free-market lines, maximizing individual choice and government responsiveness. The rationale for this view was the founders' distrust of governmental authority, especially administrative authority. This sentiment inspired work extending this critique into a practical argument for governmental decentralization and the use of market devices to provide government services. Public choice gained momentum in the 1970s and has been developed further through the work of Elinor Ostrom (1975) and students of the Ostroms such as Gordon Whitaker (1980). Because this point of view was grounded in the worldview of economics and as such was explicitly antibureaucracy, it could be considered more to the "right" than the equity perspective. However, this is an intellectually nontraditional idea, outside the frame of any part of the Old PA, and hence I place it to the left of the equity advocates. It suggests, after all, that Men of Reason are not only unnecessary but are inherently ineffective because they are compromised by their own self-interest.

Such an implication is made vivid by other work in this school, grounded in the idea that a rational process of policy implementation by bureaucracies is simply impossible. In what became a classic study of the Oakland jobs creation project, Jeffrey Pressman and Aaron Wildavsky (1973) argued that a complex interplay of self-interest prevents programs from achieving their objectives. Policy objectives will always be subverted at the level of implementation because the bureaucrats administering the policy have only a peripheral interest in achieving them. Other objectives, such as furthering careers, will have higher priority. The result is that the implementation process becomes displaced onto objectives that are not necessarily complementary to policy and that can be flatly inconsistent with them. Eugene Bardach presented an elaboration of this critique in his *The Implementation Game* (1977), a novel and biting analysis of bureaucratic behavior. The prescription following from this line of analysis was to design policies that avoided the administrative process as much as possible, such that successful implementation did not depend on bureaucrats.

Theodore Lowi's widely read and influential book *The End of Liberalism* (1969) must be counted as striking a similar neoconservative chord. Following Grant McConnell's analysis of the coterminous rise of interest group power and administrative authority, Lowi argued for the establishment of a juridical democracy, one in which law would be explicit, administrative discretion minimized, and presidential power and responsibility greatly enhanced. The role of bureaucracy as an arena for policy development would thereby be virtually eliminated.

Farther still to the left is a position holding that bureaucrats should *directly involve* citizens in the process of designing and implementing policy. This could be called simply the "participatory administration" movement (Pateman, 1970). It had a widespread impact in the real world of administration, especially at the local level in urban areas, through various community action programs of Lyndon Johnson's Great Society. The approach is radical in advocating an ostensible shift in policy discretion from administrators to citizens. It seems, then, to be a direct assault on the position of the Man of Reason. The problem, however, is that though there were some imaginative and interesting attempts to do so (Friedmann, 1973), advocates of participation never theorized the details of an effective participatory process and the role that relevant expertise needs to play in it. The result was that actual experiments in participation frequently resolved into interminable meetings according to Robert's Rules of Order or incoherent "rap sessions" of intolerable length. The participationists actually fit traditional thinking about democratic process and administration, and as such, the novelty of their argument was more its mood and tone than any theoretically informed prescription for action that it contained. In the end, this perspective was radical only in a relative sense. Indeed, I have witnessed many instances in which Men of Reason have arranged participatory events just to let them run their inevitably disastrous course—demonstrating that "given that human nature is what it is, participation always fails." The lesson, of course, is that Men of Reason are needed; nothing will ever get accomplished without their leadership.

Continuing to the left on the continuum of approaches that arose from the New PA is a body of thinking that *did* represent a departure from the conventional frame: a new approach to organization development (OD). The version of OD that arose in the Modernist context was the programmed or "canned" variety that used standardized development processes aimed at bringing target organizations closer to a predefined ideal management style, such as the Blake-Mouton grid mentioned in the previous chapter. This change strategy was widely accepted largely because it offered no surprises: The process and the objectives were set beforehand; those buying it knew what they were getting. The alternative to this that arose in the context of the New PA was "situation-emergent OD" (Kirkhart & White, 1974). Its defining premise was that no one on the outside of an organization, such as a consultant, could accurately determine an organization's key issues and what should be done to resolve them. Effective change must be grounded in self-diagnosis and treatment. The role of the situation-emergent OD consultant was to set up and facilitate the processes (the structured conversations that would or could not otherwise occur) by which organizational self-development could be carried out.

To many, situation-emergent OD appeared simply to be a version of the "participationism" that I described. There is, however, a fundamental difference. Whereas participation involved the kind of rhetorically free-swinging, democratic rough and tumble of a political caucus session conducted under Robert's Rules of Order, situation-emergent OD prescribed a highly structured and tightly managed process for consensus building and collective decision making. Such a structure and process were seen as the best, even the only, way to ensure that all points of view, all preferences, in short, all relevant contributions by members of the group, could be brought to bear on a situation. Its decision rule was collective commitment rather than the "majority rule" idea of democratic theory.

Identifying this difference suggests that the situation-emergent OD approach was grounded in a fundamentally different set of orienting assumptions. Its "radical" axiology was composed of the following beliefs: First, social realities are subjectively held and hence accurately discernible only "from the inside"; second, the answers to problems are better found in direct response to them than in generalized and objective expertise alone; third (a corollary to the second), all people have a capacity for generative action, for creating new approaches to situations rather than just responding to them.

It seems fairly obvious how such an axiology strikes at the foundation of the Man of Reason approach to collective life. For "reasoned leadership" to seem sensible as a method of governance, reality must be singular and standard so that the Man of Reason can comprehend it from his objective position of leadership. The rejection of expertise and the socially determined behavioral model make leadership irrelevant. Situation-emergent OD contained the kernel of a theory of social reality and process that could, if articulated sufficiently, undercut the Man of Reason ideology. The articulation of ideas, however, must always be projected into a social context, and where the context is highly incompatible, it presents an impossible double bind: If the ideas are presented truly, they will not be understood; if they are shaped so that they can be understood, they lose their integrity and are incorporated into the standing orthodoxy.

The sticking point for situation-emergent OD was the third axiom, having to do with ontology. The social constructionist viewpoint, even though it was a marginal perspective in sociology, had enough tradition to give it a certain prima facie weight. Also, the development of the 1960s counterculture seemed to many to validate this understanding of social process. It remained, however, to connect the idea of multiple social realities to the world of administration. The difficulty was to theorize, without appealing to religious arguments, the human personality as containing the generative, creative capacity that could ground the idea of socially constructed realities. Though many turned to interpretivist social theory, they did not find the image of the human being they sought. Interpretivism only revealed the person as having a retrospective sense-making capacity, not an ability to act with fully positive intention into the future. As a result, situation-emergent

OD, even though it often produced excellent results in its application to the organizational setting, remained a marginal OD practice and had little or no impact in reshaping the theory of administration at a broader level.

One other development of interest to the Man of Reason issue arose in the New PA period: a revisionary extension of Traditionalism. The vestiges of Traditionalism had persisted in the field through an interest in the case study approach and in the analytical understanding of "policy decision making." What faded from the scene was the implicit "structuralist" orientation previously central to Traditionalist thought—that is, the emphasis on understanding administrative events as the playing out of structural dynamics rooted in the deep repetitive patterns that defined administrative situations. Some New PA theorists who had been trained as Traditionalists moved into an exploration of Jungian thought as an elaborated structuralist frame of reference and a promising ontological grounding for situation-emergent OD. A "transformational" approach to administrative life was created (McSwain & White, 1993; White & McSwain, 1983) emphasizing personal development (in Jungian terms, a fundamental restructuring of personality) as the key to understanding conflict and conflict resolution based in psychological projection, and the analysis of organizational dynamics driven by symbolic (which is to say, mythic) archetypes. (Denhardt's *In The Shadow of Organization*, 1981, is an example of this line of thought.) Yet even though it inspired dissertation research, numerous conference papers, and a number of journal articles, this aspect of the New PA remained undeveloped and marginal to the professional mainstream.

Summary View: What Were the Results of the New PA?

The year 1980 marked a major turning point in American public administration; it is a convenient concluding point for the New PA episode. Where were things intellectually in the field as the decade of the 1970s ended? To provide perspective, recall that the legitimacy issue for public administration was eclipsed by the history of the Roosevelt administrations, World War II, and the postwar recovery period. Government in general could not have been more legitimate than it was during this era, and this grace extended to public administration. Although the legitimacy issue never went away, and although dialogue about it remained active, the central focus shifted. The Traditionalists, influenced by their experience in wartime administration, felt that legitimacy for administrative action was to be found in the character of the public administrator and in his struggle to do the right thing by diligently working to place decisions in a proper context. In the postwar period, however, a consensus on the right thing to do seemed clear: Implement the material good life for all. In this climate, the legitimacy of administration seemed assured as long as it was based on expert, technical, effective management. This is the condition that made Simon's Modernism seem so appropriate and timely. After 1964, this moral consensus broke apart. The most direct response seemed (a) to assert concern with the normative dimension of administration more actively and (b) to seek a supporting rationale for this in an ontology that depicted people as able to be good, creative (proactive), and sensitive. The problem with this answer, which is the overall approach adopted by the New PA, was that activism by bureaucrats on behalf of their normative beliefs seemed as scary and as problematic as it ever had. The New PA movement felt that the clear facts of social injustice that had come to light in the 1960s had finessed the legitimacy issue—anyone could see what had to be done. In addition, the humanistic psychology (gestalt especially) on which the New PA drew was defiantly *American*—that is, highly individualistic and hedonistic—a kind of belief that everyone could somehow naturally have anything he or she wanted if the constraints (both physical and psychological) could just be lifted. The psychologist Fritz Perls's famous "Gestalt Prayer"—"You do your thing and I'll do mine," and so on—was widely disseminated and became a kind of emblem of this viewpoint. At the level of social organization, utopian communitarianism seemed to be the desirable and available theory. Specific approaches ranged from "neutral" methodological designs such as B. F. Skinner's Walden II (which a number of groups, most notably the Twin Pines Commune, sought to implement) to an assortment of other, more typically ideological approaches, such as varieties of Marxism, revised standard religions, primitivism, the Age of Aquarius philosophy of "Love," and so on.

Where humanistic psychology and communalism and consequently the New PA failed, of course, was in theorizing and dealing with the inevitable reality of conflict. The standard answer was to discuss things, which, because there was no understanding of how to make the process of discussion work, led to the same deadening results that had brought the participation movement to bankruptcy.

The experience of the 1960s and 1970s was by no means a complete loss, however. Although much of the intellectual struggle I have been describing took place far outside the public administration mainstream and intersected with it only in the arena of organizational change, a great deal of relevant learning occurred, especially about the various issues to be confronted in constructing an alternative to the Man of Reason orthodoxy. Also, those involved in developing alternative approaches to organizational change based on theories such as gestalt were provided with working laboratories for developing techniques, testing them experimentally, and theorizing the results. Such efforts met with substantial success, which reinforced the belief that workable alternatives were possible. Finally, given that nothing really changes in social life until human consciousness changes, and given that human consciousness evolves slowly and is only partially led by theory, little should have been expected from the New PA. This period was a confusing catharsis for America, an adolescent episode. It is usually in the phase of life after adolescence, the struggle of young adulthood, that meaningful change toward a lasting personal identity or reactionary retreat into the attitudes of the parents occurs. Which direction PA would go is the question that the next era, the Reagan presidency, posed.

The Reagan Era: The Social and Intellectual Context

The historian and social philosopher Christopher Lasch (1978), in naming the 1970s the "Me Decade," was off the mark but prescient about the immediate future. The 1970s was the time in which young people sought to make contact with the transcendent aspect of the human personality (the "I"); it was the 1980s that saw the ascendancy of the "Me"—the ego.

Ronald Reagan's election marked a sharp end to the approximately fifty-year effort to build a capacity for positive government within the constitutional frame. One slogan of the Reagan movement was "It's a good system; it's the people who are the problem." This meant that the people who had taken control of the national government had subverted the true intent of the founders and twisted the constitutional system out of its natural shape. The mandate of the new regime was to get back to the original design of America as a nation where the role of government was to foster and protect free commercial enterprise. Its plan for doing this was to rebuild the military so as to protect capitalism from the threat of communism, devolve problematic aspects of government to the states so as to put it more under control of the people, and retract the national government's perceived overinvolvement in furthering economic fairness and protecting stability. In addition, Reagan brought a social agenda to his presidency: to revitalize through law what he and his supporters saw as the foundational moral values of the American way of life. The intimate interventionism entailed by this (e.g., taking personal choice about abortion away from women) appears to contradict the more antigovernment tenets of the program, but from within the worldview of the Reagan movement, the enactment of traditional values was essential to good business.

The first apparent intellectual development—though some professional economists at the time balked at according it that much credibility—was George Gilder's (1981) propagation of the theory of supply-side economics. Inspired by a concept in economic theory known as the "Laffer curve," Gilder argued that the economic dynamic involved in putting goods on the shelf would create the means, the income and the disposition, for clearing them from the shelf. The best way to achieve economic growth was to help the economy on the "supply side." This was a direct assault on Keynesian "demand-side" economics, which held that economic growth is best ensured when government intervenes to create demand by making money available to consumers. Armed with this theory, the Reaganauts (as they were appropriately called) felt justified in pursuing a program of tax cuts, reduction in welfare subsidies, and deregulation of business activity.

Simultaneously, conservative "think tanks" across the nation began presenting a political theory rationale for Reagan conservatism. The theme of this was a return to the Constitution and the original Federalist definition of the relation of government to the economy and society (Schambra, 1982). The conservative interpretation was that the founders' plan was for government to provide only support and standardization so that commercial process could flourish. Social well-being was left to the institutions of indigenous communities. This plan had been violated when Franklin Roosevelt's New Deal attempted to build the entire nation into one large consensual community that supported providing a guaranteed floor of social equity protections. The Reagan mandate was to roll back the changes that Roosevelt had initiated and reinstitute the Constitution. Reagan conservatives argued that they were not against welfare but that social well-being was best handled by private charitable organizations and individuals.

The Christian religious right also entered the political and intellectual scene in the 1980s, and its effectiveness in building a constituency and an agenda marked a definite change in the landscape of public discourse. The religious right community appropriated the term *political correctness* to refer (with intended disdain) to what they saw as the unacknowledged orthodoxy sustained by liberals on university campuses. This term was used in direct retaliation to the growth of diversity movements in the academic setting that urged dropping "the Western Civ canon" in favor of teaching the histories and literatures of women, gays, people of color, ethnic groups, and so forth as part of the standard university curriculum. Conservatives argued that diversity-based curricula represented a dominating orthodoxy and denounced requirements to include heretofore excluded groups as litmus tests of one's political correctness. A plethora of often-fragmented discourses burst forth, many emphasizing separatism and a new exclusionism. The truly distinguishing aspects of the 1980s, however, were raw commercialism and the dearth of genuine intellectual activity that seemed to follow it. The "Harvard MBA syndrome" was commented on as a sign of the times. (There was widespread complaint that new business graduates were being trained only for "get rich quick" careers in banking and finance and showing little interest in learning how actually to manage productive corporations over the longer term.) Social and political discourse was dominated by talk of corporate takeovers, mergers, junk bonds, arbitrage, and, in general, the gigantic game of "Monopoly" that seemed to be going on in the American business community. The book and movie *Bonfire of the Vanities* (Wolfe, 1987) described this world and brought the moral issues it raised into sharp focus—issues highlighted by the Ivan Boesky-Michael Milkin insider trading scandals and the nationwide savings and loan failures scandal. The reaction to these issues seemed rather mild during the 1980s, as if the value of free enterprise overrode such blemishes.

On the political front, of course, there were major—indeed, monumental—shifts in the direction of making the market the core of social life. Chief among these were the transformation of the Soviet Union, the dismantling of the Berlin Wall and the reuniting of Germany, and the movement toward European economic union. The way now seemed open for the world to become one economic system organized around the principles of commerce. A distinctive, implicit step toward seeing social life as grounded in enterprise had been taken with the Reagan presidency. This was part of what gave him his famous "Teflon shield." In a day when moralism was prominent in social discourse and ethical codes were proliferating in government agencies, not one of the many scandals within his two administrations could touch him. He represented where the world was going; to challenge him was to challenge history itself.

Developments in the Field of Public Administration

The shape the world began to take as the Reagan presidency proceeded had little place in it for public administration. Within the field, "downsizing" and "cutback management" became key words. An interest arose in strategic planning and decentralization strategies, though it apparently led to little in the way of implementation. The Grace Commission on economy and efficiency in government launched yet another campaign to bring the presumed superior efficiencies of private business practice to government administration (Goodsell, 1984). Consistent with this emphasis, Reagan appointed Don Devine, DPA, the new head of the Office of Personnel Management (OPM). Devine immediately attacked the New PA publicly, saying that it had propagated the idea that bureaucrats should be activists for public interest values such as equity, that this was a wrong-headed idea of the administrative role, and that it was time to return to the classical model of the administrator as neutral professional.

The public bureaucrat was once again coming under direct attack, continuing a trend that resurged with the Nixon presidency and escalated during the Carter years. This time, however, the effort was programmatic and carried out forcefully. (One high-level bureaucrat told me at the time that he felt as if the OPM under Reagan had actually been taken over by Soviet agents who had been given the mission to disable the national government from the inside out!) The field responded by marshalling a new and concerted effort to legitimize and professionalize the administrative role. One aspect of this was to define ethical guidelines. The publication of John Rohr's *Ethics for Bureaucrats* (1978) was a significant intellectual breakthrough on this front, and it was greeted with great interest, acclaim, and some criticism. Terry Cooper's *The Responsible Administrator* (1983), John

Burke's *Bureaucratic Responsibility* (1986), and Kathryn Denhardt's *The Ethics of Public Service* (1988) were also published at this time. Bayard Catron provided the intellectual leadership through which ASPA was able to marshall a productive dialogue concerning ethics in the contemporary governmental setting with a national conference on ethics in 1989. ASPA had adopted a code of ethics for administrators in 1985, and this, along with the recognition of the National Association of Schools of Public Affairs and Administration as an official accrediting body for MPA degrees, marked a significant step toward giving the field the degree of professionalization that many felt it needed and should have. Career planning and management came into the field as an additional increment on this new professional identity.

Others reacted directly to the charges leveled against the public service. In 1980, Charles Goodsell, at Virginia Tech University in Blacksburg, Virginia, organized a national conference on public administration and client-centered services delivery (Goodsell, 1981). The theme of the conference was appreciation of the excellent job public bureaucracies were doing. Subsequently, Goodsell published *The Case for Bureaucracy* (1994), a polemic in defense of public bureaucrats using an array of service evaluation and client satisfaction data to show that the public generally was quite happy with the job being done by public agencies. Shortly following this, at the 1983 national conference of ASPA, Goodsell and a number of his faculty colleagues issued the "Blacksburg Manifesto," a paper seeking a renewed sense of legitimacy for the role that public bureaucracy plays in democratic governance (Wamsley, Goodsell, Rohr, White, & Wolf, 1987). This paper served as the inspiration for *Refounding Public Administration* (Wamsley et al., 1990), which elaborated the manifesto's perspective. The Blacksburg group, led by Gary Wamsley, started a line of dialogue that focused directly on the legitimacy question and that defended the administrative function in governance. Given that the field and the role of administration in government were being defined out of hand as illegitimate by politicians and political appointees, this effort played a major role in helping to sustain the field against its attackers.

In a corollary intellectual development, a group of public administration theorists had decided at the 1978 ASPA conference in Phoenix to create a network of interested theorists to foster the community and exchange over broad theoretical issues that many felt ASPA had never supported. By the fall of 1978, Guy Adams at Evergreen State College had begun the publication of a forum for such theory exchanges, aptly named *Dialogue*. The response was strong, and *Dialogue* generated a committed following. During the 1981 ASPA conference in Detroit—but *not* connected to the conference—theorists met and officially formed the Public Administration Theory Network. By 1985, the editorship of *Dialogue* had shifted to Henry Kass and Barry Hammond, and the journal was published at Slippery Rock University. The first national Public Administration Theory Network symposium, held in Portland in 1988, was oriented toward the theme of finding a new identity for the field, one that could be raised against the criticism coming at it from the political environment. This conference was extraordinarily successful at maintaining the integrity of the theme, and a book of selected conference papers, *Images and Identities in Public Administration* (1990), edited by Henry Kass and Bayard Catron, was published. Never officially allied with ASPA, and determinedly adhering to a symposium/open meeting format for its annual gatherings, the network has grown steadily. By the early 1990s, its journal switched to the formal peer review format and was renamed *Administrative Theory and Practice*, under the editorship of Jong Jun and Richard VrMeer at California State University, Hayward. These events generated a certain amount of excitement around the prospect of a dialogue on the question of where the field should be going.

I have alluded a number of times to the selective incorporation of work from the field of organization theory into the field of public administration. In the 1980s, the field of organization theory opened up dramatically and moved rapidly away from the idea that management and organization process can best be understood through the rationalist model. The first and most influential step in this direction came with the publication of Burrell and Morgan's *Sociological Paradigms and Organizational Analysis* (1979). This book laid the foundation for heterodoxy in the field by describing four different and mutually exclusive sociological paradigmatic bases—functionalism, interpretivism, radical structuralism, and radical humanism—from which organization theory could be carried out. Though it acknowledged the predominance of the functionalist paradigm, it set out the philosophical lineage of all four paradigms and treated each as equally legitimate.

Karl Weick, working from the perspective of Garfinkel's ethnomethodology, published *The Social Psychology of Organizing* (1979) in a direct confrontation with the traditional role-theory approach to organization behavior found in Katz and Kahn's *The Social Psychology of Organizations* (1966). Ethnomethodology, as the left wing of Burrell and Morgan's interpretivist paradigm, had long denied role theory (Pfohl, 1975), but Weick, as a mainstream organization theorist, gave this critique point and immediacy by stating it in unequivocal terms, epitomized by the last two sentences in his book: "Organizations keep people busy, occasionally entertain them, give them a variety of experiences, keep them off the streets, provide pretexts for storytelling, and allow socializing. They haven't anything else to give" (Weick, 1979, p. 264). His point of view simply denied the existence of organizations as traditionally depicted. In a similar vein, James March and his coauthors offered the "garbage can model" (Cohen, March, & Olsen, 1972) for understanding organizational process, which, as the name suggests, held that action in organizations proceeds from a mishmash of information and other factors rather than from the process of linear reasoning depicted in the rationalist model. After producing some of the best work in the field from the rationalist-functionalist perspective, Charles Perrow (1972, 1980) shifted his point of view and argued that organizations were better understood nonrationally. An even more radical statement of this came from Herbert Kaufman, a professor emeritus with a long career of teaching public administration at Yale. He argued in *Time, Chance, and Organization* (1991) that processes of rational management in organizations have nothing to do with their success or failure. It is, he said, random chance, a kind of ecological fate, that determines whether organizations will prosper or die.

In the broader field of management and organization theory, there was a veritable explosion of publication and training activity. Leading this was the "excellence movement" inspired by the Peters and Waterman best-seller *In Search of Excellence* (1982), a study of the management practices of exceptionally successful firms. The emphasis that emerged here was on "soft-side management"—that is, the creation of organizational cultures so powerful that they could effectively structure worker behavior and customer relations. On the academic side, the development of the organizational culture literature was led by Edgar Schein's *Organizational Culture* (1985) but quickly proliferated in both books and journal articles (Akin & Hopelain, 1986; Allaire & Firsirotu, 1984; Beyer & Trice, 1987; Gagliardi, 1986; Gregory, 1983; Kilmann, Saxton, & Serpa, 1986; Ott, 1989; Pettigrew, 1979; Sathe, 1983; Schall, 1983; Smircich, 1983; Smircich & Morgan, 1982; Smith & Simmons, 1983; Wilkins, 1983). The key issue that emerged was the question of whether organizational culture could be controlled enough to be managed. Some felt that the only true culture was one that developed indigenously; it was overreaching to attempt to structure it so as to further organizational purposes. Others advocated cultural management as a new approach to organization development. These proponents identified themselves as members of the organization transformation (OT) movement (Adams, 1984, 1986; Owen, 1984, 1987). Traditional approaches to organizational development had involved grounding the change in data; the organization transformationists saw no need for building a database as the starting place for a change program. Their position was that change could be effected simply by manipulating key cultural symbols and icons in a way that would induce the attitudes and behaviors desired in organization members. Nothing epitomized the fascination with technique better than the best-selling management book *The One Minute Manager* (Blanchard & Johnson, 1982). This little manual, cast in the mythic form of a fable, seemed to fit the demand of the moment for the easy technique that would yield great results. It did engender a sarcastic response, however, to the implicit dismissal of the humanness of workers in *The 59 Second Employee* (Rae & Ward, 1984).

This activity in management intersected with the field of public administration for the most part only through the venue of training activities. In mainstream public administration circles, the emphasis seemed to be on building the professional image of the field as a practice of *governance*—an activity of which management is a rather minor part. There seemed to be little or no appreciation of how theory cast at the level of organization and management could confront the issues involved in defining the role of administration in democratic governance. The responses to the Blacksburg *Refounding Public Administration* volume (Wamsley et al., 1990) illustrate this. Most of the discussion and response to the book's argument was focused on the chapter by Gary Wamsley setting out an "agency perspective" on administration. The objective of this chapter was, in effect, to resolve the Friedrich-Finer debate by a careful thinking through of the problem in terms of an agential theory of responsibility, the bottom line of which was the notion of the administrator as a normatively informed "agential leader." Little attention was given to the specifics of how this might be accomplished or what it might mean at the level of organization process.

The split of the Theory Network from ASPA is also indicative of what was happening to the legitimacy issue. Mainstream public administration was committed to seeing administrators as professional experts, holding fast to the already moribund identity created at the "misfounding" of the field. Efforts to theorize alternatives had been ignored or openly rejected. This was most obvious in the internal politics of ASPA and the formation of the national conference agenda each year. PA theorists repeatedly proposed theory tracks, only to have them eliminated in the deliberative process of conference organization on the grounds that theoretical work needed no place of its own but rather should be integrated throughout the existing subfields. Given that the legitimacy issue was the central concern of theorists and that the avenues of research within this community were largely philosophical, psychological, and managerial in orientation, the refusal of ASPA conference organizers to provide a venue for further exploration reveals the lack of interest in and attention to the legitimacy issue at the most mainstream, official levels of the field.

As the theory work of the 1980s proceeded, the gap between theory and traditional political science/public administration governmental research widened, and opportunities for productive advances were missed. That is, theory work was done both within and outside of the field that could have moved the dialogue forward if connections had been made between it and the larger issue of legitimacy. Michael Harmon and Rick Mayer's text *Organization Theory for Public Administration* (1986) provided needed perspective on the discourse by inventorying and sorting available organization theories. The effect of this work was to suggest that the days of looking at organization and management theory purely in terms of narrow technique were past. Working in much the same direction, two psychoanalytic lines of theory development also emerged. One was a continuation of the application of Jungian psychology that began in the 1970s, and the other worked from a more classical Freudian foundation (Allcorn, 1992; Baum, 1987; Diamond, 1984, 1988, 1993; Hirschorn, 1988; Jacques, 1976; Kets de Vries, 1991; LaBier, 1986; Levinson, 1981; Schwartz, 1990; Zaleznick, 1989). The psychoanalytic perspective, by revealing the unconscious dimension of organization life, undercut the possibility for reducing management to technique and for seeing the organizational arena as rational. On another front, work inspired by new paradigmatic premises appeared. Notable among these was Kathy Ferguson's book *The Feminist Case Against Bureaucracy* (1984), which presented a feminist critique of traditional bureaucracy and ended by suggesting, at least in outline, what an alternative to it might be. This work was part of a broad movement toward the development of an understanding of organizations from a feminist perspective (Bologh, 1990; Brown, 1988; Franzway, Courte, & Connell, 1989; Ginzberg, 1990; Kanter, 1977; Powell, 1988; Stivers, 1993). Although this scholarship afforded tremendous possibilities for a rethinking of public administration's legitimacy issue, most of the theoretical implications remained unconsidered.

One of the most exciting developments of the 1980s at the level of practice was the growth of the negotiation-conflict mediation movement. Although the focal book of this field, *Getting to Yes,* was written in a popular vein, it proposed a number of profoundly important ideas that indicated nothing less than a shift in paradigm for thinking about human conflict (Fisher & Ury, 1991). Negotiation became a topic of broad cultural interest during this period, and a number of schools proposed making it a specific curriculum topic in public administration training (Richman, White, & Wilkinson, 1986).

Total quality management (TQM) was another innovation at the level of organization and management process that was integrated into public administration practice during this time (Aguayo, 1990; Carr & Littman, 1990; Deming, 1986; Gabor, 1990; Garvin, 1988; Juran, 1992; Lareau, 1991; Mann, 1985; Neave, 1989; Scherkenbach, 1991). Interest in it began in the military, but as TQM was noticed as a way of responding to competition with Japanese manufacturers, it became a broad movement, institutionalized with the establishment of the national Malcolm Baldrige Quality award given each year by the U.S. government. TQM is of special relevance to this book because (at least in the version that W. Edwards Deming formulated) it is a point-for-point expression of the philosophy of American pragmatism (White & Wolf, 1995). It is oriented toward the principle of cooperative collaboration rather than competition, and as such, its idea of authority relations is fundamentally at odds with the orthodox view. In application, TQM met the sad fate of many innovative approaches. It was selectively interpreted and bastardized into a form consistent with the prevailing ethos of management thought and practice—in this case, rational bureaucratic control.

By the end of the 1980s, the field of public administration was in a condition of fragmentation. This was symbolized in principle and in fact by a second Minnowbrook meeting held to commemorate the twentieth anniversary of the first. Whereas the participants at the initial meeting had been young men, almost all of whom were white, and the meeting had developed some sense of unified direction and movement, the participant group invited to the 1988 conference was much larger and diverse in gender, age, and race. The dialogue at times became contentious to the point of virtual incivility, and numerous participants left with a sense of anger and dismay. The very least that could be said about the meeting is that the group was so fractured in terms of professional identification, philosophical and theoretical positions, and personal attitude that nothing even resembling a coherent sense of direction for the group or for the field resulted from the meeting. Other evidence of the fracturing was seen organizationally—for example, in an association of policy schools, the Association of Public Policy Analysis and Management (APPAM), created in the early 1980s in response to a growing concern that ASPA and other public administration organizations paid insufficient attention to issues of policy analysis and were driven by a research orientation inconsistent with dominant policy analytic methodologies (Henry, 1987). APPAM was designed to provide an institutional venue for more focused policy study through its conferences and its journal, the *Journal of Policy Analysis and Management*. As something of a metaphor for the overall condition of disorientation in the field, ASPA itself began to experience financial and managerial difficulties as an institution as the decade of the 1980s closed.

Into the 1990s: The Current Intellectual Context

As the 1980s matured into the 1990s, existing trends evolved further. The global economy continued to elaborate itself, and as it did, everything seemed to reorient around the principle of economic efficiency. Huge amounts of money from personal savings began to flow into mutual fund equity accounts, and corporate management began managing for "investor return" as much as or more than for "profit" in the classical sense (Reich, 1995; 1996). As a result, turbulence began to hit the organizational world. Corporate downsizing and consequent career insecurity formed the core of an emerging "virtual" social reality, one in which life appears to go on normally but work remains the only thing that is truly real. There are consistent reports of high anxiety levels among the population generally, even though by many indications, the economy is stable and doing well and should be affording people a sense of increased security. There has been a marked increase in litigiousness, propagating the feeling that one could be sued at any time for anything. Tensions around racial, ethnic, gender, and other differences appear to be escalating—in America as well as in the world generally—and right-wing nationalism of the "live free or die" sort seems to be growing.

In the world of government, the fascination with economic efficiency has taken the form of the "reinventing movement," following Osborne and Gaebler's famous book *Reinventing Government* (1992).

The tendency, since the Reagan years, to define government as largely irrelevant, if not dangerous, in principle and practice, to economic and social life is continuing. The result of this is that political opinions are increasingly forming outside the traditional boundaries of the liberal-versus-conservative ideological debate (Tolchin, 1996). They are tending toward a libertarian viewpoint that sees no need for government at all. As the millennium approaches, a fundamental shift seems in the offing.

Intellectually, much is happening that mirrors these broader conditions. Though they have been on the scene for more than two decades, postmodernism and deconstruction are dominating discourse in a number of arenas. Postmodern organization theory has become a major school of thought and has inspired an exciting new journal, *Organizations.* Chaos theory, systems theory of the second-order cybernetics variety, and other nonlinear approaches applied to understanding social order have generated broad interest and an active following (Briggs & Peat, 1989; Gleick, 1988; Kauffman, 1993; Kiel & Elliott, 1996; Prigogine & Stengers, 1984; Richardson, 1991; Senge, 1990; Ulrich & Probst, 1984; Wheatley, 1992; Zohar, 1990). The work of Richard Rorty (1979, 1982) has consolidated gains in the acceptance of heterodoxy that began with Kuhn and has inspired a strong resurgence of interest in the work of the American pragmatists. In general, the intellectual scene is in high ferment, offering great potential for breakthroughs to occur.

What the History of the Public Administration Literature Reveals About How the Man of Reason Ideology Has Been Maintained

I want to reserve discussion of the current intellectual scene in the field of public administration for the concluding chapter, so I will end this review by stating what I see to be the patterns, themes, or lessons that one can draw from the history I have just recounted. Recall that the purpose of setting out this abridged story of the literature was to indicate how its development had to be distorted to maintain the plausibility of the Man of Reason ideology that functioned to misfound the field at its genesis.

In service of this objective, I offered an interpretive recapitulation of the story of public administration's literature. This history shows that the debate over defining the role of the administrator in gover-

nance has actually been a struggle of political ideology concerning who
has discretion over policy and how this discretion is to be exercised.
The original move in this game, early in the twentieth century, was to
use reform as a tactic for taking power away from party "hacks" and
giving it back to the "better element" among Men of Reason, the men
of the educated middle and upper classes. At this point, management
theory was synonymous with social theory; the shift to the idea of
scientific management or expert administration was, in effect, a shift
at the level of political theory. Management theory was used as an
ideological tool for reworking the identity of and legitimating a new
kind of Man of Reason.

The subsequent shift from the administrator as scientific manager
and technical expert to the Traditionalist model of expert policy-making professional was a logical next step. This required distorting the
potential of the reform movement for developing an alternative type
of collaborative, pragmatic government along the lines suggested by
Follett, Dewey, and others in the political arena such as Herbert Hoover.

Modernism was simply a change designed to update the Man of
Reason to fit the more "policy-neutral" climate of the day. The issues
of life seemed primarily technical, demanding rational solutions. The
debate over Simon and Modernism was quite limited; both sides,
though they felt strongly about the issues involved, agreed more
with each other than they disagreed. Because there was so much
agreement at the core, organization and management theory could still
be taken as having direct relevance to the broader question of defining
the place of administration in democratic governance. Indeed, the
various branches of intellectual endeavor—the subfields such as comparative administration—could be used as venues for elaborating the
Man of Reason ideology along new dimensions. The major distortion
of this period was the selective incorporation of theory and research
from the field of organizational sociology, which in general denied the
possibility for the kind of rationalistic control of organizations to
which Modernist theory pretended.

The New PA reaction caused a major change. Because philosophical heterodoxy at the level of epistemology and ontology became
legitimate or at least unavoidable, it was now possible to use organization and management theory and research as venues for exploring
radically new alternatives to institutional—which is to say, *political*—
relationships, alternatives that fundamentally threatened the hegemony of the Man of Reason ideology.

On the other hand, this was not true of those aspects of the New PA that advocated an enhanced normative sensitivity for public administrators. Such proposals fell well within the frame of traditional thinking and provided a safe arena for debate without the prospect that a threat to the underlying ideology would arise. These debates resulted in concrete progress toward redefining and legitimating the administrator Man of Reason as a professional with ethical training who, in addition, functioned under a "code" sanctioned by a professional association. Because other aspects of the New PA were oriented toward more radical possibilities for redefining the identity of the field, a split began to appear, involving especially those interested in the heterodox forms of organization theory that held the greatest potential for such a redefinition. The mainstream of the field remained concerned with questions of practice and "macro-level" institutional issues looked at from conventional perspectives. Work that might have bridged this gap, such as the Blacksburg "refounding" project (Wamsley et al., 1990) and the Kass and Catron (1990) book, failed to do so, because the mainstream reaction was to refuse the "legitimacy issue" as no longer of relevance or importance, apparently feeling that its own approach of legitimization through increased professionalization was sufficient. The theory community in a sense "spun off" into its own orbit, marginal to the mainstream but at the same time in a position to carry out fundamentally innovative theorizing. Very little of this has reached the mainstream. To my mind, the literature of mainstream public administration has been shaped so as to maintain the Man of Reason ideology through the devices of selectively incorporating material from related fields and marginalizing work that contained the potential to threaten its hegemony.

As I look back to the Friedrich-Finer debate, it seems clear to me that the field of public administration has never really wanted to resolve the question of how bureaucracy properly fits into democracy because keeping the question alive is essential to the identity that it wishes to maintain for the public administrator—the power-wielding Man of Reason. The administrative Man of Reason would rather have power with a weak rationale for his legitimacy ("Trust me, I'm a professional") than to be completely legitimate (as a collaborator with citizens) but be required to share power. The proof of this assertion I think is obvious: *The answer to the legitimacy question has been there all along!* It was in the air at the time of the reform movement, and Mary Follett and John Dewey articulated it clearly and in practical terms. Yet we in the field best positioned to elaborate the alternative possibility they raised refused, and are refusing, it. We want our legitimacy problem; it gives us who we are.

Conclusion: The Man of Reason Revealed

Throughout this book, I have used the term *Man of Reason* to refer to the central issue or problem the book addresses. I have said that it is Men of Reason who are responsible for the persistence of the legitimacy issue because they need it to maintain their position. I have created the impression that I am *blaming* the Men of Reason, implying that they have done something intentionally to us—their victims—and that if they had not been so selfish or evil, things would be different and better. I have also, by failing to specify otherwise, implied that by *Men of Reason* I mean actual *men* who occupy elite positions in our institutions, from which they are dominating the rest of us.

It is now time to set this straight and to specify things more precisely. The term *Man of Reason* refers to a *style of decision making*, specifically one that ultimately involves a specific kind of personal discretion or judgment. This is critically important: The Man of Reason is neither a Man of Science nor a Man of Virtue—that is, of moral philosophy. *His very raison d'être is that science and moral philosophy cannot provide clear answers to questions of policy choice.* He would like to be a Man of Science or Man of Virtue and be able to pronounce the right thing to do technically and ethically. The problem is that no one can possess such knowledge. The Man of Reason believes that empirical and moral Truth with a big "T" does exist but that usually human beings can only approximately understand it. He would be certain if he could, but because he cannot, his only claim is that he seeks to come as close to true fact and absolute value as it is possible for a human being to get. Recall the discussion of Friedrich and Finer. Though they are adversaries, they would agree on two things: (a) There is no way of settling the debate between them, and (b) because this is so, it is imperative that people in positions of institutional power base what they do on *Reason*. *Reason* here means the judgment, the discretion, that must be added to what can be known to make it complete and certain enough to take action. The Man of Reason, then, is a benevolent, even deferential or diffident, *Master*—one who is reluctantly compelled to run the show because the attitude of reason is in such short supply among human beings generally.

The Man of Reason defends himself by elaborately delineating the many ways in which he has no real power, discretion, or leeway in making choices. He is, he says, hemmed in by law, by moral and ethical principles, by (scientifically grounded) considerations of fact, by practical constraints, and so forth. To hear him tell it, he is a mere cipher. He seeks to minimize the discretion he has to exercise because the more he can do this, the more correct and legitimate his actions will be. In most cases, he sincerely believes that he exercises little or no discretion, and because he believes this, it becomes true in a sense. He is puzzled when attacked. He feels unappreciated because from his perspective, what he does is not only essential but difficult and tiring. Because people are so self-interested, quarrelsome, immature, or whatever they are that makes it difficult for them to get along, he *must* step in and make the decision. Because science does not produce clear answers, and neither do ethics or moral theory, he has to use his judgment. In the face of this, he tries hard to be a good leader, and this takes time, energy, and worry and creates a great deal of stress. He really does not understand why people seem to resent him and what they call his elite or privileged position; however, he accepts this resentment simply as a fact of life with which he must cope. It is probably due to the same deficiencies in human nature that created the need for him in the first place. In his view, if he is a Master, it is only because people need Masters; somebody has to be willing to do the job.

To say that Men of Reason decide things on the basis of their judgment rather than science, ethics, or morality is not to say that they denigrate these as sources of knowledge and guidance. On the contrary, they support them wholeheartedly and are the first to rise to their defense. This posture is essential to maintaining the Man of Reason ethos, the key axiom of which is *submission to objective reality.* Here I mean *objective* in the sense of "that which is outside us," the external world in which fact and falsehood/good and bad interact to produce an inescapable context, a reality that cannot be avoided and that must be acknowledged and respected.

For a mind-set like this to obtain, there must be a belief that the Truth and the Good exist objectively, even if our feeble minds cannot comprehend them directly. The Men of Reason are simply the ones among us who try the hardest to think, feel, and live in a way that moves them as close as possible to Truth and Good. The rest of us let our own idiosyncratic concerns shape our thoughts and feelings. This is another reason why scientific and normative theories must be protected from attack. If such attacks are carried too far, people in general will see no reason why their opinions are not as good as those of scientific and moral authorities and they will want to become involved directly in deciding how things are going to be. Respect for science and moral theory is essential for keeping things in their place and minimizing the dissonance with which Men of Reason have to cope. People must be held in the place of followers and Men of Reason in the place of leaders.

Are Men of Reason the elite of the world, then, those who occupy the very top positions of our social order? The answer is no, but they are the easiest ones to see for what they are if you are close to circles in which decisions are made. It is now (although it was not so, even in the recent past) a commonplace observation in Washington, DC, for example, that decision making in the Pentagon is a chaotic process of interpersonal negotiation. Because nearly all decisions involving military matters are essentially technical, this is not how it is supposed to be. Newcomers to the scene expect, as one told me, "the decision process to be data driven." They find that it is not; "data" take a back seat to other forms of argument and persuasion grounded in the discretion of the Men of Reason involved in the process. I saw this when I was involved in the NASA research I mentioned earlier. It would seem that space program decisions would be almost completely made on technical bases. This is certainly the impression that I had when I started the research. After I started talking to the people involved, I learned that was not the case. There was, of course, a huge amount of technical analysis, but this was not necessarily controlling. The decision on what mode to use in going to the moon, for example, is a good illustration (Logsdon, 1971). Most of the research had focused on various Earth orbit rendezvous and direct-ascent alternatives. The lunar orbit rendezvous mode was a last-minute choice and represented a major change. The technical rationale that NASA attempted to develop for it was not persuasive, so the document containing it was classified (Redford & White, 1971). Nontechnical thinking ultimately controlled the decision, and the discussion took place in the White House itself. Another example is the decision to send *three* astronauts. NASA had *no* adequate technical rationale for this choice. When questioned—behind the scenes—by the president's Science Advisory Committee about this, Jim Webb, the administrator of NASA at the time, wrote back a letter saying that the technical documentation had not had a chance to catch up with the decision-making process.

Was Jim Webb, as head of NASA, a Man of Reason? Yes, he was an excellent example, and NASA was an excellent example of how things proceed in a world governed by Men of Reason. Webb, however, was hardly the only Man of Reason in NASA. Even at those levels of decision that were most limited, where the technical seemed over-whelmingly preeminent, individual judgment always played a critical, even if implicit, role in ordering or structuring the decision context. In the original Apollo command module that caught fire during a test and killed three astronauts, the fire happened because the technical analysis on the design of the module, based mainly on the safety of the astronauts, did not take account of the fact that many of the exotic weight-saving metals used in its construction became flammable in the virtually pure oxygen environment of space flight. The Challenger disaster offers a similar recent example of the nearly invisible interplay between analysis and discretion.

What makes a person a Man of Reason is not simply that he occupies a high-level position in which decisions are more "political" and hence more discretionary than they are technical. Nor is he one because he imposes his discretion over the mandate of expertise. Further, he is not in principle an avoider of responsibility. Indeed, to his credit, he is willing to bear the heroic burden of leadership. The point is that in virtually every situation, there is likely to be ambiguity of every sort. The Man of Reason is one who employs a specific device for resolving this ambiguity. Decisions of any sort and at any level are susceptible to the distinctive decision-making style of the Man of Reason. What distinguishes the Man of Reason from other decision makers is that he refers his judgments to his individual discretion—which is to say, he *makes the decision alone*. If he is smart, of course, he listens to others, and he certainly will take into consideration all the facts and values that seem to bear on the situation. He does not isolate himself, but in the end, in the final analysis, he decides alone. Men of Reason can only truly collaborate through devices such as formal participation strategies or voting in which people are allowed to make individual choices, which are then aggregated into a collective choice.

In identifying Men of Reason as the villains, I am not launching a general attack on people in elite positions or people in positions of authority at other levels. There are Men of Reason at all levels of hierarchies. Anyone can be a Man of Reason. Also, Men of Reason are not necessarily men. (I will argue shortly, though, that there is an important gender dimension to the situation.) I personally know many Men of Reason who are women. It is true that the "worst" Men of Reason are those in elite positions, and because most of them are men, males in elite positions are by far the bigger part of the problem. This is so simply because, given the way things are organized, most damage to the human world is done from these upper-level positions, and they are occupied mostly by men.

What makes one a Man of Reason in the final analysis is a certain kind of closedness. I knew a police captain once who told me of an incident illustrating the difference between the Man of Reason style and a more open style. Some "radicals," in attempting to rob a sporting goods store of guns, had been interrupted and had taken a number of hostages, whom they held in the store with them while the police waited outside. The situation dragged on, and concern for the hostages rose. My friend, who was in charge of handling the matter, consulted with other officers at the scene. Finally, he decided to call up a tanklike attack vehicle, use it to crash through the front of the store, and, through this overwhelming show of power, intimidate the perpetrators into surrendering. It was a difficult decision, one involving technical, ethical, and moral aspects.

He was behaving like a good, responsible Man of Reason, but he felt unsettled about his decision. After the attack vehicle had rumbled into place in front of the store, he noticed that the two men inside seemed especially tense. He walked over to the vehicle and engaged the driver in conversation about the plan for the attack. He found that the driver had been briefed well, but on a hunch, he asked him how he felt about what he was about to do. The man responded that he felt ready, but he was worried because he did not think the plan would work. When asked why, he reported that he had grown up in that neighborhood, had been in the store many times to buy sports equipment, and knew that it was an old building with an ancient wooden floor. His prediction was that as soon as he drove the attack vehicle inside, the floor was going to collapse, and the vehicle was going to crash down into the basement.

My friend called a halt to the plan and convened a meeting (including the two men in the attack vehicle) to consider, in a collaborative way, what to do. As a result, they designed a different approach to the situation. I use this case to indicate a contrast with the Man of Reason style. My friend's persistent sense of doubt, the openness it created, and his disposition to collaborate in arriving at a solution are inconsistent with the approach of the Man of Reason.

By now I imagine that you, the reader, are wondering what the problem really is. Is the cure to the disease carried by Men of Reason a simple injunction to be open and collaborative? The answer is, basically, yes. The difficulty comes in revealing what this injunction might mean, because we already believe in openness and collaboration, right up to the point at which responsibility for a decision is necessary. Then it is only *reasonable* to all of us to have a procedure in place by which difficult decisions that must be made can be made. The bottom line is that, as Pogo found, in the final analysis the enemy is us. We all—men, women, the powerful and important, the lowly and insignificant—typically behave as Men of Reason. As a consequence, the history that I have recounted in this book could hardly have been different. At the most generic level, it is a history of the unfolding and institutionalization of the consciousness characteristic of our historical epoch. This is an age of reason, and it is an age that has been mediated primarily by men. Reason is the name of the very consciousness that all of us possess. What is at stake in the issue under discussion transcends the legitimacy problem in public administration. Consciousness itself is implicated in the discourse of legitimacy. We in the field of public administration are fortunate in this sense: The legitimacy problem puts the underlying issue in more vivid relief than is usually the case in academic discourses. It is easier, therefore, to identify the kind of discourse by which we can move toward escaping the trap of reason.

Consequently, my next rhetorical step, in Chapter 7, must be to move to a deeper level of analysis. The idea of reason itself must be unpacked and examined. When we do this, we will be able to understand more about who the Man of Reason is—his stance toward life and the external world, the attitudes that the ethos of reason induces, and why it is appropriate to refer to him as masculine. In doing this, I am going to venture into the philosophy of consciousness, but at the level of experience and in such a way that the issue, I trust, can be broadly understood. I want to outline a perspective on the grounding of consciousness and how it produces the pattern of life that it does. As is the case with this book generally, though, the idea is solely to evoke interest and offer a format for further conversations in other venues and along other dimensions.

7

Beyond Reason

I put myself in your place, and I can see that what I tell you
isn't at all interesting. It's still theatre. What can one do to
be truly sincere?

Antonin Artaud, January 24, 1947
(his last public appearance)

Evil is a form of the unlimited.
Aristotle

Je est un autre.
Rimbaud

DURING MY ACADEMIC CAREER, I have spent a great deal of
time working as a consultant to public organizations. Because
my original intention was to have a career as a public administration
practitioner, I have enjoyed this work as it has enabled me to connect
theory and practice in productive ways and to learn a tremendous
amount from my practitioner colleagues. In fact, it has been my
involvement in public agencies that has made me aware of the Man of
Reason "problem" and its pernicious consequences for the legitimacy

of administration in American governance. Although there are Men of Reason at every turn in public organizations, there are also instances in which the solution to the problem they pose is equally evident and available. My consulting practice has taught me much about myself and my field, and it has also given me hope and insight into the possibilities for change.

For more than fourteen years, I worked under contract to a military agency doing process consultation, team building, and executive leadership training. It was during one of the training sessions that I met "Jane." She came up to me at the end of a long afternoon and wanted to talk about her sense that the men in her small group were discounting her contributions. She was a tall and imposing woman (as she later noted, "My height is five foot fourteen") who seemed unlikely to be intimidated by any of her peers. I mentioned some small group research on gender dynamics, at which point she turned to me and said, "This is of particular interest to me because I used to be a man."

Few other professional (or personal) moments have stunned me so thoroughly. She was happy to tell me her story, and I was eager to learn it. I knew she was a high-ranking civilian in the Pentagon, but it was difficult to imagine her history. She told me that she had been a man until she was thirty-five—she was currently thirty-eight—and had served as a decorated Army Ranger in Vietnam. She was also a victim of Agent Orange, and her feet had been ruined by combat boots. (She offered this as an explanation of why she wore tennis shoes to work with her dresses.) After her time in the army, she had entered the civilian work force in one of the services. Despite her "macho" background, she stated flatly that she had never been comfortable in her man's body, had always felt she was a woman, and had tried for years to find an answer to her confusion. She was not a homosexual, either as a man or as a woman; she identified her condition as "gender dysphoria." Finally, at age thirty-three, she had been referred to a university sex-change center, and after extensive initial psychological screening, a trial period of dressing and living as a woman, and complicated hormonal treatments, she had had an operation and become a woman. She kept her job throughout this, was as open about her changes as possible, and was promoted several times. Staying in her job situation posed a number of difficulties, primarily for those around her who had to work to understand and deal with the new "Jane."

I could appreciate their difficulties. During that late afternoon conversation, I learned some important things. I tried to put myself in

Jane's place and imagine my identity ungendered; the daunting nature of this task showed me how embedded concepts of gender are in us. Jane literally embodied the extent to which gender is socially constructed. She carefully explained how she had to *learn* to be a woman. Gender changes do not affect vocal cords, which stretch in adolescence and cannot be reduced. Jane was still in speech therapy after three years to learn to pitch her voice higher and to attain proper inflection, word usage, appropriate vocabulary and syntax—all of which are markedly different between men and women, and all of which are learned. Over the years, she had realized that what we understand to be a profound source of our identity and attribute to biology is actually the result of careful social construction and maintenance.

She was so open about her experience that I invited her to lecture at my university on the topic of how one accomplishes the enactment of gender in the organizational setting. This seminar was well attended, and when Jane arrived, she looked out at the crowd studying her with gaping jaws, and cracked, "I thought I would start off by telling a joke, but you don't look as if you can *take* a joke!" She explained in her lecture that she found becoming a woman an essentially *cosmetic* task. Though she was relieved to have female biology, she found that it did not make her a woman; that was *accomplished* through training and hard work. My students, who were all practitioners, found her talk fascinating. We had been reading and discussing Garfinkel's (1967) study of Agnes and Bill (a case study of gender transformation), and Jane brought the ethno-methodological abstractions of the case to life.

Increasingly, I began to see that Jane taught us all a critical point about the "essential" boundaries reason requires, and this is the subject of this chapter. The challenge that Jane presented me, finally, was to come to terms with the reality that *my* gender identity as well as my social identity is just as "constructed" as is hers. In other words, she has no more of a gender "problem" than do I or anyone else. Knowing Jane confronts me with the reality that what separates us into discrete identities is a set of masks. Beneath these, Jane and I are one: I am Jane; Jane is me. I must also come to terms with the constructedness and boundedness of my sense of identity. My true "I" resides in a place outside my consciousness, a place of which I have no conscious apprehension and over which I have no control. Such an awareness, of course, is "unreasonable" because it is beyond reason. Consciousness may demand the making and wearing of social masks (Progoff, 1973), but it is *reason* that demands that we take them as seriously as we do.

Working with Jane has helped me understand what it means to move beyond reason to a different level of relationship, one that truly acknowledges the alterity of the other through the paradoxical realization that one *is* the other. Many of the day-to-day working bureaucrats around Jane accomplished this far better than I. What I saw them doing reminds me of a delightful incident during a lecture I attended where there was a large audience of federal bureaucrats. The lecturer, an African American psychologist, was arguing that by legal definitions, Dwight Eisenhower and a number of other famous "white" Americans were actually "Negroes." At this, a portly white gentleman from Louisiana leaped to his feet, turned to the audience and remarked excitedly, "From what he's saying, I can see that I myself am most probably a black man."

This is the kind of insight beyond reason that I mean. All that is required is moving ourselves beyond the regime of Men of Reason. In the remainder of this chapter, I want to discuss how this is so.

Sex, Gender, and the Man of Reason Problem

What is a "reasonable" comprehension of reality, and what is its relation to gender?

Any discussion of consciousness must begin by problematizing it. It is difficult to discuss something analytically that we take as a given. What I mean is simply this: How do you know, reader—as Zhuang Zi puzzled—that you are not a butterfly dreaming you are a person reading this book right now? If you feel that your consciousness is not problematic in this way, if there is no basis for doubt that you are a person reading this book right now and not someone or something dreaming that you are doing so, you will probably not relate very well to what you are about to read, no matter how commonsensical I try to make it. What I want to talk about is the nature of awareness itself and how awareness connects to our sense of reality, of objects in the world.

My belief is that no one can reasonably know with certainty when he or she is "dreaming" and when not. (If you are one who "never remembers a dream," maybe you just have not yet awakened.) Consciousness is not a given; we cannot take our sense of reality as hard and fast, relying on it without question. Of course, we all (I included) *do* on a day-to-day basis take our sense of reality for granted. The question that presents itself, though, is: How do we accomplish this certainty? How do we create our perception that reality is "out there" and that we are "in here" separate from it, taking it in, and creating meaning? This is at the heart of what we generally understand to be a "reasonable" approach to life; answering these questions is essential to understanding the nature of reason.

Let us begin the discussion by identifying what we, who are reasonable, consider to be an unreasonable way of approaching life. A good instance is the worldview of most traditional peoples—for example, Trobriand Islanders, Native Americans, or the indigenous peoples of Mexico. Although we may like them, be fascinated by them, and appreciate many things about the way they see the world, we modern, reasonable people consider their sense of reality to be naive and incorrect. We have heard that many of them believe in ghosts, spirits, the presence of their ancestors, and so on, and that they believe inanimate objects have a kind of consciousness and/or spirit. We know all this to be not "true." Here, then, is a basic demarcation line between the reasonable and the "unreasonable": A reasoned view of the world is *bounded*. The spirit world, usually, is placed outside the boundary of the world of reason. However, this is not entirely the point. Some reasonable people believe in the reality of spiritual phenomena such as religious miracles or divine intervention. They are not like traditional peoples, though, because they put a boundary around these things. They feel that some such phenomena are "true" and that others are "not true" and that there must be a way of drawing a line, a boundary, between the categories.

A sense of boundary is essential to a sense of "reason." The fact that I appreciate the validity of setting boundaries provides me with the belief that I am awake and conscious as I write this and not a butterfly dreaming it. Without a sense of boundary, everything shades into everything else, dreaming and wakefulness become the same, and the spirit world comes to inhabit the physical world, just as traditional peoples tend to believe. Reason, however, demands that we accept some things as in and reject others as out; this is what reason is all about. (Dreams are fantastic imaginings; waking consciousness is real.) Simon's model of decision rationality is an illustration of this. He, in fact, grounded his entire model on the necessity of boundedness. If you cannot draw a boundary around what is relevant to a rational analysis, you end up having to consider everything at once. This means that your decision process is ultimately going to consist of building a big fire and singing and dancing around it all night waiting for a sign from the gods—just as traditional peoples did. The essence of Aristotelian logic, which is the one that we all use, is boundedness: The terms of an argument must be bounded, defined in a way that renders them discrete from one another. Without boundary, we end up with a big conceptual mess, and we cannot have a reasoned approach to life.

Our analysis of the idea of boundary in Simon's work, though, also teaches us that the drawing of boundaries is problematic. In Simon's case, the variables that are left out of the analysis tend to come back and haunt us in the form of unintended effects from the rational actions that we take. This is why we are now doing ecological impact statements before we launch even social programs. Boundaries are also *intrinsically* problematic. If we are going to have a reasoned approach to reality, this approach must apply to *all* reality—that is, to the universe itself. This means that we must have an idea of the universe as bounded. According to reason, "everything" must have a boundary around it. The rub is this: The idea of boundary means that something is left out—on the other side—so how can "everything" be bounded? What can possibly be on the other side, outside of everything? This is the problem with the idea of the universe. What is outside the universe that gives it its identity as the universe? We have heard of multiple universes. Maybe other universes are outside of "ours," and they are what gives our universe its identity. This means, though, that the idea of universe is not universal. What about the universe of universes? What is outside it?

I think you get the idea. When you really push it, the idea of boundary becomes difficult. If we cannot have a valid idea of the universe as bounded, then doubt is cast on all the boundaries we want to draw. This ultimately problematizes the idea of reality as made up of "objects" that are discrete from one another. We can see this by going all the way to the other end of the continuum from the universe and looking at the idea of a fundamental particle, what has been called the "quark." Some physicists who are searching for the quark have mused that the whole project may be a contradiction in terms because when and if they find the quark, they will just begin to wonder what *it* is composed of, on and on. The idea of an ultimate particle, a final, fundamental object (which is derivative from the idea of boundary) is self-contradictory.

A similar situation seems to exist in the realm of numbers. To our everyday viewpoint, numbers and mathematics make up the last bastion of reason; they provide an irrefutable logic that reality is there (objects can be counted) and that a reasoned approach is valid. You cannot deny, the argument goes, that two plus two is four, that the angles of a triangle always add up to 180 degrees, and so on. (Actually, whether two and two add to four depends on the base of the arithmetic you are using, and the total number of degrees in triangles depends on the type of geometry you are using: In some, it is always strictly *more* than 180; in others, it is always strictly *fewer* than 180; McKeen, 1977.) We tend to forget, however, that the idea of number as a way of relating to reality did not come "naturally" to the human mind. Number, looked at in the scope of the total history of humankind, is a relatively contemporary idea. It has also gone through a process of evolution; originally, in the Greek idea of number—*arithmos*—the number and the thing were identical, one and the same. The number did not *refer* to the thing; it *was* the thing. This was before people had fully developed an idea of "representation." In the medieval period, similarly, paintings were thought to *be* what they depicted: God was *there*, in the painting (Rotman, 1987).

We tend to forget that mathematics is not, in any ultimate sense, logical. Kurt Gödel demonstrated that any mathematical system complex enough to be interesting rests on a flawed logical foundation in that it must be either incomplete or inconsistent (Nagel & Newman, 1968). The notion of the absolute, the universe, or infinity also is problematic for mathematics. The mathematician George Cantor demonstrated the paradoxes in which numbers become involved when one introduces the idea of an infinite number (Jones, 1982). For example, Cantor showed that there are (a) as many *odd* numbers as there are whole numbers and (b) as many *even* numbers as there are whole numbers, but, on the other hand, that the total number of odd and even numbers combined equals the total number of whole numbers. You can see this by doing a thought experiment: Imagine an infinite string of odd numbers, then imagine assigning a whole number to each of these, then do the same thing with even numbers, then imagine adding them together. Cantor delineated several other equally astonishing paradoxes, which, along with other aspects of number theory, suggest that the idea of number is best considered as a metaphor. Another approach is to consider numbers as existing in a separate "reality" from the one in which we live, a reality that happily overlaps with ordinary reality, but not perfectly.

The point of all this is that our commonsense understanding of numbers is naive. Numbers and mathematics do not actually validate the sense of consciousness that we take for granted. This is also true of physics, the science that we consider the ultimate arbiter of reality. It has become commonplace to quote astounding remarks from famous scientists, remarks that defy our ordinary understandings—to wit, Stephen Hawking's comment that given how physics conceptualizes time, questions are raised as to "How real is time? . . . Where does the difference between the past and the future come from? Why do we remember the past and not the future?" (quoted in Anglia Television, 1992; Schambra, 1961). We marvel at the magical reality of subatomic particles that respond to each other instantaneously no matter how far apart they are. The most sophisticated science we have seems to deny the ordinary consciousness that we take for granted.

One way of understanding this is simply to consider that the world of words, by which our consciousness is constituted, is so different from the world of mathematical equations that the one cannot be fully translated into the other. Another way of putting the matter is this: The consciousness of reason that we "commonsensically" take as given configures something that is *unsymbolizable*. Symbols are generated *within* the limits of reason. Thus, although reason depends on being able to establish boundaries or limits, there appears to be a limit to the act of limiting. There is a limit to reason itself, and reason cannot symbolize, cannot represent, its own limitations. Reason, therefore, rests on a problematic foundation. This foundation can be rendered solid only by finding a way of accepting and continually acknowledging the contradiction that underlies it without letting the contradiction undermine it completely. Shortly, I will discuss how this is accomplished in practice. Here I want to point out that reason is tenuous, is bothered by its limits, and is inherently unstable. As Roger Jones (1982), a physicist at the University of Minnesota, put it, "[Gödel's proof alone] . . . may well mean that mathematics can never be put on a firm rigorous foundation, let alone physics or anything else" (p. 158).

We can see this in the history of the effects of the discovery of the zero by the Hindus. Zero is something like the reverse of the idea of infinity, but it is exactly like infinity in that it is an ultimate and inconceivable limit. The idea of zero has had a tremendous effect on human consciousness (Rotman, 1987), enhancing the power of mathematics in almost magical ways and enabling the capacity for abstract representation in art. Where there is representation, there is absence; hence, the capacity for comprehension of absence is essential to the idea of representation. At the same time, though, zero is working to undercut or evacuate some of the most important meanings that people are able to create with numbers. The best example is money (Rotman, 1987). Money began as an actual (e.g., the gold coin) index of value. As consciousness has elaborated into the more and more sophisticated representation that zero enables, however, money has become an almost entirely abstract phenomenon, sustained by a delicate network of commercial relationships. Money has, at this point, been evacuated of any objective meaning; it refers only to the system of commercial transactions of which it is a part and to nothing outside this system. These days, money is an electronic blip on a computer screen.

I have painted a bizarre picture, one that makes it appear as if the world could collapse at any moment. In fact, the world is holding together fine. Remember, though, this is exactly what we are discussing: how we are able to sustain a stable sense of reasoned approach to the world even though reason is unstable, or grounded on a contradiction, or unable to comprehend and symbolize what its own limitations are. What I hope I have accomplished at this point is to have raised the idea that reason, the style of approaching reality that is grounded on the notion of boundary, is conceptually problematic.

You may not believe all I have conjured, and in fact, I hope you do not, because it would be better if you checked all this out for yourself and came to your own conclusions. I just want to make it plausible enough to engage you and to set the foundation for your making sense out of what I want to discuss next: sex.

What, in God's name, does "the Woman" represent?

I want to discuss sex and gender in relation to the issue of reason. First, as with consciousness, I must problematize gender. This means getting past the idea that the terms *male* and *female* refer to something that represents a concrete external reality. It is not my project to review the research and theory that confronts the commonsense view that gender is real. There is a large literature on this matter now (Alexander, 1993; Butler, 1990; Calas & Smircich, 1996; Fausto-Sterling, 1985). The result of this research and theorizing is that gender does not have an unarguable empirical basis in biology or anything else. Gender is a concept.

I do not mean that I deny there are biological differences among people that are discernible in reality. It is not, however, necessary or even sensible to set up a binary classification and force the range of these differences into two categories. Sexual difference, in all its dimensions (physical and psychological) occurs along a continuum that can be conceptualized as an asymptotic bimodal distribution. The differences are not concretely distinct but can be maintained only as a range of traits that vary. As many as 5% of human infants are born with physiologically anomalous genitals (Alexander, 1993), and their parents must choose which sex they want the child to be. Adjustments are then made surgically to effect their decision. Because there are many ways to average things out, experts on gender disagree on how many genders ought to be considered as "existing." One geneticist who is an expert in this area, Anne Fausto-Sterling, says flatly that "biologically speaking, there are many gradations running from male to female; depending on how one calls the shots, one can argue that along the spectrum lie at least five sexes—perhaps more" (quoted in Alexander, 1993, p. 14). The Gender Dysphoria Trust International has identified a potential fifteen sexes in its comprehensive review of the available evidence (Alexander, 1993). To say that the world is divided "naturally" into two categories is to oversimplify the matter seriously.

Despite this, I do not wish to be heard as claiming that gender is entirely a social construction that could be reconstructed along any lines we might choose. My position is that gender does have an intractable grounding, but this grounding is not the one that either physiology or the social constructionists want to give it. My definition of gender is this: *Gender is the expression in "reality" (which is to say, in the social world that we take for granted) of the model of reason that currently organizes consciousness* (Copjec, 1994). Explaining exactly what this means is a complex matter, but I can begin by saying again that the consciousness of reason that just about all of us currently employ *is all that we have.* Its possibilities and, more important, its dependence on limits are real. They will not budge. If they did, we would lose the foundation of our consciousness and the reality that it configures for us, and we would become psychotic.

My position is that gender reflects a *symbolic*—that is, a linguistic—reality rather than an *empirical* one. The consciousness of reason by which we currently function exists on a symbolic plane (we use words—that is, symbols—to represent reality) and operates semiotically—which is to say, according to the laws of signification rather than according to what we call the laws of the natural world. There is a connection between these two sets of laws, of course. What consciousness does is constellate, through the symbolic processes by which it functions, a representation of the REAL world that exists outside it. We typically refer to this representation as "reality" and (mis)take it to be the REAL world. Traditionally, this has been a difficult thing to understand, but it is easier to see these days because we have become familiar with the concept of *virtual reality,* the reality that we are able to generate with the aid of computers. The reality that we experience as "real" is actually a kind of virtual reality. Computer-generated virtual reality is even one step further removed from the REAL world in the direction of virtualness. It may be that its "virtual-ity" is apparent to us only because of its novelty. Animals, we might speculate, are the only ones around who are living directly—that is, who are in direct contact with the REAL world—at least as we understand and represent animals.

Consciousness is analogous to a trap for our attention. Somehow, when we acquired language, we moved out of the REAL world and onto the symbolic (that is, linguistic) plane of consciousness, and the door closed and locked behind us. Reason, in turn, is a specific version of consciousness, a stage in the elaboration of the symbolic logic of consciousness itself. We can speculate that there are other versions of consciousness closer to the REAL, which are, in that way, less of a trap than is reason. Some imagine the Goddess cultures of the ancient past to be illustrative of this type of consciousness (Gadon, 1989; Gimbutas, 1989, 1991; Olson, 1983). Those cultures, which apparently did not have writing, seem to have functioned fundamentally differently from the cultures that have grown up under what we currently think of as civilization. Gender and gender relations seem to have been different in the days of the Goddess as well. What this means for understanding the dynamics of reason is difficult to discern, since it is so speculative. I am arguing that consciousness as reason sets the symbolically objective constraints on which gender categories as we currently know them are based.

It is reason that cannot symbolize its own limits. We cannot know what we cannot symbolize, and it is probably this unknowable some-thing that makes it so difficult to resolve Cantor's paradoxes of infinite numbers, Gödel's paradox of the logical foundations of mathematics, and the other dead ends into which reason runs at its limits. Reason, in other words, is like our vision. The human visual system has a blind spot in it, caused by the blank space on the retina where the optical nerve connects to the eyeball. We are not aware of this blind spot because the brain fills it in with content that is an extrapolation of what it predicts *should* be there given what it sees in the surrounding visual field. We have the experience of complete vision even though it has a limit that we cannot apprehend directly. This underlines the notion that our sense of reality is virtual; computerized virtual realities are only different from real realities in that they leave some informa-tion out, just as our eyes do.

This makes for an approximate and therefore difficult connection between the reality we configure through our consciousness and the REALITY outside it. Reality only meshes with REALITY in an approximate way—which brings us back to the issue involving gender and the role that it plays in maintaining consciousness. In general, the approach of reason is to seek to refine the representation of reality that it makes so as to bring it into closer and closer—which is to say, into more accurate—contact with the REAL. This, of course, is what science is all about. Reason created science as a way of compensating for the limits of consciousness, of ferreting out its blind spots and of even more closely approximating the REAL. This is the laudable intention of science, but it cannot completely live up to this high purpose because it is impossible for reason to symbolize and understand its own limitation. As a consequence, it must seek to defend itself against its own intrinsic limit, its Achilles heel, at the level of practical action.

One way of understanding how gender supports consciousness is in terms of the psychological process of projection (Von Franz, 1980; Weinberg & Rowe, 1988). The least developed aspects of an individual's personality are inevitably pushed out of conscious awareness. As a result, they function as a limit to the person's consciousness, a "shadow side" that threatens the integrity and the functioning of the official, conscious personality—which is composed of those aspects that the person wants to show to the outside world and has therefore worked on developing. Consciousness is aware, at some inchoate level, of its limitations, however, and it seeks to come to terms with this by bringing the shadow side under control and preventing it from destroying all that consciousness has attained. Since it cannot consciously symbolize, understand, and come to terms with its own limit directly, its initial maneuver in attempting to prevent its shadow side from destroying it is to *create an exterior representation of the limit.* In everyday life, one way we do this is by creating personal enemies for ourselves—people that we "just do not like." Such animosities are actually grounded in aspects of ourselves that we dislike and do not want to acknowledge. We select other people in whose behavior we perceive these traits and project what we do not like about ourselves onto them. We establish an antagonistic relationship with them. At one level, consciousness is seeking to resolve its limit and expand and transform itself by finding a way of talking to itself about this limit. Because it cannot carry on an interior dialogue about its own shadow side, however, it embodies it in another person so that by having a dialogue with the other person, even a conflicted dialogue, it can come to understand its own neglected shadow side better. At another, more superficial and practical level, consciousness is seeking to *control* the shadow side so as to prevent its limitation from creating harm. After all, this is the problem, and it is, or at least potentially can be, a dire one. Sanity itself is at stake. If the shadow side is deeply repressed and consequently primitive and highly energized, it can wreak havoc. Since the conscious personality cannot symbolize its limit, it must create an object to represent it so that it can attempt to control it.

The reference to personal psychology (many will recognize this as specifically Jungian psychoanalytic theory) is meant only to be illustrative in a metaphorical way. In the case of reason as our current collective mode of consciousness, things are much more serious than this. Because we are talking about the collective level, there is much less possibility for transformation and development by resolving the limit than in the case of personal psychology. Also, the stakes are much higher, going so far as to include the fate of the human race.

Gender and gender relations are right at the center of this question, and that is why they constitute such a difficult issue. I stated earlier that gender is the expression in the everyday world of the limits of reason. The Jungian psychological metaphor allows us to understand more of what this means. Women stand for the limit to reason that it is otherwise incapable of symbolizing. *Symbolically speaking, then, reason is the Man, and the Woman is its (his) limit.* Actual men represent the Man, and actual women represent the Woman. Women function in everyday life as a stand-in for, a reminder of, the limitedness of reason and the dangers that lurk because of this. They also serve as a device for effecting practical measures that will prevent the potential dangers threatened by reason's limits. If reason could deal with—which is to say, symbolize and comprehend—that which sets its limit and is represented and made concrete in the sexual difference, we could do away with gender and have one sex. Why, after all, do we need two gender designations? To reproduce? Obviously, people could and would reproduce just as they do now without being called men and women. (Are women who are physiologically incapable of reproduction, or who choose not to reproduce, not women?) What benefit does the posturing that the gender designations induce yield for having babies and stable families in which to raise them? A strong argument could be made that, if anything, gender roles make human relationship more complex, difficult, and problematic and impair the process of producing healthy new members of society. The danger entailed in doing away with gender, however, at least at this point in the evolution of the human condition, seems to be nothing less than the complete loss of the world created by reason—and by this I mean reality itself (Noble, 1992).

How do women play the role in reality that I have just asserted that they do? What does the category "women" mean in everyday life? What do we associate with the term *woman?* What stereotypes attach to it? In general, the answers to all of these questions derive from an intuition we have that women are limitless, that they do not actually acknowledge boundaries. For example, they let their feelings out in instances where men do not: They cry, they become angry, they become "hysterical." Also, to the bitter dismay of men, they seem capable of generating endless strings of words; they talk fluidly. They seem never to run out of words. Interestingly, the available research suggests that the opposite is true and that deep down, we know it. In a study involving mixed-gender discussion groups, a word count of what was said showed that men talked more than women. Judges, guessing the gender of the participants from anonymous transcripts, identified the higher talkers as men. In other words, "it seems that people have an incorrect conscious stereotype of how much women and men talk, while at the same time having, at a less conscious level, the knowledge that men tend to speak more than women" (Frank & Anshen, 1983, p. 28).

There is, in sum, a stereotype that attaches a certain *extravagance* to women. Perhaps this goes back to differences in sexual capacity. Women are seen as capable of having sex in extravagant ways and to an extravagant extent. This is a deeply repressed aspect of the stereotype attached to women (men work hard to cover up the reality of women's greater capacity for sex) and suggests all the more that it is a true and important aspect of the matter. A common male fantasy is that women want to have sex with multiple partners, and in fact, in Jungian psychology, female idealizations of the male (the animus) are multiple, whereas male idealizations of the female (anima) are singular (Jung, 1958). Perhaps derived from this is also a perception of an abundance that attaches to women. As mothers, women are, of course, sources of fecundity and nourishment, and they are necessarily more concerned with nurturance than men. When things fall apart in a society through violence and revolution, it is typically women who organize sustaining economic processes (Arana-Ward, 1996; Moore, 1992). The association of women with natural abundance confounds the male view that nature is threatening and imposes limits. Women seem less capable of comprehending the reality of constraint and the lack of abundance with which men's reality is filled and by which it is constituted (White, 1972).

In these illustrations, I am not saying that women do, in fact, possess the traits that the stereotypes allege. Women vary widely. It would not be surprising to find, though, that women on the average do act out the place in reality to which they have been assigned. Certainly, there is a good deal of social psychological research that suggests that doing just this is a strong overall tendency in human psychology (Eden, 1984; Kohn, 1993; Milgram, 1974; Snow, 1969; Zimbardo, Haney, Banks, & Jaffe, 1973). This tendency is how social roles with a symbolic foundation (for example, in language and the logic of reason) become enacted in the social world, making the roles appear to be a reflection of nature rather than merely socially constructed.

This characterization of women relates to the issue of reason. What threatens reason is limitlessness, infinity. We can illustrate how "going on and on" is a threat to reason in some women's writing. A case in point is women's "fanzines" (fan magazines written and produced entirely by female fans) of the television show *Star Trek* (Bacon-Smith, 1986). These magazines, written entirely by women, display a distinctive kind of writing, completely unlike usual narrative exposition. The stories never end and in fact turn back on themselves, reinvent the past, bring dead characters back to life, revise characters, and so on. They are open and nonlinear to a degree unknown to "normal" narrative. A man I know who was a reader of these magazines at one point told me that he found the writing deeply disturbing specifically because nothing ever seemed to come to closure. This makes the point directly: Limitless strings of words and the perpetual revision to which they lead seem to men to *destroy the possibility for meaning.*

The nature of the threat posed to the consciousness of reason by "postmodernism" and postmodernist writers such as Jacques Derrida is quite similar to that posed by the woman. Deconstruction, and indeed the attitude of postmodernism in general, seeks to demonstrate that no text is capable of producing a bounded, confined, defined, and stable set of meanings (Derrida, 1974; Kamuf, 1991; Norris, 1982, 1987). The meanings of a text, on a close deconstructive reading, shift, slide, and mutate into the opposite of what a traditional, official reading of it might assert. Even authors are not in a position to confirm what their texts say. Deconstructionists are *refusing to keep up the appearance that words have bounded meanings* and, by implication, are refusing the idea of stable boundary. They are refusing the founding principle of reason itself.

Anyone or anything that does this from an active, empowered position is a threat to reason. Women are the generic representatives of the threat of limitlessness, but they have been kept under control for so long that, as a collective force, they function (as a male friend said) as a slave class that has accommodated to its masters. They are no longer a threat. Only those, such as various feminists, who want to "liberate" women, those, such as gay people, who want to ignore traditional gender boundaries, and those, such as postmodernists, who want to expose the tenuousness of the idea of boundary within the symbolic, linguistic realm pose a threat to reason. All these elements must be brought under control or—and I am not overstating my point here—we face the end of the world as constituted by reason.

So we come to this: The answer to the question posed as the topic of this section is that women represent that which must be denied or kept under control if reason is to be preserved. By extension, anyone or any group that becomes implicated with limitlessness or the denial of boundary must be regarded as a similar threat. Reason is the hinge to reality itself; if we lose reason, we lose the world. It is time now to elaborate further what this threat of losing the world means. It has two aspects: First, if we lose reason, we lose the capacity for configuring physical reality and for apprehending the objects of experience; second, if we lose reason, we will lose each other, which is to say we will lose our bearings on our relationships with each other as human beings, not be able to recognize each other as fellows, and become unable to behave in a human way.

Either of these losses alone would mean losing our minds, but the loss of reason means, to repeat, that both would happen to us. In asserting this, what am I trying to do? At first, this book presented itself as a persistent attack on Men of Reason. Then it seemed to back away from this attack by saying that because reason constitutes consciousness itself, the only consciousness we have, Men of Reason must lead us in positions of institutional power. Now I am extending this by saying, apparently, that to lose reason means to lose the world as we know it, and that keeping women and others like them in a position of oppression is essential to holding on to reality. Has this book thus far been a "setup" designed to force a grim acceptance of a distasteful status quo?

Rest assured, I am not going to end by holding that the status quo is all that is possible. The problem is so serious and deep, however, that I find it impossible to find an upbeat, practical way of discussing it. At the same time, I feel that, largely due to the development of the postmodern moment in which we find ourselves, we are at a point where we can create a new level of awareness about the trap (of reasonable consciousness) encapsulating us. This awareness will show that our cage has two intermeshed dimensions that are problems for us: (a) how to make things and (b) how to treat other people. I want now to delineate in a preliminary way the scope and nature of these two problems. Doing so will tell us a little about the size of the bars in our cage, what is involved in cutting through them, and the first tiny saw strokes that we might make.

What to Do Next?

How can we make a world (things) without using reason?

Throughout this chapter I try to avoid "philosophical" discourse and to keep the discussion within the frame of common sense, even when talking about highly unusual things. I have certainly pushed and perhaps strayed over that line already, and I will do so in this section as well. What I want to discuss here is the matter of "creating the world" when, of course, to our everyday minds, the world already exists. Just as I had to problematize consciousness and gender to discuss them, I must begin here by problematizing the world. This means I must render plausible the idea that a world is something we human beings must *accomplish;* it is not given to us.

If you want to tell me that the world is objectively "out there," I can and will agree with you or at least be happy to specify that this is not at issue. I have referred earlier to the world that is "out there" as the REAL or REALITY. This is the place where, again, I speculate, animals live. Human beings possess consciousness, which derives from the fact that we have developed the facility for signification—that is, for language. In the perspective that I work from, what human beings do is use the process of signification to make a representation of the REAL. We call this representation "reality," and because we have become so accustomed to it, we take it on a day-to-day basis to be the REAL thing, not a representation.

So when I say, "How can we 'make a world' without depending on reason?" I mean, "How can we become conscious that we create a representation of the REAL without relying on the idea of boundary?"

At the practical level, this means nothing less than the question of how we can make objects appear to our minds so that we can manipulate them. If you remember the metaphor of computerized virtual reality that I invoked earlier, this becomes easier. We face something like the kind of problem that computer programmers face in writing the code that will enable the computer to create a virtual reality. The specific issue is how we can do this without relying on the artifact of reason and its foundational axiom, boundedness.

The label under which thinkers usually attempt to discuss this question is *epistemology.* I can tell you from experience that the first matter we face is being able to establish a dialogue *at all* about this issue. I have a total of forty-eight years working in academe, and without question trying to engage the epistemological issues of the field has been the darkest and most intractable problem I have encountered. When this topic is raised, people tend to become anxious and distressed. (In fact, one of my graduate school advisers, a political theorist, warned me against becoming an epistemologist on the grounds that it would drive me to despair and ruin my life as it had his.) Because we all wanted to have amiable relations in our workplaces, a norm developed that academics would avoid discussing epistemological matters as far as possible. Traditionally, it was rare to find a writer who specified the epistemological stance from which a work was written—Simon was a standout exception to this. This norm was probably well advised, though it has been embarrassing to have to have it in an academic setting. The advent of "deconstructionism" and "postmodernism," however, has raised these issues in such pointed and unavoidable ways that people have had to engage them both in writing (Miller & Fox, 1996) and in face-to-face discussions, and tensions have escalated. (I have heard numerous stories of fist-fights among members of English department faculties in the early days of the introduction of deconstructionism. There is even a mystery novel about this written by an English professor, *Murder at the MLA;* Jones, 1993.

I have often fallen into epistemological discussions, probably because the perspectives from which I have worked were unorthodox. In public administration, these discussions are usually with people who represent the Man of Reason perspective fairly self-consciously. What has always amazed me is how loaded and confusing these encounters are (McSwain, 1995; White, 1995). The proponents of the Man of Reason perspective have consistently been *desperate* to dismiss my point of view, leading them to stereotype my position as relativist, as hedonistic (in the sense that they see me as arguing that the possibilities for socially constructing the world are unlimited and thus think that I do not acknowledge the constraints imposed by the reality of "how it is"), as antiauthority, and as denying the plain facts of reality (a point usually made by attempting to force me to acknowledge the reality of the "table right here in front of us"). Yet these are all mischaracterizations: They are not about the validity of perspectives, they are about *attitude*. What my colleagues have been trying to get me to do is to adopt a certain emotional and cognitive stance toward reality. They have been haranguing me in the way that parents lecture a child whom they feel has adopted a misguided attitude toward life. The specific issue under discussion becomes incidental to the larger issue of getting the child to change its attitude.

Let me explain what this means and its implication for the question we are considering. The issue consciousness must solve to configure reality (a stable and accurate enough representation of the REAL) is how to impose a limit on the representational process. To create an object in reality so that we can manipulate and use it, what we have to do is create a stable, language-based description of it in consciousness. If we let the describing process go on forever, the description is never accomplished, and the object never appears. I have had an experience that illustrates this process. As a youth, I once worked as an apprentice auto mechanic. My mentor took delight in introducing me to tools I had never used before by describing them to me—sometimes out of necessity, because he would be under a car and would send me to the tool board to fetch something for him. I would stand in front of the tool board and listen to his description. When it reached the point of cogency for me, the tool would "appear" in my field of vision. It, of course, had been there all along, but I could only "see" it when I got the idea of it. In some cases, his power of description failed, I could never get the idea, and I never saw (or "created") the tool. In these instances, he would talk on and on, and the more he did, the worse things became. *Interestingly, he typically blamed me for not being able to see the tool, as if I had the wrong attitude* in listening to him.

Descriptions are created, in the jargon of semiotics, through a "string of signification." Semioticians from Peirce on have pointed out that the process of signification is intrinsically unstable, because a "sign" refers to a "signified" (a concept) and a "signifier" (the word standing for the concept), but the signified always refers not to a thing (which could ground it and stop the process) but to another sign, composed of another signifier and signified (Hartshorne & Weiss, 1931). In short, words refer to other words, sometimes in a circular fashion. I discovered this directly once when I wanted to find out the difference between the meaning of the words *compose* and *comprise*. I wanted to remedy my ignorant confusion of them, so I looked up *compose* in a dictionary, then looked up the definitions of the words in its definition, on and on, until, surprisingly, I came back to *comprise*. The meaning of *compose* had "slud," as Dizzy Dean used to say, into *comprise*.

The problem is how to stop this sliding so that descriptions can be stabilized, concepts formed, and the things of the world configured into a reality. (Accomplishing this is a considerable task when we realize that, for example, the 500 most used words in the English language have more than 14,000 dictionary definitions; Dolan & Lamoureaux, 1990.) Then we can have facts, explanations, and all the rest of it. The way we do this at present is through imposing a boundary and thereby invoking the technique of reason, of being "reasonable." This technique has problems, leading to the conclusion that if reason is to work, we have to support it with a certain *attitude,* a certain commitment. This is why, when people persist in pointing out ambiguities and raising questions about the meaning of something, they are likely to be met with the admonition "Be reasonable!" (Children are geniuses at raising such endless strings of questions when they do not want to understand something. They realize that ambiguity is always present.) In putting it this way, I do not intend to parody or berate the attitude I am discussing. I simply want to highlight how high feelings can run because of what is at stake: reality itself, the world. This is why epistemological discussions are so terribly emotional. Literally "everything" is at stake in them.

For the sake of brevity, I will give a summary description of the attitude that is necessary to support reason and make it work. To begin, we can evoke an image that it is what we typically call "the scientific attitude." The emotional baseline of this attitude is *deference to the object.* (A lot is assumed in this, most notably that the object is there already, independent of our perception-measurement-definition of it.) In other words, we must approach the object humbly; let it speak to us; let it impose its "reality" on our minds; never let our mental state impose itself on the object. We must also maintain a *sense of perpetual openness.* This means that we accept the inevitable incompleteness of our perception-measurement-definition of the object. We must hold the view that we will *never* be able to know the object completely and finally. Science is an open-ended process. This perspective leads to a related aspect. We must be resigned to the idea that the conclusions we reach will be accepted because they are the only ones possible at this point. In sum, we must let reality tell us what to do, and we must do as we are told. There is a certain mood of fatalism in this attitude, as if we must bow down and let reality dominate us and by so doing play out our fate for us.

We create rationalizations that suggest that adopting this position is *essential*, even though it is not; hence, what reason finally must rely on is *pretense*. We must make it possible to stop the infinite sliding of the process of signification by behaving as if boundaries around things already exist and by holding to an attitude that rationalizes this behavior. I think it is clear that the ideology of reason acknowledges that reason is limited. It knows that neither science nor morality produces clear and final answers. Placing choice in the discretion of the Man of Reason is simply a way of compensating for the deficiency of reason itself. I do not mean to sound as if I am condemning reason because it is based on a sham or entails onerous costs such as the gender oppression that feminists write about or the forfeiture of responsibility for our fate that Kuhn (1962) revealed in the Man of Reason method. If reason were the only way that we could make a world, we would obviously be crazy not to be willing to do what it requires. "Your money or your life" is not really a choice at all.

I hold the view, though, that there is an alternative to reason or, if you prefer, an alternative way that we can compensate for reason's contradiction and limits. I call it *collaborative pragmatism*. I define it in contrast to reason specifically on the point of how it proposes to stop the sliding of signifiers that baffles reality creation. Collaborative pragmatism is the heart of the suppressed constitutional subtheme discussed in this book, the theme that began with the ethos of the colonies, was carried into the Articles of Confederation, appeared in populism and progressivism at the beginning of the twentieth century, and has reappeared in the present moment as postmodernism.

I can begin explaining this by returning to the case of perceiving-measuring-defining an object—perhaps the famous "table that is right there in front of us." It has become a commonplace observation in the discourse of epistemology that the reason that the table is so obviously "there" as an object in my and others' field of experience is that a backdrop has been set for this field that *makes* the table appear there. In other words, our perception has been structured in a standardized way. I have already learned—even though I did not realize it as it was happening—how to apprehend—which is to say, "create"—the table. Neither vision nor any other device of sensory perception functions in a purely "natural" manner; perception is socially conditioned (Crary, 1992; Elkins, 1996; Farmer, 1995; Sacks, 1995; Silverman, 1996). What is this social conditioning, and how is it accomplished? The physicist Roger Jones (1982) observed that to measure an object—to determine the length of a table, for example—one must already know its length before the measurement is taken. What he meant by this is that there can be no such thing as measurement in the abstract. When one starts to do a precise measurement on a table and goes as far as one can go, the atomic level, the edge of the table shades off imperceptibly into the surrounding environment. (The problem of limits again!) Jones concluded, therefore, that no measurement is possible *unless one brings a purpose to the project of measuring.* This is the sense in which one must "know the length beforehand." One must be able to tell, given the purpose at hand, when the measurement has reached a sufficient degree of precision. What accomplishes the measurement and brings the object into existence is a sense of *purpose.*

Even Men of Reason, I believe, would admit to this. The way that mathematicians have come to terms with the problem of the absolute limit of zero is by finding a way of approaching it as closely as they wish, given the purpose they are pursuing (Jones, 1982). We can see from this that the attitude of submitting to the object involves a deception. It is like the problem of the table: We cannot submit to it and let it tell us its length because it does not exist in our reality until we bring a purpose to it. *If we want a world, we have to actively create it by deciding what we are up to.* The pretense of submitting to objects, of being objective, is thus revealed as a way of pursuing a hidden agenda whereby an unrevealed purpose is realized through the putatively "neutral" activity of objective measurement. If this is the way it is, then should not all of us be included in setting the purpose that the measurement realizes?

Although this may shed some light, it nonetheless begs the question we are pursuing (i.e., how to make a world) because we still do not know how to achieve a sense of purpose. Where does it come from? How does it escape the problem of sliding signification? To address this matter, we must turn to the admittedly vast question of where our subjectivity is located. In the description of consciousness that I have presented so far, I have made it seem as if the human subject resides in consciousness, in the conscious attitude. This is true, but it is not the whole truth. There is an *unconscious dimension* to the subject, and this dimension can come into play in the affairs of consciousness in powerful ways. Although consciousness is an important aspect of human subjectivity, it is not the true center. This is because the conscious attitude is a creation of social discourse and as such is an artifact of society or at least of that part of society to which a specific individual has been exposed. As such, the person as a "consciousness" is determined and predictable, not really making choices, freely responding, or doing all the other things that we associate with being truly human.

This true human person must exist outside consciousness, perhaps in the unconscious. Subjectivity so located is in a position from which it could disrupt or stop the process of signification that occurs at the level of consciousness. The question is, How does it do this? I can hardly know consciously all about the subject in the unconscious, but I can suggest a few things about its paradoxical role. To do this, I draw on the cybernetic theorist Gregory Bateson (1973) and his analysis of Alcoholics Anonymous (AA). By invoking AA, Bateson wants to show that the system, in this case the human system, has a reality and a power independent of its parts. When alcoholics go to AA meetings and say, "I am an alcoholic," they dissolve as individual units and open themselves to the regulating power of the group system. AA is remarkably effective as a treatment for alcoholism. Whenever alcoholics assert their individuality, as when they subsequently claim, "I can take just one drink and handle it," they typically succumb again to alcohol.

Another way of looking at this is that when alcoholics say, "I am an alcoholic," they are creating a semiotic disruption or irruption in the conscious process. That is, because the term *alcoholic* designates one who has been taken over and no longer exists as an independent person, what this sentence means is: "I am . . . not." Such a statement creates a vacancy, a space into which something from the outside (the human subject emerging from its source in the unconscious) can enter. When this happens, it begins to do what the person consciously cannot do: stop drinking alcohol. A similar thing occurs in conflict situations when the parties give up game playing and posturing and discuss their vital interests. When they admit, like the alcoholic in AA, the emotionally grounded desire that they see as dominating them ("All I want is alcohol"), paradoxically, the conflict situation begins to become malleable, and possibilities for a negotiated settlement, a shared purpose, begin to emerge (Fisher & Ury, 1991; Follett, 1924; Richman et al., 1986).

The problem in creating the world is to stop the sliding of the conscious chain of signification so that we can achieve a sense of purpose. This can be done through a certain kind of social relationship that connects people in groups in a specific way, so that the hard edge of their individual consciousness is dissolved. This opens the door for something to come in from the outside—namely, human subjectivity—and this has the potential to stop the infinite process of signification and configure a purpose. This was C. S. Peirce's answer to the question of what can stop the endless sliding of signifiers. He put it in capital letters: the "COMMUNITY" (Hartshorne & Weiss, 1931).

This is not as mysterious as it may sound and can be put in terms of everyday experience. We can make a world by developing the kind of relationships with each other that allow us to figure out what we want to do next. Our shared purpose does not have to be a grand "once and for all time" purpose, which is to say, an ideological purpose. Indeed, purposes like this quickly lose their vitality and die because they become appropriated by consciousness and cannot continue to create things. This is what happens when people start quarreling over whether what they are doing is really progress. The purposes I mean are simply iterative, tentatively experimental choices about what we want to try doing next. If we, in short, can agree on something that we want to do next and set about doing it, then we do not need to worry. Our subsequent actions will create the world. At bottom, it is authentic human relationship that creates the world. *If we have relationship, we do not need reason.*

How do we relate to (treat) others?

The paradigmatic case of the Jew

I began the discussion of how to make a world by recalling some of the personal history of conflict I have had over the issue of epistemology. We can see a bit more clearly now what this conflict was about. It goes beyond what I mentioned above—namely, that I was not showing a proper attitude, keeping up the pretenses necessary to the maintenance of reason, and threatening, therefore, to bring down the world. We can see now that it also has an emotional loading around gender identity. Maintaining the attitude of deference toward the object and the pretense that words represent bounded meanings is a *male* task. It is this way because women represent limitlessness and unboundedness. The task of women is to submit to the controls that have to be placed on them if reason is to be maintained. *These two tasks constitute the baseline principle of social organization.*

This has critical implications for the possibility for human relationship and for escaping from the oppression of reason. Little is possible in the way of relationship under these conditions. In fact, relationship in the sense that I mean it here, pragmatic collaboration, is simply *im*possible. There can be no true collaboration or shared purpose because action must be based on instructions taken from the object—that is, "reality." Men, especially Men of Reason, are the only ones who have the potential to take such instructions, so they have to pass them on to women and "others." This puts men inevitably in the position of leaders and women in the position of followers. It denies collaboration.

Of course, women can assume the scientific attitude and play the role assigned to men in the symbolic order. The better the imitation, the more fully they will be accepted in these roles. There is good reason why women who "pioneered" in traditionally male roles acted and even dressed like men. In principle, though, a man who is a Man of Reason can never really regard a woman in the same way that he would a man. Women can certainly be Men of Reason, but until something changes to depose the consciousness of reason, they will always be imitations and somewhat suspect. As far as relationship at the personal level goes, people innovate in idiosyncratic ways, especially where sex is involved. In principle, however, there is no possibility for anything except the man as boss and the woman as subordinate helpmate.

This raises the question of how we can achieve the kind of human relationship in the social order that will allow reason to be supplanted. Men of Reason are not intrinsically evil; they are simply enacting the currently operative principle of consciousness and social organization, and it happens to have some onerous side effects such as gender and other kinds of oppression. What I have experienced personally and found so puzzling is that a great deal of anxiety and other confused, fear-laden feeling develops around anyone or any group that is out of proper gender position. "Proper gender position" means either representing the principle of limitation or boundedness (and therefore taking instruction from a reasoned approach to reality)—which means being male and in charge—or the opposite, representing the principle of unboundedness—which means being female and controlled. The essence of the matter, as we have seen, is the relationship to the word. Because it is through the word that the world, reality, is configured and brought into being, the word must be regarded as Law. Men take instruction through the Law, women are simply kept under it. Anytime someone gets outside these places, there is threat and anxiety, and this energizes a motive to do something about him or her.

There are many ways of being out of place in the symbolic order. The principle of reason was largely elaborated into the traditional, nonreasonable world through colonialism on the part of white Christian peoples. Colonialism was a carrying of the "Word" to others who had only the idiosyncratic "word" of their traditional societies. A condition developed of a word (of traditional culture) within the Word (of advanced colonizing cultures). The word of traditional cultures typically contained less emphasis on the idea of boundary. These cultures were placed in a position similar to that of the Woman in the symbolic system, where they stood for boundarylessness. They became, as in the case of women, something that required controlling. Skin color was often an aspect of this, in that the colored skin of most colonized peoples can be seen as signifying the void, limitlessness, and so on. However, this is only an incidental aspect of the matter. The opposition of reason to unreason is represented at the most fundamental level in the opposition of gender—male to female—and it superintends all other differences.

Given that the subordination of women has become so normalized, the threat of self-destruction of the regime of reason is more likely to involve not the poles of the gender opposition but the space between them. Reason establishes gender (the Woman) as the only way it can cope with or contain the effects of its own limitation. This means that women have a special or protected (though dominated) place within the regime of reason. Other groups, however, that are neither within the Word nor classifiable in the category of woman are not only not protected but may seem entirely expendable or "eliminate-able." This in-between realm is the area in which ethnic and other prejudice occurs. Alien groups (African Americans in the United States, Turks in Germany, etc.) participate in the projection that women, as representative of the Woman, the limit of consciousness, receive because, as I said, they appear as not fully under the Word, the Law, of the dominant group. As such, they are outside the domain of reason. This is why prejudice is so standard in its manifestations: The outgroup is always seen as lazy, dirty, conniving, disrespectful of property and status, holding weird beliefs, and so on. Generically, prejudice is the feeling that the other is not reasonable and does not live in a reasonable way. At the generic level, this means the other does not respect boundaries. Groups do better or worse in escaping prejudice to the extent that the "word" they bring with them—that is, their indigenous culture—approximates the Word of reason in how it emphasizes integral boundary. In practical terms, the more controlled a group is by a symbolic system (in the case of Hispanics by the Catholic church, in the case of Asians by the integration of religion with the family structure, etc.), the easier time it will have. There may always be a

vestigial prejudicial effect of skin color no matter what the relation to
the word, but this is minimal when compared to the group's relation
to the symbolic. African Americans in the United States, because
slavery virtually erased their indigenous "word" and severely damaged
their family system, appear as a most serious threat to reason.

The Jew stands in this respect in a special category. All other groups
have the possibility of placing themselves, by one device or another,
under the Word of reason, and by this, they can mitigate the prejudice
that they engender. They can accommodate in the way that women
have, and like women, though never able to escape the attitude of
domination, they will be able to attain a substantial degree of safety.
The case of the Jew is the paradigmatic case of intractable bias because
it reveals how the regime of reason can generate a prejudice leading to
its own destruction.

What is special about the case of the Jew? The distinguishing
characteristic of Jews as a group is that although they live within the
context of the Word of reason, they carry their own Word, and they
appear, at the symbolic level, to be under no mediating Man of Reason.
They have a direct relationship to God and represent a denial of the
necessity of bounded consciousness. They have no need of an attitude
of "deference toward the object," toward the bounded Word. Their
reality is their own, and it is complete in itself. The popular stereotypes
by which Jews are often depicted reflect this image. They are depicted
as supremely intellectual, giving them an aura of reason, but at the
same time their intellectualism is depicted as "off," usually in what is
suggested is a neurotic way. Jokes are made about the idea of their
"talking to God." They tend to be seen as a combination of the rational
and the irrational, the point of which is to symbolize that they are not
Men of Reason. As a result, the paranoia they generate is distinctive:
They are seen as intending to take over the whole world, the world
founded on Reason. On this plane, the Jew represents a different mode
of consciousness, one that does not acknowledge the limitation that
founds the dominant consciousness. Nothing that actual Jews do to
adjust to the "dominant culture" can compensate for what they mean
symbolically.

The Jews represent a Word that is both an Anti-Word and not the
Word and that seeks to exist, nonetheless, alongside and inside the
realm of the Word. As such, they are the contradiction, the limit of
reason, made manifest autonomously. In a sense, the Jew occupies a
category adjacent to that of the Woman. Unlike other marginal groups,
however, the Jews have attained a normalized place in the midst of

world society. Although they are under the same institutional constraints as everyone else, they are, psychologically speaking, not under these constraints but entirely free of them. The obedience they pay to our constraints can only appear ultimately as a sham; their sole genuine obedience is to their own word. They live in their own world, and because they do, they are a standing demonstration that the world of reason is not the only world, that there are other ways to create a world.

The Jew presents the paradigmatic instance of the problem of alterity, the case of the confrontation between people living in worlds of mutually exclusive meanings. This is why it is so important to understand the relationship with the Jew and the question of the consequence of anti-Semitic prejudice. It is helpful to consider the obsession with the Jewish Holocaust of World War II in this connection. Why do we pay so much attention to this event when, in the history of crimes against humanity, it is one among many? Why do we not speak of Pol Pot, Stalin, Mao (who probably killed more people than Stalin and Hitler combined), or the Turkish generals who executed the Armenians? The answer is that there is good reason to consider the Jewish Holocaust as different in an especially threatening way. What was different is that *Hitler decided consciously to eliminate the Jews, not from political expediency but as a matter of principle.* At the symbolic level, the meaning of this is that consciousness took on the project of denying its own limitation, the contradiction that makes it possible. It was as if men had decided, instead of simply controlling women, to eliminate the Woman, forgetting that it is she who makes the Man possible. A holocaust of women seems unimaginable, but it is clear that if one did occur, the remaining men would go mad. Precisely the same is true in the case of the Jew, whom apparently the human species can consider killing. *Were the Jew to be eliminated, the people remaining would become insane, psychotic.* There would be a sudden, cataclysmic end to reason and the consciousness that goes with it. This is the prospect that we warn ourselves against in our obsession with the Holocaust. The Jew represents the *possibility* for civilization by, on the one hand, epitomizing it (at the level of reality) and, on the other hand, contradicting it (at the level of the symbolic).

The topic under consideration, though, is relationship under reason. It is the connection of the issue of anti-Semitism to this matter that is significant. What anti-Semitism teaches us is that "tolerance" and "equal treatment" are probably not enough even to sustain a consciousness of reason, let alone to provide the quality of relationship required for transcending it. Reason is most secure, and provides the best possibility for its own transformation, *when it embraces its limitation and its contradiction.* This means neither demanding that signification—that is, words or language—be limited to bounded meanings by pretending that such meanings are there nor rejecting the bounded meanings of reason as sham and becoming playful postmodern anarchists. A metaphor that is useful here is *masquerade* in contrast to *pretense.* Reason is based on the pretense that through employing it we can possess a valid guide to action. Men of Reason see themselves and want to present themselves as *possessing* something that they bring to decision situations: namely, the special attitude of deference required for apprehending and acting on the instructions of reality. This is a necessary and conscious self-delusion that produces pretense. The premise of the masquerade, in contrast, is that the mask reveals an aspect of what is behind it, but never the whole thing. The whole thing, which is the human subject, is not and cannot be fully present in the conscious world. Meaning results from the perpetual interplay of the mask and what is behind it, and it is both "real" and tentative at the same time—that is, real only for the moment. Explicit acknowledgment of the contradiction of reason and its pretenses makes possible the shift to the attitude of masquerade and the creation of *poetic meaning,* meaning that derives from situational juxtapositions (in poetry, of words) rather than stable definitions. This is precisely the situational, iterative meaning that is involved in pragmatic collaboration. At the practical level of human relationship, it means overcoming alterity by *becoming the other,* by saying, and meaning it in the distinctively concrete way that poetry carries meaning, "I am a Jew" (Zizek, 1991).

The following case of becoming the other, taken from an essay written by a veteran of the Vietnam War, suggests this more powerfully:

This is analogous to the epistemological idea of "indwelling" in a paradigm, a fundamental framework of meaning, that is not one's own (Buscemi, 1978). The following case of becoming the other, taken from an essay written by a veteran of the Vietnam War, suggests this more powerfully:

> For me Vietnam now is the first person singular. . . . You ask where I am now? I answer, still in the killing zone. I am fire and I am smoke. I am a dark red spot on a dusty road. I am corpses stacked like cordwood on the fender of a tank. I am a little girl crying before my burning house. Most of all, I am afraid. A tree is moving, turning, now half tree and half man, a tree-man holding a rifle, a rifle pointed at me. I am reaching for my weapon, I am pulling back the slide to put a round in the chamber. I must kill this man before he kills me. My

hand shakes. . . . I will ask God to help me kill this man killing me. And now I am rifling his body, picking in his pockets, pulling his wallet from his pants. Here is Dong. And here is Dong's wife. And here is Dong's child. Mine was the bullet that left them alone. I, too, of course, am dead. The bullet that killed Dong killed me. I now am a hollow man, empty and alone. My psyche has a cicatrix. (From "The Hollow Man," by M. Norman, May 26, 1996, *New York Times Magazine*, p. 54. Copyright © 1996 by The New York Times Co. Reprinted by permission)

Another story from the Vietnam War, one that I know personally because it involved an acquaintance of mine, elaborates the point. My friend, a captain, happened one afternoon to find himself alone outside his camp, walking along the edge of a cane field and carrying only a side arm. Suddenly he saw a Viet Cong soldier in the typical "black pajama" uniform a short distance away in the cane. The man raised his rifle, fired, and the bullet whizzed past my friend's head. (He had not been in direct combat before.) He thought, "I am going to be killed if I don't do something," drew his pistol, and fired just as the man shot at him again. The Viet Cong soldier fell, and my friend turned to run back to camp. As he ran, he became nauseated, stopped, and vomited. He thought over what had happened. He decided to go back to the man. When he got there, he found him wounded in the chest but alive. He carried him back to the camp, where he was given medical attention and then placed in the Army's repatriation program. The Vietnamese man now lives in the Washington, DC, area, and he and my friend have been meeting periodically for thirty years to have dinner and talk.

What happened to my friend as he ran toward camp is that he became in his own way a hollow man. He reported to me that his nausea resulted from the flood of conflicted feelings and thoughts that overtook him after he fired and saw the man fall. All the certainty that had been trained into him and that he had maintained in his belief system about himself dissolved into one overwhelming feeling. He had been, in a sense, "killed" in the way that the soldier in the preceding story had been when he had killed Dong. Gone was the sense of boundary that had so clearly separated him and the Viet Cong soldier. Also, his sense of discrete action had dissolved—that is, his sense that life is a process of deciding and doing and living with the consequences. In the hollowness left by the evacuation of these aspects of his identity, new possibilities emerged. His "decision" to kill the man now simply looked like an iterative event in an ongoing flow. He was able to see the other man in a new, more open light. He had crossed the boundary of self and other, and *he had crossed the boundary of his own model of reasoned action.*

The point of telling this story is not to advocate my friend as a role model for soldiers of the future. I am making no comment about soldiering at all. That both these illustrations involve war is probably because the extreme conditions that occur in war often create experiences that can break the hold that reason and its premise of boundary have on our consciousness. These cases suggest that when this happens, meanings occur that are broader and deeper than those configured by reason. These meanings are temporary and unstable in that they are contingent. The distinctive thing about acting from this position is that meanings have to be created continuously through a process of relatedness that acknowledges the alterity of the other at the same time that it realizes that self and other are the same. All the familiar, appealing certainties of contractual relations are no longer available.

This conclusion, and the analysis on which it is based, no doubt appears strained and dire. After all, one might ask, what does it have to do with public administration? I want to move on to address this now. To set the context for it, I will return to my review of the literature of public administration as it bears on the issue of legitimacy. Where I ended the preceding chapter was at the point of discussing the current intellectual scene in the field, so it is there that I will begin.

The Current Scene in Public Administration:
The Good News and the Bad News

When I originally designed this book, my plan for the final chapter was organized around a two-part conclusion. First, I was going to outline an argument that there are direct analogues between our present-day fin de siècle and the one at the end of the previous century such that history is repeating itself in a sense, and there is a new opportunity to redefine the identity of the field of public administration. In relation to this, I was going to make linkages between the philosophy of American pragmatism and key aspects of postmodern theories. Second, by using the "pragmatism is postmodern" argument as a foundation, I was going to conclude by outlining one way to settle the legitimacy problem for public administration: Adopt a model of public administration grounded in Follett and other pragmatists that show it properly to be pragmatic collaboration with citizens. At the time, this conclusion seemed to be avant garde and theoretically sophisticated. It seemed so outré, as a matter of fact, that bringing it off effectively appeared a daunting task.

The good news is that both of these tasks have already been accomplished to a significant degree. Descriptions of America as a postmodern society abound, and the parallels between these and accounts of the 1890s appear rather obvious (Borgman, 1992; Denzin, 1991; Fox & Miller, 1995; Rosenau, 1992). Richard Rorty's (1982, 1989) work has amply demonstrated the connection between key aspects of pragmatism, especially in Dewey, with the postmodern sensibility. The literature of total quality management (TQM) has revealed aspects of both postmodern thinking and pragmatism (Scherkenbach, 1988; White & Wolf, 1995). The eminent expert on pragmatism, Richard Bernstein (1992), has made a similar and powerful argument.

On the point of elaborating a pragmatic collaborative model of public administration, work both within the field and ancillary to or supportive of it is mushrooming. Such efforts, indeed, are the most exciting things going on in the area at the moment. Camilla Stivers (1990), a scholar whose work has been discussed at a number of points in this essay, has for years been prominent in the movement to redefine the field around a citizen orientation. Her call for active relationships between citizens and administrators is now being addressed in a broad array of responses. A second book from the "Blacksburg Manifesto" group has been published (Wamsley & Wolf, 1996); it advocates a reorientation of the field toward a Jeffersonian, citizen-based model. It even suggests that the Anti-Federalists provide historical legitimacy for this position. This is a rather sharp departure from the "agential leader" model of administration that formed the heart of the original *Refounding Public Administration* (Wamsley et al., 1990) volume. Charles Goodsell, though not appearing in the new volume, has also advocated a reorientation of public administration toward the citizen as the bureaucrat's primary role sender, saying that its traditional points of reference, such as the idea of the public interest and the presidency, are no longer appropriate or effective in this role. Pat Ingraham (1996), as president of the National Association of Schools of Public Affairs and Administration, has issued a similar call, as has Robert Denhardt (1996), a past president of the American Society for Public Administration. A number of other authors in the field have offered analyses that support the move toward redefining public administration so that it can better comprehend and deal with an active citizenry (Box, 1995; Frug, 1993; Herzog & Claunch, 1996; Racine, 1995; Ventriss, 1995a). Two landmark books have appeared in the field within the two past years that are also directly on this point. These are Fox and Miller's *Postmodern Public Administration* (1995) and David Farmer's *The Language of Public Administration* (1995). Both of these books are sympathetic to the postmodern perspective, and both, in different ways, advocate a citizen-oriented public administration. Fox and Miller call for a public administration grounded in dialogue. Farmer's idea entails an "antiadministrator" whose primary point of reference is the other, the client or citizen being served.

The bulk of the work aimed at vitalizing the role of citizenship in governance, however, is being done outside the field of public administration in related disciplines such as political science and sociology. The communitarian movement that the book *Habits of the Heart* (Bellah, Madsen, Sullivan, Swidler, & Tipton, 1985) launched is gaining ground steadily through the work of Amitai Etzioni (1993, 1995) and others. The related but not synonymous "civil society" movement (cited in Chapter 3 of this volume) has overtaken the original communitarian idea and has gained center stage with works such as Robert Putnam's *Making Democracy Work* (1993) and Michael J. Sandel's *Democracy's Discontent: America in Search of a Public Philosophy* (1996). These books have been matched by a host of others written from positions across the political spectrum from far right to far left, and with not only a social but also an organizational and a personal focus.

The interest that has developed within the field in introducing nonlinear theories—for example, chaos theory, the new systems theory, and second-order cybernetics (cited in Chapter 6 of this volume)—bears directly on the question of finding a proper identity for public administration. This development is supportive of the reorientation I am discussing because it implies that an open attitude and an emphasis on the immediacies of relationship building (Wheatley, 1994) are essential for coping with the chaotic conditions that currently confront more and more organizations. It relates closely to the incorporation of family systems theory into organization theory and management (cited in Chapter 6). This long-established body of theory offers a radically innovative way to conceptualize individuals in organizations as products of networks of social relationships. The idea has powerful implications for enabling an improved quality of engagement between workers and those outside the organization.

All in all, I am much encouraged by the array that I have just sketched. Nonetheless, the bad news is that the most likely outcome is that nothing will really change (Behn, 1995; Golembiewski, 1996; Kirlin, 1996; Spicer, 1995; Stillman, 1995). First and most broadly, there is strenuous opposition to all forms of postmodernism, and my intuition is that this opposition represents the great center of theoretical opinion in the field. Second, some have begun to argue that the field should simply stop talking about the legitimacy problem: In effect, public administration in America is legitimate de facto at this point, and the problem is really a false artifact resulting from the absence of a concept of state in U.S. constitutional theory (Rutgers, 1994; Stillman, 1995; Warren, 1993). The concern with ethics as a main focal point of the field seems untouched by the radically innovative ways of thinking about ethical issues offered by various schools of postmodern theory (Bauman, 1993; D. Wood, 1987). The center of opinion seems most drawn to a "new institutionalism" that is expressed in works such as March and Olsen's *Rediscovering Institutions: The Organizational Basis of Politics* (1989) and Philip Selznick's *The Moral Commonwealth* (1992).

This approach is especially pernicious, in my view, because it appears to be something new when in fact it is reactionary, a defensive holding action against the effects of the wearing away of the epistemological foundations of the ideology of reason. The new institutionalism seeks to incorporate pragmatism into its perspective and to appear as epistemologically open-minded by grounding itself on a foundation of interpretivism (Selznick, 1992). The ambiguities of pragmatism (especially the critically important Dewey) and interpretivism render the postmodern readings of pragmatism and interpretivism vulnerable to the charge of being "controversial." Unfortunately, the charges of controversy work with much more impact against theories contending for attention than they do against standing orthodoxies even when the orthodoxy has become problematized and is controversial itself. The net effect of all this is likely to be that things in the field will change but stay the same all the more. We may even consider, though for only a while, that the legitimacy problem is solved. The field might reorient itself around a public administrator of the "Andy of Mayberry" sort—an open, community-oriented, manipulative but nice public servant who runs the world by his own discretion just like the strongest Man of Reason of the past (White & McSwain, 1993). The seeming relativism of postmodern theory is also evoking the last-ditch defense of the Man of Reason ideology: that even though facts and values are not usually clear, and discretion is required, in some cases there is certainty. The contention, then, is that this means that in principle, absolute moral and empirical truths do exist: Hitler was evil, and death is real. The conclusion is that—and it has a great deal of rhetorical appeal—any perspective that denies such things must be crazy. This is, in my view, a vulgar way to argue, but it is difficult to beat.

A Concluding Reflection

I must temper this pessimism with the observation that much of how I feel is based on my identity as a process theorist. To the extent that my career has been devoted to anything, it has been dedicated to the purpose of presenting process theory as a plausible orientation by which public administration could redefine itself. By process theory, I mean Mary Follett and the sort of collaborative pragmatism that I have been advocating in this book. What I have persistently encountered as the central resistance to process theory is that it is unacceptably "relativistic" on the two key fronts of what are generally referred to as fact and value. This resistance centers on the idea that even if it is granted that there can be no finally clear-cut factual or moral basis for the exercise of authority, any approach, such as process theory, that does not ground itself in a sense of deference to objective fact or acknowledge that in some cases facts are undeniable and evils are clear undercuts all possibility for responsible action and is unacceptable. Any call for making action situationally contingent is both dangerous and suspect.

As a process theorist, I have met these resistances by pointing out the self-contradiction of all approaches seeking to avoid wrong action through the device of certainty: "Scientific" and moral certainty has produced much of what we consider to be the most evil episodes of human history. It seems possible that evil can emerge from any quarter—from anarchistic settings to the most venerable institutions. What seems to be behind evil most often is *certainty*, and what produces certainty is the yearning to refer our thoughts and feelings to something outside the human realm, either "facts" or "values" or both. Process theory seeks to make an alternative to certainty possible by showing that when human interaction proceeds properly, a basis for action appears (what Mary Follett called the Law of the Situation) that is neither objectively certain nor ultimately tentative (McSwain & White, 1987).

Explaining process, though, does not seem to work effectively enough to quell the fear that evil will emerge and misdirect action.

That is why I approached the issue differently here. Most of this book argues that a kind of dismal intellectual history aimed at keeping Men of Reason in place was inevitable for public administration and, indeed, for American government. What made this history inevitable was that no important change could happen until we were able to see (a) how it is possible to create a world, to act, without relying on reason and (b) how to come to terms with the otherness with which our fellow human beings confront us. My underlying argument, however, has been that doing the first of these really depends on being able to accomplish the second. Everything depends on coming to terms with the issue of alterity.

I have said nothing about the details of process (White, 1990). That seems to be the wrong level from which to approach the matter. The generic issue is understanding how to confront the task of achieving the correct existential stance in our lives toward each other, the stance from which we will be able to regard persons as others and as us in the same moment. This is why I chose the approach that I did here, and specifically why I focused on the case of the Jew. Time and again, my colleagues in the field have confronted process theory with the case of Hitler and the Nazis. The question they posed was, "Why do we need process when we know Hitler was evil?" Then (suspiciously), "Why do you want us to stop and talk about what to do with him or others like him?"

My answer is that the certainty with which we regard Hitler tends to blind us to the fact that we all have a Hitler within, and it is this universal Hitler that is the most terrible danger. The question, to my mind, is not "How do we handle Hitlers, Skinheads, radical animal rights activists, violent antiabortion groups, and so on?" (the answer to which is obvious: For the present, continue doing what we can) but rather "How do we minimize the possibility that the Hitler aspect of the human psyche will erupt?"

What puzzles me is why the question of what to do about Hitler holds more interest than the question of *how to prevent him*. It seems as if our consciousness of reason *needs* the specter of Hitler as a rationale for itself, as a rationale for the idea of the "just war." Reason seems to require opposition to itself to appear meaningful. Its rhetorical power, its capacity to mobilize and direct emotion, depends on its having an antithesis that needs conquering. Process theory, because it is grounded in the idea that the "opposite" of reason resides within itself as its own limit, denies this rationale and is thus anathema to reason.

I do not see reason as some sort of ultimately bad regime. I have always regarded the opposition of process theory to reason as something like the standing battle between the Democrats and the Republicans in American politics. One might agree with one party more than the other, but it is easy to accept and live under the regime of whichever party holds power. As we approach the end of the twentieth century, however, it is becoming more difficult to hold this happy "Qué será, será" position. There are more and more signs that reason is failing. It may be that the logic of reason has elaborated itself into our patterns of social organization to the point that it has reached its own contradiction. As a process theorist, I, of course, favor the view that all ideas contain a contradiction or flaw that will ultimately come out and present the conditions for change. Irrespective of the cause, however, it seems that social relationships are becoming more problematic.

There is an alarming worldwide rise in prejudice that threatens to engulf us (Barber, 1995; Enzensberger, 1994; Kaplan, 1996). This precipitous increase in sectarian violence began with the dissolution of the Eastern Communist bloc. It appeared that democratic capitalism had won the day and that the world was going to move to a new order, the centerpiece of which would be an integrated market economy. The world economy is indeed developing apace, but at the same time tensions among national, ethnic, racial, and other groups are escalating. There seems to be little understanding of what is energizing this renewed prejudice. As one observer of this scene put the problem, "What gives today's civil wars a new and terrifying slant is the fact that they are waged without stakes on either side, that they are wars *about nothing at all* [italics in original]" (Enzensberger, 1994, p. 8).

The interesting thing about this comment is that it is precisely correct for a reason that it probably did not intend. I agree with the analysis of the problem offered by psychoanalysis. Democracy contains a contradiction at the level of individual psychology. Democracy demands that people be regarded without respect to race, gender, religion, ethnicity, age, and so forth, without regard to anything that concretely confers an identity on them. As a democratic citizen, I must look at my fellows simply as blank others (Zizek, 1991). By extension, I must regard myself in this same way. What this principle ignores, however, is that it requires an eventually complete evacuation of subjectivity, such that I have no identity at all, at least as I have been given to understand the term. The same is true of capitalism. What capitalism offers as a systemic principle is the production of the greatest degree of gratification at the lowest price. The price-to-satisfaction ratio is its ultimate ethical principle. The problem is, of course, that to accomplish this, everything must be priced, yet the act of pricing transforms the things human beings value the most—all of which have to do with relationship to others and to self—into commodities. As consumers in a capitalist order, then, we all become evacuated, satisfied things. Others are commodities to us, we are commodities to them, and we all are only consumers.

This is not to say that a capitalist democracy has no values. Indeed, its values are the highest principles of liberalism and justice. A discrepancy between moral principle and reality acts as a powerful motive for progressive development in which undeveloped nations are transformed into active trading partners. This enhances the efficiency with which the world economic order can exploit and transform resources, revealing in the process that the actual underlying consequence, if not motive, of capitalism is total exploitation of our ecosystem. It is quite natural, then, that an international corporation, Benetton, would build a major worldwide advertising campaign around the concept of advocating universal human values of equality and social and political justice.

What the ideology of democratic capitalism fails to comprehend, though, is that values have no meaning, no grip, in a "universal" context. *They must be grounded in concrete, collective human relationship.* This is why, in a news report on European television, young rebels from the former Yugoslavia announced that they wanted to send a message to the West: "We refuse the United Colors of Benetton." Because they had been faced suddenly with the prospect of a complete evacuation of identity when the ideology of communism failed, it made sense that this kind of resistance would erupt. The venue for such resistance must be to fall back on whatever traditional identities are available and assert those aggressively, if not violently, so as to make them vital and real. This is the sense in which the new civil wars are "about nothing at all." They are a struggle people are waging against being *made into* nothing at all.

The same logic holds for the reassertion of all prejudices and chauvinisms, from church burnings in the South to misplaced "live free or die" American nationalism in the West. What "reasoned" approach can be mounted to respond to these? Reason's approach is moral argument and, when this fails, the just war. The problem is that the power of moral argument has passed its zenith and no longer has the effect it once possessed. Its rhetorical efficacy depends on having a foundation in the stable group identifications that no longer exist.

For this reason, it is likely that the regime of reason will not be able to cope with the contradiction in democratic capitalism that results in evacuation of the individual. Under such conditions, against whom is the just war to be fought? This was the question poignantly raised by the Branch Davidian tragedy in Waco, Texas. The enemy ultimately is a phantom, the growing sense of nothingness within us all, and the only war that can be fought against this enemy is one against any other people who can be seen as unlike us. If this prospect is true, and if we are to save ourselves from it, we are going to have to find a new basis for identity and social relationship and a venue for expressing these so that they can be broadly learned.

So now we come full circle back to the legitimacy issue in public administration. As long as we hold on to this issue by arguing it in the terms of its traditional framing, Men of Reason and their regime will continue, and the contradiction of reason could well consume us. Moving past this issue presents a huge task of transformation, but it may be possible to accomplish. We first must realize that the starting place for the change is *not* adopting a new theory. In this sense, this book and others like it are rather unimportant to the task at hand. Richard Rorty (1994) has written recently that the main problem that the Left (which he wants to revive) has at present is that it has no party to invite people to join, no concrete program of action that it can offer. His point is that theory has little impact in bringing about actual change because unless there is something different to *do,* our energy will be vented in useless theoretical quibbling. This is exactly how the legitimacy problem has functioned to keep us arguing pointlessly.

This is why I want to end by reiterating my purpose: to invite the theory community in public administration to adopt a different style of dialogue. Involving ourselves with the legitimacy issue, since its hidden premise is that people must be held to account, disposes us to sit in judgment on one another and the value and validity of our points of view as we discuss and write about the concerns of our field.

The practical alternative to this is opening ourselves to one another. The practical starting place for this has been identified already by Camilla Stivers, by Fox and Miller (1995) on the last page of their book, and by David Farmer (1995) in his discussion of alterity. The alternative is to *listen,* to become hollowed out, and to receive the other as oneself (Stivers, 1994). This reveals that what I am talking about here is not so much the end of reason as its transformation through the open acknowledgment and embrace of its own contradiction and terrible flaw. By making people and their lives an object in its contemplations, reason separates us from one another when the reality of the human condition is: I am you.

Postscript

I realized as I concluded this project that I had a number of feelings about having written such a book as this. I was reading an excellent article in the *New York Review of Books* last night, and I put it down feeling bothered. I reflected on how different was the discourse of this book from that of the typical intellectual. I like the affectation of formality and coldness that intellectuals present. It took me time and a lot of work to learn it even to the modest degree that I have. Also, I have always considered myself blessed in both my intellectual friends and my enemies, and I want to keep all this as it is. A part of me does not want to take the message of this book to heart and embark on the program of change that it entails. This part just wants my friends to say "Great book, O.C.!" and my enemies to make their usual inane and off-the-point remarks about my work so that things can go as usual.

At the same time, though, I am critical of intellectuals. They tend to have a highly ambivalent attitude toward people in general. Most of them want to be critical—this, indeed, is their vocation—and advocate for the increased welfare of "common" people, but at the same time they want to feel that they are better than the average guy. The result is that they end up working inadvertently to support the pattern of privilege of which they want to be critical, and in the process they let themselves become addicted to the "perks" of the petty bourgeois lifestyle that those in power give them.

I have come to this viewpoint directly from experience as an organization development consultant. People in organizations usually relate to each other as academics do, and this is largely the cause of the problems that OD consultants get called in to help fix. The problems start resolving, it is my observation, when people start changing the way they talk and relate, becoming less reasonable and more real. As I have conducted sessions in which this occurs, I often think of how alien this way of talking is to academics (they are notorious among OD consultants as difficult clients). I also have frequently had the thought that the people I work with in organizations have much more important, responsible jobs than academics do, yet they are willing to drop their pretenses to get their work done responsibly. Are our ego needs as professors so great that even with the low-stakes situations we face we cannot do likewise? I do not know, but our tendency seems to be to hold to the posture of elite figures and by this protect those who are the real power holders. We thereby become simply the schoolmarms and masters of the ruling sector of society.

We in public administration have, I think, a special responsibility to resist this tendency. The true inspiration of our field is the magical but practical task of turning the authority of government to the furtherance of human purposes. The special charity involved in this definitely begins at home. It is time for us to start talking to each other, and this means learning to drop our intellectual pretenses. I doubt that there is much hope for taking this change very far among people of my generation, no matter how much we might wish it. But there are students, and in the final analysis a book that demands the kind of change this one does must be directed toward them. So, to students in the field of public administration, I say: Although the world you face is potentially more problematic than any world faced by a new generation, it is your world, you own it to a degree that no other generation has. You can make it what you want it to be, and do not let anyone tell you any differently.

Don't let it end like this. Tell them I said something.
                                   —*The last words of Pancho Villa*

References

Adams, J. D. (Ed.). (1984). *Transforming work.* Alexandria, VA: Miles River.

Adams, J. D. (Ed.). (1986). *Transforming leadership.* Alexandria, VA: Miles River.

Agrippa [pseud.]. (1966). Letters: December 3, 1787. In C. Kenyon (Ed.), *The antifederalists* (pp. 131-160). New York: Bobbs-Merrill.

Aguayo, R. (1990). *Dr. Deming: The American who taught the Japanese about quality.* New York: Carol.

Akin, G., & Hopelain, D. (1986, Winter). Finding the culture of productivity. *Organizational Dynamics*, pp. 19-32.

Alexander, J. (1993, October). The five sexes. *New Woman*, pp. 14-17.

Allaire, Y., & Firsirotu, M. (1984). Theories of organizational culture. *Organizational Studies, 3*, 193-226.

Allcorn, S. (1992). *Codependency in the workplace.* Westport, CT: Quorum.

Anglia Television & Gordon Freedman Productions (Producer), & Morris, E. (Director). (1992). *A brief history of time* [Film].

Appleby, P. (1945). *Big democracy.* New York: Knopf.

Arana-Ward, M. (1996, September 1). Mothers know best. *Washington Post*, Outlook Section, p. C1.

Astley, W. G. (1985). Administrative science as socially constructed truth. *Administrative Science Quarterly, 30*, 497-513.

Bacon-Smith, C. (1986, November 8). Spock among the women. *New York Times Book Review*, pp. 25-28.

Barber, B. (1984). *Strong democracy.* Berkeley: University of California Press.

Barber, B. R. (1995). *Jihad vs. McWorld.* New York: Time.

Bardach, E. (1977). *The implementation game.* Cambridge: MIT Press.

Barnard, C. (1968). *The functions of the executive.* Cambridge, MA: Harvard University Press. (Original work published 1938)

Barnes, B. (1982). *T. S. Kuhn and social science.* New York: Macmillan.

Bateson, G. (1973). *Steps to an ecology of mind.* St. Albans, NY: Paladin.

Baum, H. S. (1987). *The invisible bureaucracy.* New York: Oxford University Press.

Bauman, Z. (1993). *Postmodern ethics.* Oxford, UK: Blackwell.

Bayley, S. (1991). *Taste: The secret meaning of things.* New York: Pantheon.

Beard, C. A. (1913). *An economic interpretation of the Constitution of the United States.* New York: Macmillan.

Beeman, M. (1987). Introduction. In R. Beeman, S. Botein, & E. Carter II (Eds.), *Beyond confederation: Origins of the Constitution and American national identity* (pp. 3-19). Chapel Hill: University of North Carolina Press.

Beer, S. H., Ulam, A. B., Spiro, H. J., Wahl, N., & Eckstein, H. (1958). *Patterns of government: The major political systems of Europe.* New York: Random House.

Behn, R. D. (1995). The big questions of public management. *Public Administration Review, 55,* 313-324.

Bellah, R. N., Madsen, R., Sullivan, W. M., Swidler, A., & Tipton, S. M. (1985). *Habits of the heart.* Berkeley: University of California Press.

Berger, P., Berger, B., & Kellner, H. (1974). *The homeless mind.* New York: Vintage.

Berger, P., & Luckmann, T. (1966). *The social construction of reality.* Garden City, NY: Doubleday.

Berne, E. (1961). *Transactional analysis in psychotherapy.* New York: Grove.

Berne, E. (1970). *Games people play: The psychology of human relations.* New York: Grove.

Berne, E. (1972). *What do you say after you say hello.* New York: Grove.

Berne, E. (1976). *Beyond games and scripts.* New York: Grove.

Bernstein, R. J. (1992). *The new constellation: The ethical-political horizons of modernity/postmodernity.* Cambridge: MIT Press.

Beyer, J. M., & Trice, H. M. (1987, Spring). How an organization's rites reveal its culture. *Organizational Dynamics,* pp. 5-24.

Black, M. (Ed.). (1961). *The social theories of Talcott Parsons.* Englewood Cliffs, NJ: Prentice Hall.

Blake, R. R., & Mouton, J. S. (1964). *The managerial grid: Key orientations for achieving production through people.* Houston, TX: Gulf.

Blanchard, K., & Johnson, S. (1982). *The one minute manager.* New York: William Morrow.

Blau, P. M. (1965). *The dynamics of bureaucracy.* Chicago: University of Chicago Press.

Blau, P. M., & Scott, W. (1963). *Formal organizations: A comparative approach.* New York: Routledge & Kegan Paul.

Bloom, A. (1987). *The closing of the American mind.* New York: Simon & Schuster.

Bologh, R. W. (1990). *Love or greatness: Max Weber and masculine thinking—a feminist inquiry.* London: Unwin Hyman.

Borgman, A. (1992). *Crossing the postmodern divide.* Chicago: University of Chicago Press.

Bowen, M. (1978). *Family therapy in clinical practice.* Ann Arbor: University of Michigan Press.

Box, R. C. (1995). Critical theory and the paradox of discourse. *American Review of Public Administration, 25*(1), 1-19.

Bragdon, H. N., McCutchen, S. P., & Ritchie, D. A. (1994). *History of a free nation.* New York: Glencoe.

Braibanti, R. (1969). *Political administrative development.* Durham, NC: Duke University Press.

Braybrooke, D., & Lindblom, C. E. (1963). *A strategy of decision: Policy evaluation as a social process.* Glencoe, IL: Free Press.

Briggs, J., & Peat, F. D. (1989). *Turbulent mirror.* New York: Harper & Row.

Brown, R. D. (1987). Shay's Rebellion and the ratification of the federal Constitution in Massachusetts. In R. Beeman, S. Botein, & E. Carter II (Eds.), *Beyond confederation: Origin of the Constitution and American national identity* (pp. 113-127). Chapel Hill: University of North Carolina Press.

Brown, W. (1988). *Manhood and politics: A feminist reading in political theory.* Totowa, NJ: Rowman Littlefield.

Brutus Junior [pseud.]. (1965). The New York journal: November 8, 1787. In M. Borden (Ed.), *The antifederalist papers* (p. 103). East Lansing: Michigan State University Press.

Buck, A. E. (1921). *Public budgeting.* New York: Appleton.

Burke, J. P. (1986). *Bureaucratic responsibility.* Baltimore: Johns Hopkins University Press.

Burns, J. M., Peltason, J. W., & Cronin, T. E. (1984). *Government by the people* (12th ed.). New York: Prentice Hall.

Burrell, G., & Morgan, G. (1979). *Sociological paradigms and organizational analysis.* Portsmouth, NH: Heinemann.

Buscemi, W. I. (1978, Fall). Political theory: Impact of the philosophy of science. *ASPA News,* pp. 1-5.

Butler, J. (1990). *Gender trouble: Feminism and the subversion of identity.* New York: Routledge.

Caiden, G. E. (1971). *The dynamics of public administration: Guidelines to current transformations in theory and practice.* Hinsdale, IL: Dryden.

Calas, M. B., & Smircich, L. (1996). From "the woman's" point of view: Feminist approaches to organization studies. In S. Clegg, C. Hardy, & W. R. Nord (Eds.), *Handbook of organization studies* (pp. 218-257). Thousand Oaks, CA: Sage.

Campbell, A., Converse, P. E., Miller, W. E., & Stokes, D. E. (1960). *The American voter.* New York: John Wiley.

Carr, D. K., & Littman, I. D. (1990). *Excellence in government: Total quality management in the 1990s.* Arlington, VA: Coopers & Lybrand.

Carson, R. (1962). *Silent spring.* Boston: Houghton Mifflin.

Catron, B., & Harmon, M. M. (1981). Action theory in practice: Toward theory without conspiracy. *Public Administration Review, 41,* 535-540.

Centinel [pseud.]. (1965). Letters to *The Independent Gazetteer:* October 5, 1787 and November 8, 1787. In M. Borden (Ed.), *The antifederalist papers* (pp. 110-134). East Lansing: Michigan State University Press.

Centinel [pseud.]. (1966). Letter to *The Independent Gazetteer:* October 5, 1787. In C. Kenyon (Ed.), *The antifederalists* (pp. 2-14). New York: Bobbs-Merrill.

Cohen, M. D., March, J. G., & Olsen, J. P. (1972). A garbage can model of organizational choice. *Administrative Science Quarterly, 17,* 1-25.

Connolly, W. (1969). *The bias of pluralism.* New York: Atherton.

Cooper, T. (1983). *The responsible administrator.* Port Washington, NY: Kennikat.

Copjec, J. (1994). Sex and the euthanasia of reason. In J. Copjec (Ed.), *Supposing the subject* (pp. 16-44). London: Verso.

Copley, F. B. (1923). *Frederick W. Taylor, father of scientific management.* New York: Harper.

Corwin, E. S. (1957). *The president: Office and powers, 1787-1957.* New York: New York University Press.

Crary, J. (1992). *Techniques of the observer: On vision and modernity in the nineteenth century.* Cambridge: MIT Press.

Croly, H. (1963). *The promise of American life.* New York: E. P. Dutton.

Cross, G. (1993). *Time and money.* New York: Routledge.

Crozier, M. (1964). *The bureaucratic phenomenon.* Chicago: University of Chicago Press.

Czarniawska-Joerges, B. (1992). *Exploring complex organizations: A cultural perspective.* Newbury Park, CA: Sage.

Dahl, R. A. (1956). *A preface to democratic theory.* Chicago: University of Chicago Press.

Dahl, R. A. (1961). *Who governs? Democracy and power in an American city.* New Haven, CT: Yale University Press.

Dahl, R. A. (1967). *Pluralist democracy in the United States: Conflict and consent.* Chicago: Rand McNally.

Dahlberg, J. S. (1966). *The New York Bureau of Municipal Research: Pioneer in government administration.* New York: New York University Press.

Damrosch, D. (1995). The scholar as exile. *Lingua Franca, 5*(2), 56-60.

Davis, C. R. (1996). The administrative rational model and public organization theory. *Administration & Society, 28,* 39-60.

Deming, W. E. (1986). *Out of crisis.* Cambridge: MIT Center for Advanced Engineering Study.

Denhardt, K. G. (1988). *The ethics of public service: Resolving moral dilemmas in public organizations.* New York: Greenwood.

Denhardt, R. B. (1981). *In the shadow of organization.* Lawrence: Regents Press of Kansas.

Denhardt, R. B. (1996). Denhardt opens Atlanta conference. *P.A. Times, 19*(8), 16.

Dennard, L. (1995). Neo-Darwinism and Simon's bureaucratic antihero. *Administration & Society, 26,* 464-487.

Denzin, N. K. (1991). *Images of postmodern society.* Newbury Park, CA: Sage.

Derrida, J. (1974). *Of grammatology.* Baltimore: Johns Hopkins University Press.

Diamond, M. (1979). Ethics and politics: The American way. In R. H. Horowitz (Ed.), *The moral foundations of the American republic* (2nd ed., pp. 38-72). Charlottesville: University of Virginia Press.

Diamond, M. A. (1984). Bureaucracy as externalized self-system: A view from the psychological interior. *Administration & Society, 16,* 195-214.

Diamond, M. A. (1988). Organizational identity: A psychoanalytic exploration of organizational meaning. *Administration & Society, 20,* 166-190.

Diamond, M. A. (1993). *The unconscious life of organizations: Interpreting organizational identity.* Westport, CT: Quorum.

Dolan, S. L., & Lamoureaux, G. (1990). *Initiation à la psychologie du travail.* Bourcherville, Quebec: Gaetan Morin.

Dolbeare, K. (1974). *Political change in the United States: A framework for analysis.* New York: McGraw-Hill.

Douglas, M. (1986). *How institutions think.* Syracuse, NY: Syracuse University Press.

Drucker, P. F. (1995). *Managing in a time of great change.* New York: Truman Talley.

Dumenil, L. (1995). *The modern temper: American culture and society in the 1920's.* New York: Hill & Wang.

Duverger, M. (1955). *Political parties.* New York: John Wiley.

Dvorin, E. P., & Simmons, R. H. (1972). *From amoral to humane bureaucracy.* San Francisco: Canfield.

Eden, D. (1984). Self-fulfilling prophecy as a management tool: Harnessing Pygmalion. *Academy of Management Review, 9*(1), 64-73.

Eisenach, E. J. (1994). *The lost promise of progressivism.* Lawrence: University Press of Kansas.

Eliot, T. S. (1971). *T. S. Eliot: The complete poems and plays, 1909-1950.* Orlando, FL: Harcourt Brace Jovanovitch.

Elkins, J. (1996). *The object stares back: On the nature of seeing.* New York: Simon & Schuster.

Ellis, R. E. (1987). The persistence of antifederalism after 1789. In R. Beeman, S. Botein, & E. Carter II (Eds.), *Beyond confederation: Origins of the Constitution and American national identity* (pp. 295-314). Chapel Hill: University of North Carolina Press.

Enzensberger, H. M. (1994). *Civil war.* London: Granta.

Esman, M. J. (1972). *Administration and development in Malaysia: Institution building and reform in a plural society.* Ithaca, NY: Cornell University Press.

Etzioni, A. (1960). Two approaches to organizational analysis: A critique and a suggestion. *Administrative Science Quarterly, 5,* 257-278.

Etzioni, A. (1961). *Complex organizations: A sociological reader.* New York: Holt, Rinehart & Winston.

Etzioni, A. (1964). *Modern organizations.* Englewood Cliffs, NJ: Prentice Hall.

Etzioni, A. (1993). *The spirit of community: Rights, responsibilities and the communitarian agenda.* New York: Crown.

Etzioni, A. (Ed.). (1995). *New communitarian thinking: Persons, virtues, institutions, and communities.* Charlottesville: University Press of Virginia.

Fagas, J., & Shepherd, I. L. (Eds.). (1971). *Gestalt therapy now.* New York: Harper & Row.

Fainsod, M., Gordon, L., & Palamountain, J. C. (1959). *Government and the American economy.* New York: Norton.

Farmer, D. (1995). *The language of public administration.* Tuscaloosa: University of Alabama Press.

Fausto-Sterling, A. (1985). *Myths of gender.* New York: Basic Books.

The Federal Farmer [pseud.]. (1965). The quantity of power the Union must possess is one thing; the mode of exercising the powers given is quite a different consideration: 1787. In M. Borden (Ed.), *The antifederalist papers* (pp. 113-114). East Lansing: Michigan State University Press.

Ferguson, E. J. (1979). The nationalists of 1781-1783 and the economic interpretation of the Constitution. In G. S. Wood (Ed.), *The Confederation and the Constitution: The critical issues* (pp. 1-14). New York: University Press of America.

Ferguson, K. E. (1984). *The feminist case against bureaucracy.* Philadelphia: Temple
    University Press.
Ferkiss, V. (1974). *The future of technological civilization.* New York: George Brazilier.
Finer, H. (1940). Administrative responsibility in democratic government. In
    C. Friedrich (Ed.), *Public policy* (pp. 247-275). Cambridge, MA: Harvard
    University Press.
Fisher, R., & Ury, W. (1991). *Getting to yes: Negotiating agreement without giving in*
    (2nd ed.). New York: Penguin.
Follett, M. P. (1918). *The new state.* New York: Longmans, Green.
Follett, M. P. (1924). *Creative experience.* New York: Longmans, Green.
Follett, M. P. (1940). *Dynamic administration: The collected works of Mary Parker
    Follett* (H. C. Metcalf & L. Urwick, Eds.). New York: Harper.
Foss, P. O. (1960). *The grazing fee dilemma.* Indianapolis: Bobbs-Merrill.
Foucault, M. (1970). *The order of things.* New York: Pantheon.
Foucault, M. (1977). What is an author? In D. F. Bouchard (Ed.), *Language, counter-
    memory, practice: Selected essays and interviews* (pp. 113-138). Ithaca, NY:
    Cornell University Press.
Foucault, M. (1979). *Discipline and punish* (A. Sheridan, Trans.). New York: Vintage.
Fox, C. J., & Miller, H. T. (1995). *Postmodern public administration.* Thousand Oaks,
    CA: Sage.
Frank, F., & Anshen, F. (1983). *Language and the sexes.* Albany: State University of
    New York Press.
Franzway, S., Courte, D., & Connell, R. W. (1989). *Staking a claim: Feminism,
    bureaucracy and the state.* Sydney, Australia: Allen & Unwin.
Frederickson, H. G. (1980). *New public administration.* University: University of
    Alabama Press.
Freeman, L. (1955). *The political process: Executive bureau-legislative committee
    relations.* Garden City, NY: Doubleday.
Friedman, E. H. (1985). *Generation to generation.* New York: Guilford.
Friedmann, J. (1973). *Retracking America.* Garden City, NY: Doubleday.
Friedrich, C. (1940). Public policy and the nature of administrative responsibility.
    In C. Friedrich (Ed.), *Public policy* (pp. 221-245). Cambridge, MA: Harvard
    University Press.
Frug, J. (1993). Decentering decentralization. *University of Chicago Law Review, 60,*
    253-338.
Gabor, A. (1990). *The man who discovered quality.* New York: Random House.
Gadon, E. W. (1989). *The once and future goddess.* San Francisco: Harper & Row.
Gagliardi, P. (1986). The creation and change of organizational cultures: A concep-
    tual framework. *Organizational Studies, 2,* 117-134.
Gans, H. (1971, May-June). The uses of poverty: The poor pay all. *Social Policy, 2,*
    20-24.
Gardner, N. (1963). *Effective executive practices.* New York: Doubleday.
Gardner, N. (1965). *The art of delegating.* New York: Doubleday.
Gardner, N. (1974). Action training and research: Something old and something
    new. *Public Administration Review, 34,* 106-115.
Garfinkel, H. (1967). *Studies in ethnomethodology.* Englewood Cliffs, NJ: Prentice
    Hall.
Garvin, D. A. (1988). *Managing quality.* New York: Free Press.
Gilder, G. (1981). *Wealth and poverty.* New York: Basic Books.

Gilmore, T. (1982). A triangular framework: Leadership and followership. In R. R. Sagar & K. Wiseman (Eds.), *Understanding organizations: Applications of Bowen family system theory* (pp. vii-xii). Washington, DC: Georgetown University Family Center.

Gimbutas, M. (1989). *The language of the goddess*. San Francisco: Harper & Row.

Gimbutas, M. (1991). *The civilization of the goddess*. San Francisco: Harper & Row.

Ginzberg, L. D. (1990). *Women and the work of benevolence: Morality, politics and class in the 19th century United States*. New Haven, CT: Yale University Press.

Gleick, J. (1988). *Chaos: Making a new science*. New York: Penguin.

Goldwin, R. A. (1979). Of men and angels: A search for morality in the Constitution. In R. H. Horwitz (Ed.), *The moral foundations of the American republic* (pp. 1-18). Charlottesville: University of Virginia Press.

Golembiewski, R. T. (1996). The future of public administration: End of a short stay in the sun? Or a new day a-dawning? *Public Administration Review, 56,* 139-148.

Goodnow, F. (1900). *Politics and administration*. New York: Macmillan.

Goodsell, C. T. (1981). *The public encounter*. Bloomington: Indiana University Press.

Goodsell, C. T. (1984). The Grace Commission: Seeking efficiency for the whole people? *Public Administration Review, 44,* 196-204.

Goodsell, C. T. (1994). *The case for bureaucracy* (3rd ed.). Chatham, NJ: Chatham House.

Goodwyn, L. (1976). *Democratic promise: The populist movement in America*. New York: Oxford University Press.

Gouldner, A. W. (1954). *Patterns of industrial bureaucracy*. Glencoe, IL: Free Press.

Gregory, K. L. (1983). Native-view paradigms: Multiple cultures and culture conflicts in organizations. *Administrative Science Quarterly, 3,* 359-376.

Guba, E. G. (Ed.). (1990). *The paradigm dialog*. Newbury Park, CA: Sage.

Guerin, P. (1976). *Family therapy: Theory and practice*. New York: Gardner.

Guess, G. M. (1989). Comparative and international administration. In J. Rabin, W. B. Hildreth, & G. J. Miller (Eds.), *Handbook of public administration* (pp. 477-498). New York: Marcel Dekker.

Gulick, L., & Urwick, L. (Eds.). (1937). *Papers on the science of administration*. New York: Columbia University, Institute of Public Affairs.

Habor, S. (1964). *Efficiency and uplift: Scientific management in the Progressive Era*. Chicago: University of Chicago Press.

Hall, J. A. (Ed.). (1995). *Civil society*. Cambridge, UK: Polity.

Hardy, R. J. (1992). *Government in America*. Boston: Houghton Mifflin.

Harmon, M. M. (1981). *Action theory for public administration*. New York: Longman.

Harmon, M. M. (1995). *Responsibility as paradox: A critique of rational discourse on government*. Thousand Oaks, CA: Sage.

Harmon, M. M., & Mayer, R. T. (1986). *Organization theory for public administration*. Boston: Little, Brown.

Harrington, M. (1962). *The other America: Poverty in the United States*. New York: Macmillan.

Hartshorne, C., & Weiss, P. (Eds.). (1931). *The collected papers of Charles Sanders Peirce* (Vols. 1 & 5). Cambridge, MA: Harvard University Press.

Hartz, L. (1948). *Economic policy and democratic thought: Pennsylvania, 1776-1860*. Cambridge, MA: Harvard University Press.

The Harwood Group. (1991). *Citizens and politics: A view from Main Street America.*
    Bethesda, MD: Author.
The Harwood Group. (1995, November). *America's struggle within: Citizens talk
    about the state of the Union.* Bethesda, MD: Author.
The Harwood Group. (1996, January). *The public realm: Where America must address
    its concerns.* Bethesda, MD: Author.
Hatcher, C., & Himmelstein, P. (Eds.). (1976). *The handbook of gestalt therapy.* New
    York: Jason Aronson.
Hawley, E. W. (1994). Herbert Hoover and American corporatism, 1929-1933. In
    R. F. Himmelberg (Ed.), *Business-government cooperation 1917-1932: The
    rise of corporatist policies* (pp. 121-149). New York: Garland.
Heady, F. (1966). *Public administration: A comparative perspective.* New York:
    Marcel Dekker.
Heady, F. (1989). Issues in comparative and international administration. In
    J. Rabin, W. B. Hildreth, & G. J. Miller (Eds.), *Handbook of public adminis-
    tration* (pp. 499-522). New York: Marcel Dekker.
Heer, C. (1926). *The post-war expansion of state expenditures.* New York: National
    Institute of Public Administration.
Heilbroner, R. (1974). *An inquiry into the human prospect.* New York: Norton.
Henry, N. (1987). The emergence of public administration as a field of study. In R. C.
    Chandler (Ed.), *A centennial history of the American administrative state*
    (pp. 37-85). New York: Free Press.
Henry, P. (1966). Debates in the Virginia convention 1788. In C. Kenyon (Ed.), *The
    antifederalists* (pp. 240-251). New York: Bobbs-Merrill.
Heritage, J. (1984). *Garfinkel and ethnomethodology.* Cambridge, UK: Polity.
Herman, S. M., & Korenich, M. (1977). *Authentic management: Gestalt orientation
    to organizations and their development.* Reading, MA: Addison-Wesley.
Herzog, R. J., & Claunch, R. C. (1996). Stories citizens tell: New and old directions
    for city management. In J. Jung (Ed.), *Proceedings of the Ninth National
    Symposium on Public Administration Theory* (pp. 212-225). Hayward, CA:
    Public Administration Theory Network.
Hicks, J. D., & Mowry, G. E. (1956). *A short history of American democracy.* Boston:
    Houghton Mifflin.
Himmelberg, R. F. (1976). *The origins of the National Recovery Administration.* New
    York: Fordham University Press.
Himmelberg, R. F. (Ed.). (1994). *Business-government corporations 1917-1932: The
    rise of corporatist policies.* New York: Garland.
Hirschorn, L. (1988). *The workplace within.* Cambridge: MIT Press.
Hirschorn, L., & Gilmore, T. (1980). The application of family therapy concepts to
    influencing organizational behavior. *Administrative Science Quarterly, 25,*
    18-27.
Hofstadter, R. (1955). *Age of reform: From Bryan to F.D.R.* New York: Knopf.
Homans, G. C. (1950). *The human group.* New York: Harcourt Brace Jovanovitch.
Hummel, R. P. (1977). *The bureaucratic experience.* New York: St. Martin's.
Ingalls, J. D. (1976). *Human energy.* Reading, MA: Addison-Wesley.
Ingraham, P. (1996, April 13). Address to Center for Public Administration and
    Policy, Annual High Table, Blacksburg, VA.
Jacobson, N. (1963). Political science and political education. *American Political
    Science Review, 57,* 561-569.

Jacques, E. (1976). *A general theory of bureaucracy.* London: Heinemann.

Jamison, A., & Eyerman, R. (1994). *Seeds of the sixties.* Berkeley: University of California Press.

John De Witt [pseud.]. (1966). To the free citizens of the Commonwealth of Massachusetts: November 5, 1787. In C. Kenyon (Ed.), *The antifederalists* (pp. 89-109). New York: Bobbs-Merrill.

Jones, D. J. (1993). *Murder at the MLA.* Athens: University of Georgia Press.

Jones, R. S. (1982). *Physics as metaphor.* New York: New American Library.

Jordan, W. P., Greenblatt, M., & Bowes, J. S. (1985). *The Americans.* Evanston, IL: McDougal, Littell.

Jun, J. (1986). *Public administration: Design and problem solving.* New York: Macmillan.

Jun, J. (1994). *Philosophy of administration.* Seoul, Korea: Daeyoung Moonhwa International.

Jung, C. G. (1958). The syzygy: Anima and animus. In V. S. de Laslo (Ed.), *Psyche and symbol: A selection from the writings of C. G. Jung* (pp. 9-22). Garden City, NY: Doubleday.

Jung, C. G. (1963). *The collected works of C. G. Jung* (2nd ed., Vol. 14; R. F. C. Hull, Trans.). Princeton, NJ: Princeton University Press.

Juran, J. M. (1992). *Juran on quality by design.* New York: Free Press.

Kahn, M. (1979). Organizational consultation and the teaching of family therapy: Contrasting case histories. *Journal of Marital and Family Therapy, 5*(1), 69-80.

Kakar, S. (1970). *Frederick Taylor: A study in personality and innovation.* Cambridge: MIT Press.

Kaminski, J. P. (1983, February). Antifederalism and the perils of homogenized history: A review essay. *Rhode Island History, 42,* 30-37.

Kamuf, P. (Ed.). (1991). *A Derrida reader.* New York: Columbia University Press.

Kanter, R. M. (1977). *Men and women of the corporation.* New York: Basic Books.

Kaplan, R. D. (1996). *The ends of the earth: A journey at the dawn of the 21st century.* New York: Vintage.

Kass, H. D., & Catron, B. L. (Eds.). (1990). *Images and identities in public administration.* Newbury Park, CA: Sage.

Katz, D., & Kahn, R. L. (1966). *The social psychology of organizations.* New York: John Wiley.

Kauffman, S. A. (1993). *The origins of order: Self-organization and selection in evolution.* New York: Oxford University Press.

Kaufman, H. (1991). *Time, chance, and organization: Natural selection in a perilous environment* (2nd ed.). Chatham, NJ: Chatham House.

Keirsey, D., & Bates, M. (1978). *Please understand me.* Del Mar, CA: Prometheus-Nemesis.

Kenyon, C. (1979). Men of little faith: The anti-federalists on the name of representative government. In G. S. Wood (Ed.), *The Confederation and the Constitution: The critical issues* (pp. 56-85). New York: University Press of America. (Original work published 1955)

Kerr, C. (1967). *The university in America.* Santa Barbara, CA: Center for the Study of Democratic Institutions.

Kets de Vries, M. (Ed.). (1991). *Organizations on the couch.* San Francisco: Jossey-Bass.

Key, V. O. (1959). *Politics, parties, and pressure groups.* New York: Thomas Y. Crowell.

Kiel, D., & Elliott, E. (Eds.). (1996). *Chaos theory in the social sciences: Foundations and applications.* Ann Arbor: University of Michigan Press.

Kilduff, M. (1993). Deconstructing organizations. *Academy of Management Review, 18,* 13-31.

Kilmann, R., Saxton, M., & Serpa, R. (1986, Winter). Issues in understanding and changing culture. *California Management Review, 2,* 87-94.

Kirkhart, L., & White, O. F., Jr. (1974). The future of organization development. *Public Administration Review, 34,* 129-140.

Kirlin, J. J. (1996). The big questions of public administration in a democracy. *Public Administration Review, 56,* 416-423.

Kohn, A. (1993). *Punished by rewards: The trouble with gold stars, incentive plans, A's, praise and other bribes.* New York: Houghton Mifflin.

Kownslar, A., & Smart, T. (1983). *Civics: Citizens and society* (2nd ed.). New York: McGraw-Hill.

Kronenberg, P. S. (1977, April). *Toward a theory of the interorganization.* Paper presented at the meeting of the National Conference of the American Society for Public Administration, Atlanta.

Kuhn, T. (1962). *The structure of scientific revolutions.* Chicago: University of Chicago Press.

LaBier, D. (1986). *Modern madness.* New York: Touchstone.

Lacan, J. (1977). *Ecrits* (A. Sheridan, Trans.). New York: Norton.

Lacan, J. (1978). *The four fundamental concepts of psycho-analysis* (A. Sheridan, Trans.; J.-A. Miller, Ed.). New York: Norton.

Laing, R. D. (1960). *The divided self.* London: Tavistock.

Laing, R. D. (1967). *Politics of experience.* New York: Penguin.

Lane, L. M., & Wolf, J. F. (1990). *The human resource crisis in the public sector.* New York: Quorum.

Lapolambara, J. G. (1963). *Bureaucracy and political development.* Princeton, NJ: Princeton University Press.

Lareau, W. (1991). *American samurai.* Clinton, NJ: New Win.

Lasch, C. (1978). *The culture of narcissism.* New York: Norton.

Lasswell, H. D. (1971). *A preview of policy sciences.* New York: American Elsevier.

Lawrence, P. R., & Lorsch, J. W. (1969). *Organization and environment: Managing differentiation and integration.* Homewood, IL: Richard D. Irwin.

Lawrence, S. A. (1962). *The battery additive controversy.* Indianapolis: Bobbs-Merrill.

Lederer, W. J. (1958). *The ugly American.* New York: Norton.

Lee, R. H. (1966). Letters from the Federal Farmer: October 8, 1787 and October 10, 1787. In C. Kenyon (Ed.), *The antifederalists* (pp. 197-233). New York: Bobbs-Merrill.

Leonard, W. N. (1969). *Business size, market power, and public policy.* New York: Thomas Y. Crowell.

Levinson, H. (1981). *Executive.* Cambridge, MA: Harvard University Press.

Lieberson, J. (1982a). Postscript to the logic of scientific discovery. *New York Review of Books, 29*(18), 67-69.

Lieberson, J. (1982b). The romantic rationalist. *New York Review of Books, 29*(19), 51-57.

Lienesch, M. (1980). The constitutional tradition: History, political action, and progress in American political thought 1787-1793. *Journal of Politics, 42*(1), 2-30.

Lienesch, M. (1983). In defence of the antifederalists. *History of Political Thought, 4*(1), 65-87.

Lienesch, M. (1988). *The new order of the ages: Time, the Constitution, and the making of modern American political thought.* Princeton, NJ: Princeton University Press.

Lindblom, C. A. (1959). The science of muddling through. *Public Administration Review, 19*, 79-88.

Lippmann, W. (1937). *The good society.* New York: Little, Brown.

Little, J. H. (1994). Administrative man faces the quality transformation: Comparing the ideas of Herbert A. Simon and W. Edwards Deming. *American Review of Public Administration, 24*(1), 67-84.

Lockhard, D. (1976). *The perverted priorities of American politics.* New York: Macmillan.

Logsdon, J. (1971, June). Selecting the way to the moon: The choice of the lunar orbit rendezvous mode. *Aerospace History.*

Lowi, T. (1969). *The end of liberalism.* New York: Norton.

Lowndes, R. (1981). Speeches of Rawlins Lowndes in the South Carolina legislature: January, 1788. In H. J. Storing (Ed.), *The complete anti-federalist* (Vol. 5, pp. 149-150). Chicago: University of Chicago Press.

Lux, K. (1990). *Adam Smith's mistake: How a moral philosopher invented economics and ended morality.* New York: Random House/Shambala.

MacIntyre, A. (1984). *After virtue: A study in moral theory* (2nd ed.). Notre Dame, IN: Notre Dame University Press.

Madison, J. (1952). Federalist #10. In R. M. Hutchins (Ed.), *American state papers* (pp. 49-53). Chicago: Encyclopedia Britannica.

Mann, N. R. (1985). *The keys to excellence: The story of the Deming philosophy.* Los Angeles: Prestwick.

March, J. G., & Olsen, J. P. (1989). *Rediscovering institutions: The organizational basis of politics.* New York: Free Press.

March, J. G., & Simon, H. A. (1958). *Organizations.* New York: John Wiley.

Marini, F. (Ed.). (1971). *Toward a new public administration.* London: Chandler, Scranton.

Marshall, G. (1996). Deconstructing administrative behavior: The "real" as representation. *Administrative Theory and Praxis, 18*(1), 117-127.

Martin, J. (1992). *Cultures in organizations: Three perspectives.* New York: Oxford University Press.

Maslow, A. (1968). *Toward a psychology of being.* Princeton, NJ: Van Nostrand.

Mason, A. T. (1979). The Constitutional Convention. In G. S. Wood (Ed.), *The Confederation and the Constitution: The critical issues* (pp. 37-55). New York: University Press of America.

Mason, G. (1966). Objections to the proposed federal Constitution. In C. Kenyon (Ed.), *The antifederalists* (pp. 191-195). New York: Bobbs-Merrill.

Maurer, R. (1996). *Beyond the wall of resistance.* Austin, TX: Bard & Stephen.

May, R. (1953). *Man's search for himself.* New York: Delta.

May, R., Angel, E., & Ellenberger, H. F. (Eds.). (1958). *Existence.* New York: Simon & Schuster.

McCombs, C. E. (1927). *City health administration.* New York: Crowell, Collier, & Macmillan.

McConnell, G. (1966). *Private power and American democracy.* New York: Vintage.

McKeen, R. L. (1977). Behavioral objectives and non-behavioral objectives: A case of when and where. *College Student Journal, 11*(2), 139-145.

McMath, R. C. (1993). *American populism: A social history 1877-1898.* New York: Hill & Wang.

McSwain, C. J. (1995). Men, mom, meaning and marginalization. *Administration & Society, 27,* 283-289.

McSwain, C. J., & White, O. F., Jr. (1987). The case for lying, cheating and stealing: Personal development as ethical guidance for managers. *Administration & Society, 18,* 411-432.

McSwain, C. J., & White, O. F., Jr. (1993). Transformational organization theory. *American Review of Public Administration, 23*(2), 81-98.

McWilliams, W. C. (1979). On equality as the moral foundation for community. In R. H. Horowitz (Ed.), *The moral foundations of the American republic* (2nd ed., pp. 183-213). Charlottesville: University of Virginia Press.

Merkle, J. A. (1968). The Taylor strategy: Organizational innovation and class structure. *Berkeley Journal of Sociology, 13,* 59-81.

Merton, R. K. (1936). The unanticipated consequences of purposive social action. *American Sociological Review, 1,* 894-904.

Merton, R. K. (1940). Bureaucratic structure and personality. *Social Forces, 18,* 560-568.

Merton, R. K. (1949). *Social theory and social structures.* Chicago: Free Press.

Milgram, S. (1974). *Obedience to authority: An experimental view.* New York: Harper & Row.

Miller, H. T., & Fox, C. J. (Eds.). (1996). *Postmodernism, "reality," and public administration: A discourse.* Burke, VA: Chatelaine.

Mills, C. W. (1959). *The sociological imagination.* London: Oxford University Press.

Montgomery, J. D., & Siffin, W. J. (Eds.). (1966). *Approaches to development: Politics, administration and change.* New York: McGraw-Hill.

Moore, M. (1992, August 16). Bangladesh Bank: A woman's domain. *Washington Post,* Section A, p. 1.

Morris, R. B. (1987). *The forging of the Union: 1781-1789.* New York: Harper & Row.

Morstein-Marx, F. (1946). *Elements of public administration.* Englewood Cliffs, NJ: Prentice Hall.

Mosher, F. C. (Ed.). (1980). *American public administration: Past, present, future.* University: University of Alabama Press.

Mosher, W. E. (1937). Government without patronage. *Annals, 189,* 35-41.

Mund, V. (1965). *Government and business.* New York: Harper & Row.

Nagel, E., & Newman, J. R. (1968). *Gödel's proof.* New York: University Press.

Naisbitt, J. (1982). *Megatrends.* New York: Warner.

Neave, H. R. (1989). *The Deming dimension.* Knoxville, TN: SPC.

Nedelsky, J. (1982). Confirming democratic politics: Anti-federalists, federalists, and the Constitution. *Harvard Law Review, 96,* 340-360.

Nelson, D. (1980). *Frederick W. Taylor and the rise of scientific management.* Madison: University of Wisconsin Press.

Neustadt, R. (1960). *Presidential power: The politics of leadership.* New York: John Wiley.

Noble, D. F. (1981). *The progressive mind.* Minneapolis, MN: Burgess.

Noble, D. F. (1992). *A world without women: The Christian clerical culture of Western science.* New York: Oxford University Press.

Norman, M. (1996, May 26). The hollow man. *New York Times Magazine,* Section 6, p. 54.

Norris, C. (1982). *Deconstruction: Theory and practice.* New York: Routledge.

Norris, C. (1987). *Derrida.* Cambridge, MA: Harvard University Press.

Olasky, M. (1992). *The tragedy of American compassion.* Wheaton, IL: Crossway.

Olson, C. (1983). *The book of the goddess.* New York: Crossroad.

O'Neill, W. L. (1971). *Coming apart: An informal history of America in the 1960's.* New York: Quadrangle/New York Times.

Osborne, D., & Gaebler, T. (1992). *Reinventing government: How the entrepreneurial spirit is transforming the public sector.* Reading, MA: Addison-Wesley.

Ostrom, E. (1975). The design of institutional agreements and the responsiveness of police. In L. Rieselbach (Ed.), *People vs. government* (pp. 274-299). Bloomington: Indiana University Press.

Ostrom, V. (1973). *The intellectual crisis in public administration.* University: University of Alabama Press.

Ott, J. S. (1989). *The organizational culture perspective.* Chicago: Dorsey.

Owen, H. (1984). Facilitating organizational transformation: The uses of myth and ritual. In J. D. Adams (Ed.), *Transforming work* (pp. 209-244). Alexandria, VA: Miles River.

Owen, H. (1987). *Spirit: Transformation and development in organizations.* Potomac, MD: Abbott.

Parenti, M. (1974). *Democracy for the few.* New York: St. Martin's.

Parsons, T. (1949). *The structure of social action.* Glencoe, IL: Free Press.

Parsons, T. (1951). *The social system.* New York: Free Press.

Pateman, C. (1970). *Participation and democratic theory.* Cambridge, UK: Cambridge University Press.

Perls, F., Hefferline, R. F., & Goodman, P. (1951). *Gestalt therapy.* New York: Delta.

Perrow, C. (1961). The analysis of goals in complex organizations. *American Sociological Review, 26,* 854-866.

Perrow, C. (1972). *Complex organizations: A critical essay.* Glenview, IL: Scott, Foresman.

Perrow, C. (1980). Zoo story or life in the organizational sandpit. In G. Salaman & K. Thompson (Eds.), *Control and ideology in organizations* (pp. 259-277). Cambridge: MIT Press.

Peters, T. J., & Waterman, R. H., Jr. (1982). *In search of excellence.* New York: Warner.

Pettigrew, A. M. (1979). On studying organizational cultures. *Administrative Science Quarterly, 24,* 570-581.

Pfiffner, J. M. (1935). *Public administration.* New York: Ronald.

Pfohl, S. J. (1975). Social role analysis: The ethnomethodological critique. *Sociology and Social Research, 59,* 243-265.

Pinkney, H. R. (1969). *Christopher Gore: Federalist of Massachusetts: 1758-1827.* Waltham, MA: Gore Place Society.

Piszkiewicz, D. (1995). *The Nazi rocketeers.* Westport, CT: Praeger.

Playford, J., & McCoy, C. (1967). *Apolitical politics.* New York: T. Crowell.

Polanyi, M. (1958). *Personal knowledge.* New York: Routledge & Kegan Paul.

Powell, G. (1988). *Women and men in management.* Newbury Park, CA: Sage.

Pressman, J. L., & Wildavsky, A. B. (1973). *Implementation.* Berkeley: University of California Press.

Prigogine, I., & Stengers, I. (1984). *Order out of chaos: Man's new dialogue with nature.* New York: Bantam.

Progoff, I. (1973). *Jung's psychology and its social meaning.* Garden City, NY: Doubleday.

Publius [pseud.]. (1952). The Federalist papers. In R. M. Hutchins (Ed.), *American state papers* (pp. 29-259). Chicago: Encyclopedia Britannica.

Putnam, R. D. (1993). *Making democracy work.* Princeton, NJ: Princeton University Press.

Racine, D. P. (1995). The welfare state: Citizens and immersed civil servants. *Administration & Society, 26,* 434-463.

Rae, A., & Ward, P. D. (1984). *The 59 second employee: How to stay one second ahead of your one minute manager.* Boston: Houghton Mifflin.

Rawls, J. (1971). *A theory of justice.* Cambridge, MA: Harvard University Press.

Ramos, A. G. (1981). *The new science of organizations: A reconceptualization of the wealth of nations.* Toronto: University of Toronto Press.

Redford, E. S. (1958). *Ideal and practice in public administration.* University: University of Alabama Press.

Redford, E. S. (1965). *American government and the economy.* New York: Macmillan.

Redford, E. S. (1969). *Democracy in the administrative state.* New York: Oxford University Press.

Redford, E. S., & White, O. F., Jr. (1971). *What manned space program after reaching the moon? Government attempts to decide: 1962-1968.* Syracuse, NY: Inter-University Case Program.

Reich, C. A. (1995). *Opposing the system.* New York: Crown.

Reich, R. B. (1996, February). *Pink slips, profits and paychecks: Corporate citizenship in an era of smaller government.* Speech delivered at the George Washington University School of Business and Public Management, Washington, DC.

Remy, R. C., Elowitz, L., & Berlin, W. (1984). *Government in the United States.* New York: Scribner.

A Republican Federalist [pseud.]. (1966). To the members of the convention of Massachusetts: January 19, 1788. In C. Kenyon (Ed.), *The antifederalists* (pp. 125-128). New York: Bobbs-Merrill.

Rhoads, S. E. (1985). *The economists' view of the world.* Cambridge, UK: Cambridge University Press.

Richardson, G. P. (1991). *Feedback thought in social science and systems theory.* Philadelphia: University of Pennsylvania Press.

Richman, R., White, O. F., Jr., & Wilkinson, M. H. (1986). *Intergovernmental mediation: Negotiations in local government disputes.* Boulder, CO: Westview.

Richter, A. (1970). The existentialist executive. *Public Administration Review, 30,* 415-422.

Riesman, J. A. (1987). Money, credit and federalist political economy. In R. Beeman, S. Botein, & E. Carter II (Eds.), *Beyond confederation: Origins of the Constitution and American national identity* (pp. 128-135). Chapel Hill: University of North Carolina Press.

Riggs, F. W. (1965). *Administration in developing countries: The theory of a prismatic society.* Boston: Houghton-Mifflin.

Riggs, F. W. (1991). Public administration: A comparativist framework. *Public Administration Review, 51*, 473-477.

Riggs, F. W. (1994). Bureaucracy and the Constitution. *Public Administration Review, 54*, 65-72.

Rohr, J. A. (1978). *Ethics for bureaucrats: An essay on law and values.* New York: Marcel Dekker.

Rorty, R. (1979). Kuhn and incommensurability. In R. Rorty, *Philosophy and the mirror of nature* (pp. 322-333). Princeton, NJ: Princeton University Press.

Rorty, R. (1982). *Consequences of pragmatism.* Minneapolis: University of Minnesota Press.

Rorty, R. (1989). *Contingency, irony, and solidarity.* Cambridge, UK: Cambridge University Press.

Rorty, R. (1994). Feminism, ideology, and deconstruction: A pragmatist view. In S. Zizek (Ed.), *Mapping ideology* (pp. 227-234). London: Verso.

Rosenau, P. M. (1992). *Post-modernism and the social sciences.* Princeton, NJ: Princeton University Press.

Rotman, B. (1987). *Signifying nothing: The semiotics of zero.* New York: Macmillan.

Rutgers, M. R. (1994). Can the study of public administration do without a concept of the state? Reflections on the work of Lorenz Von Stein. *Administration & Society, 26*, 395-412.

Sacks, O. W. (1995). *An anthropologist on Mars: Seven paradoxical tales.* New York: Vintage.

Safford, J. L. (1987). *Pragmatism and the progressive movement in the United States.* Lanham, MD: University Press of America.

Sandel, M. J. (1996). *Democracy's discontent: America in search of a public philosophy.* Cambridge, MA: Harvard University Press.

Sathe, V. (1983, Autumn). Implications of corporate culture: A manager's guide to action. *Organizational Dynamics*, pp. 5-23.

Schaef, A. W. (1988). *The addictive organization.* San Francisco: Harper & Row.

Schall, M. S. (1983). A communication-rules approach to organizational culture. *Administrative Science Quarterly, 28*, 557-581.

Schambra, P. E. (1961). Effects of heavy ions on cellular systems relative to lightly ionizing radiation. *Radiation Research, 14*, 126-131.

Schambra, W. A. (1982, Spring). The roots of the American public philosophy. *Public Interest, 67*, 36-48.

Schattschneider, E. E. (1960). *Party government.* New York: Holt, Rinehart & Winston.

Schein, E. H. (1985). *Organizational culture and leadership.* San Francisco: Jossey-Bass.

Scherkenbach, W. W. (1988). *The Deming route to quality and productivity.* Rockville, MD: Mercury.

Scherkenbach, W. W. (1991). *Deming's road to continual improvement.* Knoxville, TN: SPC.

Schmidt, M. R. (1993). Government: Alternative kinds of knowledge and why they are ignored. *Public Administration Review, 53*, 525-530.

Schuman, D. (1973). *A preface to politics.* Lexington, MA: D. C. Heath.

Schwartz, H. (1990). *Narcissistic processes and corporate decay.* New York: New York University Press.

Selznick, P. (1949). *T.V.A. and the grass roots*. Berkeley: University of California Press.

Selznick, P. (1992). *The moral commonwealth: Social theory and the promise of community*. Berkeley: University of California Press.

Senge, P. M. (1990). *The fifth discipline*. New York: Doubleday.

Sheldon, C. (1984). *In his steps*. Uhrichsville, OH: Barbour.

Shepard, H. (1965). Changing interpersonal and intergroup relationships in organizations. In J. G. March (Ed.), *Handbook of organizations* (pp. 1115-1143). Chicago: Rand McNally.

Siffin, W. J. (Ed.). (1957). *Toward the comparative study of public administration*. Bloomington: Indiana University Press.

Siffin, W. J. (1966a). *Approaches to development: Politics, administration and change*. New York: McGraw-Hill.

Siffin, W. J. (1966b). *The Thai bureaucracy: Institutional change and development*. Honolulu: East-West Center.

Silverman, D. (1970). *The theory of organizations*. London: Heinemann.

Silverman, K. (1996). *The threshold of the visible world*. New York: Routledge.

Simon, H. A. (1952). Development of theory of democratic administration: Replies and comments. *American Political Science Review, 46*, 494-496.

Simon, H. A. (1976). *Administrative behavior: A study of decision-making processes in administrative organizations* (3rd ed., rev.). New York: Free Press.

Simon, H. A., Smithburg, D. W., & Thompson, V. A. (1950). *Public administration*. New York: Knopf.

Sjoberg, G. (1960). *The preindustrial city: Past and present*. New York: Free Press.

Sjoberg, G. (1989). Notes on the life of a tortured optimist. *Journal of Applied Behavioral Science, 25*, 471-486.

Skowronek, S. (1982). *Building a new American state*. New York: Cambridge University Press.

Smircich, L. (1983). Concepts of culture and organizational analysis. *Administrative Science Quarterly, 28*, 339-359.

Smircich, L., & Morgan, G. (1982). Leadership: The management of meaning. *Journal of Applied Behavioral Science, 18*, 257-273.

Smith, B. (1925). *State police*. New York: Crowell, Collier, & Macmillan.

Smith, E. W. L. (Ed.). (1977). *The growing edge of gestalt therapy*. Secaucus, NJ: Citadel.

Smith, J. A. (1907). *The spirit of American government*. New York: Macmillan.

Smith, K. K., & Simmons, V. M. (1983). A Rumpelstiltskin organization: Metaphors in field research. *Administrative Science Quarterly, 28*, 377-392.

Smith, M. (1966). Debates in the New York convention: 1788. In C. Kenyon (Ed.), *The antifederalists* (pp. 370-389). New York: Bobbs-Merrill.

Snow, R. E. (1969). Unfinished Pygmalion. *Contemporary Psychology, 14*, 197-200.

Spicer, M. W. (1995). *The founders, the Constitution, and public administration: A conflict in worldviews*. Washington, DC: Georgetown University Press.

Spiro, H. J. (1959). *Government by constitution: The political systems of democracy*. New York: Random House.

Stanley, M. (1972). Technicism, liberalism, and development. In M. Stanley (Ed.), *Social development*. New York: Basic Books.

Stein, H. E. (1952a). The disposal of the aluminum plants. In H. Stein (Ed.), *Public administration and policy development: A case book* (pp. 313-362). New York: Harcourt Brace.

Stein, H. E. (1952b). Introduction. In H. Stein (Ed.), *Public administration and policy development: A case book* (pp. ix-xiv). New York: Harcourt Brace.

Stein, H. E., & Arnow, K. S. (Eds.). (1948-1951). *Case studies in public administration and policy formulation.* New York: Inter-University Case Program, Polygraphic Company of America.

Stewart, F. M. (1950). *A half century of municipal reform: The history of the National Municipal League.* Berkeley: University of California Press.

Stillman, R. J., II. (1995). The refounding movement in American public administration: From "rabid" anti-statism to "mere" anti-statism in the 1990's. *Administrative Theory and Praxis, 17*(1), 29-45.

Stivers, C. (1990). Active citizenship and public administration. In G. L. Wamsley, C. T. Goodsell, J. A. Rohr, P. Kronenberg, O. F. White, Jr., J. F. Wolf, & C. Stivers, *Refounding public administration* (pp. 246-273). Newbury Park, CA: Sage.

Stivers, C. (1993). *Gender images in public administration: Legitimacy and the administrative state.* Newbury Park, CA: Sage.

Stivers, C. (1994). The listening bureaucrat. *Public Administration Review, 54,* 364-369.

Stivers, C. (1995). Settlement women and bureau men: Constructing a useable past for public administration. *Public Administration Review, 55,* 522-529.

Stone, A. B., & Stone, D. (1975a). Appendix: Case histories of early professional educational programs. In F. C. Mosher (Ed.), *American public administration: Past, present, future* (pp. 268-290). University: University of Alabama Press.

Stone, A. B., & Stone, D. (1975b). Early development of education in public administration. In F. C. Mosher (Ed.), *American public administration: Past, present, future* (pp. 11-48). University: University of Alabama Press.

Storing, H. J. (1979). Slavery and the moral foundations of the American republic. In R. H. Horowitz (Ed.), *The moral foundations of the American republic* (2nd ed., pp. 214-233). Charlottesville: University of Virginia Press.

Storing, H. J. (Ed.). (1981a). *The complete antifederalist* (Vols. 1-7). Chicago: University of Chicago Press.

Storing, H. J. (1981b). *What the anti-federalists were for.* Chicago: University of Chicago Press.

Studensky, P. (1920). *Public pension systems.* New York: Appleton.

Taylor, F. W. (1947). *Scientific management.* New York: Harper.

Terreberry, S. (1968). The evaluation of organizational environments. *Administrative Science Quarterly, 13,* 590-613.

Thayer, F. (1981). *An end to hierarchy and competition: Administration in the post-affluent world* (2nd ed.). New York: Franklin Watts.

Thompson, J. D. (1959). *Comparative studies in administration.* Pittsburgh: University of Pittsburgh Press.

Thompson, J. D. (1967). *Organizations in action.* New York: McGraw-Hill.

Thompson, J. D., & McEwen, W. J. (1958, February). Organizational goals and environment: Goal setting as an interaction process. *American Sociological Review, 23,* 23-31.

Thompson, V. A. (1975). *Without sympathy or enthusiasm: The problem of administrative compassion.* University: University of Alabama Press.

Toffler, A., & Toffler, H. (1995). *Creating a new civilization.* Atlanta: Turner.

Tolchin, S. J. (1996). *The angry American: How voter rage is changing the nation.* Boulder, CO: Westview.

Tompkins, J. (1992). *West of everything.* New York: Oxford University Press.

Ulrich, H., & Probst, G. J. B. (Eds.). (1984). *Self-organization and management of social systems: Insights, promises, doubts, and questions.* New York: Springer-Verlag.

U.S. Department of Labor, Office of Planning and Research. (1965). *The Negro family: The case for national action.* Washington, DC: Government Printing Office.

Uveges, J. A., Jr., & Keller, L. F. (1989). The first one-hundred years of American public administration: The study and practice of public management in American life. In J. Rabin, W. B. Hildreth, & G. J. Miller (Eds.), *Handbook of public administration* (pp. 1-42). New York: Marcel Dekker.

Ventriss, C. (1995a). Emerging perspectives on citizen participation. *Public Administration Review, 45,* 433-440.

Ventriss, C. (1995b). Modern thought and bureaucracy: *The bureaucratic experience: A critique of life in modern organization. Public Administration Review, 55,* 575-581.

Ventura, M. (1995, December 12). Trapped in the time machine. *Washington Post,* Outlook Section, pp. 1-3.

Ver Steeg, C. L. (1964). *The formative years: 1607-1763.* New York: Hill & Wang.

Vidal, G. (1976). *1876.* New York: Ballantine.

Von Franz, M. L. (1980). *Projection and re-collection in Jungian psychology.* London: Open Court.

Waldo, D. (1948). *The administrative state.* New York: Ronald.

Waldo, D. (1952). Development of theory of democratic administration. *American Political Science Review, 46,* 81-103.

Waldo, D. (1955). *The study of public administration.* New York: Random House.

Waldo, D. (1971). *Public administration in a time of turbulence.* London: Chandler, Scranton.

Waldo, D. (1975). Political science: Tradition, discipline, profession, science, enterprise. In F. I. Greenstein & N. W. Polsby (Eds.), *Handbook of political science: Vol. 1. Political science, scope and theory* (pp. 1-130). Reading, MA: Addison-Wesley.

Walker, J. (1966, June). Critique of the elitist theory of democracy. *American Political Science Review, 60,* 285-295.

Wamsley, G. L., Goodsell, C. T., Rohr, J. A., Kronenberg, P., White, O. F., Jr., Wolf, J. F., & Stivers, C. (1990). *Refounding public administration.* Newbury Park, CA: Sage.

Wamsley, G. L., Goodsell, C. T., Rohr, J. A., White, O. F., Jr., & Wolf, J. F. (1987). The public administration and the governance process: Refounding the American dialogue. In R. C. Chandler (Ed.), *A centennial history of the American administrative state* (pp. 291-317). New York: Free Press.

Wamsley, G. L., & Wolf, J. F. (Eds.). (1996). *Refounding democratic public administration: Modern paradoxes, postmodern challenges.* Thousand Oaks, CA: Sage.

Wamsley, G. L., & Zald, M. (1973). *The political economy of public organizations.* Bloomington: Indiana University Press.

Warren, K. F. (1993). We have debated ad nauseum the legitimacy of the administrative state—but why? *Public Administrative Review, 53,* 249-254.

Weick, K. E. (1979). *The social psychology of organizing* (2nd ed.). Reading, MA: Addison-Wesley.

Weinberg, G., & Rowe, D. (1988). *The projection principle.* New York: St. Martin's.

Wells, H. G. (1975). *Things to come.* Boston: Gregg. (Original work published 1935)

West, C. (1989). *The American evasion of philosophy.* Madison: University of Wisconsin Press.

Wheatley, M. J. (1994). *Leadership and the new science: Learning about organization from an orderly universe.* San Francisco: Berrett-Koehler.

Whitaker, G. P. (1980). Coproduction: Citizen participation in service delivery. *Public Administration Review, 40,* 240-246.

White, L. (1926). *Introduction to the study of public administration.* New York: Harper.

White, O. F., Jr. (1972). Beyond power politics: Vive la difference as political theory. *Maxwell Review, 8*(2), 57-63.

White, O. F., Jr. (1973a). The problem of urban administration. In G. Frederickson (Ed.), *Neighborhood control in the 1970's* (pp. 117-137). New York: Chandler.

White, O. F., Jr. (1973b). *Psychic energy and organizational change.* Beverly Hills, CA: Sage.

White, O. F., Jr. (1983). Communication induced distortion in scholarly research: The case of action theory in American public administration. *International Journal of Public Administration, 5,* 119-150.

White, O. F., Jr. (1990). Reframing the authority/participation debate. In G. L. Wamsley, R. N. Bacher, C. T. Goodsell, P. S. Kronenberg, J. A. Rohr, C. M. Stivers, O. F. White Jr., & J. F. Wolf, *Refounding public administration* (pp. 182-245). Newbury Park, CA: Sage.

White, O. F., Jr. (1991, March). *The semiotic way of knowing and public administration.* Paper presented at the annual meeting of the Public Administration Theory Network, Washington, DC.

White, O. F., Jr. (1995). Public administration's gender identity problem. *Administration & Society, 27,* 277-282.

White, O. F., Jr., & McSwain, C. J. (1983). Transformational theory and organizational analysis. In G. Morgan (Ed.), *Beyond method* (pp. 292-305). Beverly Hills, CA: Sage.

White, O. F., Jr., & McSwain, C. J. (1990). The Phoenix Project: Raising a new image of public administration from the ashes of the past. In H. D. Kass & B. L. Catron (Eds.), *Images and identities in public administration* (pp. 23-60). Newbury Park, CA: Sage.

White, O. F., Jr., & McSwain, C. J. (1993). The semiotic way of knowing. *Administrative Theory and Praxis, 15*(1), 18-35.

White, O. F., Jr., Waggaman, J. S., & Hofstetter, C. R. (1967). *Rush County, Indiana voting in general elections: 1890-1964.* Indianapolis: Indiana Historical Society.

White, O. F., Jr., & Wolf, J. F. (1995). Deming's total quality management movement and the Baskin Robbins problem. *Administration & Society, 27,* 203-225, 308-321.

Wiebe, R. H. (1967). *The search for order.* New York: Hill & Wang.

Wildavsky, A. (1984). *The politics of the budgetary process* (4th ed.). Boston: Little, Brown.

Wildavsky, A. (1993). On the Articles of Confederation. *Public Affairs Report, 34*(6), 13-14.

Wilkins, A. L. (1983, Autumn). The culture audit: A tool for understanding organizations. *Organizational Dynamics,* pp. 24-38.

Williams, A. (1983). An Election Sermon, Boston: 1762. In C. S. Hyneman & D. S. Lutz (Eds.), *American political writing during the founding era: 1760-1805* (Vol. 1, pp. 3-5). Indianapolis, IN: Liberty.

Willoughby, W. F. (1927). *Principles of administration.* Washington, DC: Brookings Institution.

Wills, G. (1971). *Nixon agonistes.* Boston: Houghton Mifflin.

Wilson, W. (1978). The study of administration. In J. M. Shafritz & A. C. Hyde (Eds.), *Classics of public administration* (pp. 3-17). Oak Park, IL: Moore. (Original work published 1887)

Wolfe, T. (1987). *Bonfire of the vanities.* New York: Farrar, Strauss.

Wolff, R. (1968). *The poverty of liberalism.* Boston: Beacon.

Wood, D. (1987). Beyond deconstruction? In A. P. Griffiths (Ed.), *Contemporary French philosophy* (pp. 175-194). Cambridge, UK: Cambridge University Press.

Wood, G. S. (Ed.). (1979a). *The Confederation and the Constitution: The critical issues.* New York: University Press of America.

Wood, G. S. (1979b). The worthy against the licentious. In G. S. Wood (Ed.), *The Confederation and the Constitution: The critical issues* (pp. 86-112). New York: University Press of America.

Wood, G. S. (1987). Interests and disinterestedness in the making of the constitution. In R. Beeman, S. Botein, & E. Carter II (Eds.), *Beyond confederation: Origins of the Constitution and American national identity* (pp. 69-109). Chapel Hill: University of North Carolina Press.

Wood, G. S. (1993). *The radicalism of the American Revolution.* New York: Vintage.

Yankelovitch, D. (1991). *Coming to public judgment: Making democracy work in a complex world.* Syracuse, NY: Syracuse University Press.

Zaleznik, A. (1989). *The managerial mystique: Restoring leadership in business.* New York: Harper & Row.

Zimbardo, P. G., Haney, C., Banks, W. C., & Jaffe, D. (1973, April 8). The mind is a formidable jailer: A Pirandellian prison. *New York Times Magazine,* pp. 38-60.

Zinn, H. (1995). *A people's history of the United States: 1492-present* (rev. ed.). New York: Harper.

Zizek, S. (1991). *Looking awry.* Cambridge: MIT Press.

Zohar, D. (1990). *The quantum self.* New York: Quill/William Morrow.

Zuckerman, M. (1970). *Peaceable kingdoms: New England towns in the eighteenth century.* New York: Knopf.

Index

About the Author

"O. C. McSwite" is a pseudonym for Orion F. White, Professor of Public Administration at the Center for Public Administration and Policy at Virginia Polytechnic Institute and State University, and Cynthia J. McSwain, Professor of Public Administration at The George Washington University. Individually or together, they have previously taught at The University of Texas at Austin, The University of Southern California, Syracuse University, The University of North Carolina at Chapel Hill, North Carolina State University, and the University of California at Berkeley. They have published widely on the topics of organization development and change, the application of psychological theory to public administration, and the connection of public administration to broader issues of social process. Their current research interest involves the application of postmodern theories, especially the psychoanalytic thought of Jacques Lacan, to problems in public administration. In addition to their research, they have accumulated more than forty years of experience working as consultants to organizations of all types both in the United States and internationally.